Writing Interactive Fiction with TWINE

Melissa Ford

800 East 96th Street,
Indianapolis, Indiana 46240 USA

Writing Interactive Fiction with Twine

Copyright © 2016 by Melissa Ford

ISBN-13: 978-0-7897-5664-0
ISBN-10: 0-7897-5664-1

Library of Congress Control Number: 2015956273

1   16

Trademarks

Warning and Disclaimer

Special Sales

For information about buying this title in bulk quantities, or for special sales opportunities (which may include electronic versions; custom cover designs; and content particular to your business, training goals, marketing focus, or branding interests), please contact our corporate sales department at corpsales@pearsoned.com or (800) 382-3419.

For government sales inquiries, please contact governmentsales@pearsoned.com.

For questions about sales outside the U.S., please contact intlcs@pearson.com.

Editor-in-Chief
Greg Wiegand

Acquisitions Editor
Rick Kughen

Development Editor
Todd Brakke

Managing Editor
Sandra Schroeder

Project Editors
Tonya Simpson
Seth Kerney

Copy Editor
Kitty Wilson

Indexer
Works Publishing

Proofreader
The Wordsmithery LLC

Technical Editor
Chris Klimas

Editorial Assistant
Cindy Teeters

Cover Designers
Mark Shirar
Chuti Prasertsith

Compositor
Bronkella Publishing

Contents at a Glance

Table of Contents

Foreword

Some people set out to change the world when they build something new. I didn't. I built the first versions of what would become Twine with an audience of one in mind: myself. I had experimented with writing traditional interactive fiction (IF), the kind exemplified by games like *Zork*, that ask the reader to explore a world by typing commands. I wanted to try experimenting with IF in a different way, to create something that ran lighter on puzzle solving and heavier on storytelling.

The best reference point I had was an immensely popular series of books I had devoured when I was in elementary school, Choose Your Own Adventure *(CYOA)*. Though many of the stories they told were haphazard and madcap, there was something inescapably intriguing to me about stories that have no fixed plot, whose content is changed by the process of reading them.

Of course, this idea—which we'd now think of as a branch of the hypertext medium—has a history that stretches back much further than the CYOA series. It runs back nearly a century, in fact. But just as I had no great ambitions when I first started with Twine, I also had no great knowledge of the medium. My thoughts were humble. I saw a hill and wondered what was past it. Twine was the walking-stick I built to help myself get there.

Twine has grown and grown since then, to my delight. What I'm most proud of is how many people have used Twine to write their first interactive story. Some of these people only know the medium of interactive fiction in the same terms I did, with examples like CYOA and *Zork*. Many more, I suspect, come to the medium completely fresh. Whoever you are, it's truly a privilege to be able to offer a first glimpse of this territory. I hope you'll fall in love just as I did.

But there are hazards to exploration. False trails and dead ends abound. A wise explorer draws on every resource available—and this book, though there are no maps printed in its pages nor any descriptions of flora or fauna, is an excellent guidebook to have at your side on your first foray.

—Chris Klimas, creator of Twine

About the Author

Melissa Ford is the author of numerous works of fiction and nonfiction. She has been a huge interactive fiction fan since 1982, when her dad gave her a copy of *Zork* to help her become a better speller. She is the blogging and social media editor at *BlogHer*, a contributor at *GeekDad*, and the Twine mentor at her local computer club. She is also the author of the award-winning blog *Stirrup Queens*. She earned her MFA from University of Massachusetts–Amherst.

Dedication

For my Dad, who brought home Zork and said, "Play this."

Acknowledgments

First and foremost, a huge thank you to the Que team for all of your hard work: Rick, Todd, Tonya, Laura, Sandra, Seth, Cindy, Mark, Michelle, Greg, and Kitty. A shout-out to Charlotte Kughen, who helped with the middle of the book, and an enormous separate thank you to Rick Kughen for believing in this project when I wrote him, "So I have this idea for a book..." and he brought me into the Que family. I have never had so much fun working on a book.

Thank you to James Floyd Kelly, who held my hand when I needed to jump and made sure I landed somewhere good. And an enormous thank you to Chris Klimas for jumping with me. I would not have done this without you.

And on that note, there literally wouldn't be a book without Twine itself. Thank you to Chris Klimas for making a program that even someone with no coding background can pick up within minutes. You've really leveled the playing field. Thank you to Leon Arnott and Thomas Michael Edwards for your work with the two formats in Twine, and to Dan Cox and Greyelf for answering questions when I was first learning my way around Twine.

I would have never found Twine if not for Frank Hunleth and Josh Westgard asking, "Hey, Mel, want to learn an interactive fiction language?" And a huge thank you to Dave Lebling for answering questions during early days to get the next generation of interactive fiction creators on their way.

Thank you to one very special teacher, Andrea Siska, who not only nurtured the best in my kids but brought out the inner programmer in me.

No book would ever get finished without the help of my siblings and their families—Randall, Morgan, Wendy, Jonathan, Olivia, and Penelope—as well as my parents. In fact, most aspects of life would never get finished without the help of my parents, so thank you for everything from making me learn how to spell so I could play interactive fiction games to giving me writing days. I love all of you so much.

Much love and one thousand thank yous to Josh, who gives me space to dream and supports every outlandish idea that pops into my head. I love you for always having my back, for letting me vent when I get stuck, and for giving me the energy to try again. And thank you, of course, to the twins, who made me see computers as more than plastic and wire. There is no chance in a million years that I would have found Twine if not for you two, and the biggest happiness in my day is seeing the projects you create and the creativity that spills out of your brains. I love you two to pieces.

And, last but never least, Truman, my furry confidante who squeaks his many thoughts, especially ones about cookies.

We Want to Hear from You!

As the reader of this book, *you* are our most important critic and commentator. We value your opinion and want to know what we're doing right, what we could do better, what areas you'd like to see us publish in, and any other words of wisdom you're willing to pass our way.

We welcome your comments. You can email or write to let us know what you did or didn't like about this book—as well as what we can do to make our books better.

Please note that we cannot help you with technical problems related to the topic of this book.

When you write, please be sure to include this book's title and author as well as your name and email address. We will carefully review your comments and share them with the author and editors who worked on the book.

Email: feedback@quepublishing.com

Mail: Que Publishing
ATTN: Reader Feedback
800 East 96th Street
Indianapolis, IN 46240 USA

Reader Services

Register your copy of *Writing Interactive Fiction with Twine* at quepublishing.com for convenient access to downloads, updates, and corrections as they become available. To start the registration process, go to quepublishing.com/register and log in or create an account*. Enter the product ISBN, 9780789756640, and click Submit. Once the process is complete, you will find any available bonus content under Registered Products.

*Be sure to check the box that you would like to hear from us to receive exclusive discounts on future editions of this product.

Introduction to Interactive Fiction

Have you ever loved a book so much that you wanted to step inside it? Do you sometimes wish that you could walk around Narnia or become a student at Hogwarts? Do you think about alternate paths for the narrative or wish you could see the choices not taken for characters? What if all the bells and whistles were stripped away from a game, and all you were left with was the perfect, engaging story? What if I told you that there's a type of computer game that allows the player to enter and control the story, like in a Choose Your Own Adventure book?

It's called interactive fiction.

In this book you'll learn how to make your own interactive fiction using Twine.

Wait a Second...What Is a Choose Your Own Adventure Book?

Choose Your Own Adventure books are unique novels that allow the reader to guide the story. After each page or two of text, you face a choice.

Let's pretend you're reading a Choose Your Own Adventure mystery set in a scary old house. After reading a few pages about the house, you get a choice: If you want to go in the kitchen, go to page 7. If you want to go to the living room, go to page 12.

If you turn to page 7, the story goes in one direction. If you turn to page 12, it goes in another. Every few pages, you make another choice. You can get 40 or so different story experiences inside a single book.

Of course, Twine doesn't operate with page numbers, but you can create a story with hyperlinked text that allows the reader to play over and over again, getting a different story outcome based on different choices.

That's just the jumping off point for Twine. Unlike with a Choose Your Own Adventure book, with Twine you're not limited to making a game where the player simply makes choices until reaching the end. By adding scripts, which are bits of programming used to run tasks within the game, you can have the player collect objects in an underground kingdom, race a timer to fix a space ship before it explodes, or have words wash off the screen in a story set on a beach.

Twine projects at their core are text based, but you can also add images or use the CSS and HTML code that you'll learn in this book to change the way the words appear on the screen.

Even if you've never written a line of code in your life, by the time you get to the end of this book, you will know how to build a text-based world, bring characters to life, and drop the player into a puzzle of your own creation. Sound good?

Are They Games or Stories?

So are the projects made with Twine games or stories? Answer: Yes! Why do they have to be one or the other? With Twine, you get to play with your words.

In this book, I switch between the words *game* and *story*, but both words always apply. Some people like to think of using Twine as writing interactive stories and other people structure their projects more like games.

There are a lot of similarities between game structure and story structure. The same traits that make a good game also make a good book. Think about your favorite book and what you like about it. I'm willing to bet that it has interesting characters who have goals, action that moves the story along, and a plotline that makes sense. (For instance, characters learn there are problems first and find the solution later rather than the other way around.) In this book you'll learn how to use story structure in your Twine game, too.

I use a lot of writing terms in this book, and I promise that playing with Twine will make you a better writer, a better reader, a more logical thinker, and a generally more inquisitive and thoughtful person in the analog world.

I know, big promises, but I plan to deliver.

What Type of Games Can I Make with Twine?

There's a whole wide world of interactive fiction out there, and it's divided into two main categories: choice-based games and parser games.

Choice-based games are digital versions of Choose Your Own Adventure books. The player reads some text and then clicks on a link to get the next piece of the story.

Parser games are another type of text-based adventure. Instead of clicking on a choice, the user types at a command line to tell the character what to do, such as "pick up the sword" or "go north." Lateral thinking is a hallmark of parser games, and many people find them difficult to play because they require the reader to solve puzzles by telling the character what to do in the game. If you can't guess the solution to the puzzle or find the right words, you can't move the story forward.

Twine straddles these two categories, offering the best of both worlds. You can make a straightforward Choose Your Own Adventure story, and you can also borrow elements of traditional parser games and incorporate them into a Twine project. Twine allows you to give the player the freedom and complexity of a parser game even though all of the answers are technically right there on the screen, simultaneously giving it the simplicity of a choice-based game.

By adding scripting to Twine, you can have different text appear to the reader based on objects they're holding or tasks they've performed. You can create random events, such as the rolling of a virtual set of dice, which means you can make a complex role-playing game similar to *Dungeons and Dragons*, or you can make a scene where two wizards duel one another and have the game keep track of gained and lost points. You can build task puzzles, which are a hallmark of parser games, or you can create mazes. The type of game or story you make is limited only by your imagination.

Linear Storytelling Versus Interactive Storytelling

I'm going to guess that you're pretty familiar with linear stories, in which you open the book on the first page and read straight through until you reach the last page.

You're probably also familiar with the first person and third person points of view. A first-person story uses pronouns such as *I* or *me*, and the reader understands the story through the main character's point of view. *The Hunger Games* is written in first person, with the story flowing through Katniss. If she doesn't experience it, the reader doesn't experience it. The book begins "When I wake up, the other side of the bed is cold." The pronoun *I* indicates first person.

Third person uses pronouns such as *he*, *she*, and *they*. The narrator floats above the story, usually following the main character but like an invisible ghost. Harry Potter is written in third person; the invisible narrator usually tells us what is happening in Harry's world, though every once in a while, we're following someone else who connects with Harry's story, such as Professor Snape. That series begins "Mr. and Mrs. Dursley, of number four, Privet Drive, were proud to say that they were perfectly normal, thank you very much." The pronoun *they* indicates third person.

Unlike most linear stories, interactive stories are written in second person. By using the second-person pronoun *you*, an interactive story makes the reader feels as if he or she has been dropped into the story.

Look at how the first page of my favorite Choose Your Own Adventure book, *The Mystery of Chimney Rock*, begins: "Vacation is here, and you're visiting your cousins Michael and Jane for a few days at their new home in Connecticut." The story says you're visiting your cousins, so the main character is you.

When you construct a Twine story, you write it in second person so that the player becomes the main character in your story.

How to Use This Book

Unlike an interactive story where you jump around the book, this one is a linear tale: You start here with the introduction and keep reading until you get to the last chapter.

But wait! This book is also interactive, in the sense that many times in each chapter, you'll set the book down and open up Twine on your computer and try writing scripts. These exercises come in the form of Try It Out sidebars, like this:

TRY IT OUT: HERE'S WHAT A TRY IT OUT LOOKS LIKE

When you see this element in this book, you'll know you've reached a point at which you can try creating your own interactive fiction code. You'll receive a story prompt to get you started, though feel free to change the details to suit your literary tastes. The point is to get comfortable with the cool tasks you can do in Twine while simultaneously strengthening your writing abilities.

Make sure you do all the Try It Out exercises in the book because doing them will help you understand other ways you can creatively use scripting to construct unique aspects to your games.

I want to warn you now that there is a lot of information in this book, and if you try to perfect every aspect of storytelling in one fell swoop, you will quickly become overwhelmed. Authors and game makers spend many years trying to get all these aspects of storytelling to line up. My advice is to focus on getting comfortable with each facet of storytelling individually rather than trying to master everything at once. Once you're strong at creating memorable characters or building vivid settings, you will find that these skills are easy to pluck from your virtual toolbox each time you sit down to start a new project. Writing skills get under your skin the more you practice.

Ready to start making your first story? Turn the page.

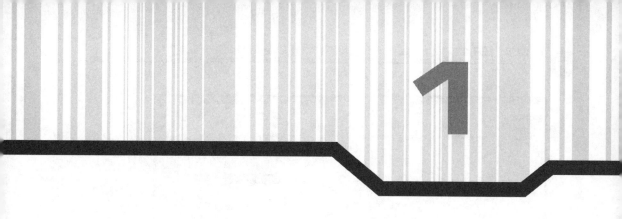

The Nuts and Bolts: Getting Started with Twine

Using Twine is a lot like playing with Legos. It takes only a few seconds to learn how to snap Lego bricks together and build a simple house. Spend a little more time with Legos and their instructions, and you can put together a set. Spend a lot more time with Legos, and you can design your own projects that utilize engineering concepts.

In this chapter, you're going to start by snapping together a quick story with Twine. Afterward, you'll backtrack and learn your way around the Twine site. As you read this book, you'll learn how to do more and more complicated things with Twine by adding scripting. Building a simple story is cool, but creating a role-playing game that you can play with friends is even cooler.

Ready to get started?

Installing Twine

Although there is an online version, downloading Twine allows you to use it even if you're offline. Head to twinery.org and look for Download in the upper-right corner.

Click the correct version under Download for your computer (Windows, Mac, or Linux) to download the zipped file. Unzip the file and put the application somewhere that you can find it on your computer, for instance, moving the folder to your Documents folder in Windows. Click on the index.html file to open it.

When Twine opens for the first time, it brings up a brief tutorial. Click Skip, and Twine takes you to a white screen, as shown in Figure 1.1.

In addition to the Twine file you download, you also need an Internet browser in order to test and play your game. Twine works well with Chrome, Firefox, Internet Explorer (version 10 and later), Safari, and Microsoft's new Edge browser in Windows 10.

Once you have Twine and a compatible browser, you're ready to get started with Twine.

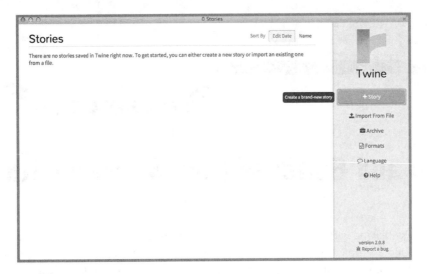

FIGURE 1.1   The Twine Stories screen.

Starting Your First Story

Let's try your hand in building a simple story so you can become accustomed to Twine. In the future, you'll let your imagination soar when it comes to the exercises in this book. But for this first story, simply type the example word for word so you can see how the program plays out on the screen.

Start by clicking the large green +Story button on the right sidebar to start a new story. Name it Doors and click the +Add button. Twine automatically takes you to the blue grid screen shown in Figure 1.2.

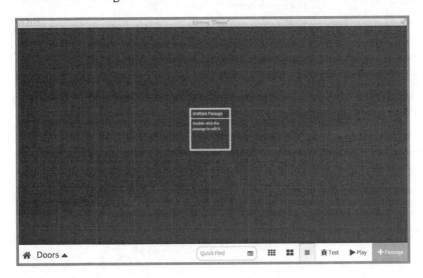

FIGURE 1.2   Blue grid screen.

Double-click the box on the blue grid screen to open it. You can also hover over the box and click the pencil icon from the pop-up menu that appears. Either way allows you to open the box so you can begin writing your story.

Currently in the body of the box, you should see a brief passage that begins with the words `Double-click this passage to edit it`. Erase those placeholder words so you have a clean screen to begin typing.

I'd like you to start your story *in medias res*, which is just a fancy way of saying in the middle of the action. Type the following text in the box:

```
You are facing two doors. One is a beautiful, shimmery blue that
looks as if it is made out of water. The other is a dark, dingy
door with a spider web clinging to the edge.
```

In a normal story you, as the author, determine what happens next. With interactive fiction, you need to give the player some options. In order to give options in Twine, you need to place square brackets around the words you want to be clickable within the game, add a vertical bar (the pipe keyboard character, |), and give the name for the target passage to the right of that bar. You don't want any space before or after the vertical bar. Here's a template that shows how:

```
[[hyperlinked words|Passage Name]]
```

Then you start a new paragraph and write the following options directly below the text you already have in the body of the box:

```
Do you want to open [[the blue door?|Blue Door]]
Or do you want to open [[the black door?|Black Door]]
```

Click the X in the upper-right corner of the box. This causes two new boxes, or passages, to open on the screen, as shown in Figure 1.3.

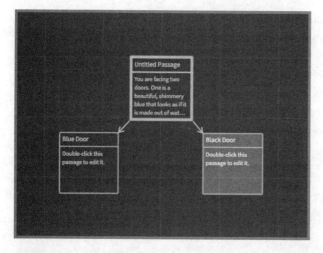

FIGURE 1.3 New boxes appear on the screen after you create a choice in the passage.

Open by double-clicking the one labeled Blue Door and type this:

```
You open the blue door and come face-to-face with a dragon
that devours you in one gulp.
```

Click the X in the upper-right corner and now open by double-clicking the box labeled Black Door. Type the following in that box:

```
You open the black door and a hooded figure hands you a silver ring,
buzzing with magic. He says, "You can now make any wish.
Welcome to your adventure."
```

Again click the X in the upper-right corner and then navigate down to the menu at the bottom of the screen and click the Play button (refer to Figure 1.3). Your story opens in a new Twine window. You should see your starting text along with your two choices, as shown in Figure 1.4.

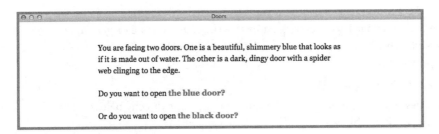

FIGURE 1.4 A playable version of your story appears when you click the Play button.

At this point if you click the text `the blue door`, the dragon devours you. Click `the black door`, and you get the magic ring.

You're playing your game on your computer at this point, and no one else can access this game yet. At the end of this book in Chapter 23, "Finishing Up and Clicking Publish," you'll find instructions on how to host your game on the Internet so anyone can play, but right now the game is using your local storage, which means that only you can see it.

Click the house icon on the lower-left corner of the screen to return to the Stories screen where you can start a new game.

Congratulations! You now know how to make a basic story in Twine. You could just keep writing the story, offering options, and creating new passages. But Twine lets you do a lot more, as you'll learn in the following pages.

Saving in Twine

Twine automatically saves your stories to your computer. But what if you want to move your stories to another computer, send a copy of your game to a friend to upload into their copy of Twine, or make a backup copy of your projects to be safe?

In the Stories screen, click the Archive button to create a single file that contains a copy of each of your stories. Keep your archive file in a safe place on your computer, such as the Documents section of Windows.

Navigating Twine Menus

The Twine menus run along the bottom of the screen when you're on the blue grid screen and along the right sidebar when you're on the Stories screen. There is also the pop-up menu that can be seen when you hover over a box.

Getting to Know the Stories Screen

The Stories screen is your home base; it provides links to all your individual projects. As you've just seen, you can click Archive to save your stories in a single file. In addition, you can click Import from File to either bring in a saved version of your stories (perhaps because it was previously deleted) or upload your stories onto a different computer.

Every time you want to start a new project, you click the green +Story button. Click it, name your story, and click the +Add button. (Don't worry...you can rename your story later.)

Double-click back on your first story, Doors, to return to the blue grid screen.

Getting to Know the Blue Grid Screen

As you've already seen, the blue grid screen is where you write your stories. There are a few important actions associated with the menu bar at the bottom of the screen. The little house icon in the bottom-left corner takes you back to the Stories screen.

To the right of the little house is the story menu. Currently it should be showing the name of your story, Doors, along with a triangle. Click the triangle, and you can see some more options in Figure 1.5, including Edit Story Stylesheet or Publish to File, that you'll use later in this book.

On the bottom-right side of the screen is a bug icon with the word Test beside it. When you click this button, you can test play your game from a certain point in the story. Next to that is the Play button, which plays your story from the beginning. Finally, the bright green +Passage button in the bottom-right corner allows you to add additional passages to your story if they don't automatically generate.

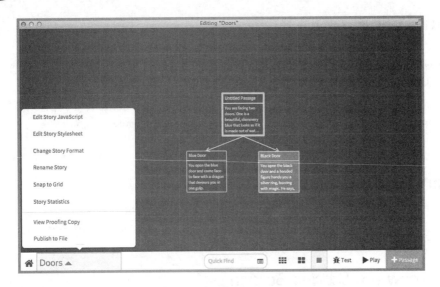

FIGURE 1.5 Additional options in the story menu.

Getting to Know the Hover Menu

The last of Twine's basic features you'll learn about in this chapter is the hover menu. If you hover over any of the boxes in your story, you'll see a small menu with commonly used options pop up over the box, as shown in Figure 1.6.

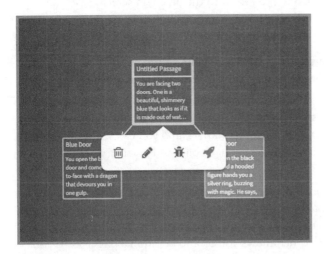

FIGURE 1.6 Hover over the passage box to trigger an additional menu.

The first icon is a garbage can. Click that to delete the passage from the story. Click the pencil icon to edit a passage; you can get the same effect by simply double-clicking the box. The bug icon plays the story starting at the active passage so you can see how your game appears for the player.

Finally, there is the rocket ship icon, which you use to create a starting point for a story. By default Twine marks the first box you create as the starting point for your story. You'll notice that the first box you created has a slightly thicker border, which indicates that it's the starting point for your story. You can, if you want, designate any passage as the starting point, and you can change the starting point at any time. To see how this works, go back to the Doors story and hover over the Blue Door passage. Click the rocket ship icon, and you should see the border of the white box grow a little thicker, indicating that it is now the start passage. Now click the Play button at the bottom of the screen. What happens?

Instead of seeing your opening text and the two options, you should see the passage where the dragon devours you. Go back to the blue grid screen and hover over your original starting passage and click the rocket ship icon again. You should see the thicker border switch to that box, and when you click the Play button, your original opening appears on the screen.

Believe it or not, that's pretty much it in terms of getting started with Twine's most basic features. You're now ready to blast off and learn new and interesting things about links that will help you further develop your interactive storytelling skills.

Using Choice to Create Agency

Choice makes interactive fiction different from other storytelling mediums. In a traditional book, an author writes a single path for a story to take, but interactive fiction authors give that power to the reader. The reader gets to choose which way the story goes, and that simple act creates *agency*, which refers to how much a person can influence their world.

Take, for example, Infocom's interactive fiction game *Moonmist*. In it, you are a detective, and your friend asks you to investigate strange occurrences at her home, which just happens to be a haunted castle. Every choice you make means something, including the answer you give when asked your favorite color at the beginning of the story. The direction you walk, the characters you question, and the objects you pick up or move will determine your unique experience with the game.

Moreover, the main character in the story also has a different experience. With interactive fiction, the need for agency happens on two levels. You need to give players a lot of agency and allow them to make meaningful choices, but you also need to allow the characters in the story to have agency and influence their fictional world. One way to do this is by giving everyone and everything in your story a purpose.

A very famous playwright named Anton Chekhov once gave writing advice to an actor that is still used to this day: "One must not put a loaded rifle on the stage if no one is thinking of firing it." What that means is that readers are curious and notice everything, and they are constantly trying to figure out why everything is in the story or game. Don't distract them by putting a gun into the story if the gun serves no purpose.

As you write something new in your story, ask yourself *why*. For instance, why are you setting your story on Mars? Why are you giving your main character a sister? Why is there an apple on the table? You don't need to always tell the reader why, but you, the author, should know why you're including something. Think of a reason for why you include every detail in your story.

This one word—*why*—will help you shape a story that keeps the reader engaged in discovering the purpose of every character and object. As you write, think about what is motivating your characters. What do your characters want? Do they want to discover treasure, get off an island, or seek revenge? If you define your characters' purpose, players will feel as if they serve a purpose, too. When you know the purposes of each character and object, you can craft meaningful choices—and that is the most important thing you can do as an interactive fiction writer: Create choices that allow players to feel that their decisions actually matter.

NOTE

Understanding Key Terms

It's important that you understand some important interactive fiction terminology. The *player* is the person reading the story or playing the game. The *player character* (abbreviated *PC*) is the character that the player controls. Any characters that the player doesn't control are called *non-player characters* (abbreviated *NPCs*).

In this book, I often talk about *story levels*. Every time you offer a choice to the reader that leads to a new passage, you create a new level to your story. The first passage is the first story level. All the passages attached to that passage are in the second story level, and so on.

Most interactive fiction is written in present tense because the action is unfolding as the player is reading. That immediacy lends automatic urgency to the choices. Unlike a book where the reader can clearly see that the story continues after the page they're reading, with interactive fiction, the rest of the story doesn't exist until the player makes a choice.

Let's dive deeper into how you create exciting choices for the reader.

Designing Agency

By giving your players meaningful choices, you give them a greater sense of agency while exploring your story. Remember that *agency* in terms of game design refers to a person's capacity to affect his or her world—or, in this case, the story's world.

The more the reader can affect a story, the higher his or her sense of agency. So think about letting the player make big decisions that come with big consequences. The player character may become the ruler of the land or may die a watery death at sea; the choice is in the player's hands, much as in real life. At the same time, a choice may not appear big in the moment. You can have a seemingly small choice lead to big consequences for the player character, such as choosing one route to the store over another but having very different events affect the player character's life along each way.

If you create lots of agency for your players, they'll feel like active, important figures in your story, and that's the point of writing interactive fiction in the first place. Agency is all about making things happen and letting your player shape the story. You impose the limits, but ultimately you should craft a game that lets the player choose the way the story goes.

Just to be clear, agency isn't about freedom; you can have a prisoner with high agency who is actively working to escape from jail, and you can write a story about a girl skipping through a field, who doesn't really do anything or affect the world around her. Agency refers to how much a character can make things happen. It's more exciting to have characters do things than to have characters have things done to them. It's even more exciting for characters to change the world around them with their choices.

Agency is the difference between actively and passively interacting with the world. If a character chooses to steal a magic axe and then use it to chop down a beanstalk, that's an active interaction, one where the character is actively making a choice, an example of high agency. If the character is handed a magic axe and told to chop down the beanstalk, that's a passive interaction, or a low-agency story.

TRY IT OUT: CHOICE AND CONSEQUENCE

To try creating a simple scene with high agency, open a new story in Twine by clicking the green +Story button on the right sidebar, naming your story Beanstalk, and clicking the +Add button, as shown in Figure 2.1. (If you need a refresher on Twine basics, take a look back at Chapter 1, "The Nuts and Bolts: Getting Started with Twine.")

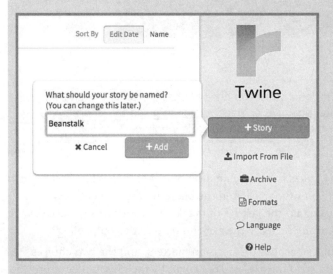

FIGURE 2.1 Creating a new story in Twine.

Say that the giant at the top of the magic beanstalk has threatened to come down and kidnap your bratty sibling. What happens in your scene? What choices do you give the player?

In the first box, write two choices. In those next two boxes, write two more choices. Finish the story with four possible endings. You will have three story levels, for a total of seven boxes, as with the story shown in Figure 2.2.

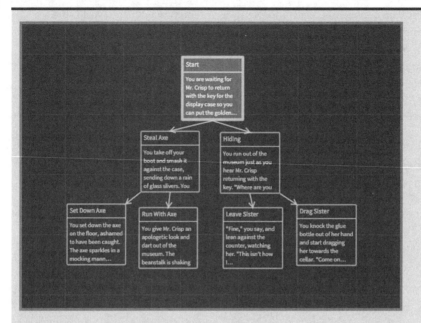

FIGURE 2.2 This story has three story levels.

When you're finished writing, ask yourself if the choices matter. Does the character truly affect his or her world (high agency), or does someone guide the character's actions so he or she isn't really making a choice at all (low agency)?

How does your story go? My story starts in a museum after the giant makes his threat. On the wall is a magic axe with a little bit of magic left in the blade—enough to cut down the beanstalk. Do you steal the axe, using up the last bit of magic the town owns to save your bratty sibling that no one likes? Or do you leave the axe and try to hide your sibling?

Both choices are high-agency choices because the decision matters, and the two choices have different consequences. If you steal the axe, you're caught by the museum curator, who demands that you drop it. You can cooperate and drop the axe, or you can choose to run with it.

On the other hand, if you go home and try to hide your sibling, will your sibling balk? Will you let him/her be kidnapped (and hopefully learn a lesson!) or force your sibling to hide? This is a high-agency story because the player's various choices result in different things happening.

A lower-agency story would give the reader less control, perhaps by overruling the player's decision to run. The museum curator might tackle the player to the floor, no matter which choice he or she makes. In that case, the story doesn't really let the player make a decision because dropping the axe or having another character force the player to drop the axe results in the same conclusion. A story with low agency doesn't really give many choices. If the only way forward is to rescue your sibling with sword drawn, the story isn't so interactive, is it?

There are some things you can do to increase the player's sense of agency while they play your game.

Providing Clues

Players should be able to predict what will happen when they make a choice so they can make the choice they want. If every choice leads to a random result, the players might get frustrated, since they'll soon realize that their choices don't really matter.

Of course, sometimes you might want to surprise players. Maybe you're writing a fantasy thriller game, and the players are trying to escape a fire-breathing monster. If they choose to open a door and find themselves facing a magically constructed brick wall they didn't expect, you'll add to the suspense of the escape. But if nothing in your story is predictable, players might get frustrated and stop caring because they have no way of guessing what will happen when they make a choice. Balance is important.

One way to help your players make good decisions is to leave clues for them. Let's say you're writing a game about a detective investigating a mystery inside an English manor. In one of your passages, you mention that the detective's stomach is rumbling. Later, when a wealthy family member invites the detective to dinner, the players might remember that the detective was hungry and take the invitation. During dinner, the detective learns an important clue. This way, you reward the players for reading closely, and the readers feel like savvy detectives themselves.

On the other hand, if you don't mention that the detective is literally starving to death and needs to eat, it wouldn't be fair to punish the players for not going to dinner by having the detective keel over midway through the investigation.

At their core, choices need to be fair. If you've given players some warning, it's completely fair to make a decision have a huge consequence. But players quickly become frustrated if the consequences come out of nowhere, or if the consequence to a seemingly small decision brings a quick end to all the work they've put into playing the game.

TRY IT OUT: PLAYTESTING YOUR STORY

To create a game that provides clues for players to make a smart guess, open a new story and name it Fair Guess.

Plant an important clue in the opening of your story: Convey to the readers that the character is tired. Don't overdo it; you don't want to make it too obvious. Make sure you add a lot of other description to the passage so that being tired is just one fact the players know about the character.

Now give the readers two choices: one that allows them to go to sleep and the other to leave and do something exciting.

Ask a few people to play your game, and afterward, ask them which choice they made. Ask them why they made the decision they made and see if they noticed that the player character is tired.

If most of your test players mention that the character is tired, you've done a good job adding in the clue. If they don't, you may want to go back and see if you can change the game around a bit and have a few new people play to try it again.

Crafting Meaning

Players know when a choice they've made is meaningful, so if a character does something, make sure that the action has some kind of consequence. You don't always have to make the consequence known immediately, but you, the writer, should know why you included a choice and how it affects the story.

For example, what if the players have to choose whether to save themselves and run out of a burning building or go back in and save a dog trapped inside? There are a lot of possible consequences that could play out in the long run and in the short term. The players may be killed in this heroic act, or they may survive and get the dog to safety, too. Later in the game, the owner of the dog may be so grateful that she gives the players a reward for saving the dog, or she may be so angry that the player didn't try to help that she becomes an obstacle.

Of course, not every choice needs to carry such high stakes. There are all kinds of choices. Inject a little humor into your story by making some of the choices lighthearted. Ridiculous choices can serve a point by lightening the mood, especially in a scary story. Romantic choices can create a bond between a player character and a non-player character that influences the stakes of the story.

Sometimes you may want provide just one option in a passage. Let's say the player reaches a door that you want him or her to walk through because it's a key point of your story. You can place just one link, such as `[[open the door|Door Open]]`, at the end of the passage.

This is also a good way to break up a long passage into two smaller, more manageable passages.

TRY IT OUT: FOUR CHOICES

To create a game that allows players to make a fair, smart guess, open up a new story and name it Consequence.

In this game, your main character is a knight who encounters a dragon. Make sure you take some time to give the knight's backstory before you present your choices.

At the end of the first scene, give the player four choices: run, attack the dragon, try to befriend the dragon, or sneak past the dragon. For each of the four choices, write a very different consequence. For instance, if a player decides to sneak past the dragon, he or she may find that the dragon loses all trust in the player. Or, if the player tries to befriend the dragon, he or she might discover that the dragon has been lonely for a long time and is so happy that it gives the player some gold to celebrate.

In other words, make the choices meaningful by having the dragon react to the actions of the main character.

How different were your endings? Were there four very different outcomes based on the actions of the main character? Think about your own life and how there are natural consequences for your choices.

World-Building with Optional Details

Links don't always have to appear at the end of a passage. You can create links in the middle or at the beginning of a passage, too. Mixing up where you place your links keeps players engaged as they search for them.

In fact, placing links throughout your passages is a great way to give players opportunities to find out more information about various objects in the passage. You can also create links to what I call *detail passages*. These are side passages that lead to more information instead of moving the story forward.

For instance, let's say I want to describe a spaceship. I could place links throughout the passage that take the player to detail passages that give them more information about objects in the room before taking them back to the original passage:

```
You enter the cargo hold of the empty spaceship and stare at the wall of
[[space suits|Space Suits]] and [[helmets|Helmets]], all neatly hanging on hooks
```

```
as if waiting for the crew to return. There are [[oxygen tanks|Oxygen Tanks]] and
boxes of [[freeze-dried food|Food]]. A light above your head flickers on and off.

Do you want to continue to the [[flight deck|Flight Deck]] or go back to
exploring the [[airlock|Airlock]]?
```

If you play my game and click on `helmets`, the story takes you to a brief passage and then
back to the main passage:

```
You take down one of the helmets and try it on. It feels heavy on your head.
[[Back to Cargo Hold|Cargo Hold]]
```

In Figure 2.3, the detail passages fan out from the main cargo hold passage, giving more
information about the contents of the room. Each detail passage leads back to the cargo
hold passage rather than branching out to continue the story. This is a great way of
spreading out descriptions, and it lets players explore as much or as little as they want.

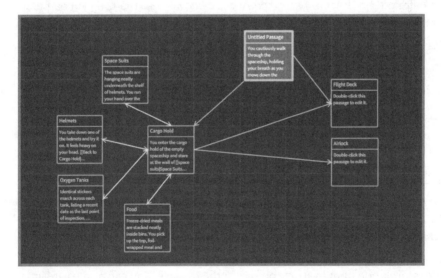

FIGURE 2.3 Detail passages fan out from the main story passage to provide
more information.

TRY IT OUT: WORLD-BUILDING

Try creating a game that involves detail passages by opening a new story and naming it Vacation.

In this story, it's the first day of your vacation. Give the player six options for what to do, such as going to a museum or going to the beach.

Flesh out these six choices a bit and try placing your links in different places throughout your passage. Allow the player to explore a space by creating detail passages that give more information about the objects they encounter. (Don't forget to include a link back to the main passage.)

Was it more difficult to write out six choices instead of two? How did you decide which facts to put upfront in the passage and which facts to place in a detail passage?

Using Choice to Affect Pacing

Another way to build agency is to make sure to give choices frequently. If a passage is getting very long, consider moving some information to detail passages. This way you place control in the hands of the players because they get to decide how much to read and how much to just keep moving.

How long should each passage be before you offer a choice? Think about how much *you* would want to read before you're itching to click something or take action.

TRY IT OUT: PACING AND CHOICE

To try creating a game that keeps things moving quickly, open up a new story and name it Speed.

The situation for this game is that the main character is running. Why? That's up to you! Convey the sensation of running to the readers by keeping the passages brief—no more than three sentences per main passage. This is an active game, so make sure there is a lot of danger and action.

Ask a few people to play your game and ask them how they felt playing the game. Did the short bursts of text make them feel as if they were running, too? Did they like having a lot to do?

It's not always easy to write brief passages. In fact, it's often difficult to convey enough information using a limited number of words. Experienced Twitter users understand this lesson very well. Keep looking at your story and try to think of ways to make your word choices more specific.

Imagining Different Choices

You've now had practice constructing many different types of choices. The following sections outline some categories of choice that can help you decide how you want to move your stories forward in the future. Consider using a mix of the different kinds of choices to add depth and texture to your game.

Giving Preference Choices

Preference types of choices come down to likes and dislikes, such as options at a restaurant: Would you like to order the chicken tenders, or would you like to order the hamburger? This kind of choice generally has low consequences. That is, unless the chicken tenders have a bone that causes the player to choke to death, or the hamburger has a clue written in ketchup on the bun. It's up to you how you make use of seemingly insignificant choices!

Giving Value Choices

Value decisions ask players to designate worth. Worth, of course, is not only measured in money. Worth can take into account sentimental value or usefulness. A check for $100,000 is worthless to an astronaut trapped, alone, on a moon base, but more food or oxygen tanks may be priceless. Likewise, when you ask a player whether to save a book or a diamond, you're asking the player to decide what he or she values more.

Giving Adventure Choices

Adventure types of choices take players into the heart of danger and set action in motion. Players who are a bit nervous can choose the safer route, and players who love excitement can take the riskier option.

Giving Ethical Choices

Ethical choices may be the most interesting ones you give players in a game. With these choices, you're asking them to listen to their conscience and decide what feels "right." When you're writing games, you have a lot of freedom to explore these kinds of choices. Playing games is a way of trying something out that you would never do in the real world. You can construct a game that allows players to behave unethically without having to face real-world consequences.

Giving Cause/Effect Choices

Cause-and-effect types of choices may seem unimportant on the surface but can hide new paths. Say that you're given the option to water a crop of carrots or rip the plants out of the ground. The first choice takes you on a path where you have food to eat in the future. The second choice takes you on a path where you discover a magic ring hidden in the dirt under the carrots. These types of choices are set up the same way: Do *X*, and *Y* happens. Make sure that both choices lead to equally cool (but different) adventures.

Giving Exploratory Choices

Exploratory choices allow readers to explore the setting in the story and learn as many details as they want about the space. You can create these kinds of choices, as described earlier, by linking to detail passages. You can also use links to give more description about objects, people, or situations.

Giving Obtainable Choices

Obtainable decisions allow the player to procure items that can come when you let players decide if they want to pick up or drop objects they encounter in the game. In Chapter 5, "Building Objects with Variables," you'll learn how to code a game so it remembers which objects the player is carrying.

Giving Directional Choices

Directional choices ask players if they want to go north or south, in or out, up or down. You can also name a space instead of a direction by asking things like whether players want to go into the kitchen, living room, or bedroom.

Plotting Your Story's Choices

With so many kinds of choices to consider writing for your players, it's a good idea to organize your ideas before you buckle down and start writing your game. Every smart writer starts with an outline. An outline helps you plot out your story or game so you can build it efficiently when you sit down to write. When you have a solid outline, you know where each plot point is going to go.

You may prefer to write a very detailed outline to keep track of all the choices you're going to present to the player, or you may just want to jot down the big plot points. Either way, making an outline helps make the actual writing of your game go smoothly.

One of my favorite planning tools is the decision tree. A decision tree looks like an upside-down tree. What do I mean by that? Consider the beanstalk story plotted out as a decision tree in Figure 2.4.

The tree begins with a single passage (think of it like a stabilizing trunk) and then branches out to each decision and its consequences.

To make your own decision tree for a new story, start by writing the opening action at the top of a piece of paper. You can be very detailed or just jot down a general sense of what will happen. Each time you offer a decision, draw a line off the passage and write down what happens next.

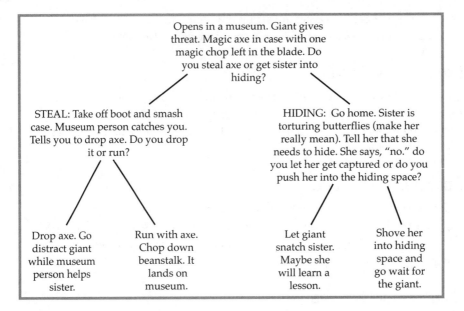

FIGURE 2.4 A sample decision tree for the beanstalk story.

While it's certainly helpful to make a decision tree even if you're only dealing with three levels of story, it becomes invaluable once you start building long and detailed games. Creating decision trees not only ensures that you won't forget to include the great ideas you have bubbling around in your brain, but it frees your mind to concentrate on creativity rather than trying to remember what you want to have happen next. Plus, once you create an outline, you can walk away from your story and come back to it, knowing exactly what you need to write next.

You can use decision trees to keep track of other elements of your story, such as characters, character background stories, objects, or even a point system.

TRY IT OUT: WRITE A DECISION TREE

Take out a piece of paper and practice making a decision tree for the story situation below. Build at least five story levels.

Say that a candy maker has stolen a priceless jewel from a museum and covered it in chocolate so it looks identical to the millions of other chocolate candies in his shop. The museum has hired you to find the jewel and return it to the museum. How do you solve this problem?

Name the candy maker as well as any extra characters in your story. Keep a running list of any objects that you include in your game, and if you want to assign points, make sure you mark which tasks will earn the player points.

Handling Endings

Take a look at the decision tree you made in the last exercise. Did you need to turn your paper horizontally in order to contain all the events in your story? Was the fifth level enormous compared to the second level? Managing the number of endings to your story is something you can plot out with a decision tree, too.

By making a few tweaks to the way you present decisions, you can change the story shape and alter the number of endings.

Using the Fan Story Shape

The story shape you've been using up until this point is the classic *fan shape*. The first story level contains one passage. The second story level contains two passages. The third story level contains four passages, and the fourth story level contains eight passages. The story gets wider and wider, fanning out as it grows.

If you have only a few story levels, the fan arrangement is manageable. But what happens when you go beyond five story levels? How do you keep yourself from having to write 64 different endings on the seventh story level?

Sometimes you might want to give the player more than two choices. More choices means more variation in the game, but it also means more work for you since you need to build all the choice paths! If you find yourself getting overwhelmed writing so many different choices, the next story shape can help you slim things down.

Using the Hourglass Story Shape

The bottleneck, or *hourglass shape,* is commonly used in longer stories and games. Imagine an hourglass: It's wide at the top, then narrows to a thin neck that slows down the falling sand, and then widens again at the bottom.

You can build a story with chokepoints by giving options in two or more different passages that lead to the same place. You can repeat this pattern whenever the number of passages in a story level is growing unmanageable.

Say that your candy story starts out at the museum where the player character gets an assignment. The player character can grab their friend, Peter, to help sort through the candies in the shop; they can go home and get their trusty candy-eating robot, Sweetie; or they can ask their friend Sarah if she will help.

In Figure 2.5, you can see how some of the choices lead to the same point before branching out again later in the story.

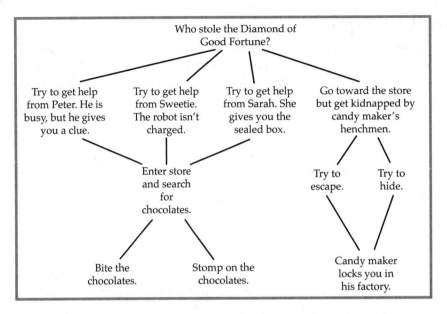

FIGURE 2.5 A sample decision tree that has an hourglass shape.

While the second story level contains four passages, the third story level contains only three instead of the eight or more passages that would normally appear in a fan-shaped story. This is because three of the options in the second story level—getting help from Peter, getting help from Sweetie, and getting help from Sarah—all lead to the same place: entering the store to search for chocolates. The fourth option in the second story level—going toward the store and getting kidnapped—leads to two more choices.

This shape is like the narrowing neck of an hourglass, with entering the store acting as a chokepoint bringing many threads of the story together.

You might be wondering if this shape takes away a little agency from the players if any path they take ultimately brings them to the same place. Yes and no. For example, if players have the clue from Peter, they'll make different choices in the future than players who took the robot route. Even if the players end up in the same place, they still get to decide how they get there. This way, you have to write only a handful of endings, but the players can have many different experiences while playing your game.

TRY IT OUT: STORIES THAT CONVERGE

Go back to your evil jewel-hiding candy maker story and change it up by making a new decision tree. How can you keep key elements from your first version of the story while trying out this new method for writing fewer endings?

If you can't bring the entire level together to meet at a certain point, consider using the same two options in a variety of passages.

Delaying Branching

I like to think of the delayed branching technique as producing a maze-like story shape. When you're walking through a maze, you don't always know how each turn will affect your next move. This type of decision-making is known in interactive fiction as *delayed branching*, and it makes for a rich, complicated game. With delayed branching, the outcome of a choice isn't revealed until much later in the game. In other words, early choices set the player on a new path, but that path isn't clear until much further along in the story. You can build this type of structure by encouraging players to pick up objects that will be important later on in the story, or you can have players visit certain locations in order to unlock new paths.

For instance, you may have players go to the store and buy ingredients at the beginning of the game. If they happen to purchase sugar, they'll be able to bake cookies later for their neighbor. Or you may have players learn a password at the beginning of the game, but they won't be asked to use the password until the middle of the game.

This type of story structure has a lot of twists and turns, so you should try dropping clues in the passage to direct players toward objects or information they may need later in the game.

Creating Another Type of External Link

Up until this point, you've been giving options this way:

```
[[hyperlinked words|Passage Name]]
```

But there is a second way you may see people use when creating Twine games. In this case, you create an arrow using an angled bracket and hyphen that points toward the room name. It can look like this:

```
[[hyperlinked words->Passage Name]]
```

or this:

```
[[Passage Name<-hyperlinked words]]
```

Giving options this way may help you visualize where the player is headed as you construct your story, or you may find it more helpful to see the two chunks of text divided by a vertical bar. This is just a second, useful option to know to help you find your "Twine style."

Creating a Vivid Setting

One of the first interactive fiction games, *Adventure*, explored a real space: Bedquilt Cave in Kentucky. The original author, Will Crowther, loved caving and wanted to re-create the sensation of cave exploration as a text-based game. So, he mapped out a real cave and coded the game, and he threw in some fantasy elements like an annoying dwarf and the magical word XYZZY. Later on, Don Woods expanded the game, giving gaming adventurers hours of play.

Players felt as if they were really crawling through a cave. It didn't matter if they had never been spelunking; Crowther acted as the player's eyes and ears. He led them through the subterranean scenery so they could imagine what it was like to crawl through narrow rock passages. I've played that game so many times that I think if I were ever to go to the real Bedquilt Cave, I could find my way around it just because of this game.

It's time to turn your eye toward *setting*, which refers to the physical space of a story. By writing a vivid description of a place, you help your players feel as if they're being transported there. Stories and games are magical because they make you feel as if you are traveling without leaving your home.

This chapter teaches you how to write a strong setting and how to organize map-based games. Once you learn how to build a space out of words, you can forge off the beaten path and chart your own unique trail; maybe you'll even create your own land or planet.

Understanding the Importance of Setting

Have you ever woken up somewhere unfamiliar and needed to take a few seconds to figure out where you are? Well, readers go through that sensation every time they start a Twine game.

The setting helps players figure out what's happening and helps them guess what will happen next. Location sets readers' expectations. For example, a story set on a distant planet is going to be very different from one set in a cave, or a futuristic restaurant, or a gloomy English manor.

You can use players' expectations to your advantage: You can give them exactly what they expect, or you can twist their expectations to surprise them. (This is called *subverting* expectations.)

Setting is the first thing readers encounter, so you have to make it good, and that means making it vivid. You need to make readers feel as if they're standing in a new place even though they're still sitting in their living room. Think about your favorite settings: What makes you want to enter Narnia, or go to Hogwarts, or visit Mars?

A simple set of prompts can help you get started imagining a place and help you figure out what information you need to convey to your reader.

Creating Setting from Prompts

These are some questions to ask yourself when you sit down to start writing a story or game:

What's the location?   This is the general place or places where the game is set, such as New York City, Narnia, the beach, or the moon.

Where does the player character start?   This is the specific place the game begins, such as the lamppost in Narnia or the front door of a house.

Where does the game end?   Once you've decided the specific location where the game ends, you can focus on what motivates the characters in your story. Why do they want to get to that endpoint? More importantly, how do they get to that endpoint?

What buildings are there?   What human-made structures are there? Which buildings are important to your story? Consider monuments, parks, and stores—anything built or shaped by humans.

What does the geography look like?   Are there mountains that will become obstacles for the player? Water and coral reefs around the submarine? Giant canyons on the surface of the planet?

What time is it?   Is your story set in the middle of winter? Is it near a holiday? Is your story taking place during the day, or at night, or both?

What is the weather like?   Think about the climate and weather of your setting, which will impact how the player moves through the story. Is it a rainy place? Is it very hot? What do players need to wear to be comfortable?

What are the other people like?   Maybe there aren't any other inhabitants in your story (creepy!), but if there are, what are they like? Are they helpful? Distrustful? Do they speak the same language as the player character or a different language? Of course, aliens count in this category, too.

What is the culture of the area?   How does your player character relate to the culture of the area? Is the player character from that area and accepted by others? Is he or she an outsider from an area at war with the people in your setting?

What is the area's past?   Think about the place's history. If your story is set on a distant planet, have other outsiders passed through there, changing the way the aliens think about outsiders?

Now that your imagination is percolating, I'll walk through two new Twine tools and how you might use them to create a space: `(link:)` and `(display:)`.

Adding Descriptions with `(link:)`

You've already learned how to use a little scripting, though you may not have realized that your foray into coding a game has already begun. The `[[link]]` tool that you've been using to connect two passages, `[[hyperlinked words|Passage Name]]`, is a kind of script. Those double brackets around the words tell the program to link the current passage to the passage named on the right side of the vertical bar.

Now, however, you need to learn some scripting that involves using parentheses to set a tool apart from the plain text in the passage. The `(link:)` tool allows an action to occur inside the existing passage; namely, it allows you to give the reader small, optional details to the story without troubling the reader to enter a whole new passage.

With the `(link:)` tool, the text still appears as hypertext on the screen, and players instinctively know to click the links in order to explore where they go. But unlike the `[[link]]` tool, the `(link:)` tool keeps the player in the same passage (and, therefore, all the other text remains on the screen, too) and expands the paragraph to include the new text.

To create an internal link, write the link's text inside the quotation marks inside the parentheses and write the words you want to appear when the link is clicked inside single square brackets, like this:

```
(link: "Words you want linked.")[New words that appear and replace the linked text.]
```

You'll notice that the order of the hypertext word or words and the passage name mirrors the same order seen in the `[[link]]` tool, with the hypertext listed first and the name of the passage to the right.

What if you want quotation marks to appear with the link? For example, what if you want the linked text to be part of a conversation between two characters? For this, you put single quotation marks around the double quotes, as shown here:

```
(link: '"What the character is saying."')[New words that appear and replace the linked piece of dialogue.]
```

Now the quotation marks remain as quotation marks when they appear onscreen. Try both of the preceding examples on your computer and click Play to see the `(link:)` macro in action.

Next try the following example. Open a new story in Twine and call it Link and type the following:

```
Every wall of the room is covered in ceiling-to-floor bookcases filled with old,
dusty books. (link: "You pull an untitled book off the shelf.")[You stare at the
strange symbols that dot the spine of many of the books, and feel a breeze move
through the room even though all the windows are closed. The book you have pulled
from the bookcase feels heavier than a normal book.]
```

When you play this example, you should see two sentences, one in plain text and one hyperlinked, as shown in Figure 3.1.

> Every wall of the room is covered in ceiling-to-floor bookcases filled with old, dusty books. **You pull an untitled book off the shelf.**

FIGURE 3.1 Example text using the `(link:)` tool.

When you click the hyperlinked sentence, it's replaced by the text you put in brackets, as shown in Figure 3.2.

> Every wall of the room is covered in ceiling-to-floor bookcases filled with old, dusty books. You stare at the strange symbols that dot the spine of many of the books, and feel a breeze move through the room even though all the windows are closed. The book you have pulled from the bookcase feels heavier than a normal book.

FIGURE 3.2 Once the linked text is clicked, the new text appears.

Notice that the hyperlinked text disappears from the screen when you click it. If you want any hyperlinked text to stay on the screen, you need to repeat it inside the brackets.

The small but mighty `(link:)` tool can help you build your setting by placing the power in players' hands. They can get as much description or as little description as they wish. When using the `(link:)` tool, remember to additionally use the `[[link]]` tool to continue the story and move players out of the current passage.

Repeating Text with `(display:)`

Sometimes you might want to repeat the description of a complicated space, especially if you want the player to visualize the layout and have access to the same choices several times. The `(display:)` tool gives you an easy way to repeat text. It's perfect for creating small spaces in a story, such as looking at a room in detail or describing the layout of a town square.

In fact, Anna Anthropy's Twine game called *Town* does just that. You start out in a plaza and see a palace, an armory, and a bank. Each time you click on one of the links, you get a little bit of information about that building but still see the description of the plaza. You feel as if you're turning to examine each building while staying in the same space, since the overall description of the setting doesn't change. Of course, there is a link to the next part of the story in the description of one of the buildings, so you can continue once you've explored the small area as much as you like.

To create using this tool, add this line to any passages where you want to repeat the text of another passage:

```
(display: "Name of Passage")
```

Get ready to work through an example that shows how you might use the `(display:)` tool. Open a new story in Twine and call it Alien Restaurant. Change the title of the first passage from Untitled Passage to Restaurant and type this in it:

```
Every table is occupied by [[squid-like aliens|Aliens]] dining in pairs.
There is an aquarium filled with [[neon-blue fish|Aquarium]] dividing the
restaurant. The only empty table is set with the expected [[plate|Plate]],
[[silverware|Silverware]], and [[napkin|Napkin]], but also has a
[[strange box|Meal Box]] with dozens of knobs sticking out of the top,
a [[bowl|Meal Bowl]] filled with tiny metal balls, and a [[stick|Meal Stick]]
with a suction cup on the end.
```

This is the passage that you repeat when you use the `(display:)` tool. Every time you add `(display: "Restaurant")` to future passages, this entire passage repeats on the screen, as shown in Figure 3.3.

> Every table is occupied by **squid-like aliens** dining in pairs. There is an aquarium filled with **neon-blue fish** dividing the restaurant. The only empty table is set with the expected **plate**, **silverware**, and **napkin**, but also has a **strange box** with dozens of knobs sticking out of the top, a **bowl** filled with tiny metal balls, and a **stick** with a suction cup on the end.

FIGURE 3.3   This passage repeats every time you use the `(display:)` tool in a future passage.

You want players to be able to click on any of the links in the passage to receive more information about the squid-like aliens, the neon-blue fish, or the strange box, but you also want players to be able to make second, third, and fourth choices instead of moving into another section of the story. In other words, you want them to stay right here in this restaurant and explore.

To make this happen, you need to start filling the newly created passages that describe parts of the restaurant. You're going to keep the description simple and then display the description of the restaurant again. The reason for keeping the description brief is that the Restaurant passage is already pretty long, and you don't want to give readers too much text to read through.

In the passage titled Aliens, add the following description and script:

```
You try not to stare at the alien couple sitting at the table closest to the door,
but it's impossible not to gape at their waving tentacles. They sense you staring
at them, and turn around to stare back at . . . YOU.
(display: "Restaurant")
```

You can see the additional passages fanning out around the Restaurant passage in Figure 3.4, even though only the Aliens passage is filled.

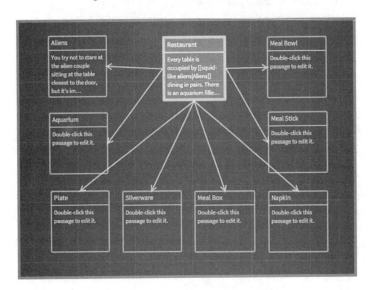

FIGURE 3.4 The additional passages fanning out around the repeating Restaurant passage in the blue grid screen.

You need to play this story so far to make sure everything is working. Click the Play button and then click the text `squid-like aliens`. Your screen should look like the one shown in Figure 3.5.

Not only do players see the description of the squid-like aliens, but they can now choose to learn more about the silverware or that bowl filled with tiny metal balls, since you've repeated the Restaurant passage. This way, players can continue to explore the restaurant. Fill in the additional information in the other passages and make sure to always end each passage with `(display: "Restaurant")` so the player can keep exploring.

Be sure the capitalization of the title and the capitalization of the room name inside the display tool match. For instance, because the passage title is Restaurant, you need to capitalize *restaurant* when you write the name of the passage with `display:`, like this:

```
(display: "Restaurant").
```

> You try not to stare at the alien couple sitting at the table closest to the door, but it's impossible not to gape at their waving tentacles. They sense you staring at them, and turn around to stare back at... YOU.
>
> Every table is occupied by **squid-like aliens** dining in pairs. There is an aquarium filled with **neon-blue fish** dividing the restaurant. The only empty table is set with the expected **plate, silverware,** and **napkin,** but also has a **strange box** with dozens of knobs sticking out of the top, a **bowl** filled with tiny metal balls, and a **stick** with a suction cup on the end.

FIGURE 3.5   The passage shows new text in addition to all the text and links in the Restaurant passage.

Remember that Twine is case-sensitive, and if the capitalization doesn't match, Twine gives you an error message telling you that a passage doesn't exist. Your first stop whenever you receive an error message should be to ensure that the capitalization in links matches the capitalization in a passage title.

Setting Tips and Exercises

It's time to dive deeper into how location influences readers' experiences. The following exercises are meant to spark your creativity and to encourage you to look at setting in a whole new way. All the exercises use (link:), (display:), and [[link]], or a combination of those tools. (If you need a refresher on how to use [[link]], refer to Chapter 2, "Using Choice to Create Agency.")

Writing What You Know

Writers are always told to write what they know. If you took that advice literally, you could never write fantasy stories or science fiction. Books would have no unicorns or dragons or magical schools. Fiction would be a little dull.

Still, it does make sense to draw from personal experience, even when you're trying to write about imaginary things. Maybe you've never been inside a real castle, but you've been inside a house. Use the layout of a house you know well, change the walls to worn stone and the grass outside the front door into a moat, and you've got yourself a castle!

If you want to write about something that you don't have any firsthand experience with, do a little research. Maybe you won't be able to go up in space, but you can certainly read firsthand accounts so you can accurately describe what liftoff feels like.

TRY IT OUT: BUILD A CASTLE

To turn your home into a castle, open a new story and name it Castle.

Pretend your house or apartment is a castle. Using the layout of your actual home, create rooms in the house and change the description so it sounds like what you imagine a person would see if he or she were standing in an old stone castle.

Ask someone in your home to play the game. After they've gotten a chance to explore, ask them if they recognize the space.

Being the Player's Eyes

Here's a cool fact: There is a longstanding relationship between the interactive fiction and blind communities. Text adventures—unlike graphical games—don't require a lot of work to become accessible to all players. Because of this, many blind gamers gravitate toward interactive fiction. Keep this in mind when building your game because you, the writer, are always the player's eyes.

When you're building setting, you're describing a place for someone who can't see it. Imagine a very specific place—real or fictional—and then start describing it to yourself. How detailed can you be? Focus on each small unit of the space, describing it as fully as possible before moving on to the next section.

TRY IT OUT: DETAILED DESCRIPTIONS

Open the Castle game you created earlier. Choose one of the rooms and open the passage. Describe it in close detail; try creating passages for at least eight objects in the room. Describe the walls, the floors, the ceiling, and any fixtures or furniture. What things are out of place in the room? Don't stop describing until you sense that the reader would see the room exactly as you see it in your head.

Use either the `(display:)` tool or the `(link:)` tool to accomplish this exercise.

Considering What a Character Would Notice

Consider what your player character is like and how that might affect what he or she notices. A short player character isn't going to be able to see high places, for instance, whereas a tall player character may not be focused on looking at the floor. Take a walk around the room you're in right now, taking note of what you notice at your eye level. Now drop down to the floor and crawl through the room. Do you see how your description of the same place would change depending on your height?

Now factor in the player character's personality. Is the player character someone who is very neat and tidy? A neat character would probably comment on a messy space or notice that things are out of place. Is the player character someone who moves quickly through an area, or is the character nervous or scared? A fast-moving or nervous player character may not notice the tiny details while running through the space.

TRY IT OUT: NEW POINTS OF VIEW

Open the Castle game you created earlier. Choose one of the eight objects in the room described in a passage and have that object magically shrink or enlarge the player character temporarily. Describe the room from this new vantage point and then have the player character return to normal size before the player character heads back to the main description of the room.

Combining Motion with Surroundings

The world looks very different when you're walking slowly through an area than when you're seeing it from the window of a moving train. Creating settings that keep changing can help capture the reader's interest. People might get restless staying in one place for too long, so think about keeping your players moving.

It's easy to keep players moving; all you need to do is give your characters a reason to explore. Why do they need to get out of the spaceship or go into the cave? Why do they need to move from one room to another? Are they looking for clues, trying to escape another character, or merely exploring?

TRY IT OUT: GAZING OUT THE WINDOW OF A TRAIN

Start a new story and name it Train.

Set your player character on a moving train. Where is the player character going? Is the player character excited to be traveling or dreading arriving at the destination? Have your player character look out the window. What does the player character notice in the passing landscape? Give the player character the magical ability to slow down time using a spell so he or she can take a closer look at the world outside.

Use the (link:) tool to reveal more information. For instance, if the player character notices a shed outside the train window, he or she can use a spell to slow down the train, click the linked text, and reveal the inner contents of the shed.

Using Your Other Senses

You're not just the players' eyes. You're also their ears, nose, tongue, and hands. Setting isn't just about what you see; it's about what you hear, smell, taste, or feel in the setting. What are the sounds of the forest? What is the smell of the Irish countryside after a rainstorm? What does a strawberry taste like? Does the tabletop feel bumpy or smooth?

TRY IT OUT: EXPLORING OTHER SENSES

Open the Train game you created earlier. Visit the dining car. What does the character see, hear, smell, taste, and feel? Make sure to utilize all five senses and use the (link:) tool to reveal more sensory information.

Considering the Mood of a Place

Some places are quiet and creepy, especially at night. Other places feel lonely, like a desolate planet on the edge of the solar system. Other places are lush and relaxing, like a jungle landscape thinning out onto a pristine beach.

Think of your setting as an extra character. What is the personality of your setting? Is it a loud place, a quiet place, an isolating place, a crowded place? Is your society a utopia or a dystopia? Is it a formal place where characters are dressed up or a casual place where jeans rule? Is the architecture ornate or plain? Is it an unforgiving landscape with prickly, unwelcoming foliage, or is it a warm, embracing small town surrounded by farmland? Is the place exciting like an amusement park or relaxing like a library?

Just as people have personalities, places do, too. The personalities of the characters may clash or work well with the setting, and the setting may even help you to create your characters. Think about the type of people who are drawn to or repelled by your setting.

TRY IT OUT: DESCRIBING MOOD

Open the Train game you created earlier. Leave the dining car and find yourself in an empty compartment. The emptiness fills you with dread. Where did all the people go? Why did the door suddenly lock behind you, trapping you inside the train car? Describe the creepiness of the space.

You can use a fun little trick to hide the exit of a room. Place it inside a (link:) by nesting the passage choice using this template:

```
(link: "hyperlinked words")[words to replace linked words plus
[[exit to another passage|Passage Name]]]
```

Notice that there are three square brackets at the end of the line. The first two close off the link to the next passage, and the last square bracket closes off the new words that replace the original linked words. As you type, you'll see the linked text change color to help you keep the brackets straight.

In Figure 3.6, you can see that the links to the passages that leads out of the room, Open Door and Leave Door, appear only when the player clicks on "lift the rug".

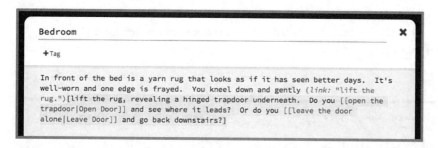

FIGURE 3.6 The passage hides the links to other passages from the player inside the (link:) tool.

You could use this trick in your game to hide the exit by placing numerous links into the passage so the player needs to find the one that contains the exit out of the passage. Here's how you could create one where the exit is hidden inside a book left behind on a seat:

```
The train car is completely empty except for a (link: "book left behind on the
first seat.")[book that fans open as you pick it up, revealing a [[tiny door|Exit]]
drawn on the page.] There are four windows, two on the [[left side|Left Windows]]
of the train and two on the [[right|Right Windows]], though all of them appear to
be locked.

There is a light flickering from the ceiling with an (link: "odd hinged door in
the glass cover.")[odd hinged door that breaks off in your hand when you try
to open it.] All of the seats are covered in [[plush velvet|Velvet]]; strange
for an ordinary passenger train.
```

The additional links in the passage help the reader visualize the space, but only one of them contains a way out of the train car. The extra passages, such as Left Windows, Right Windows, and Velvet, are all detail passages that give the player a little bit more information about the space and bring the player back to the train compartment passage.

Drawing the Player's Attention

Vivid description doesn't necessarily mean long description. In fact, most people don't like to receive the setting as one big chunk of text at the beginning of the story. Write so that different aspects of the setting appear as the player character moves through the story. When you start your story, your player doesn't need to know about every feature of the land. Instead, as the character moves around and encounters new locations, you can gradually reveal that there is a cave guarded by a dragon, that mountains blot out the sky, or that a town of fairy houses is nestled deep in the forest.

Balance barebones, practical descriptions of unimportant places with vibrant descriptions of important places. This helps draw the reader's attention to whatever it is you want them to notice.

Let's say that you're describing a town. You may write a long description of the important buildings where the action will take place (the library, school, and bakery) but merely mention the fact that there is also a post office and hospital since the story will never enter those spaces.

TRY IT OUT: GUIDING THE PLAYER THROUGH THE TOWN SQUARE

Start a new story and name it Town Square.

Pretend your player character is an alien who has landed in a sleepy little town on Earth. The alien is standing in the town square, trying to figure out the landscape. Remember, the player character has never been to Earth and has no clue what he or she is looking at.

Using the (display:) tool, label a repeating passage Town Square. Then create links to the various buildings around the town square so that the alien player character can get a bit more information about each building. Give a deeper description for each important building and give a cursory description of each unimportant building.

Don't forget to include (display: "Town Square") at the bottom of each passage so the player can see all the options over and over again. Ask a friend to play your game and see if he or she can tell which are the important buildings.

Using Descriptive Words

The more descriptive the words you use, the fewer of them you need to use. Write out a description of the setting and then judge each word. Ask yourself if there's a more specific word that says the same thing but goes a step further. For example, red is certainly a specific color, but crimson or maroon goes a step further in helping the reader visualize the shade of red you have in mind.

A thesaurus can come in handy! Look up synonyms for any words you think you could replace with something better.

TRY IT OUT: A VERY DESCRIPTIVE HAT STORE

Returning to the Town Square story you began earlier, you're going to create a few new buildings. The first building is the movie theater. Create a passage for the movie theater (titling it Movie Theater) and write a brief description of the space. Create a second space called Hat Store 1 and link it to the movie theater.

Now create a passage for a library (titling it Library) and write a brief description of the space. Create a space called Hat Store 2 and link it to the library.

Now open the passage titled Hat Store 1. Write a basic description of the store, keeping it as simple as possible. Copy that description and also place it in the passage for Hat Store 2, but this time, edit that description to make it specific. For instance, you could say that it's a milliner, which is a store that specifically sells women's dress hats. See, the description has gone from general hats, which could include everything from top hats to baseball caps, to fancy women's hats, like fascinators. How specific can *you* become?

Which hat store description a player receives is dependent on whether the player enters the store through the movie theater or the library as seen in Figure 3.7. Pretend that the library in this town instantly fills your brain with great vocabulary words, just by walking through the doors.

If the player has been to the library, he or she will see a descriptive paragraph. If the player has been to the movie theater, he or she will see a basic paragraph.

For example, for Hat Store 1, you could write something simple like this:

```
You enter the hat store. The shelves hold a lot of hats in many different colors.
There is a woman behind the counter who looks up from her book as you enter.
```

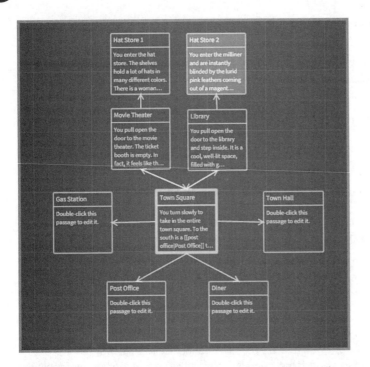

FIGURE 3.7 The two Hat Store passages give readers two very different levels of description on the same space.

In Hat Store 2, you can kick that description up a notch by choosing very specific words:

You enter the milliner and are instantly blinded by the lurid pink feathers coming out of a magenta, velvet cloche set on a shelf by the front door. The store bell tinkles like laughter as you enter, and the elderly woman behind the counter lifts one gnarled finger in the air as she continues to read her book, indicating that you should wait to speak until she is done with the page.

Which description gives you a very specific visual of the space?

Distinguishing Static and Dynamic Settings

Sometimes the setting remains exactly the same throughout a whole story; this is known as a *static* setting. In other stories, the setting may change a lot, and this is known as a *dynamic* setting. Whether or not the setting changes plays a big role in the action of the story.

There are two ways a setting can change: An event may change the landscape, such as a fire burning down an important building, or the player character may move, traveling from place to place. Both options create a sense of movement, which keeps the story trucking along. Static landscapes are great for conveying drudgery, and landscapes that transform help move the action.

TRY IT OUT: TRAVEL THROUGH TIME

Want one story with a lot of settings? Consider a time travel tale! Open up a new story and title it Time Travel. Start the story in a time machine. Where will you go? This passage will be repeated using the (display:) tool, so make sure that your wording works and that you've labeled the starting passage Time Machine.

Give the reader six possible destinations and repeat the code (display: "Time Machine") at the bottom of each of the six passages.

So how could you tackle this exercise? First, set up the passage you need to repeat and title it Time Machine:

```
There is a time machine here with six buttons, each a different color.
Do you want to press the [[red button|Red]], [[orange button|Orange]],
[[yellow button|Yellow]], [[green button|Green]], [[blue button|Blue]],
or [[purple button|Purple]]?
```

Then, in the new passages that you just created, describe what happens when someone pushes one of those buttons. Make sure you add (display: "Time Machine") at the bottom of the paragraph so the player can still see the description of the time machine.

For instance, in the green button passage, I wrote a brief introduction that sends the player on his or her way or gives the player the option to choose a different button, using (display: "Time Machine"):

```
You press the green button and an image of the rolling fields of Ireland flash
on the screen. A cool voice comes out of the speakers: "Would you like to
[[visit Ireland|Ireland]] in the year 2045?"

You debate what to do. You have always wanted to visit [[Ireland|Ireland]].
(display: "Time Machine")
```

Sketch out the diverse settings, write layers of description with the (link:) tool, and write short passages. How does the player character interact with these very different settings? Does the player character enjoy some settings more than others?

This is your longest, most complicated story yet, so take your time with this exercise before going onto the next section.

Building a Map-Based Game

Creating a map-based game involves creating a physical setting that the player can explore. With directional choices like north, south, up, down, in, or out, the player controls where he or she goes. A map-based game may not have a plotline; rather, it may be fun because it allows a player to "travel" to a space and explore without leaving home. For example, you could construct an interactive fiction Hogwarts and allow players to move from room to room in the castle.

You can practice this process by turning your home into a game space. Think of this as an unofficial but more elaborate Try It Out. Start by constructing a map of your house or apartment. Draw the layout of the rooms and pay attention to the flow of the space so you know how players can move from room to room. Figure 3.8 shows an example of a map of a house.

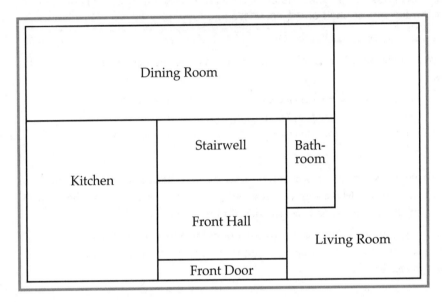

FIGURE 3.8 A map of a house.

Once you have a rough sketch of your house, you can translate it into Twine. Create a passage for each room on your map. Figure 3.9 shows what the map from Figure 3.8 looks like all set up in Twine. Click and drag the boxes to arrange them so they're in the same order as the rooms on your map.

Link the rooms together as you would actually walk through them. In Figure 3.9, the player can only go to the dining room or front hall from the kitchen, but he or she can go to four different rooms from the front hall.

Now write some choices for your player to make when navigating this house. You can give the player directional choices such as go left or go right, or you can write room-based choices, such as "enter the living room" or "enter the bathroom."

Open each passage and write a description of the room. Try actually walking to that room in your house and taking a look around. Where do your eyes go first when you enter that room? What furniture is in that room? Remember that you are not only the players' eyes, but also their ears, nose, tongue, and hands. Use all five senses when writing your descriptions.

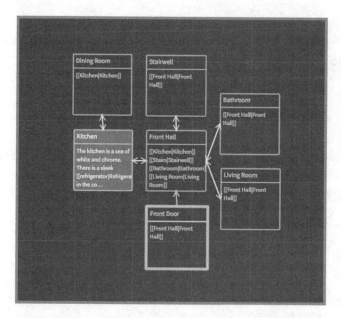

FIGURE 3.9 The earlier house map now constructed out of Twine boxes.

Now that you've written some description to start, you can add even more details to create opportunities for deeper exploration. Write a few short detail passages that connect to each room or use the (link:) tool to hide information for the player to discover.

Although there are only seven locations in this house, each passage may have dozens of detail passages that provide further detail. Each of those passages may have multiple passages connecting to them, as you can start to see in Figure 3.10.

In the kitchen, the player can look in the cabinets. In this case I've used detail passages to give additional information, but I could just as easily use the (link:) tool to create richer description.

Unless you're talking about places that people would love to visit, such as Hogwarts or the Shire, moving from room to room probably isn't very interesting if there isn't a goal, so you should give the player a goal. The player character could discover a ripped piece of paper with part of a secret message on it, and they must search the house to find the rest of the pieces. Don't make it too easy! Create nested links to make players poke around to accomplish the goal.

Houses are often small, but you can use the technique just described with larger spaces, such as a town or a country. Just draw your map, create your corresponding passages, arrange the boxes on the grid screen, and then add shorter passages to the main passages.

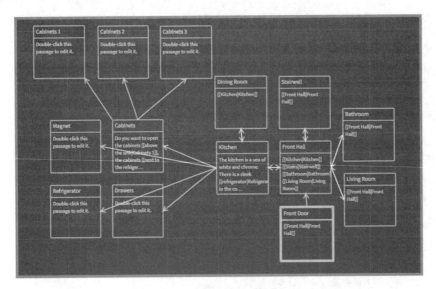

FIGURE 3.10 The house contains several rooms. Each of those rooms has detail passages connected to the rooms to encourage deeper exploration.

Creating a Maze

Mazes are a beloved and dreaded hallmark of interactive fiction. They have fallen out of vogue in contemporary interactive fiction because people find them fun to make but annoying to play. Still, they played a huge role in the early interactive fiction games, and, therefore, it's a rite of passage to make your own.

In fact, *Adventure*, that interactive fiction game I mentioned at the beginning of this chapter, contains a "maze of twisty little passages, all alike." What makes mazes interesting is that the path through them isn't obvious, so players must pay attention and keep track of where they've been.

TRY IT OUT: DESIGN YOUR OWN MAZE

Make a simple maze by arranging a grid of 16 boxes on the Twine screen, with 1 additional box to serve as the exit. Designate one of the passages as the entrance to the maze and then link various passages together. Try making some of your paths go diagonally (do you want to go northeast, or do you want to go southwest?) and throw in a few one-way options and dead ends.

Subtly change the text in the passages to convey that the reader is in a similar but slightly different space. A player wins when he or she gets to the exit passage, so make sure you have some fun text in that box to reward the player for making it through the maze.

Some other common spatial tropes in interactive fiction are caves and tunnels. It's good to know what commonly pops up in text adventure games so you can get creative and twist these elements into something new.

Map-based games are a great blank slate for exploring other aspects of Twine, including collecting objects or creating a points system for a traditional adventure-style role-playing game (RPG). As long as the exploration is meaningful and the players have a goal, they'll keep coming back to your game to play it again and again.

You've only scratched the surface of using Twine. You may be worried that the tasks are going to get harder, but I have a secret to tell you: Without even realizing it, you've been using macros, hooks, and strings. In other words, you've already done a lot of computer programming! I'll discuss those things further in the next chapter and teach you what macros are and how they work in Twine. Soon you'll be able to do some pretty cool things in your stories.

Designing Puzzles

Puzzles have always played a large role in interactive fiction, and dozens of types of puzzles commonly pop up in interactive fiction games.

For instance, Brian Moriarty's 1985 classic *Wishbringer* opens with you, the reader, standing on top of a hill with your boss, who is instructing you to deliver a letter to the Magick Shoppe on the other side of town. After you take the letter, you can head down the hill toward the cottage or the graveyard.

You quickly learn that your path to the Magick Shoppe is obstructed when you encounter the first puzzle in the game. A yapping dog blocks your path to town, and a creepy gravedigger locks the back gate of the cemetery before you can exit. How can you deliver the letter if every route to the Magick Shoppe is blocked?

This puzzle requires you to find an object that will distract the dog so you can pass. Luckily, there is a bone at the bottom of an open grave in the graveyard, and if you give the dog the bone, it will be too busy chewing on it to chew on you.

This type of puzzle is sometimes called a collection puzzle, an object puzzle, or a lock-and-key puzzle, but for the sake of defining some very specific categories of puzzles, let's call this type of puzzle a useful-item puzzle.

It's an easy one to kick off the game. Okay, so maybe it isn't *easy*; after all, I also tried jumping over the dog, kicking the dog, and racing the gravedigger, none of which worked. But it's *simple* in the sense that the object and its use are in close proximity. You pick up the bone in the graveyard, and you use it a turn or two later at the cottage.

In other puzzles, the object may come early in the story, but you don't encounter the puzzle until close to the end, which makes discovering the solution a little more difficult. It also means that one of your choices early in the story might make it impossible to solve a puzzle later in the story; for example, early on you might have a choice of weapon and take the sword when what you really need to advance to the end of the story is the bow and arrow.

In some games, the entire story is one big puzzle, like in the game *80 Days* by the game company Inkle. In *80 Days*, a game with connections to Jules Verne's *Around the World in 80 Days*, the player character is Phileas Fogg's servant, Passepartout. You need to make choices that will help your boss circumnavigate the globe in 80 days so he can win his bet.

It seems easy on the surface, but every choice you make has the potential to move you forward or cost you days of travel on your journey. For instance, I almost killed my boss, Mr. Fogg, by taking him across Egypt on a camel without the proper gear (oops!), and I stranded us in India without any money. Needless to say, I didn't make it around the world in 80 days the first time I played, though I made better choices the second time around, once I understood how my choices affected the outcome of the story.

Of course, plenty of interactive fiction doesn't include puzzles. You should take a close look at this hallmark of interactive fiction even if you don't think right now that you will add puzzles to your games. Making your own puzzles is a rite of passage for an interactive fiction writer, and this chapter aims to get you testing your players' creativity.

Finding Puzzle Ideas

Instead of learning a new Twine tool in this chapter, you're going to focus on understanding how writing scripts works so you can better use Twine to construct puzzles. In particular, you'll learn about macros and hooks—two pieces of script that you've already been using, even if you don't know these tools by name yet.

Understanding how to spot and create macros and hooks will help you dive into each new macro and hook in upcoming chapters. In fact, learning how you can fit these pieces of code together to create your own game will feel like solving a particularly satisfying puzzle.

First, however, you need to understand how to generate puzzle ideas and how to fit them into the framework of your story.

Finding Puzzles in Everyday Life

Whether you realize it or not, you solve puzzles all the time. For instance, you solve a certain type of puzzle three times every day: a series of sustenance puzzles. You've probably never thought about your lunch choice as a puzzle, but that's exactly what it is. You might solve your daily lunch puzzle by eating a highly portable peanut butter sandwich, or you may solve it by consuming leftovers from last night's dinner in order to clear out the refrigerator.

The best puzzles make sense outside the game as much as they make sense inside the game. People need to eat in order to live; therefore, it makes sense that your player character also needs to eat in order to live. Humans can't see in the dark, so it makes sense to require a light source in order to see in an unlit space.

Puzzles in interactive fiction games usually require the player to think hard or collect objects before they can begin to solve the puzzle. In a game, you might hide a peanut butter sandwich in a lunch bag in your friend's school locker, or you might have the player run out of bread and then need to work hard to make the sandwich.

The key to creating clever puzzles is to make sure the solution isn't too obvious. For instance, if the player encounters a locked door (a popular puzzle in interactive fiction), instead of allowing a simple solution like "turn the knob," you may choose to make the player utter a secret magic word, wave a wand, or search for a hidden key. You can make the player think and explore in order to find the best solution.

So to begin, consider all the puzzles around you that can be incorporated into a game. You solve problems all the time; make your players solve problems, too.

Making Your Puzzles Matter

Players tend to get cranky about pointless puzzles in games. Although all puzzles are meant to slow down game play and challenge the player to be clever or pay attention to the small details, there is a big difference between a necessary puzzle and a pointless puzzle. Sometimes pointless puzzles are called "soup can" puzzles, named after a game that had the player arrange soup cans in a certain order. These types of puzzles seem out of place in the general storyline.

Say that you're playing a game based on the book from *Alice's Adventures in Wonderland*. Alice sees a tiny door at the end of the hall but can't fit through it. Ah, a puzzle! There is a bottle on the table that contains a liquid that shrinks down Alice until she is small enough to fit through the door.

This would be a purposeful puzzle if this appeared in a game. There is a reason given for why Alice wants to be small enough to fit through the door: She wants to enter the beautiful garden on the other side of the door. Moreover, while drinking a liquid usually doesn't shrink a person, Lewis Carroll keeps the theme of strange things happening after ingestion going throughout the book, so this isn't a random event free floating in the narrative.

In a ridiculous, weird, wacky world puzzles can be ridiculous, weird, and wacky. Even in the normal, everyday world, readers can suspend their disbelief and roll with the idea that they may need to do tasks in games that they wouldn't necessarily do in real life, such as breaking into a house and stealing a priceless painting. The point is to make the puzzle part of the game and give readers a clear reason for why they are doing the task.

In the example of Alice, most girls don't go around drinking from random bottles they find as they move through their day. But her actions make sense in context because she's trying to get through the door, the bottle says, "Drink Me," and she's in a moment of desperation since she's stuck underground.

So what would be a soup can puzzle in this case? Say that Alice enters the hall and wants to go through one of the many normal-sized doors without a clue as to what she'll find on the other side. So she already is without a purpose, which, if you remember from Chapter 2, "Using Choice to Create Agency," is a low-agency situation. This puzzle would be particularly pointless if the door were locked until Alice drinks a vial of liquid that's sitting on the table. How does drinking liquid have anything to do with unlocking doors? Plus, her path to the door seems clear until this random event is thrown in her way. This is a soup can puzzle.

So how do you know if a puzzle is worth including? First and foremost, make sure that it moves the story forward. Does the player learn more about the world, more about the character, more about the situation at hand? Does the solution make sense, and does the puzzle meld with the plot? If you can answer "yes" to these questions, then the puzzle serves a purpose.

If a puzzle isn't part of the plotline, if it is solely meant to slow down game play, take it out. Puzzles aren't serving their purpose if they're only annoying the reader.

Building Puzzles in Twine

How exactly do you build a puzzle? Let's start by creating a choice puzzle, like in *80 Days*, where every decision brings you closer to or farther from your ultimate goal.

In this situation, say that you're a weary space traveler who has stumbled into an inn, called The Lonely Asteroid, on a distant planet, looking for a hot meal and a bed for the night. You run into a fierce alien who is cranky because you took his favorite seat at the bar. He challenges you to a duel, which hardly seems fair because he has capabilities that go beyond that of a tired space traveler. Still, this alien stands between you and your ultimate goal: a little peace and quiet.

Let's call this type of puzzle a troublesome-person puzzle, where a character in the story blocks the player character from reaching his or her goal. How will your character talk or act his or her way out of this scenario?

Finding the Starting Point and End Goal

Begin constructing your puzzle by identifying the starting point and the end goal. The starting point is the confrontation with the alien—it's the moment that kicks off the puzzle and makes it clear that there is a problem to be solved—and the end goal is getting your meal at the inn.

You can dive right into the opening scene. Open a new story and label it Alien Encounter. Title this first passage Encounter:

```
The alien balls his hands into fists. "I could beat you to a bloody pulp for
taking my seat," he says casually, "but I'll give you a chance to get out of
this bar alive. Just give me my seat if you want to live."

He's tiny, but most Naxons are. You know from your travels that Naxons emit a
dangerous green goo from their fists that burns through human skin in seconds.
Couple that with their ability to turn invisible and your overwhelming
exhaustion and you have a recipe for disaster.
```

Okay, so the scene is set, and you have a starting point, but what sort of choices can you give players that will either take them closer to or farther away from solving the puzzle and getting to the end goal?

Add these choices at the bottom of the same passage:

```
You could always move to a different spot in the restaurant, beg him to resolve
this peacefully, lie and say that you have some erbium in your pocket (deadly to
most Naxons), or grab something off a nearby table to use as a weapon. Or run.
There's always running.

What do you want to do? [[Move|Move]]? [[Beg|Beg]]? [[Lie|Lie]]? [[Grab|Grab]]?
Or [[run|Run]]?
```

Now you have the complete opening. When you click Play, you should see the opening description of the situation as well as five choices (see Figure 4.1).

The alien balls his hands into fists. "I could beat you to a bloody pulp for taking my seat," he says casually, "but I'll give you a chance to get out of this bar alive. Just give me my seat if you want to live."

He's tiny, but most Naxons are. You know from your travels that Naxons emit a dangerous green goo from their fists that burns through human skin in seconds. Couple that with their ability to turn invisible and your overwhelming exhaustion and you have a recipe for disaster.

You could always move to a different spot in the restaurant, beg him to resolve this peacefully, lie and say that you have some erbium in your pocket (deadly to most Naxons), or grab something off a nearby table to use as a weapon. Or run. There's always running.

What do you want to do? **Move**? **Beg**? **Lie**? **Grab**? Or **run**?

FIGURE 4.1   The opening of a troublesome person puzzle.

So how do you make this puzzle difficult? Well, if you were to play *80 Days*, you would notice that, while the outcomes of your choices always make sense, they don't always match your expectations. For instance, there are times in *80 Days* when you're kind but it backfires, and there are times when you're kind and it leads you closer to the end goal. You can't always predict how another person (or, in this case, alien) will react to your actions. So in this example, you need to decide if deferring to the alien by moving or begging will help or hinder the player.

Adding Layers to Your Puzzle

Open the first new passage—which is called Move—and write a consequence that makes sense and either brings the player character closer to the end goal or farther away:

```
"I don't want any trouble," you tell the alien, gathering your bag.
"I'll just move to this seat over here."

Before you can even bend your knees to sit down at the new table, you can tell
that you've made a terrible mistake. There's an invisible Naxon exactly where you
were aiming to sit. As he makes himself corporeal, you can see that he's not
only glaring at you, but has green goo oozing from between his fingers.

Do you [[jump behind the bar|Behind Bar]] to put some distance between you,
do you [[fight this new Naxon|Fight New Naxon]], or do you [[run|Run]]?
```

So physically moving away from the alien doesn't stop the player character's problems. In fact, I would say this takes the player farther away from the goal.

The more choices offered, the more complicated the puzzle, which is a good thing for the player, even if it's more work for the writer. To lessen the work on my end, I've linked one of the choices in this new passage to the Run passage that appears in the story opening. In this way, it becomes a choice in two places, but I have to fill only one passage. In Figure 4.2, you can see that the reader has three choices, but I only need to write two new passages in addition to the already existing Run passage. It also means that the Run passage becomes part of the second and third story levels at the same time due to the way the story branches as well as merges those branches by offering the same passage as a link in two different places.

Now you can work on what happens if the player character chooses to beg. Open up the passage Beg and write this:

```
"Hey, I'm sure we can solve this peacefully. You seem like such a kind,
understanding -- and did I mention, handsome -- Naxon. Please spare my life.
You can have the contents of my backpack if you leave me unharmed."

"Naxon?" the alien says. "You think I'm a Naxon?"

The alien grins at you gleefully and transforms himself into a Deerdon,
a boring, chameleon-like alien that can change itself to resemble whatever
it encounters. Deerdons aren't dangerous at all, and now you look ridiculous
for groveling to a lowly alien.

"Though I will take your backpack. Thanks!" he says, grabbing your bag from the
floor. Before you can react, he's out the door, and you're out on the streets.
Without any money or possessions, you have no chance of staying in the
Lonely Asteroid tonight.

The end.
```

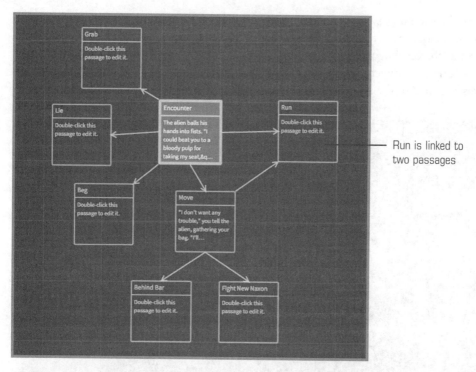

Run is linked to two passages

FIGURE 4.2 By linking a new choice to an old passage, you limit the number of passages the writer needs to fill.

Again, this is a possible consequence, but maybe not one that the player expected. And it neatly wraps up that choice to make it an ending for the game. Sometimes when I offer a lot of choices in a scene, I write some dead-ends. Without them, the story may become too unwieldy.

So what happens if the player character lies? Write the following in the passage Lie:

```
"I'm happy to give you this seat," you tell the alien, "though I'm not sure you
want it considering that I'm about to smear erbium all over the tabletop.
Are you sure?"

The alien gulps and glances at your pocket. "I guess it depends on the erbium.
Can I see it?"

You don't actually have any erbium.

You start to panic and look around for a potential weapon, something heavy that
you can chuck right at this Naxon. You see a salt shaker, but unfortunately,
it is several seats away, and the alien is staring right at you.

Do you [[distract the alien|Grab Shaker]] and grab the salt shaker? Or do you
admit that [[you don't have any erbium|Admit]] after all?
```

This time there are only two choices, but each requires a new passage. You're currently up to four extra passages that create a third story level to this puzzle, as you can see in Figure 4.3. Start at the opening passage, Encounter, and follow the arrows from box to box. The passages connected directly to the opening passage make up the second story level. The passages attached to the second story level passages make up the third story level.

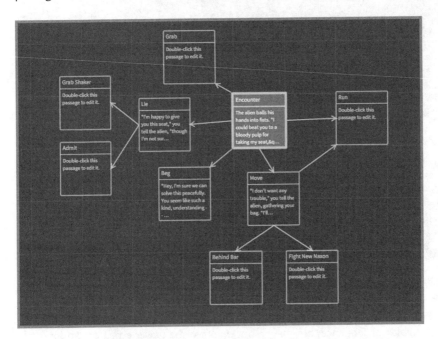

FIGURE 4.3 There are four passages in the third story level.

In this figure, you can see each story level by following the arrows. There are four passages in the third story level: Behind Bar, Fight New Naxon, Grab Shaker, and Admit. You don't want to give the player an easy path through this puzzle, so none of the passages in the second story level lead directly to the goal of a quiet meal. The player will have to keep making difficult choices.

If the player character grabs a weapon and prepares to fight the original alien, one problem is solved and a new problem opens. So write this in the passage Grab Shaker:

```
You point over the alien's shoulder and shout "look out!" Luckily the Naxon is
quite gullible. While he turns to look, you snatch a metal salt shaker and
brandish it over your head as if about to throw it. It isn't exactly the most
frightening weapon, but it does the trick. The alien backs away, croaking about how
it is hard to tell the difference between salt shakers and erbium shakers.

You forgot how much salt resembles erbium!
```

You sigh with relief and try to sit down in your seat, but something is occupying
the spot. Remember how Naxons can make themselves invisible? Well, one has slipped
into the vacant chair while you argued with the other Naxon.

As he makes himself corporeal, you can see that he's not only glaring at you
but has green goo oozing from between his fingers.

Do you [[jump behind the bar|Behind Bar]] to put some distance between you,
do you [[fight this new Naxon|Fight New Naxon]], or do you [[run|Run]]?

Here you write the same problem that cropped up in the passage titled Move. You just
tweak the text a bit to give the same situation with the same alien new life, and by providing
the player with the same response options, you limit how many new passages you need to
write in the third story level, as you can see in Figure 4.4.

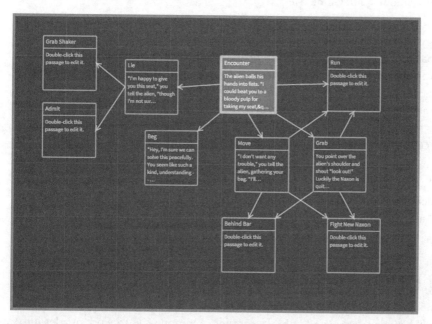

FIGURE 4.4 Arrows show the connections between the story levels.

Figure 4.4 shows the Grab passage moved over so you can clearly see that the choices in the
Move and Grab passages both lead to the same passages in the third story level. Without
writing a lot of new passages, you can make a situation more complicated and the path
toward the solution more convoluted.

Finally, you need to fill in the passage titled Run:

```
"Nice to meet you," you call hastily over your shoulder as you dart out of the
inn. You don't realize until you're on the street that you left your bag at the
bar. There's no way that you're going back inside, but there's also no way off
this planet without your spaceship key and wallet.

Do you risk [[returning to the inn|End]] and having to deal with the Naxon?
Or do you [[wander around the planet|End]], trying to find another way to get home?
```

Finishing the Puzzle

Both of the choices included in the Run passage lead to the end of the story. Whether you return to the inn or look for another way home, you walk into the gaping maw of an alien that swallows you in one gulp. Game over!

Well, it's game over when it comes to this series of choices. There are still multiple passages in the third story level that need to be filled in with text, such as Behind Bar and Fight New Naxon. Now that the story is started, you can fill in these passages by offering choices that lead to a fourth story level or closing them off by writing an ending. Remember, you can merge branches of the story by linking to the same passage in multiple places. This ensures that the fourth and fifth story levels (or however many levels the puzzle unfolds until the player finds resolution) don't become too large and complicated. Return to Chapter 2, "Using Choice to Create Agency," to review the hourglass story shape and delayed branching.

The puzzle ends when the player finds the solution that allows him or her to eat dinner and get to bed, which gives a brief respite before the game throws another puzzle the player's way. Now take a few minutes to complete this game.

Congratulations! You've made your first interactive fiction puzzle.

Building Other Types of Puzzles

There is a lot of variation in puzzle type names in the interactive fiction community, but the following list will help you get started in brainstorming common ways to work puzzles into your games:

Transportation puzzle—The player is moved from Point A to Point B by solving the puzzle or is moved from Point A to Point B against his or her will for not solving the puzzle.

Useful-item puzzle—In these types of puzzles, the player gets an item in one part of the game and uses it to solve a puzzle in another part of the game.

Hidden-object puzzle—Rather than having an item appear in plain sight as in a useful-item puzzle, the object is hidden, and obtaining the object is part of the puzzle.

Rationing puzzle—Objects need to be used at a certain time, and if they're used in the wrong place, the later puzzle cannot be solved.

Interacting-objects puzzle—This type of puzzle is similar to the classic logic puzzle that involves taking a fox, a chicken, and a bag of feed across a river. Leaving two wrong items together causes the player to fail.

Locked-door puzzle—This type of puzzle blocks the player's path. A locked-door puzzle doesn't have to involve an actual locked door. Be creative! The "locked door" could be a grouchy landlord who demands the rent before you can pass into your apartment.

Manipulation puzzle—These types of puzzles require the player to manipulate something, like a machine or a switch, in order to change the situation.

Escape puzzle—These types of puzzles trap the player in a physical space from which he or she needs to escape.

Narrow-space puzzle—The player's motion is limited based on the objects being held, such as carrying too many items to fit through a door.

Sequencing puzzle—The player needs to put objects in the correct order.

Cryptogram—The player needs to crack a code or read a secret cipher.

Sustenance puzzle—The character is unable to keep going unless he or she has food.

Light-source puzzle—The player can't enter certain areas of the game without carrying a light source, or the player can't enter certain areas of the game because he or she is carrying a light source (such as trying to carry a torch in water).

As you play interactive fiction games, you'll encounter a lot of puzzles and discover which ones *you* like to solve.

Using Macros and Hooks

Now it's time to switch gears and talk about how macros and hooks work together to create scripts. Each new macro and hook is easier to learn if you go through how all macros and hooks work so you can see the pattern.

There are actually three Twine formats—Harlowe, SugarCube, and Snowman. Although games in each format display differently on the screen, each format also has its own unique way of writing scripts. The default format, and the one you'll use for the time being, is Harlowe, which was designed by Leon Arnott. Twine opens in the Harlowe format. Each time you start a new story, it will automatically be set to the Harlowe format. This format has built-in macros and hooks that enable you to do some pretty cool things in your games.

You've been using macros and hooks for the last few chapters. Up until this point, I've been calling them *tools*, as in the (link:) tool and the (display:) tool. While they certainly are handy tools, the more accurate term for them is *macro*.

A *macro* is basically a shortcut to performing a specific task. Macros extend the way Twine stories work so that you don't have to write long pieces of code in order to pull off neat tricks, such as the links between passages or making new text appear on the screen, as you do with `(link:)`. In both cases, those are macros at work. To distinguish between the text of a story and macros, you'll sometimes see the macros referred to as TwineScript, though in this book, I generally call the code in the passage the script.

Hooks are the words inside the single brackets, and they're called hooks because you can hook actions (which are the macros) onto them.

With the exception of the double square brackets for the `[[link]]` macro that connects two passages, all macros in Harlowe follow the same format: They begin with a parenthesis, a word, and a colon. Take, for example, the macro `(font:)`, which you can use to change the font for your story:

```
(font: "monospace")[These words look like they came from a typewriter.]
```

Let's take a look at this example of a macro and hook, part by part. The macro opens with a parenthesis, the word `font`, and a colon. Macros are commands. In other words, a macro tells Twine what you want it to do. The example above tells Twine to use the font that appears inside the quotation marks: monospace. Monospace is a typewriter-like font, so I used the font to write the words "These words look like they came from a typewriter," as shown in Figure 4.5.

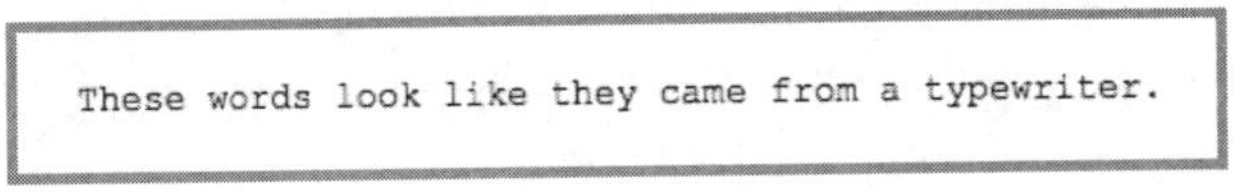

```
These words look like they came from a typewriter.
```

FIGURE 4.5 A macro and a hook in action.

The macro acts on the hook and changes the words that appear inside the single brackets so they display in a monospace font.

Whatever appears inside the single brackets is affected by the macro, and whatever is outside the single brackets is not affected by the macro. In fact, if you place more text outside the single brackets, as shown here, you can see in Figure 4.6 that it displays in the default font and not in monospace, like the words inside the hook:

```
(font: "monospace")[These words look like they came from a typewriter.]
But these words appear in the default font.
```

```
These words look like they came from a typewriter. But these words
appear in the default font.
```

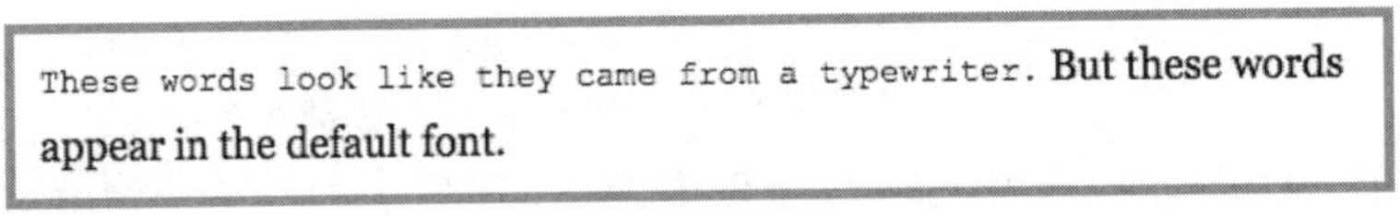

FIGURE 4.6 A macro and a hook with text outside the hook.

The macro acts only on whatever is contained inside the single brackets.

You can practice using macros and hooks by making a puzzle. Remember that you're not doing anything new here; you're just looking at the tools you've been using through new eyes. By having this vocabulary and understanding of how scripting works, you'll be able to quickly learn new macros because they all behave the same way and have similar syntax.

TRY IT OUT: CREATE A TRANSPORTING PUZZLE

To make a transporting puzzle, open a new story and name it Transporting.

Create a scene where there are eight different colored potions on a table. Three of the potions trap the player in the room. Four of the potions poison the player and end the game. The last potion allows the player to move through the exit. A player can test potions until he or she gets through the exit or dies trying.

Use the (link:) macro and hook to keep the player in the room. Use the [[link]] macro to move the player to a passage called Poisoned and use another [[link]] macro to move the player to a passage called Exit.

Of course, you'll need to provide the player with hints to help him or her make an informed decision.

How did you give clues to the player to help with the potion decision? One way you could do it is to write a little rhyming riddle for the player, like this:

```
You enter the hallway and the door immediately melts into the wall,
trapping you inside. The only furniture in the room is a small table with eight
brightly colored potions and a note. You pick up the note and read:
We are eight potions in a locked hall.
Three of the potions do nothing at all.
Four potions are poison (if you believe).
One potion, of course, will allow you to leave.
Primary colors won't make you sick.
Secondary colors may contain a trick.
The colors of fire should keep you around.
The color of water may cause you to drown.

Do you want to drink the (link: "red")[red potion does nothing],
(link: "orange")[the orange potion does nothing], [[yellow|Exit]],
[[green|Poisoned]], (link: "blue")[the blue potion does nothing],
[[purple|Poisoned]], [[pink|Poisoned]] or [[silver|Poisoned]] potion?
```

It is clear from the rhyme that red, yellow, and blue are safe to try: They'll either keep you in the same place or transport you to the exit. The orange, green, and purple potions, according to the rhyme, are potentially dangerous. The player can reason that the orange potion is safe due to the "colors of fire" line, whereas the final line insinuates that despite its safe nature that the player doesn't want to choose blue if the goal is to get out.

These sorts of clues still leave things open to chance. The player can eliminate choices without having an easy answer in the game.

Using Named Hooks

Up until this point, you've been using what are called *anonymous hooks*. The majority of hooks that I like to use in Twine are anonymous hooks. They are called anonymous because they don't have a label. Anonymous hooks are only connected to the macro immediately in front of the hook. In other words, you will always see a macro in front of an anonymous hook.

But a few hooks you'll use later in this book are *named hooks*. Named hooks aren't attached to a macro, so they are not preceded by a word enclosed in a parentheses. They're called named hooks because each one comes with a nametag. You can use that nametag to reference the hook anywhere inside the passage. Here's a named hook in action:

```
You reach into your satchel, feeling around for your magic wand...
Where is it? It has to be [in here somewhere.]<think|
(click: ?think)[But you realize you left it on your workbench next to
your spell book!]
```

The named hook is `[in here somewhere]`. This hook isn't attached to a macro. Instead, it has a tag attached to it: `<think|`. The tag begins with an angled bracket (`<`), contains the name of the hook (`think`), and ends with a vertical line (`|`), also called a pipe. When you put it all together (`<think|`), you get the nametag. That tag makes this a named hook.

That nametag allows you to refer to the hook somewhere else in the passage. For instance, instead of attaching the hook directly to a macro, you can place the macro later in the passage when you tell Twine how you want it to modify that named hook. This is handy when you have a long passage and you want to tuck the code toward the bottom of the passage and keep it out of the way. Named tags let you separate cause from effect on the page.

In the case of the example, the code appears toward the bottom of the passage so the `(click:)` macro can act on the hook named `?think`. Each named hook is named with a tag-shaped bit of punctuation (doesn't `<think|` look like a tag?), and all named hooks are referenced in the macro with a question mark in front of the tag name. The question mark was chosen because it looks a little bit like the sort of hook Captain Hook uses in place of his hand in *Peter Pan*.

In the preceding example, the `(click:)` macro creates a clickable link for the words inside the named hook: "in here somewhere." The `(click:)` macro transforms what would normally be plain text into a hyperlink. When those words, which are marked by ?think, are clicked, the macro shows the text contained in the hook attached to the macro. In other words, the words "in here somewhere" stop being a link once they're clicked, and the words in the anonymous hook appear on the screen: "But you realize you left it on your workbench next to your spell book."

You've probably noticed that (click:) and (link:) behave in a similar manner from the reader's point of view: the reader sees hyperlinked text on the screen, and when he or she clicks it, new words appear. However, their usage on the blue grid screen looks very different from the writer's point of view. The biggest difference is that (link:) works with anonymous hooks, and (click:) works with named hooks.

Named hooks are always acted upon by a macro, but the macro and the hook are set apart. This comes in handy when you want the code to be tucked away, apart from the rest of the text.

How does this look when it plays out on the screen? In Figure 4.7, the player sees the plain text and the named hook, which appears on the screen as blue hypertext.

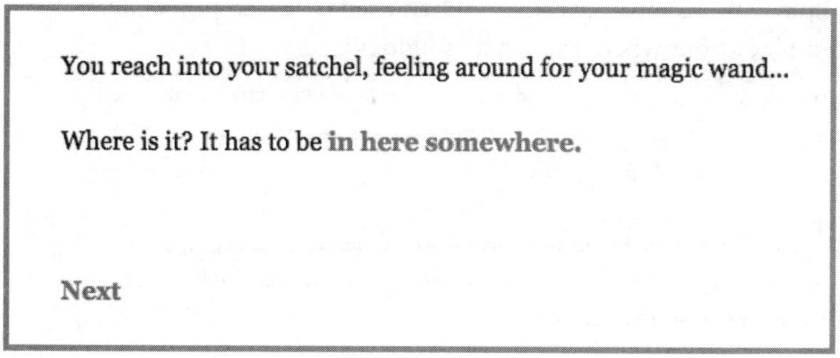

> You reach into your satchel, feeling around for your magic wand...
>
> Where is it? It has to be **in here somewhere.**
>
>
>
> **Next**

FIGURE 4.7 A named hook, appearing as hypertext on the screen.

Then, when the named hook is triggered by being clicked, the hypertext turns into plain text and remains on the screen. In addition, the words that were inside the anonymous second hook are displayed, as shown in Figure 4.8.

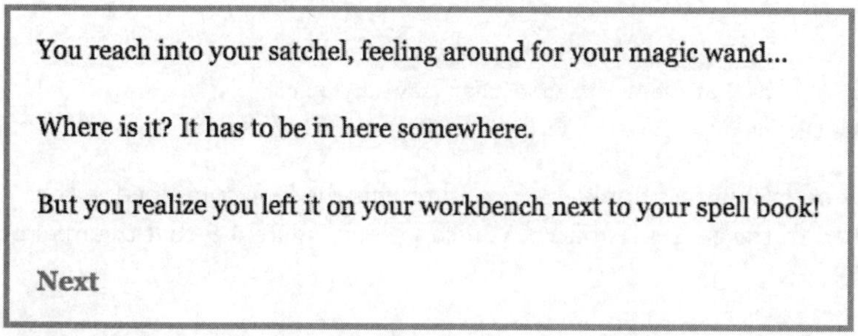

> You reach into your satchel, feeling around for your magic wand...
>
> Where is it? It has to be in here somewhere.
>
> But you realize you left it on your workbench next to your spell book!
>
> **Next**

FIGURE 4.8 The named hook is triggered, displaying the text in the second hook.

You can use named hooks to create a hidden-object puzzle.

TRY IT OUT: CREATE A HIDDEN-OBJECT PUZZLE

To make a hidden-object puzzle, open a new story and name it Hidden Object.

The scene opens with a busker on the boardwalk, offering a chance to play a dangerous game. The player gets one chance to find the magic stone that the busker has hidden underneath one of his three cups. But there's a catch: The other two cups contain an explosive powder that will ignite and blow the player off the boardwalk.

Use a named tag to ask the busker for a hint so you'll know which cup to choose. Use `[[links]]` for the cups to transport the player to an explosion passage or a winning passage.

How did you construct your passage so all the cups looked alike to the player at first glance? I set up my example with a simple lead-in and then used a named hook called `?hint` to have the busker drop a hint about where the stone is hidden:

```
"I need that stone," you tell the busker. He drops it underneath the center cup
and begins to shuffle them around the table. You watch carefully at first but soon
grow confused, unable to tell where the stone is located.

You start to point to a cup, but the busker holds up his hand. "Remember, two
of these cups contain enough explosive powder to blow you into the center of
the ocean. Sure you know where the stone is?"

You aren't sure, but you don't really have a choice to walk away. You need to
get that stone.

You wonder if he'd give you a [hint.]<hint|

Do you choose the [[first cup|Explosion]], [[second cup|You Win]],
or [[third cup|Explosion]]?

(click: ?hint)[The busker winks at you. "What's that saying? First
is the worst, second is the best, third is the one with the hairy chest?"]
```

The `(click:)` macro acts on the named hook `<hint|` and reveals the hint contained in the anonymous hook attached to the `(click:)` macro. You can see in Figure 4.9 that the macro is below the named hook.

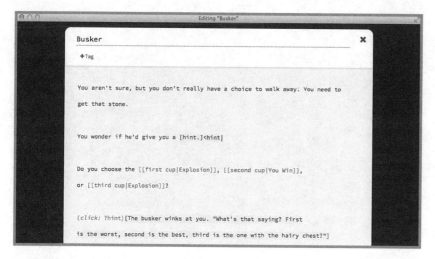

FIGURE 4.9 The (click:) macro in Twine.

Now that you've expanded your Twine vocabulary and understand how Twine's macros and hooks work, the new macros you'll learn in future chapters will be easy to understand because they all follow the same format. The more macros you learn, the more fun things you can do with Twine, including, of course, making puzzles.

Building Objects with Variables

A wand, a golden snitch, and round black glasses. Even with only three objects to identify the character, you probably thought of Harry Potter. Let's try this again: deerstalker hat, magnifying glass, and pipe. Sherlock Holmes, right? What about lightsaber, blaster, and droid? Luke Skywalker from *Star Wars*. Kryptonite, cape, and phone booth? Superman.

Objects define a character and give them a purpose. For example, in *The Lion, the Witch, and the Wardrobe* by C.S. Lewis, the character Edmund is associated with Turkish delight. Turkish delight would have been a luxury candy in 1940s London—difficult to obtain and enjoyed only by the very rich. With this simple object, the author conveys to the reader that Edmund is greedy. He requests a delicacy instead of penny candy, even when there's a sugar shortage back home. The candy also gives him a purpose, as he quickly becomes addicted and promises to bring his siblings to the evil White Queen in exchange for more Turkish delight. This single object not only tells us a lot about Edmund but also drives the plot forward, giving Edmund a reason to do what he's going to do.

Using Objects in Interactive Fiction

Objects play a huge role in interactive fiction. What would *Enchanter* be without the spell book? Or *Wishbringer* without the wish stone? Or *Hitchhiker's Guide to the Galaxy* without the towel? Not only do objects help the player solve puzzles or explore, but they also serve as the details that make the story memorable. Infocom, an early maker of interactive fiction games, knew that players love objects so much that it included tangible versions of them—called feelies—packaged with its games. If you bought the game, you could own your very own lab report from *Deadline* or a balloon from *Ballyhoo*.

Collecting objects was a huge part of early interactive fiction games like Infocom's *Zork*. The object of the game was simple: Go to an underground kingdom and collect treasures and then come back above ground and deposit said treasures in the trophy case. The game ended when you found all the objects.

Of course, it was rarely as easy as simply walking into a room and taking an object. You often needed to solve puzzles. For instance, there was a knife you needed to pick up in the house above ground and carry with you to use later in the game to kill a thief. However, if you were still carrying that knife when you got in a raft later in the game, it punctured the raft and made it useless.

Still, it didn't take long for interactive fiction makers to realize that collecting objects without a purpose beyond putting them in a trophy case is sort of boring. At some point, the readers take a step back and wonder *why* they should keep walking around, picking up every treasure that's not nailed down. You can circumvent this boredom by building your object collection around a quest.

The word *quest* may make you think about knights riding off to slay a dragon and save a princess. After all, *quest* is often used in fantasy stories to describe the impossible task the brave main character needs to do to save someone or something.

But in the literary sense, *quest* simply describes the motivation of the player character. What does the player character want? What is he or she trying to do? What is the player character's goal? The type of quest not only answers these questions but gives the player a reason for collecting objects during a game, just as Turkish delight gave Edmund a reason to keep moving through Narnia.

You can add objects to your Twine games by using variables. With a bit of scripting, you can offer players options to pick up (or drop) objects. In this chapter, you'll learn a few new macros that will be invaluable in adding, subtracting, and tracking objects in your game as well as learn how to frame them in a quest.

Building Interactive Objects with Variables

Think of a *variable* as an empty box in which you can store information. In fact, a variable really is just a virtual storage system. Unlike a macro, a variable doesn't exist in Twine until *you* make it exist. To see how it works, in the next section you'll make one and use it in a story.

Creating a Variable

Let's say that you want to have a ring in your story. It's a good idea to name the variable the same name as the object so that you remember the name of the variable every time you want to use it. In Twine, you write a variable name with a dollar sign in front, so the variable for a ring might be written as `$ring`.

After you create the variable `$ring`, you have to give it a value. A *value* is the information you're storing in the virtual storage system of the variable. You may want to track the number of rings and assign a *number value* such as 1. You may instead want to track the way the ring looks and assign a word value (known as a *string* in programming) such as `"gold"` or `"big"`. Or you can track a fact about the ring and assign a *Boolean* value, such as true if the player character has the ring and false if she doesn't.

To set the value of the variable, you use the `(set:)` macro. Here's how you assign a number value:

```
(set: $ring to 1)
```

The nice thing about this code is that it's practically written in plain English. Here you're basically telling Twine to set a variable called $ring to the value 1. There is no hook after this macro.

Changing a Value

Once you set the value of a variable, Twine remembers it from passage to passage. Right now, Twine remembers that you told the program that the player character is holding one ring in the story. What if a character finds two more rings? You can either change the number by assigning a new number with the (set:) macro, or—even better—use operators (such as addition or subtraction symbols) to add to the value. This example resets the value of the variable $ring so it takes into account that two more rings were found:

```
(set: $ring to 3)
```

And this gives you the same effect:

```
(set: $ring to $ring + 2)
```

The second example tells Twine to take whatever the original value was for $ring and increase it by two. This is the preferred way of adding to the existing value of the variable.

These are the operators you commonly use in Twine:

+	Add
-	Subtract
/	Divide
*	Multiply
>	Greater than
<	Less than
>=	Greater than or equals
<=	Less than or equals
is	Equals
is not	Does not equal

Say that the player character drops a ring. You can use the subtraction symbol to reduce the value much the way you use the addition symbol to add to the value:

```
(set: $ring to $ring - 1)
```

Here's how you could have a character tell the player character that he is going to wave his wand and double the number of rings the player character is currently holding:

```
(set: $ring to $ring * 2)
```

Or your player character could encounter a really mean wizard who steals half the rings the player character is holding:

```
(set: $ring to $ring / 2)
```

Note that the division operator really will divide the value in half, so if the value of $ring was 3, Twine will now think that your character has 1.5 rings, which is a little odd. You can work around this by telling Twine to round the final amount to a whole number, like this:

```
(set: $ring to (round: $ring / 2))
```

Now, when Twine divides that initial value of 3, instead of saying that you have 1.5 rings, it rounds up and states that you have 2 rings. Notice that there are two closing parentheses at the end of the line of code. That is because this code uses a nested macro—a macro within a macro. The first closing parenthesis closes off the (round:) macro, and the second one closes off the (set:) macro. Nested elements are very common in code.

Using Strings

All the variables you've looked at so far are number values. What if you wanted to describe a ring and save your description in the $ring variable? You could do that with a word or a set of words known as a *string*. Strings are written inside quotation marks.

Let's say that there are three rings in a box: a silver ring, a gold ring, and an iron ring. You want to give the player character a choice between the various rings and then have the game track which ring was chosen so you can display different text based on which ring the player chose. You use the (set:) macro to assign a word to the variable, like this:

```
(set: $ring to "gold")
```

This example sets the variable $ring to "gold". But if the player character changes his or her mind and picks the silver ring the next time there's a choice, you just use the (set:) macro again to reset the value:

```
(set: $ring to "silver")
```

Now, unless you change it again, Twine remembers that the ring is silver from passage to passage.

Using Boolean Values

You can assign a true/false value, or Boolean value, to a variable. Essentially, any question where true or false fits as the answer ("The player has the ring, true or false?") can use this type of value. For instance, you may want to assign a true value to $ring if the player character has taken the ring:

```
(set: $ring to true)
```

Booleans are written without quotation marks. In fact, if you put quotation marks around a Boolean value, Twine interprets it as a string. So, as with numbers, simply write the word true or false without quotation marks.

When you use a Boolean value, it can be a good idea to create a variable name that reflects its possible true/false status. You aren't limited to a single word when it comes to naming variables. In fact, the point of the variable's name is to remind you what you're tracking, so you can link together as many words as you need without spaces between them. Instead of naming the variable $ring, name the variable something that reflects its state of being, such as $hasRing:

```
(set: $hasRing to true)
```

You may wonder why the variable in this example has strange capitalization. You can't have spaces between the words in a variable's name, so programmers write multiple-word variables like this, with the first letter of the first word lowercased and the first letter in each subsequent word capitalized. This makes it easy to quickly see where one word ends and next word begins.

Booleans can't tell you a numerical amount, nor can they tell you anything descriptive about an object, but they're very handy when all you want to do is track an either/or situation such as having an object or not.

Here's another example of a Boolean value, used to track whether a door is open:

```
(set: $doorOpen to false)
```

By creating a variable for the door, you can track whether the door is open (true) or closed (false).

Using Variables in Passages

So how does the (set:) macro look in action inside a passage? To find out, you will write a search quest for a story. In a search quest, the main character goes looking for something that is lost or unknown. The player may search for a physical object, such as a missing book, or information. In this case, the player character wants to know if the magical land of Pyradin is real.

The scene opens in your tutor's study. Old Harrington has taken out a box of tarnished rings, their stones missing, and tells you that they are the last doors into Pyradin.

Unfortunately, because the stones are missing, Old Harrington is no longer able to tell the rings apart, though each ring will transport you to one of the five districts of Pyradin. In addition, because it has been dozens of years since he has last stepped foot in Pyradin, Old Harrington cannot tell you what sort of danger will meet you when you enter.

Still, you've been waiting all your life for an opportunity to find out for yourself whether Pyradin is real, and you're not going to let a little danger stand in your way.

Open a new story and label it Pyradin. You can also go ahead and title the first passage Harrington Study, and type this in it:

```
Old Harrington shakes the box, and the jingle of metal against metal sounds like
a welcoming bell tinkling as you open a door. You clasp your hands behind
your back as if you don't trust yourself not to grab the whole boxful and slide
them onto your fingers, one by one. You know what happens to people who can't
make a decision, who try to go too many places at once, hedge their bets.

They get ripped apart.
```

```
You try to distinguish between the stoneless rings to make your choice. There
is the [[silver one|Silver Ring]], the [[gold one|Gold Ring]], the
[[iron one|Iron Ring]], the one with the [[broken metal flower|Flower Ring]],
and the one with the [[odd design carved into its side|Design Ring]].

Which one to do you want to take?
```

At this point, you've set the scene and given five choices corresponding to the five rings. Doing so creates five new passages, as shown in Figure 5.1.

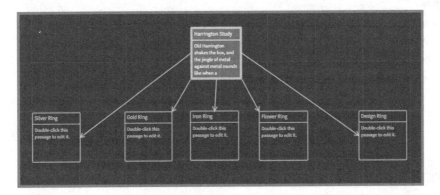

FIGURE 5.1 The five new passages off the first passage create the second story level.

You now need to place the variable $ring and its value at the start of each of the passages in this newly created second story level. When the player makes a choice in the opening story passage and clicks on one of the links corresponding to the different rings, he or she goes to one of the five new passages shown in this figure. When the player opens the new passage, the variable and its value is set using the (set:) macro. Although the variable name remains the same from passage to passage, its value is a different string depending on the passage. In the Silver Ring passage, the value is "silver", and in the Gold Ring passage, the value is "gold".

Consider the passage Silver Ring as an example:

```
(set: $ring to "silver")You pick up the silver ring and weigh it in your hand.
It's lighter than you expected. You move to slip it onto your ring finger,
but Old Harrington grabs your wrist to stop you.

"Before you leave, you can take one more object from my magical box to aid
you in your travels."
```

He opens another box revealing three ordinary objects. There is a feather,
a pair of glasses, and a hat. You can't see how any of them will help you
in your journey, but you don't want to be rude.

Do you take the [[feather|Feather]], [[glasses|Glasses]], or [[hat|Hat]]?

At the start of the passage, you can see the (set:) macro being used to set the value of the
variable, $ring: (set: $ring to "silver"). Although you could place the variable anywhere
inside the passage, here it is at the top so you wouldn't forget that the purpose of this new
passage is to set the value of the variable based on the choice the player made in the first
passage. It's important to make sure you remember to tell Twine the outcome of the player's
choice so you can track it through the game.

The rest of the passage gives another three choices at the bottom of the screen. These open
up three new passages in the third story level, as shown in Figure 5.2.

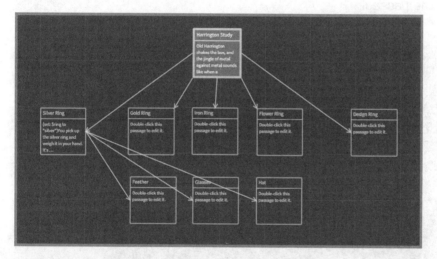

FIGURE 5.2 Three new passages make up the third story level.

To keep things simple, you can repeat the same text inside each of the subsequent passages
in the second story level and just change the value to a corresponding string. In the Gold
Ring passage, the string is "gold", and in the Iron Ring passage, the string is "iron". In the
Design Ring passage shown in Figure 5.3, the string is "design".

Because all five passages contain the same text with the exception of the setting of the
variable at the beginning of each passage, all the choices at the bottom of the passage link
to the same three passages in the third story level, as shown in Figure 5.4.

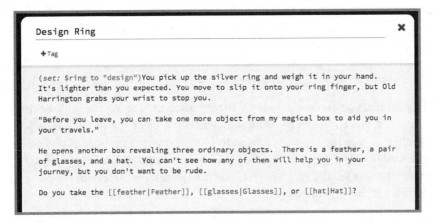

```
Design Ring                                                          ✕
─────────────────────────────────────────────────────────────────────
  ✚ Tag

(set: $ring to "design")You pick up the silver ring and weigh it in your hand.
It's lighter than you expected. You move to slip it onto your ring finger, but Old
Harrington grabs your wrist to stop you.

"Before you leave, you can take one more object from my magical box to aid you in
your travels."

He opens another box revealing three ordinary objects. There is a feather, a pair
of glasses, and a hat. You can't see how any of them will help you in your
journey, but you don't want to be rude.

Do you take the [[feather|Feather]], [[glasses|Glasses]], or [[hat|Hat]]?
```

FIGURE 5.3 The variable $ring being set with the string "design" at the beginning of the passage.

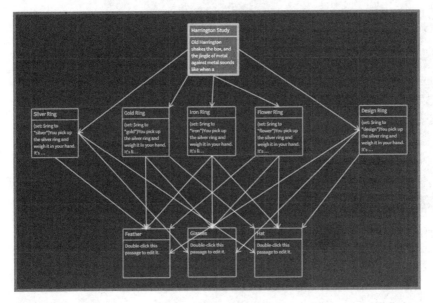

FIGURE 5.4 All five passages in the second story level lead to the same three passages that make up the third story level.

Note that although you can see the code on the grid-like passage screen, the player does not see the code while playing the game but instead sees what is shown in Figure 5.5.

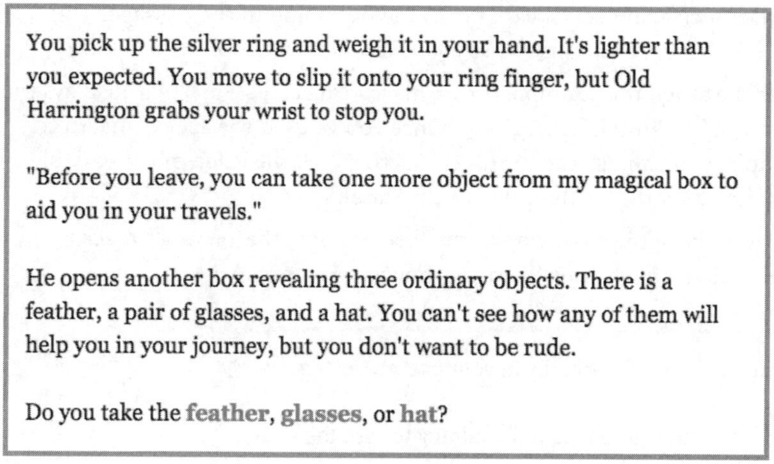

> You pick up the silver ring and weigh it in your hand. It's lighter than you expected. You move to slip it onto your ring finger, but Old Harrington grabs your wrist to stop you.
>
> "Before you leave, you can take one more object from my magical box to aid you in your travels."
>
> He opens another box revealing three ordinary objects. There is a feather, a pair of glasses, and a hat. You can't see how any of them will help you in your journey, but you don't want to be rude.
>
> Do you take the **feather**, **glasses**, or **hat**?

FIGURE 5.5 The `(set:)` macro in action in the Silver Ring passage.

Twine can track an unlimited number of variables, so to make things a little more interesting in this example, you can track a second variable, `$magicalItem`. The value of the `$magicalItem` variable gives the player a superpower he or she can use upon entering Pyradin. The feather allows the player to fly, the glasses let the player become invisible, and the hat lets the player walk through walls.

So, if the player chooses the feather, he or she can't become invisible to a monster in Pyradin, and if the player encounters a locked door, he or she won't be able to walk through the wall in order to get in the building. Making the `$magicalItem` choice influences the outcome of the player's story.

Just as you set the value of the variable `$ring` within the passages of the second story level, you set the value of the variable `$magicalItem` in the passages of the third story level. Again, you can mostly keep the same language in each passage, tweaking just a few words and the value of the variable. All the passages in the third story level lead to a single passage in the fourth story level: Pyradin.

Open the passage Feather and fill in the following text:

```
(set: $magicalItem to "feather")You pick up the feather and place it carefully
in your pocket.

"It's now time to go," Old Harrington tells you, nodding toward the
(print: $ring) ring in your hand.

You place the (print: $ring) ring on your finger and instantly feel your
body jerked towards [[a brightly lit space|Pyradin]].
```

The code in this passage once again sets a variable at the beginning of the passage. This time the variable is $magicalItem, and it uses a string as its value: "feather".

In order to personalize the story, this example uses a macro called (print:) that displays the value of the listed, set variable—in this case, $ring. Once you've used the (set:) macro to set the value of a variable, you can ask the (print:) macro to tell the value of the variable. In this case, it returns the string that is the value of the variable.

If, for instance, the player chose the silver ring in the first passage, the (print:) macro states that you have the silver ring in your hand, as shown in Figure 5.6.

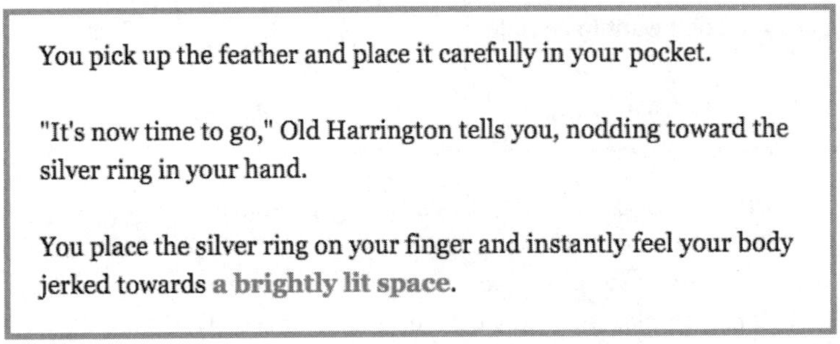

> You pick up the feather and place it carefully in your pocket.
>
> "It's now time to go," Old Harrington tells you, nodding toward the silver ring in your hand.
>
> You place the silver ring on your finger and instantly feel your body jerked towards **a brightly lit space.**

FIGURE 5.6 The (print:) macro displays the value of the $ring variable.

Think of the (print:) macro as the opposite of the (set:) macro. With the (set:) macro, the writer assigns the value of the variable, and with the (print:) macro, Twine displays the value of the already set variable. Think about these two macros in terms of a lemonade stand: With the (set:) macro, you make a sign stating that lemonade is 50 cents per cup, and with the (print:) macro, you check the sign to remember how much you priced your lemonade.

This example uses the (print:) macro just to add a personalized touch to the story. The player chose the silver ring in the opening passage, and the player is reminded of this in the third passage with the description of the ring in his or her hand.

Technically, Twine is programmed to allow you to write the name of the variable without specifically using the (print:) macro by using the variable in the plain text of the passage and having Twine display the value of the variable. For instance, this sentence displays in the same way onscreen:

```
You have a $ring ring.
```

as this one:

```
You have a (print: $ring) ring.
```

So why get in the habit of using the (print:) macro at all? Not only does it give you practice with this macro, which will be more useful to you in the future when you combine it with other macros, but the (print:) macro helps you structure your sentence properly. Remember that the macro is simply printing the value, and it's easy to accidentally leave off the name of the object in the plain text since the name of the object is also the name of the variable. For instance, the following appears on the screen as "You are holding the silver.":

```
You are holding the $ring.
```

Before continuing, fill in the other two passages in the third story level—Glasses and Hat— with the same text you placed inside the passage titled Feather, but change the value of the variable $magicalItem to the string "pair of glasses" or "hat" in its respective passage. As said earlier, all three passages in the third story level lead to the same place: Pyradin (see Figure 5.7).

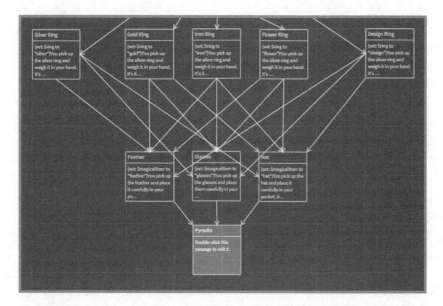

FIGURE 5.7 All passages in the third story level lead to a single passage, Pyradin, in the fourth story level.

Since this is a search quest, you'll continue the story with the player character motivated to explore Pyradin and learn new information applicable to the quest.

Building Conditional Statements

Once you've created variables, you can display different text based on the values of your variables. In Twine, you can use the assignment macros (if:) and (else:) to write conditional statements. A conditional statement checks whether a fact is true or false.

You've probably encountered a lot of conditional statements in your day-to-day world, such as "*if* you do your work, *then* you can go to the movies." In that case, the condition is whether or not you've done your work. If the answer is yes, you can go to the movies. If the answer is no, you can't go to the movies. Twine works in the same way, looking to see whether the statement's conditions have been met, and if they have, performing a task or displaying certain text. Conditional statements are common in programming languages.

In this section you'll continue the Pyradin game by changing the player's experience based on which magical object he or she chose back in Old Harrington's study. When entering Pyradin, the player is standing next to a tree that has tiny brass keys dangling like apples. If the player took the feather, he or she can fly up and grab one of the keys. If the player took the glasses or the hat, he or she won't see the choice to fly up into the tree, and the only option is to go down the hill toward the town.

Adding a Conditional Statement

Let's set up a conditional statement. The condition is whether or not the player has the feather, or, to put it in Twine terms, whether the variable $magicalItem has a value of "feather".

Open the passage named Pyradin and write this:

```
You are standing on top of a windy hill, overlooking the valley and, beyond that,
the sea. The high spires of the Dunningham Castle rise over the rest of the hamlet,
casting shadows on the houses arranged in a semi-circle around the seat of power.

You cannot believe you are actually here.

Suddenly, your brain catches up with your body, and you start to feel doubtful.
After all this time, it was so easy getting here. Too easy. You wonder if this
is really Pyradin at all.

You look around and finally notice the odd tree behind you casting a shadow
over the grass. Dangling from each branch are dozens of tiny brass keys.

(if: $magicalItem is "feather")[You feel the feather knocking against your leg
in your pocket, almost as if it's trying to tell you that you can fly. Do you
want to [[hold the feather|Fly]] and attempt to fly and get a key? Or do you
want to [[head down the hill|Town]] into the town and explore?](else:)[Too bad
you can't reach any of the keys. You should probably [[head down the hill|Town]]
into the town and explore.]
```

Remember learning about macros and hooks in Chapter 4, "Designing Puzzles"? This passage contains two anonymous hooks attached to two different macros that often work together: (if:) and (else:). These macros work together to create a conditional statement. The structure for the conditional statement sounds very much like plain English:

> If the $magicalItem variable has the value "feather", display the text and links on the screen that appear inside the first hook: "You feel the feather knocking against your leg in your pocket, almost as if it's trying to tell you that you can fly. Do you want to

[[hold the feather|Fly]] and attempt to fly and get a key? Or do you want to [[head down the hill|Town]] into the town and explore?" If the $magicalItem variable has any other value except "feather", display the text and link that appear inside the second hook: "Too bad you can't reach any of the keys. You should probably [[head down the hill|Town]] into the town and explore."

Go ahead and play this example on your computer. The first time, choose to take the feather in the second story level. The second time, don't take the feather. When you take the feather, you should see toward the bottom of the passage the text shown in Figure 5.8.

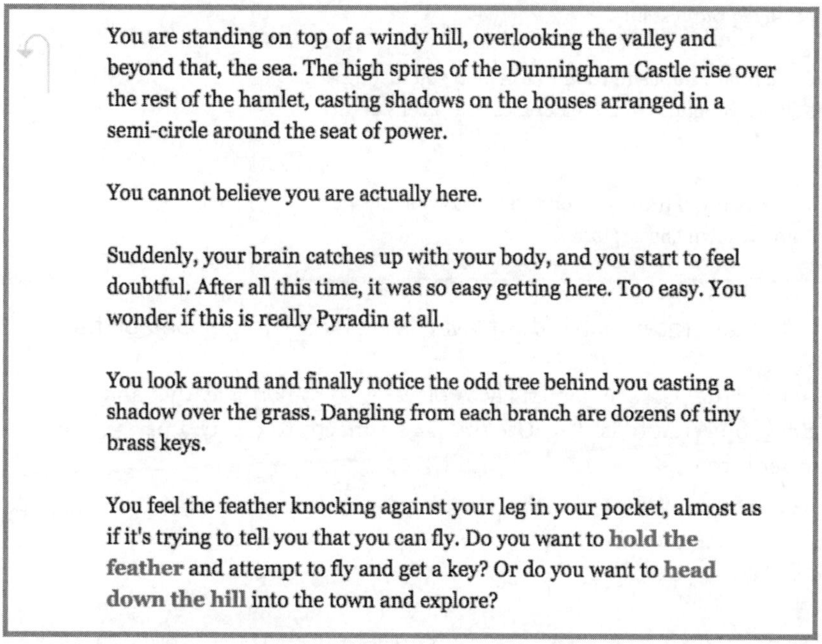

You are standing on top of a windy hill, overlooking the valley and beyond that, the sea. The high spires of the Dunningham Castle rise over the rest of the hamlet, casting shadows on the houses arranged in a semi-circle around the seat of power.

You cannot believe you are actually here.

Suddenly, your brain catches up with your body, and you start to feel doubtful. After all this time, it was so easy getting here. Too easy. You wonder if this is really Pyradin at all.

You look around and finally notice the odd tree behind you casting a shadow over the grass. Dangling from each branch are dozens of tiny brass keys.

You feel the feather knocking against your leg in your pocket, almost as if it's trying to tell you that you can fly. Do you want to **hold the feather** and attempt to fly and get a key? Or do you want to **head down the hill** into the town and explore?

FIGURE 5.8   Conditional statement if the player is holding the feather.

You see the text and choices in the first hook because you've chosen the feather. If you took the glasses or the hat, you don't have the option to fly. Instead, as shown in Figure 5.9, your only choice is to go down the hill and explore.

As the writer, you know that there is a piece of code in that passage containing two possible statements, but the player sees only the hook that applies to his or her situation.

> You are standing on top of a windy hill, overlooking the valley and beyond that, the sea. The high spires of the Dunningham Castle rise over the rest of the hamlet, casting shadows on the houses arranged in a semi-circle around the seat of power.
>
> You cannot believe you are actually here.
>
> Suddenly, your brain catches up with your body, and you start to feel doubtful. After all this time, it was so easy getting here. Too easy. You wonder if this is really Pyradin at all.
>
> You look around and finally notice the odd tree behind you casting a shadow over the grass. Dangling from each branch are dozens of tiny brass keys.
>
> Too bad you can't reach any of the keys. You should probably **head down the hill** into the town and explore.

FIGURE 5.9 Conditional statement if the player is holding the glasses or hat.

You now need to fill out the passage named Fly. A player who took the feather and chose to fly now gains a new object: a brass key. Use the (set:) macro to create a new variable called $gotKey and set it to true:

```
(set: $gotKey to true)You take the feather out of your pocket and immediately
feel your body rise off the ground. The feather seems to be interacting with
the magical ring to allow you to fly.

You soar up to the tree and pluck a key off one of the higher limbs. You slip
it into your pocket as you float back down.

You're now ready to [[head down the hill|Town]] into the town and explore.
```

When the player encounters a door later in the game, use conditional text to make it possible to open the door if the variable $gotKey is true. If the value of $gotKey is false, the player needs to find a different way inside, or he or she will not be able to enter at all.

You can link this passage to the other passage in the fifth story level to ensure that the variation in the story depends on the objects found along the way; this prevents you from having to create dozens of possible storylines. With very few passages, as shown in Figure 5.10, you can create a lot of play variation.

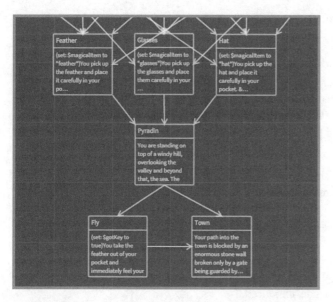

FIGURE 5.10 Variation in the story depends on the objects found instead of on having a lot of passages.

Adding More Than One Condition

Sometimes you enter a point in a story where you want a number of possible things to happen based on variables. In that case, you can chain together "if" statements by using the (elseif:) macro. There is no limit to the number of (elseif:) macros that you can chain together.

Say that the pathway to town is blocked by a stone wall being guarded by an orc. How the player will get over the wall depends on the value of the variable $magicalItem. Remember that $magicalItem can have one of three different values: "feather", "pair of glasses", or "hat":

```
Your path into the town is blocked by an enormous stone wall, broken only by a
gate being guarded by a mean-looking orc.
```

```
The (print: $magicalItem) in your pocket twitches as if it wants you to take it
out and use it.
```

```
(if: $magicalItem is "feather")[You take out the feather and feel your body rise
off the ground. You sail over the wall and land on the other side, unnoticed.]
(elseif: $magicalItem is "pair of glasses")[At that moment, a troop of orcs comes
marching toward the gate. You slip on the glasses to see them better and find that
the glasses make you invisible! You slip in with the troop of orcs and march through
the gate, unseen.] (elseif: $magicalItem is "hat")[You put on the hat and feel your
```

body turn gelatinous. You wonder if you could walk through the stone wall. You head down a few yards away from the orc and ooze inside the wall, unseen.]

Take a look at the conditional text in the code. You first state that if the value of the variable `$magicalItem` is the string `"feather"`, Twine should display the text inside that first anonymous hook attached to the `(if:)` macro. If the player is holding the feather, he or she will see the words in Figure 5.11: "You take out the feather and feel your body rise off the ground. You sail over the wall and land on the other side, unnoticed."

Your path into the town is blocked by an enormous stone wall broken only by a gate being guarded by a mean-looking orc.

The feather in your pocket twitches as if it wants you to take it out and use it.

You take out the feather and feel your body rise off the ground. You sail over the wall and land on the other side, unnoticed.

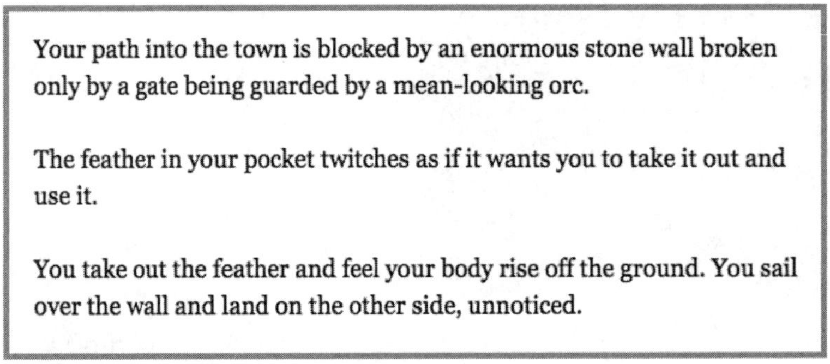

FIGURE 5.11 The game displays the text inside the first hook, which is attached to the `(if:)` macro.

Next, instead of using the macro `(else:)`, which would take care of any other possible value, you give another specific value for `$magicalItem`, using the `(elseif:)` macro. In this case, you give the next possibility. If the player is holding the glasses, he or she will see the words in Figure 5.12 that appear in the hook attached to the first `(elseif:)` macro: "At that moment, a troop of orcs comes marching toward the gate. You slip on the glasses to see them better and find that the glasses make you invisible! You slip in with the troop of orcs and march through the gate, unseen."

Your path into the town is blocked by an enormous stone wall broken only by a gate being guarded by a mean-looking orc.

The pair of glasses in your pocket twitches as if it wants you to take it out and use it.

At that moment, a troop of orcs comes marching towards the gate. You slip on the glasses to see them better and find that the glasses make you invisible! You slip in with the troop of orcs and march through the gate, unseen.

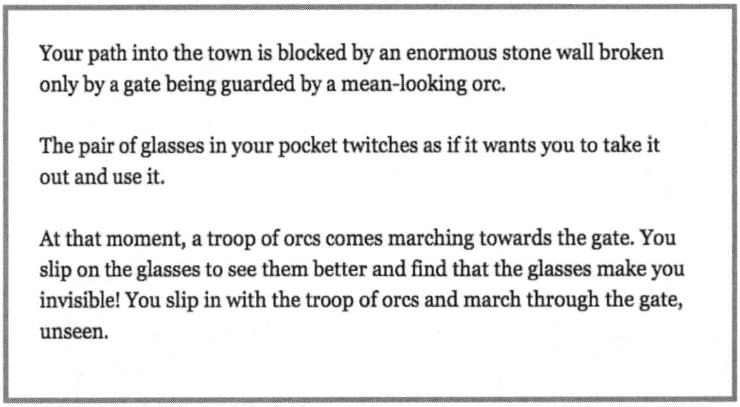

FIGURE 5.12 The game displays the text inside the second hook, which is attached to the first use of the `(elseif:)` macro.

Finally, you give another (elseif:) that accounts for the third possible value for $magicalItem. If the player is holding the hat, he or she will see the words in Figure 5.13 that appear in the hook attached to the second (elseif:) macro: "You put on the hat and feel your body turn gelatinous. You wonder if you could walk through the stone wall. You head down a few yards away from the orc and ooze inside the wall, unseen."

Your path into the town is blocked by an enormous stone wall broken only by a gate being guarded by a mean-looking orc.

The hat in your pocket twitches as if it wants you to take it out and use it.

You put on the hat and feel your body turn gelatinous. You wonder if you could walk through the stone wall. You head down a few yards away from the orc and ooze inside the wall, unseen.

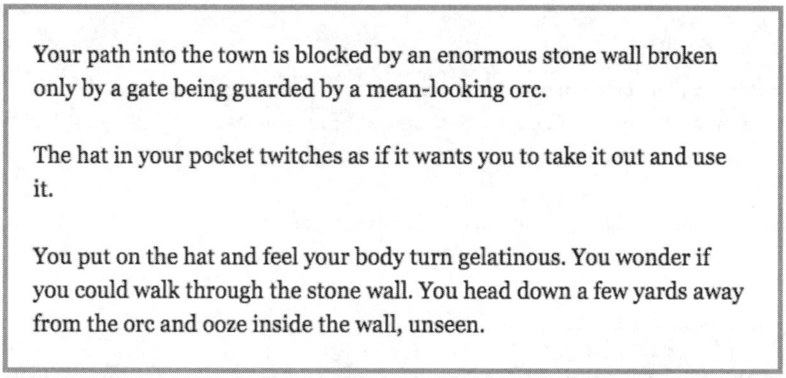

FIGURE 5.13 The game displays the text inside the third hook, which is attached to the second use of the (elseif:) macro.

The (elseif:) macro always requires that an (if:) macro has been used to start the chain. As you've seen, you can use the (if:), (else:), and (elseif:) macros to make picking up objects in your story a meaningful act for players that changes their experience with the story.

Keeping Track of the Player

Conditional statements aren't only tied to what the character is holding. They're also used, along with the (history:) macro, in Twine to track where the character has been. This is a handy macro if you want the player to experience different text based on where he or she has been in the story, much like seeing different text based on which objects the character is holding.

Now you're going to jump ahead in the story and have the player character reach the castle where the king has been holding the prince captive in a dark turret. If the player character has been to the turret, you want the player character to confront the king. If the player character has not been to the turret, you want the player character to ask about the prince's whereabouts.

Create a new sample story called Pyradin Castle. The first passage begins in the front hall of the castle, so label it Front Hall and fill it with this text:

```
You enter the castle and look around. You can go to the [[left|Turret]] up a
steep stone staircase, or you can go to the [[right|Lobby]] and wait for the
king's guards to invite you into the throne room.
```

Fill in the Turret passage with this text:

```
You climb the steps and enter the turret. You're shocked to find the prince
chained to the wall. You quickly free him while he explains that his father
tied him up to keep him from interfering with the king's plan to seal off the
kingdom. The moment the prince is free, he races to the throne room, and you
[[follow quickly on his heels|Throne Room]].
```

In the Lobby passage, write this:

```
You enter the lobby outside of the throne room and nod at one of the guards.
"I've come here from another land. I need to see the king," you say.
The guard enters the throne room and returns a moment later.

"The king is most curious as to how you entered Pyradin," he comments.
"He'll see you now."

[[You enter the throne room|Throne Room]].
```

Both passages lead to the final destination, the throne room. The four passages form a little diamond shape, as shown in Figure 5.14.

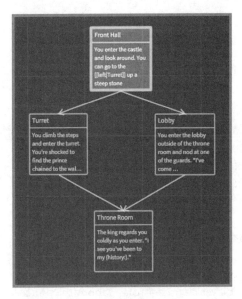

FIGURE 5.14 The three story levels are contained in four passages.

This is where (history:) comes into play. You need to track where the player character has been so you can display different text depending on the path the player took.

Open the Throne Room passage and practice using `(history:)` so you can understand how it works. Type this inside the passage:

```
The king regards you coldly as you enter. "I see you've been to my (history:)."
```

What happens when you play the game? Go to the turret and then enter the throne room. When you do, you should see the words in Figure 5.15: "The king regards you coldly as you enter. 'I see you've been to my Front Hall,Turret.'"

> The king regards you coldly as you enter. "I see you've been to my Front Hall,Turret."

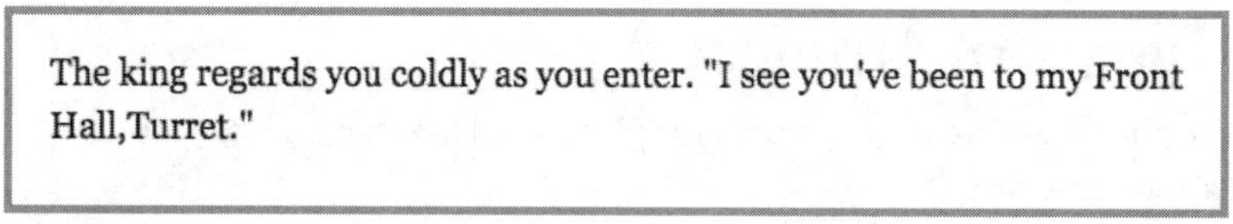

FIGURE 5.15   The `(history:)` macro displays which passages the player has visited.

So the syntax is a little odd, but you get the point: The `(history:)` macro lists the passages where the player has been. In this case, the player starts in the front hall, enters the turret, and continues into the throne room. The king recites this list, leaving out the throne room since the player is currently in that passage.

Now that you understand that `(history:)` is just a list, you're ready to use it a different way. Instead of telling the player where he or she has been, you can have Twine think about the passages the player has visited and display specific text based on this information, using the `(if:)` and `(else:)` macros.

Remember that you want the player character to either confront the king or ask about the prince's whereabouts. To ask Twine to check if the player has been to the turret and encountered the prince, erase the text currently in the Throne Room passage and replace it with this:

```
(if: (history:) contains "Turret")[You burst into the room with the prince,
surprising the king. "You tied up your own son?" you yell as you rush the
throne.](else:)[The king looks up at you as you enter. "Where is the prince?"
you question.]
```

Take a look at the code above. The first piece (`if: (history:) contains "Turret"`) checks to see if the passage Turret is part of the history list; in other words, has the player character read the passage called Turret? If so, the player sees the following text: "You burst into the room with the prince, surprising the king. 'You tied up your own son?' you yell as you rush the throne."

The next part of the code states what happens if the player character hasn't been to the turret. You do this with `(else:)`. Instead of seeing that first bit of text, the player sees the second bit of text: "The king looks up at you as you enter. 'Where is the prince?' you question."

Play the game to see it in action. Try going through the lobby and then restarting the game and entering the throne room through the turret. Does the text change based on your history?

It's time to start trying your hand at setting variables and constructing conditional statements. The best way to quickly create purpose and give the character a reason for collecting objects is to give the player character a quest.

Setting Up Types of Quests

Quests give the player a purpose: The player must complete a task, escape a dangerous situation, or discover a hidden truth.

You've already explored a search quest in this chapter, and in the following sections, you'll create a variety of types of quests.

As you build games, think about what the characters want and how they're going to get it. What tools will they need to complete a task? What valuable objects define the character or the situation? Why are characters collecting items, and how will they use these items once they're collected?

Collecting objects is a common task in interactive fiction games. Think about giving objects in your stories a purpose to help move the story forward.

Writing Search Quests

As stated earlier in this chapter, in a search quest, the character goes looking for something that is lost or unknown. The lost component may be a physical object, such as a missing book, or it might be information.

To try creating a search quest, you're going to plant a *red herring*—something that is meant to distract the reader from noticing important objects or information. Make sure you include an object that looks useful but merely distracts the reader from seeing the truth too easily.

TRY IT OUT: CREATE A SEARCH QUEST

The player character is on a boat in Scotland, looking for definitive proof of the Loch Ness Monster. You need to decide which tools the main character needs to complete the task and whether the player ever finds the monster...or something much worse!

Writing Fetch Quests

With a fetch quest, the player needs to get stuff, which is a very common trope in role-playing games (RPGs). It may be a quest for one important object, or the player may need to collect a lot of objects that are scattered around an area.

TRY IT OUT: CREATE A FETCH QUEST

Rewrite a fairy tale. You could set the fairy tale characters in the real world and have them collect the important objects from their respective story in order to get back to their fairy tale world. For instance, if you were rewriting "Jack and the Beanstalk," you'd create variables for the magic beans, the goose that lays golden eggs, and the harp. Once the player character collects these items, he or she can get back home. Or, if you were rewriting "Hansel and Gretel," you could have the witch collect all the candy she needs to make her house.

Writing Drop-off Quests

A drop-off quest is pretty much the opposite of a fetch quest. Instead of collecting things, the player character needs to give objects to other people or place them in special locations.

TRY IT OUT: CREATE A DROP-OFF QUEST

You are a spy who needs to drop off the information you've gathered around the city so other spies can collect the information and use it to stop a major crime from destroying the palace. Create three variables called $hasClueOne, $hasClueTwo, and $hasClueThree. Set all of their values to true to indicate that the player starts the game holding the three clues. As the player drops off a clue, change the value of the variable to false. Put some danger in the game by using conditional statements that end the game if the character is caught still holding a clue when encountering a character who is working for the bad guys.

Writing End Quests

End quests involve putting an end to something or someone. The object of the game or story is to stop something from happening.

TRY IT OUT: CREATE AN END QUEST

It's the last day of school, and your best friend has set up an elaborate, terrible prank that you know will get her in trouble if she goes through with the plan. Using variables for the pieces she has scattered around the school, send the player character on an adventure, disassemble the components of her prank, and save your friend from expulsion.

Writing Rescue Quests

The point of a rescue quest is to protect a non-player character and move that player where he or she needs to go. Think of this type of quest as escorting someone out of danger.

TRY IT OUT: CREATE A RESCUE QUEST

Create a steampunk game where the clockmaker has been imprisoned inside one of his own timepieces. How will you help him escape before he is crushed by the turning gears? What objects will the player need to complete the quest, and what will happen without the right tools?

Writing Escape Quests

An escape quest sends the player character on a journey. The main character is either trying to run away from a dangerous situation or trying to run toward a place.

TRY IT OUT: CREATE AN ESCAPE QUEST

The player character is a letter of the alphabet, stuck accidentally in the world of numbers. What will the player use to escape Numberopolis? How will the player get back to Alphabet City? And why does the player want to escape rather than explore this new land? What sort of objects would be useful to a letter of the alphabet?

Writing Transformative Quests

During a transformative quest, the player character changes. Maybe the main character starts out the story very timid and eventually finds their voice. Or maybe the main character is a villain who decides to come over to the good side by the end of the story.

TRY IT OUT: CREATE A TRANSFORMATIVE QUEST

The main character is a pirate who discovers that he doesn't really want to be a pirate. In fact, he'd much rather be a baker, but his parents expect him to live out his days on the high sea. Try to use variables and conditional statements in your story to reveal how the player changes from blood-thirsty pirate to cake maker. For instance, perhaps the player finds baking supplies on one of the ships he invades, or maybe he eats a delicious cookie that brings him more joy than stealing treasure. What makes the pirate change his mind?

Writing Creation Quests

A creation quest focuses on building something that wasn't there before. It could involve finding all the parts to build a really fantastic robot, construct a building, or even build something intangible, such as hope, that wasn't there at the beginning of the story or game.

TRY IT OUT: CREATE A CREATION QUEST

The player character lands on a desolate planet and needs to build a new space station and hook up an oxygen generator to the building before he or she runs out of portable oxygen. But things aren't exactly as they seem on the planet, and the player character isn't alone. Are the alien life-forms friendly and helpful, or do they undo all of the player character's hard work if the player character hasn't collected certain objects?

Now that you've had a lot of practice with mimicking real-life objects with variables, you can focus those variables on something a little less tangible: time.

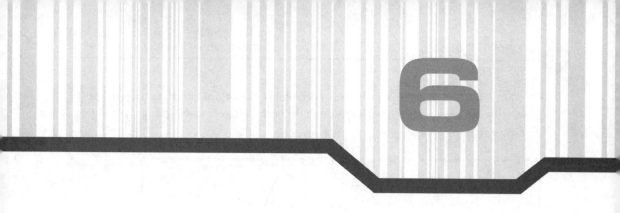

Stasis, Catalyst, and Climax: Understanding Story Arc

Fiction has a set shape; in fact, stories follow a structural formula. The shape of a story is called the *story arc*, and understanding the traditional structure of a story can help you organize your games into tales that make sense to the player.

Readers expect to enter a story or game and get a sense of the situation. Where are they? Who are they? What is happening around them? That initial information-gathering place in the story is called *stasis*. Then something happens that triggers the action—otherwise known as the *catalyst*. Finally, the action is tied up with a moment of resolution called the *climax*, and the players relax into an ending that lets them know that all will be fine in the story world (or not), and *stasis returns*.

In the past, you may have seen plot diagramed with different terms, maybe beginning with *exposition*, continuing to *rising action*, reaching a *climax*, and then dropping down into *falling action*. But this labeling is confusing when applied to story arc because, for example, exposition can actually happen anywhere in the story, not just in the opening chapters.

Exposition is what you call those backstory details that explain the situation. So exposition can happen anywhere in the story that you are explaining background information. It could even happen at the end of the story, as it often does in the Harry Potter stories, when Dumbledore sits down in each book and explains a little more about Voldemort to Harry.

Still, exposition is particularly important during the period of stasis because it gets readers caught up on what is happening, where they are, and who they are. This is why people sometimes use that term *exposition* in place of the more accurate term, *stasis*.

This chapter focuses on the action of the story and therefore uses terms that convey action and inaction, such as stasis, catalyst, and climax. You're also going to turn up the volume on time with a few new macros—namely the `(live:)` and `(goto:)` macros, which you will use to delay the appearance of a link and create a timer inside your game.

Drawing a Story Arc

If you were to draw story arc as a shape, it would start as a flat line (stasis), dip down (catalyst), shoot upward (climax), and finally return to a flat line (stasis returns), as shown in Figure 6.1.

Of course, the end of the story will look nothing like the beginning of the story since the characters will change throughout the book. In both cases of stasis, though, the action is no longer in flux.

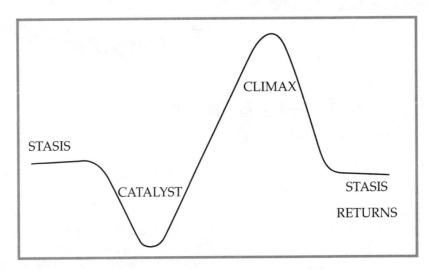

FIGURE 6.1 The shape of a story.

Just like any book on your bookshelf, interactive fiction games and stories follow this structure. Take, for instance, *Mrs. Pepper's Nasty Secret* by Jim Aikin and Eric Eve. The game begins with four short paragraphs of exposition in a period of stasis to get readers caught up on important details such as what is happening, where they are, and who they are.

In *Mrs. Pepper's Nasty Secret*, you as the player are a skateboarding kid who lives near cranky Mrs. Pepper, whom everyone suspects is a witch. She has stolen your skateboard, and you want to get it back. You're outside her house, and you can hear strange noises coming from inside. All this information sets the scene.

Getting into Mrs. Pepper's house is a bit of a puzzle, but once you lure her out of the way and step inside by climbing in through the open window, you kick off the action. That moment of climbing into the house, the catalyst, changes the story. You're no longer begging a mean, old witch for your skateboard. You're a clever kid taking matters into your own hands. You're going to get that skateboard back as well as figure out what is making the noises. You find your skateboard and then determine that a garden elf is the source of the noise. You help him by bringing him outside, and this creates a moment of resolution (climax). The game ends with you quickly tidying up so Mrs. Pepper doesn't know you were inside the house and then leaving with your skateboard (stasis returns).

This game goes a step further in helping the reader notice the arc by breaking up the storytelling moments into different physical spaces. You move from outside the house (stasis) to inside the house (catalyst) to finally back outside the house (climax) before you leave for home (stasis returns).

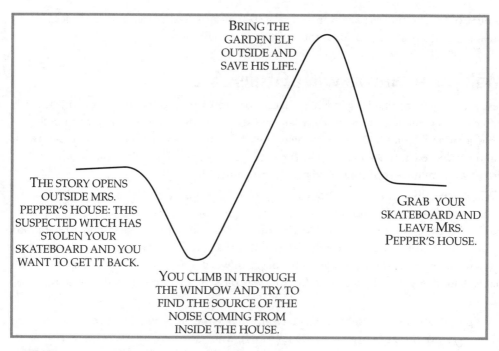

BRING THE GARDEN ELF OUTSIDE AND SAVE HIS LIFE.

THE STORY OPENS OUTSIDE MRS. PEPPER'S HOUSE: THIS SUSPECTED WITCH HAS STOLEN YOUR SKATEBOARD AND YOU WANT TO GET IT BACK.

GRAB YOUR SKATEBOARD AND LEAVE MRS. PEPPER'S HOUSE.

YOU CLIMB IN THROUGH THE WINDOW AND TRY TO FIND THE SOURCE OF THE NOISE COMING FROM INSIDE THE HOUSE.

FIGURE 6.2   The story arc for Mrs. Pepper's Nasty Secret.

Placing the defining moments in different places is an easy way to divide up the story and define the arc. Similarly, the game *Zork* by Infocom begins above ground (stasis), moves to an underground kingdom when you go through the trapdoor (catalyst), and finally resolves back above ground when you put the final treasure in the trophy case and have the secret passage open (climax). And then you exit the area through the stone barrow (stasis returns). If you're struggling with building arc, consider placing these sections in three or four different locations, as described in the story example that follows.

Understanding Time and Pacing

It's important to think about the aspect of time in a story. Time inside a story is called *pacing*, and the purpose of time in a story is to create tension. Of course, there are ways to do this outside the story, such as counting moves, but you also need to think about ways you can convey that time is passing inside a story and that the passing of time matters. Set a deadline for your character; it will pique the player's interest because now there is something at stake: Will the character resolve the conflict in time? Humans are forever racing against clocks and calendars, trying to beat time, and that natural tension from the real world will help you set a good story pace in the fiction world.

Not only can you write about the passing of time in a game, but you can set actual timers into your game with macros. Nothing gets hearts pounding quite like having a limited amount of time to find the solution and save the day. The best place for one of these thrilling moments is at the peak of the action: the climax.

Making a Game with Story Arc

Next you're going to build a game that focuses on story arc so you can see how the action unfolds. This game is a modern-day, Viking ghost-pirate adventure. The player character is the great-grandchild of Count Emil, who once hid part of his vast fortune on a remote island off the coast of Denmark, while trying to outwit some pirates. Yes, the very same pirates who are now appearing as ghosts in the game.

You know that the buried box contains priceless jewelry and bars of gold, but it also contains items of sentimental value to your family, namely a locket that belonged to Count Emil's wife, the glamorous and well-loved Countess Katrine, who vanished under mysterious circumstances. Your great-grandfather always said that the key to solving that mystery lay in the word engraved on the inside of the locket—a word that he had never understood and that was long forgotten by the time the story was passed down to your father and, now, to you.

To help separate the story segments and clearly define the arc, you can set the story in three locations. Have the story begin on a boat (stasis), where the player gathers the background information. Then have the story move to the island, where the player character seeks the treasure (catalyst) but encounters the Nordic ghost pirates. There are multiple ways for the story to resolve (climax), depending on choices made during the game; among the options are helping the pirates and obtaining the locket. Ultimately, the player character leaves the island to sail off into the sunset, back toward mainland Denmark (stasis returns).

Opening a Game in Stasis

Open a new story and label it Locket. You can also go ahead and title the first passage Set Sail and type this in it:

```
You turn your face into the wind and adjust the bag over your shoulder as
you head to the remote island where your great-grandfather, Count Emil, buried
a piece of your family's great fortune many years ago.

You set sail from Hirtshals a few days ago. You know from your great-grandfather's
notes, which contain the coordinates for the uninhabited island where he hid the
treasure, that you'll know you are close when you see Risin og Kellingin -- the
giant and the witch -- the name for the two large rocks jutting out of the water.

You scan the horizon for pirates. Though the Viking pirate encampments died out
hundreds of years ago, there have been stories, told in the local pubs, about
unmanned ghost longships floating on the water, their wooden planks being bleached
by the sun.
```

```
They're just stories, right?

Anyway, pirates are the reason your great-grandfather hid this treasure in the
first place. If there are any lurking around, they can have the priceless jewelry
and the gold bars your great-grandfather buried there. You're after only one thing:
your great-grandmother Katrine's locket. She disappeared not long after your
grandfather was born, and Emil always said that the locket he buried there held
the key to the mystery. One word, engraved inside the locket, by now forgotten so
many generations later, will tell you what happened to your great-grandmother.

That's your treasure.

You look up at the lookout nest above you. Do you want to [[climb up|Lookout Nest]]
to see if you can get a better view, or do you want to
[[stay on the deck|Stay on Deck]]?
```

This long passage sets the scene and provides stasis. Despite the rocking boat, this establishes a time of internal steadiness (stasis) for your player's character. The opening is a snapshot or a peek into the character's world.

The player now can answer three vital questions: Where am I? Who am I? What am I doing and why? The player character is on a boat, heading to an island. He or she is the great-grandchild of Count Emil and Countess Katrine, and he or she is going to retrieve the locket his or her great-grandfather hid on the island. The player character is then going to look for the word engraved on the inside of the locket and solve the mystery of the great-grandmother's disappearance. The player now knows what he or she needs to know before getting to the catalyst.

But before you get to that changing moment of the catalyst, you give the player two choices at the bottom of the scene: He or she can go up to the lookout nest or stay on the deck. By doing this, you stretch the stasis period another story level. Each choice will change the course of the story once the player reaches land.

If the player goes up to the lookout, he or she sees a ghost ship on the horizon and will try to avoid it; if the player remains on deck, he or she receives a visit from Ailios, the mermaid, who warns that the player should leave the treasure on the island alone because danger lies ahead. Pause for a moment to write your own version of the story, making sure that you end this section of the story with a passage that has the player character transferring to a smaller boat and landing either on the north side of the island or the south side.

So the opening passages create a period of stasis, letting the players know who they are, where they are, and their goal. Stasis is the place where the reader gets their footing. Next, it's time to shake things up with the catalyst.

Continuing to the Catalyst

Let's speed forward a few passages in the story. The catalyst gets right to the meat of the story. If stasis is a moment in the story where the action is standing still and all is steady, catalyst is the point where the story is set into motion.

Action doesn't refer just to those hold-your-breath moments in the story such as when an asteroid is about to hit a planet or the knight is charging into battle. In storytelling, the action is what is happening to move the story forward. You've probably had all sorts of things happen today that weren't heart-stopping or remarkable moments but were nonetheless events that moved your day forward.

All around the action are things like descriptions of settings, people, or situations (otherwise known as exposition) or conversations (otherwise known as dialogue). But driving the story forward is the action—those moments that change the course of the story and keep moving the player closer to (or farther away from) his or her goal.

Back in the sample story, the player now approaches the uninhabited island and either takes the north landing or the south landing. Here's what happens if the player continues the story by following the south landing:

```
You wait until the smaller boat runs aground before slinging your bag over your
shoulder and leaping lightly into the frigid water. You pull the boat to shore
on the rocky beach.

The island has been uninhabited for hundreds of years, which is probably why your
great-grandfather chose it to hide his treasure. It is nameless, though in his
notes he called it hjarta holmur. Heart Island? The island's heart? You don't
know much Faroese, and you can't tell if he is naming that for the shape of the
land or because he buried part of his heart in the rocky ground.

There are two poorly maintained paths leading away from the beach: a steeper path
to the left and a grassy path to the right. But before you can consult Count Emil's
notes and choose the correct direction, you feel a cold wind wrapping itself around
your legs and then your waist, and finally your arms, binding them to your side.

Do you [[try to run|Run]]? Or do you [[bow your head|Bow Head]] to the ghostly
presence?
```

The original plan to sail to the island, get the treasure, and get home has been thwarted by the cold wind wrapping itself around the player's legs. Everything has changed; what started out as a journey to learn about a great-grandmother has become a tale about fighting ghost pirates. That type of quick change, where the situation goes off the rails, is the catalyst.

If the player tries to run, the ghost pirates will hold him or her to the spot. They are only made of memories, but they drain the player of all his or her energy, preventing escape. If the player bows his or her head and listens to the ghost pirates, they will trust the player and allow him or her to negotiate freedom in exchange for releasing them from this earth. They are still here on this island only because of the buried treasure, and if the player works with them, the player can send the ghosts to the afterworld, Helheim. Once again, pause to write these passages in your sample game.

At this point, you need to think about how the story will go from catalyst to climax—that is, from problem to solution. To make things interesting, you should include multiple paths to get to the resolution of the situation. How will each of the choices you offer lead to a different outcome?

There will be many passages in the catalyst section of the story; in fact, the vast majority of your story will take place between the catalyst and the climax. To limit the number of endings you need to write, feel free to tie off a few threads early while carrying other storylines through the story arc to their end.

Building to the Climax

The climax is the story's dramatic conclusion. The word *climax* comes from the Greek word for "ladder." Think of this as a moment of heightened tension. Will things work out, or will they fall apart for the player character? If the catalyst is the problem, the climax is the solution, attempting to bring back the steadiness of stasis.

Although there will be many resolutions for the story, depending on choices made in earlier passages, for now you can take the path from where the player bows his or her head and works with the ghost pirates to release them from this world while simultaneously getting the locket.

As the player navigates the route to the treasure over several passages (with a few obstacles thrown in for good measure), he or she learns that the pirates are still here on earth only because the player's great-grandfather wrote about his encounters with the pirates in cursed ink inside his diary. By writing their names on the page, he unknowingly bound them to this world, even after death.

The pirates don't want to harm the player; they just want help getting released from this world. The solution is pretty simple: The player can stab the diary found among the rest of the treasure with the silver dagger he or she is carrying.

Now the player gets to the climax, reaching the moment of unearthing the treasure (hidden in the ruins of a church in the center of the island) and needs to stab the leather-bound book. It's important for the player to be quick because there are terrible consequences for hesitating.

To make the time aspect fair for the reader, before the player reaches the current passage, the main pirate, Brynjar, tells the player character to be careful when opening the box that contains the treasure and warns that time will be of the essence. Time is important for player character and player alike because this passage includes a timer that will transport the player to an unwanted ending if he or she doesn't click the link in time:

```
"Be careful," Brynjar warns as you set down your bag and move to open the box.

You pull the lid and see a leather-bound book nestled atop bags of coins, gold
bars, and velvet jewelry boxes. You look up to make sure that Brynjar hasn't
tricked you, that he isn't planning to steal the treasure now that you've gotten
the box open.

But Brynjar and the rest of the pirates aren't circling the box with their smoky
energy. They are writhing in pain, their ghostly faces contorted as the book is
exposed.

"Please," Brynjar manages to gasp.

[[Stab the book!|Take Locket]]
(live: 20s)[(goto: "Dead")]
```

This passage includes two new macros: (live:) and (goto:). Because the (goto:) macro doesn't automatically create new passages for you like the [[link]] macro does, you have to go down to the green +Passage button and add a passage. Title this passage Dead—and remember that capitalization matters with Twine.

Fill in your own sad ending for the Dead passage. Don't forget to include a link to the first passage in the story (Do you want to [[play again|Set Sail]]?) if you want to give the player a chance to start over and make new choices.

Now try playing the story without clicking anything on the screen. In 20 seconds, you are transported to the Dead passage. Try it again by clicking the link. As long as you do it within 20 seconds, you move to the Take Locket passage.

The (live:) macro uses real time—in this case, 20 seconds—to wait to do whatever is in the hook. Inside the hook is a second macro: the (goto:) macro, which simply takes the player to the listed passage, in this case, Dead. If you were to write that code in plain English, it would be "In 20 seconds, take the player to the Dead passage."

Of course, the (goto:) macro doesn't have a chance to transport the player to a new passage if the player clicks Stab the book! because the [[link]] macro takes the player to the Take Locket passage. The (live:) macro only works inside the passage where it is used. Once the player leaves that passage, the (live:) macro stops counting time.

You can see how the timer adds an element of tension. In fact, you can make things even more tense by not having the link appear on the screen at first. The (live:) macro can also delay text from appearing until a set amount of time has passed.

By tweaking the ending of the passage as shown here, you can delay `[[Stab the book!|Take Locket]]` from appearing until after 15 seconds has passed, giving the reader only a 5-second window to click the link before being transported to the Dead passage:

```
But Brynjar and the rest of the pirates aren't circling the box with their
smoky energy. They are writhing in pain, their ghostly faces contorted as the
book is exposed.

"Please," Brynjar manages to gasp.

(live: 15s)[[[Stab the book!|Take Locket]] ]

(live: 20s)[(goto: "Dead")]
```

Make sure you place the proper number of square brackets around the `[[link]]` macro. The first square bracket begins the hook, and the other two square brackets are attached to the `[[link]]` macro. Tweak the amount of time you give the reader to heighten the tension.

Of course, be fair about time. Timers can quickly move from being a clever trick to a frustrating distraction when they are used as punishment for slow reading. Give the player enough time to get through the passage and make a choice.

Where does the story go from here? It begins its conclusion—also known as stasis returns—with the next passage, Take Locket.

Returning Back to Stasis

The story wraps up with the player character taking the locket and the player receiving a choice: Open the locket and see the word or keep the word a mystery because there's been enough emotion for one day?

If the player chooses to open the locket, he or she sees that the word is *maighdean mhara*, which is "mermaid" in Gaelic. Of course, the player's great-grandfather wouldn't have known this word because he only spoke Danish. So the player's great-grandmother either began as a mermaid and spent some time pretending to be a human on land or started as a human and transformed into a mermaid. Either way, the mystery of her disappearance is solved: Like Ailios, the mermaid who warned you to leave the treasure alone at the beginning of the game, the player's great-grandmother lived out the rest of her days somewhere in the water.

The game closes with the player character reboarding the ship and setting sail for mainland again, his or her internal steadiness returned, along with the original state of stasis that started the game.

Diagramming the Story

You can apply the sample game to the shape shown back in Figure 6.1. Figure 6.3 shows that classic story shape for the sample story, with the background information setting the scene (stasis), the encounter with the ghost pirates kicking off the action (catalyst), the ghost pirates being released from their limbo when and the player stabs the book and gets the locket (climax), and finally the player leaving the island with newfound knowledge about his or her great-grandmother.

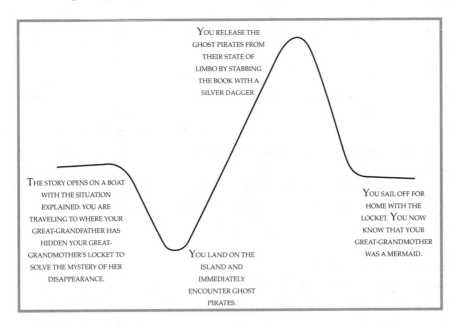

THE STORY OPENS ON A BOAT WITH THE SITUATION EXPLAINED: YOU ARE TRAVELING TO WHERE YOUR GREAT-GRANDFATHER HAS HIDDEN YOUR GREAT-GRANDMOTHER'S LOCKET TO SOLVE THE MYSTERY OF HER DISAPPEARANCE.

YOU LAND ON THE ISLAND AND IMMEDIATELY ENCOUNTER GHOST PIRATES.

YOU RELEASE THE GHOST PIRATES FROM THEIR STATE OF LIMBO BY STABBING THE BOOK WITH A SILVER DAGGER.

YOU SAIL OFF FOR HOME WITH THE LOCKET. YOU NOW KNOW THAT YOUR GREAT-GRANDMOTHER WAS A MERMAID.

FIGURE 6.3   A plot diagram of the sample story.

By placing each of these elements in a different location, you further aid the reader in sensing when a new twist will happen in the story.

TRY IT OUT: STRANGENESS AT THE HAPPY BURGER

Write a story that focuses on arc. Place each section of the story in a different location.

Say that Happy Burger is the worst restaurant of all time. The French fries are greasy, the hamburgers are microscopic, and a cockroach just crawled into the milkshake machine. Sadly, it's also where the player character works. Take your time to set the scene over a few passages so the reader gets a sense of the player character's personality as well as the restaurant. All of this is stasis.

Things get very interesting when a batch of French fries accidentally land on the floor and the player goes into the closet to get cleaning supplies. The back wall of the closet is missing, and the player character can see a dark corridor stretching into the distance. This catalyst poses a turning point for the reader: Should the player ignore what he or she saw and clean up the mess, or should the player trot on down that corridor (possibly into danger)?

Every path out of the catalyst situation needs to have its own climax since every problem ultimately finds a solution in a story. If the player character stays to clean up, French fry grease may melt holes in the player character's uniform, which might lead him or her discover that Happy Burger has been frying those potatoes in something other than oil (poison? alien goo? the boss's magic concoction?). If the player character goes down the corridor, he or she may end up in a strange land or another planet or inexplicably standing in a random room at a nearby museum. The choice is up to you, but whatever you choose, be sure to make the climax a resolution of the situation.

Finally, bring the story to a conclusion by wrapping up the action and stating the new normal.

Remember, as the writer, you're guiding the player through a story, from the flat plateau of stasis to the dip of catalyst to the climb toward climax, and finally back to the plateau of stasis again. Feel free to create dead ends for some choices (perhaps if the player doesn't go down the corridor, he or she is fired in another passage or two and is left wondering, while walking home, what the boss is up to) while taking others all the way out to resolution.

TRY IT OUT: BEWARE THE DRAGON

Once again, focus on building story arc. Every day after school, the player character visits the magical land of Chandar by walking into the painting that hangs on the bedroom wall. Convey to the reader how exciting it is to get to Chandar, how beautiful the painting is, and what the player can see or do in Chandar. All of this scene setting is stasis.

The catalyst occurs when the player character enters Chandar. He or she can immediately tell that something is wrong. The magical animals that normally appear are missing, and the air is distinctly warmer than usual. There are burn marks on many of the trees, and the fields have a scorched look to them. The only message, spelled out in stones, is ominous: Beware the dragon.

Have the story move toward a nail-biting climax. Allow the player to suspect that the dragon is hiding inside the library and that he or she needs to hunt it down and kill it with a magical sword before it breathes fire on the player character and turns him or her into toast. Use the (live:) macro to build your own timer into this game to give the player 10 seconds to stab the dragon before being burned to a crisp and transported to an ending passage.

Finally, have the story resolve by banishing the dragon and restoring Chandar for its magical animals (stasis returns).

Remember to lead players through the four stages of story arc, moving them to a new physical location each time you begin a new segment of the story.

Extending Story Arc

Longer games simply extend the story arc, layering more pieces between the catalyst and climax, while sometimes creating dead-ends in the narrative to vary the length of the arc. All begin with the traditional story arc:

stasis → catalyst → climax → stasis

But in longer stories, you can layer in obstacles by moving between attempts to solve the problem and setbacks, or you can introduce new twists to the problem midstory, so your arc looks something like this:

stasis → catalyst → attempt → setback → new solution → climax → stasis

The story still begins by setting the scene (stasis) and moves to present the main problem (catalyst). But now a fuller story shows you the character trying to solve the problem (attempt). The first solution doesn't work, maybe because a new obstacle comes into play (setback). The character tries to solve the problem again (new solution), succeeds in a really big way (climax), and wraps up by telling what life is like now (stasis).

You can repeat the middle three sections (attempt, setback, and new solution) as needed. A longer game or story may have four or five cycles of attempt, setback, and new solution before wrapping up, each attempt giving the character new knowledge and shedding light on aspects of the main character's personality.

Counting Turns with the (history:) Macro

Using a timer isn't the only way you can add tension to a game. You can use the (history:) macro to count the number of turns a player takes overall as well as how many times a player has been in a certain passage.

Remember that (history:) is simply a list of the passages the player has seen. It can list those passages individually by title, as you saw with the example in Chapter 5, "Building Objects with Variables," of the king stating that the player had been through the front hall and turret.

You can also ask Twine to see where the player has been by checking that list and then displaying text if it sees that the player has been to a certain passage. This was the case in Chapter 5 when the player character said different things based on whether he or she entered the throne room through the lobby or the turret.

In addition, (history:) can count up all the passages on the list by checking the length of the list. If the player has been through 3 passages, the length of the list is 3. If he or she has been through 80 passages, the length of the list is 80.

Let's say that you want the player to know how many moves it took to finish a game. You can do this with (history:), which counts each visit to a passage as a turn. So at the very end of the story, in the very last passage, you can print the total number of turns by using this code:

```
It took you (print: (history:)'s length) turns to finish the game.
```

The command print tells Twine to display the length of the current history path. In this case, the length of (history:) is a count of the number of passages a person has read. If a player keeps revisiting the same passage, (history:) counts each visit as a separate visit, even if nothing changes on the screen. At the same time, (history:) only measures moving to a new passage. Therefore, if you use (display:), it does not increase the count for those passages.

TRY IT OUT: MAZE

Return to the maze you created in Chapter 3, "Creating a Vivid Setting," which contains the grid of 16 boxes on the screen, with an additional box to serve as an exit. In the exit passage, tell the player how many turns it took him or her to get through the maze by printing the length of (history:). Give the player a scale to give an idea of how well he or she did. For instance, perhaps 0 to 10 moves makes a player an expert explorer, whereas 30+ moves points to the player being navigationally challenged.

Controlling Time with `(history:)`

You can use the `(history:)` tool to display different text based on how many times a player character has been in a room, which can also convey the passing of time.

Say that the player character is exploring an empty house alone. The first time he or she goes through the living room, the light doesn't work and the living room is dark. The second time he or she goes through the living room, though, three candles are lit.

Open a new story, call it Multiple Visits, and label the first passage Living Room. Write the following in the passage:

```
(if: (count: (history:), "Living Room") is 0)[You walk into the living room but
can barely make out the furniture in the dim light. You flip the light switch but
nothing happens. You think you hear a mouse scurry under a chair as you approach.
Do you want to go into the [[library|Library]] or the [[hallway|Hallway]]?](else:)
[You enter the living room and see three votive candles burning on the low table,
casting soft light into the corners of the room. Your heart starts pounding as you
look around to see who lit them. You thought you were alone in the house.]
```

Let's take a quick look at the code. When a player first starts the story, the history list will be empty because he or she hasn't been to a passage yet. If you ask Twine the count from the history list, it will return the number zero.

But every time the player goes to a passage, this increases the sum of the history list by one. Twine makes a calculation in real time, and every time the player asks it to count the history, it delivers the number of passages read.

You can also have Twine check the number of times a player has been to a specific passage. The preceding example asks Twine to display text based on whether it's the first time the player is seeing the Living Room passage: `(if: (count: (history:), "Living Room") is 0)`. It asks Twine to check the history list and see how many times the Living Room passage appears. If the answer is zero, it displays the following text:

```
You walk into the living room but can barely make out the furniture in the dim
light. You flip the light switch but nothing happens. You think you hear a mouse
scurry under a chair as you approach. Do you want to go into the
[[library|Library]] or the [[hallway|Hallway]]?"
```

On your first visit to the living room, the first bit of text displays, as shown in Figure 6.4.

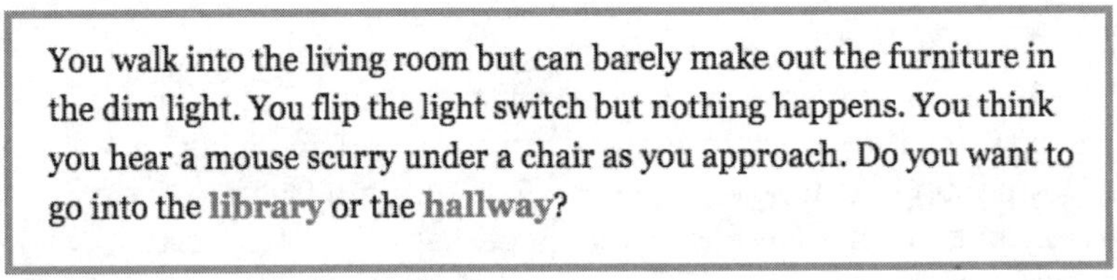

> You walk into the living room but can barely make out the furniture in the dim light. You flip the light switch but nothing happens. You think you hear a mouse scurry under a chair as you approach. Do you want to go into the **library** or the **hallway**?

FIGURE 6.4 Counting visits with `(history:)`.

But what if Twine checks the history list and sees that the Living Room passage has already been read at least once? In that case, it displays the other text in the hook attached to (else:):

```
You enter the living room and see three votive candles burning on the low table,
casting soft light into the corners of the room. Your heart starts pounding as
you look around to see who lit them. You thought you were alone in the house.
```

Figure 6.5 shows the second text option for the living room passage.

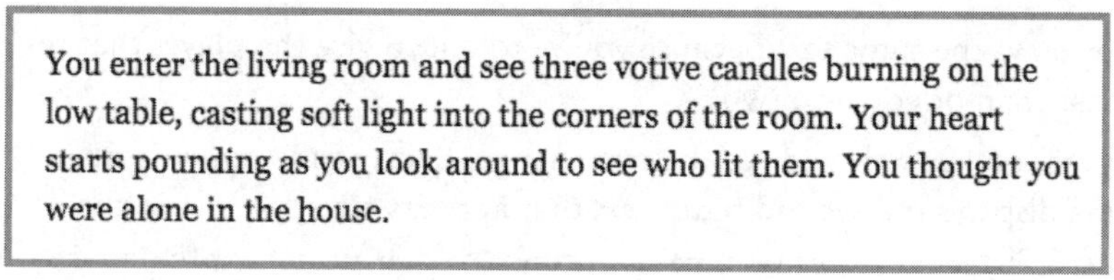

> You enter the living room and see three votive candles burning on the low table, casting soft light into the corners of the room. Your heart starts pounding as you look around to see who lit them. You thought you were alone in the house.

FIGURE 6.5   The second visit to the living room.

Controlling Links with (history:)

You can use the (history:) tool to control when links appear, which is a different take on the delay you created earlier in this chapter by using the (live:) macro.

Let's say you want a link to appear after some time has passed. For example, maybe the player character is printing a photograph. The link to pick up the picture appears only after the player character has waited a few minutes.

The way you can simulate waiting is to add a link to the current passage inside the passage. This keeps the reader looping in the same passage rather than having the [[link]] tool send the player to a new passage. In other words, if the passage title is Start, instead of giving a choice that links to a different passage, you can give a choice that links to the Start passage.

To see how this works, open a new story, call it Photo, and label the opening passage Start. Type this in the Start passage:

```
(if: (count: (history:), "Start") <= 2)[You are waiting for your picture to be
ready. [[Do you still want to wait?|Start]]](else:)[The picture is finally ready.
Do you want to [[pick it up?|Take Picture]]]
```

This stationary link [[Do you still want to wait?|Start]] adds Start to the history list each time the hyperlinked text (Do you still want to wait?) is clicked, adding to the length of the list.

So what happens when you play the story? You should see the opening sentence on the screen, along with the hyperlinked text, Do you still want to wait? If you click the hyperlinked text, it displays the same message again, as shown in Figure 6.6, because you've looped back through the current passage.

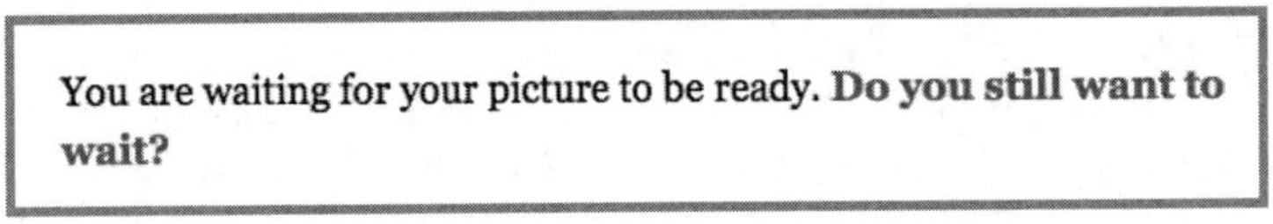

> You are waiting for your picture to be ready. **Do you still want to wait?**

FIGURE 6.6   Showing delayed text with `(history:)`.

Click it again, and it displays the same text because you've told it to give the player that text as long as the visit is less than or equal to two.

Now click it one last time, and you should see the text change. Because the count is now greater than two, Twine displays the second bit of text that appears after `(else:)` in the script, as seen in Figure 6.7: `The picture is finally ready. Do you want to pick it up?` This text contains a link to another passage, `(pick it up|Take Picture)`, so after all that waiting, the player character can be on his or her way.

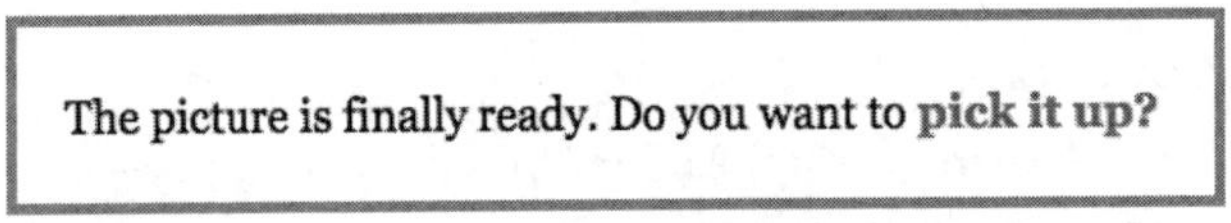

> The picture is finally ready. Do you want to **pick it up?**

FIGURE 6.7   The delayed text appears after the third click.

Now that you know how to keep the game moving and present the action in a way that draws the reader into the story, it's time to learn how to add a little randomness to the game play in order to create a unique experience every time someone sits down to read one of your creations. Twine has macros that you can use to create chance whenever the player clicks a link, a trick that pairs nicely with many story genres.

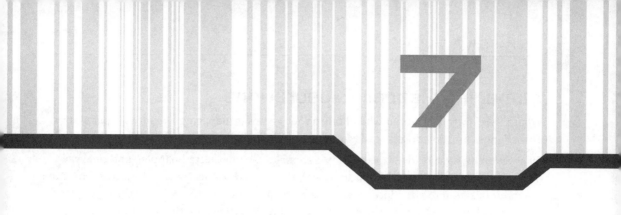

Exploring Interactive Fiction Genres

A good way to understand how interactive fiction genres can be used to fulfill or twist a player's expectations is to think about genres as if they are ice cream flavors.

Let's say that you enter an imaginary ice cream shop and peer into the case. There, tucked behind the glass, is a container of vanilla ice cream mixed with chunks of broken Oreos. You can easily identify that flavor as cookies and cream, even if you've never before bought ice cream in this particular shop.

Knowing that the flavor is cookies and cream conjures certain expectations about taste and texture. You also know what the ice cream is *not*; in other words, you don't expect to see marshmallows and almonds in your cookies and cream, even though those ingredients would be at home in a scoop of Rocky Road.

Some people love cookies and cream, and other people prefer different flavors. Luckily, an ice cream store has lots of flavors, and hopefully one appeals to *your* sense of taste.

Now snap your fingers and turn that imaginary ice cream shop into a store serving up scoops of interactive fiction. *Genres* are a story's *flavor*. Fantasy, science fiction, horror, and adventure are all genres, and each one comes with certain attributes that are associated with that type of story, such as common objects, types of characters, or plot devices. These elements help the player identify the genre of the story.

For instance, say that a game opens with a crime scene. The player is supposed to collect evidence and interview the non-player characters in the house. The player character is carrying a magnifying glass, vials, latex gloves, and fingerprint dusting powder. It's clearly a detective or mystery game, right? In this case, you don't expect to see a unicorn, an orc, or a magical sword, all items that would be suited to a fantasy game but out of place in the Sherlock Holmes universe.

If you learn the identifiable features associated with a genre, you can use them to create shortcuts to understanding. For instance, if the player character is a detective in a mystery, his or her motivation is immediately clear, based on the hallmarks of the genre: The goal is to solve the crime. Although you don't have to worry about the genre police arresting you for mixing the wrong items into your story, it is good to know the common attributes of each genre so you can fulfill or exploit the reader's expectations.

Managing Reader Expectations

What I'm really talking about when I talk about genres is managing a reader's expectations. This chapter aims to address reader expectations on a multitude of levels.

One way to manage reader expectations is to make the unexpected happen, and one way to do this is to introduce randomization with the `(either:)` and `(random:)` macros. You can use randomization to introduce an element of surprise into a story. What if the description of a room changes each time the player passes through it because the description is randomly generated from a list of possible options? Or what if the player character opens a box a second time, and something else is inside? You've been letting the reader make the choices up until this point, but you can also introduce an unexpected element by allowing the program to make a choice behind the scenes, too. This means that you, as the author, can play your own game without knowing for certain what you'll find on the screen.

In this chapter you'll practice using those new macros by learning about and trying your hand at writing some of the common genres in interactive fiction. Of course, as with ice cream flavors, some genres will not appeal to you. But in this chapter you have a chance to sample many types of stories and see which ones hold your interest.

In this chapter you'll also learn about generating randomization at the plot level by introducing plot twists—those moments when the reader's mouth drops open because something unexpected has happened. Throughout the story, the reader is building a base of information about the character and comes to expect certain facts to be true. Readers expect good people to keep making good choices, and they expect villains to always take the evil option. But just as you can twist expectations within a genre by leaving behind well-worn *tropes*—common storylines that pop up in a genre—you can twist expectations on the micro level by having your characters make choices that surprise the reader. Those twists are important because they encapsulate internal tension.

Your characters will have tension with other characters, and you can think of that as external tension, but they'll also struggle internally to do the right thing, which gives birth to a constant, underlying question: Will he or won't he (or will she or won't she)? You don't want the reader to be certain of the answer to this question because, even in the most non-suspenseful of situations, the reader needs to be held on the edge of will he/won't he in order to be interested enough to continue making choices in the game. Readers will keep reading if they want to see how everything turns out within that tension.

In other words, managing expectations is also about ensuring that the reader can't completely guess the outcome until the final word of the story. So make your good characters do some ethically questionable things and make your villains secretly have a heart of gold in a crucial moment. These small plot twists don't just generate interest for the reader but give the reader a deeper understanding of more complex characters who are therefore more believable. After all, real people rarely behave only one way, and your characters should mirror humans in being unpredictable, too.

In the next section you'll learn how to get random by using the (either:) and (random:) macros. You can take advantage of these macros across genres, using them for everything from virtual dice rolls in a fantasy role-playing game to monsters jumping out of the closet unexpectedly in a horror game.

Creating Chance with the (either:) and (random:) Macros

There are two macros in Twine that randomize the player's experience with the game. The (either:) macro can display randomized text or transport the player to a randomly chosen passage. The (random:) macro can imitate the rolling of dice or assign a random numeric value to a variable. The (either:) macro is more flexible because it can be used with numbers, strings, or Booleans, whereas the (random:) macro can only be used with numbers. Both macros infuse unpredictability into the story since Twine chooses which option to display or value to assign to a variable.

Using the (either:) Macro

The (either:) macro can randomly display text on the screen if you first produce a series of options. It chooses from the list and displays one of the available options, forgoing the rest. To see this in action, start a new story called Creepy Room and type this in the first passage:

```
You see a ghostly apparition in the (either: "mirror", "window",
"doorway", "shadows", "fog").
```

Now if you play your game, rather than seeing those five options, you see the one that is randomly chosen by the program to display (see Figure 7.1).

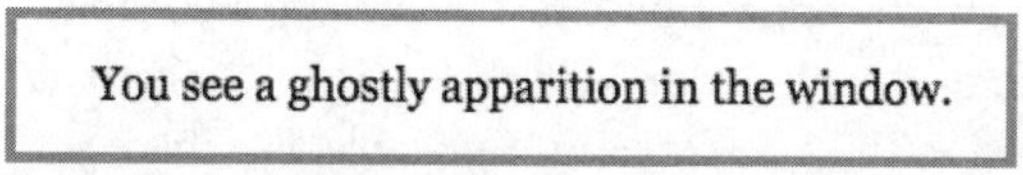

> You see a ghostly apparition in the window.

FIGURE 7.1 Randomly displayed text on the screen.

If you refresh the passage again, you're likely to see a new statement on the screen, such as `You see a ghostly apparition in the shadows` or `You see a ghostly apparition in the doorway`. But I have to couch it with the term *likely*; you still have a one in five chance of seeing the same option again.

So how does the (either:) macro work?

Twine randomly chooses one option and prints the word (or words if there are multiple words) enclosed inside one of the sets of quotation marks. The example above shows only a single word—mirror, window, doorway, shadows, or fog—in each set of quotation marks. But you can also place many words between the quotation marks to, for example, have the

Twine game print whole sentences randomly. For instance, you could type this to have the description of the room change every time a person reenters the passage:

```
You walk into the bedroom and see (either: "a four-poster bed covered in a soft,
white blanket", "an empty space where a bed should be", "a child-sized bed in the
shape of a pirate ship", "a mattress on the floor").
```

This example has Twine shuffle through four descriptions and display one on the screen in addition to the regular text that starts the passage, as shown in Figure 7.2.

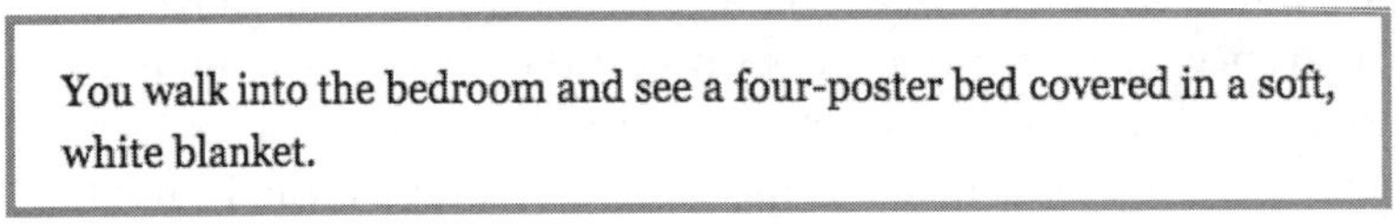

> You walk into the bedroom and see a four-poster bed covered in a soft, white blanket.

FIGURE 7.2   A randomly displayed chunk of text.

Twine allows you to list an unlimited number of possible options with the (either:) macro. The more options you list in the macro, the more variation in the game. You can use the (either:) macro at this most basic level to simply print one of the listed options to add a little variety to the text. This adds a new, somewhat unnerving dimension to your game as the description of a space keeps changing. However, this setup *can't* track which text the player received and refer to it in a later passage.

To refer to the text the player received later in the passage, you can use the (either:) macro to set a value for a variable and then have the story print the value of that variable in the future. This means you need to create a variable, use the (set:) macro in conjunction with the (either:) macro to assign a value to the variable, and then print the randomly chosen value for the variable. To see how this works, you can go back to the first example and play with it so the game remembers where the person saw the ghostly apparition. Start by making a variable called $ghostSighting. Then use the (set:) macro in conjunction with the (either:) macro at the start of the passage to assign a random value to the $ghostSighting variable, like this:

```
(set: $ghostSighting to (either: "mirror", "window", "doorway", "shadows", "fog"))
You see a ghostly apparition in the (print: $ghostSighting).
```

The passage now opens with the (set:) macro assigning a value to the $ghostSighting variable. It randomly assigns one of the five possible values (mirror, window, doorway, shadows, or fog) by using the (set:) macro in combination with the (either:) macro. Finally, it prints the value of the recently assigned variable in the text of the passage. Figure 7.3 shows how it appears on the screen.

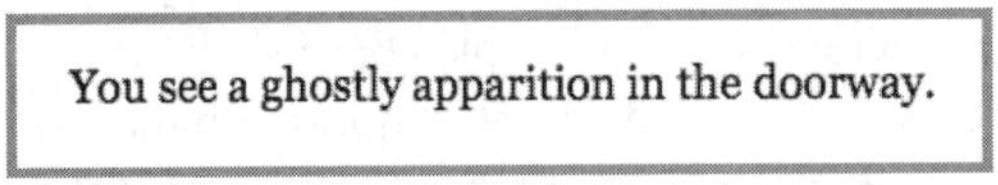

> You see a ghostly apparition in the doorway.

FIGURE 7.3   Randomly displayed text on the screen that utilizes the value of a variable.

As you can see in Figure 7.3, the player sees the text the same way as in Figure 7.1, despite the passages looking very different on the back end. Figure 7.4 shows the text written in the simplest utilization of the `(either:)` macro, and Figure 7.5 shows the text written using the `(set:)` macro to remember the randomly chosen text by making it the value of a variable.

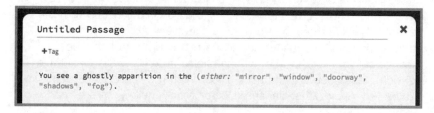

FIGURE 7.4 A passage using only the `(either:)` macro.

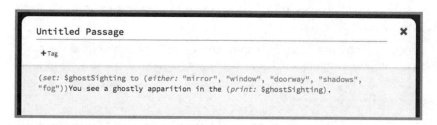

FIGURE 7.5 A passage using the `(set:)` macro together with the `(either:)` macro.

With the example in Figures 7.3 and 7.5, you can keep utilizing the variable—in this case, the `$ghostSighting` variable—in future passages because the game will continue to track it from passage to passage. In other words, you could have the player character tell a non-player character about the ghost sighting many passages later, like this:

```
"I'm telling you that I saw a ghost in the (print: $ghostSighting)," you tell
Amelia as she rolls her eyes.
```

This way of utilizing the `(either:)` macro is especially helpful when the randomized text becomes a key part in the story. For instance, what if you were writing a digitalized version of the game *Clue*? You could have the machine randomly generate the person, room, and weapon, and then have the game check the randomly assigned value of the variable throughout the game as the player character interacts with all of the non-player characters. It could remember that Professor Plum did it in the library with the wrench, or, in the following example, Mrs. Bread did it at the grill station with the peanut butter.

TRY IT OUT: COOKED AT THE RESTAURANT

Write a game, called *Cooked*, in which the player character is a detective in a *Clue-*like game set in a cooking school. Use the `(either:)` macro in conjunction with the `(set:)` macro to assign a value to each of the three variables. With the variable `$weaponUsed`, the options should be peanut butter, carrot, shrimp, milk, coffee, or baguette. With the variable `$roomUsed`, the options should be grill station, vegetable prep, sink, dining room, long counter, and back office. With the variable `$personUsed`, the options should be Mr. Apple, Chef Banana, Doctor Marshmallow, Mrs. Bread, Miss Pineapple, and Professor Cucumber.

Have the detective interact with each of the characters as they move around the kitchen, exploring the various stations. Do the interactions change if the character is guilty or innocent? How could you use the `(if:)` and `(else:)` macros to have different text appear on the screen?

At the end of the game, reveal the person, room, and weapon by printing the values of those variables. The player can check his or her guess against the answer on the screen.

In the *Cooked* game, after setting the value of the variable at the beginning of the story, how did you use that value in each subsequent passage? A simple way is to provide two text options in each passage using the `(if:)` and `(else:)` macros. For instance, the conversation between the detective and Mr. Apple might look different depending upon whether the game randomly assigned the value of `"Mr. Apple"` to `$personUsed`:

```
(if: $personUsed is "Mr. Apple")[Mr. Apple looks nervously around the kitchen, his
eyes resting on the (print: $weaponUsed) for a moment before looking at Miss
Pineapple. "I have no idea what you mean by that.](else:)[Mr. Apple wrings his
hands and glances at the ceiling while he speaks, as if he is addressing the
stucco, "I don't remember where I was that night."]
```

If the game randomly assigned the value `"Mr. Apple"` to the variable `$personUsed` at the beginning of the game, the player sees the text in the first hook. If the game randomly assigned any other value to the variable `$personUsed` at the beginning of the game, the player sees the text in the second hook.

Don't forget to provide instructions to the player at the beginning of the game, telling him or her to try to solve the crime while playing. Also remember to print the answer to the crime in the final passage, perhaps like this:

```
I know who did it! It was (print: $personUsed) in the (print: $roomUsed) with
the (print: $weaponUsed)!
```

This game can be played over and over again, with a different result each time, just like the famous board game. You as the author get to play a little, too, since you won't know which value the program assigned at the start of the game.

You can also use the (either:) macro to send the player to a random passage. To do so, you provide a link, but the link transports the player to one of the passage options listed with the (either:) macro. To see how this works, open a new game, call it Falling, and type this in the opening passage:

```
You run through the door into the room and feel yourself falling through the
[[floor.|(either: "Dark Room", "Water Room", "Small Room")]]
```

With the (either:) macro, Twine does not automatically generate new passages as it does for the [[link]] macro. Therefore, much like with the (goto:) macro from Chapter 6, "Stasis, Catalyst, and Climax: Understanding Story Arc," you need to use the green +Passage button at the bottom of the screen to add three passages. Make sure you pay attention to capitalization and match the names of the passages. Notice that Twine generates an extra passage named "(either: "Dark Room", "Water Room", "Small Room")" because it believes you intended to create such a passage until you provide Twine with passages that match the options used in the (either:) macro. Be sure to delete this extra passage.

Fill in a sentence or two in the three additional passages and then play your game. Figure 7.6 shows what it looks like when you play: You get a single link on the screen. This link transports the player to one of the three passages Dark Room, Water Room, or Small Room.

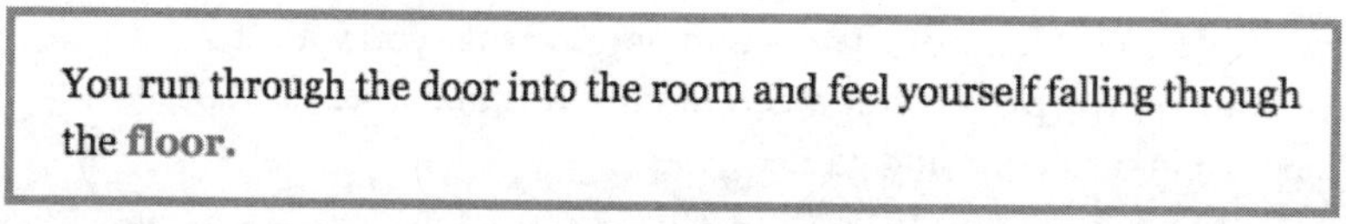

> You run through the door into the room and feel yourself falling through the **floor.**

FIGURE 7.6 A single link appears on the screen when the game uses the (either:) macro to send the player to a random passage.

At this point, you can continue writing the game, creating three unique plot threads that take the player in different directions upon falling fall through the floor.

Don't feel limited to creating only one link. You could add even more variation in the story by giving the reader two or three choices in a single passage and having each of the links lead to a random passage within a set of choices.

Using the (random:) Macro

The (random:) macro is very similar to the (either:) macro, except that it is used exclusively with numbers. One way it differs from the (either:) macro is that you can give Twine a range of numbers instead of listing each possible numerical option.

To see how the (random:) macro works, open a new story and call it Dice Roll. In the first passage, write the following opening:

```
You pick up the dice and weigh them in your hand. They feel lighter than usual.
You toss them onto the table and look at the results: a (random: 2,12).
```

You give the macro the range 2 through 12 because 2 is the lowest number a person can roll with a pair of dice, and 12 is the highest number a person can roll with a pair of dice. The program randomly chooses a number within that range and displays it on the screen.

When you now click the Play button, you see the text shown in Figure 7.7, with a single number between 2 and 12 listed.

You pick up the dice and weigh them in your hand. They feel lighter than usual. You toss them onto the table and look at the results: a 9.

FIGURE 7.7 The (random:) macro can be used to simulate the rolling of a pair of dice.

Much like with your first example with the (either:) macro, the (random:) macro in this case merely displays text. The game doesn't track the number, nor could another character refer back to the dice roll in a later passage and state the results. To make those things happen, you need to once again combine forces with the (set:) macro and assign a value to a variable.

Open a new sample story and call it Random Traits and assume that you want to use the (random:) macro to start off the player with a certain amount of $strength, $beauty, $intelligence, and $cunning in a role-playing game.

You want the game to track the original level of each characteristic so you can have the player character either win or lose in future situations, based on their characteristic level. You need to once again create variables—in this case, $strength, $beauty, $intelligence, and $cunning—and then use the (set:) macro to place a random value between 1 and 10 for each characteristic. Here's what this looks like:

```
(set: $strength to (random: 1, 10))(set: $beauty to (random: 1, 10))
(set: $intelligence to (random: 1, 10))(set: $cunning to (random: 1, 10))
You come to life. Your strength is (print: $strength), your beauty is
(print: $beauty), your intelligence is (print: $intelligence), and your
cunning level is at (print: $cunning).
```

If you now play this game, as shown in Figure 7.8, despite all the code, only a small amount of text is shown on the screen, stating the player character's levels in these four categories. As the player moves through the game, you can have certain events occur if the player's levels are above or below a certain amount by using the (if:) and (else:) macros to check the value of the variable and display the appropriate text.

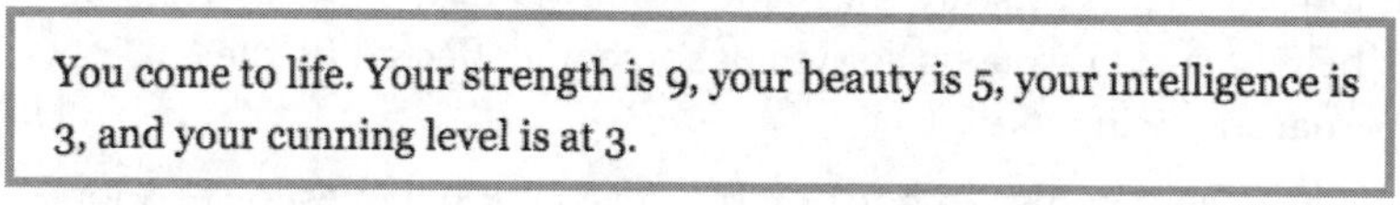

> You come to life. Your strength is 9, your beauty is 5, your intelligence is 3, and your cunning level is at 3.

FIGURE 7.8   The (random:) macro assigns level amounts to the characteristic variables.

You can also have events add or subtract from these randomly assigned base levels as a reward or punishment for choices by using the traditional way of adding or subtracting value from a variable: (set: $strength to $strength + 1) or (set: $strength to $strength - 1). Try adding this additional sentence below the original paragraph:

```
(set: $strength to (random: 1, 10))(set: $beauty to (random: 1, 10))
(set: $intelligence to (random: 1, 10))(set: $cunning to (random: 1, 10))
You come to life. Your strength is (print: $strength), your beauty is
(print: $beauty), your intelligence is (print: $intelligence), and your
cunning level is at (print: $cunning).
```

```
(set: $strength to $strength + 1)Actually your strength level is (print: $strength).
```

Now when you play the game again, the first paragraph states your strength level as one number, and the second paragraph states your strength level as one number higher than the first.

Now that you know a few possible uses for these new macros, you can try them out within a multitude of genres.

Delving into Genres

The word *genre* comes from the French for "kind" or "sort," and this is a perfect way of looking at interactive fiction genres. The label is meant to tell the player what kind of story to expect.

There are dozens of genres and *subgenres*, or smaller categories inside larger, more general categories. The following sections cover only a few of the possibilities. If you examine the common traits, character types, goals, and storylines within each genre, you'll soon start noticing categorical differences between games and seeing how the writer can either play into or twist the player's expectations.

Exploring Horror

Gloomy castles, abandoned buildings, and eerie, empty towns are the classic settings for horror games. Of course, the castles, buildings, and towns are populated by monsters, demons, vampires, werewolves, or ghosts, plus there are usually a few hapless main characters running from the terror they find as they move through the story.

Although the goal of a horror writer is to scare the reader, the goal of the reader depends on whether the game is being played through the eyes of someone affected by the supernatural or the supernatural being itself.

The horror genre, especially when it comes to horror interactive fiction games, owes a lot to the writer H.P. Lovecraft. Lovecraft never wrote interactive fiction, of course, but authors today use many of the hallmarks of early twentieth-century Lovecraftian fiction.

Lovecraftian tales are known for using dread as the primary fear tactic, relying on the idea that what you don't know is much scarier than what you know. The creaking of floor boards when you know you're alone in the house, the empty town where everyone has mysteriously vanished, or the monster you sense is lurking somewhere in the dark are all Lovecraftian tropes that pop up again and again in interactive fiction games.

Words that will help set the tone in a horror story: dank, fetid, rotting, corpse, hideous, creak, lurk, stench, slimy, gloomy, and spooky.

TRY IT OUT: THE EMPTY THEATER

A strange person takes your ticket when you arrive at the theater. You get an uneasy feeling after you take your seat as the rest of the theater remains empty. As the clock ticks closer to curtain time, you almost don't want the show to start, terrified of what you might see on stage. As you start to explore the theater, you wonder where the rest of the audience is and what they know about this theater that you don't.

Write this story, using the `(either:)` or `(random:)` macro to add an element of creepiness to your story by having the description of the player character's surroundings change.

Exploring Fantasy

Lush rolling hills, forests that twinkle with magic, stone castles, and fairy houses are all common settings for fantasy stories. There are usually rulers—kings and queens—as well as wizards, elves, fairies, naiads, and dwarves. Animals often talk, and you may catch sight of a unicorn or two (better than a dragon!) in a fantasy story.

The goal of the writer is to build a world readers wish could be real, like J.R.R. Tolkien's Middle Earth, while the goal of the reader is tied to the adventure that moves the player through the landscape. Good vs. evil, magic vs. non-magic, and a quest to save a person, kingdom, or precious artifact is often at the heart of a fantasy game.

Words that will help set the tone in a fantasy story: sparkle, twinkle, glint, beast, amulet, realm, valiant, conjure, lore, and spell.

TRY IT OUT: THE WISH

You're exploring a magical realm you entered though a strange door in the attic of your friend's house. You're somewhat nervous because right after you stepped into the magical land, the door slammed shut and disappeared. Yes, you appear to be stuck, with no ability to get home. You encounter a pixie who grants you three wishes. Do you wish to get home? Do you wish to stay in the magical land forever?

Write this story, using the (either:) macro along with the (set:) macro to have the player character randomly blurt out a wish.

Exploring Science Fiction

Science fiction features spaceships floating past millions of stars, crash landings on desolate planets, and, of course, encounters with aliens. Yes, science fiction has plenty to do with outer space, but sci-fi stories can also remain close to home and grapple with robots, computers, and technology gone awry.

The goal of a sci-fi writer is to explore fears and wonder related to the unknown, while the goal of the reader may be to get back to Earth, stop an evil robot from killing humanity, or nurture a lost alien who just wants to find his way home.

Often science fiction involves returning to a known and comfortable place, such as getting a weary space traveler back home or exploring new information on something people thought they knew, such as finding their happiness with computers turned on its head as artificial intelligence grows smarter than the humans who created it. Man vs. machine and earthling vs. alien are among the infinite universe of science fiction tropes.

Words that will help set the tone in a science fiction story: spaceship, rocky, empty, parallel universe, travel, alien, blaster, android, lonely, amazement, weird, and bleak.

TRY IT OUT: FRIENDSHIP

A lonely scientist is trying to create a robot that can simulate real conversation, perhaps even one day speaking for itself. Sometimes the robot's answers so closely mirror real speech that the scientist is sure that he has built a lifelong friend, but other times, the robot's answers stray off course, reminding the scientist that he is only hearing echoes of his own programming and not the feelings of the actual robot.

Use the (either:) macro to create a story that randomly chooses whether the robot's answer is what the scientist wants to hear or whether it goes far off course.

Exploring Mystery

A crime has been committed, and it's your job to investigate. From the London alleys where Sherlock Holmes used his keen powers of observation to hunt for clues to the wisecracking, coffee-drinking detective interviewing suspects at the county jail, this genre requires a writer to be clever enough to stay three steps ahead of readers at all times, lest they see the answer before the writer is ready for the big reveal.

The goal of the mystery writer is to enter the mind of the criminal, while the goal of the reader is to figure out how and why the crime occurred. A hallmark of mysteries and detective stories is that things are rarely as they seem on the surface; readers need to consume a mystery story with a careful eye to avoid missing important clues.

Words that will help set the tone in a mystery story: capture, hardened, clue, crumpled, case, forge, laboratory, sabotage, weapon, vice, musty, and homicide.

TRY IT OUT: THE DINNER GUEST

You are a detective, and you're staying at a quaint bed-and-breakfast, trying to unwind from your last case. As luck would have it, your B&B host is murdered, and you're tossed back on the job and need to work to figure out what happened. You have a limited amount of time before the other guests at the B&B check out. Is the culprit the host's son, who wanted to inherit the business? Is it the scientist who brought a strange suitcase filled with vials on her vacation? Or is it the troubled young man who talked about trying to escape his past?

As in the earlier Try It Out where you created the *Cooked* game, you can use the (set:) macro and (either:) macro in combination in order to randomly set a new murderer each time at the beginning of the story.

Exploring Espionage

Discreet meetings in alleyways, high-tech devices snapping microscopic photos of documents, and alluring villains trading secrets to gain power are just a few of the hallmarks of spy thrillers. In this genre, the ever-present question "Will he or won't he?" gets an extra twist, with two extra words: "Will he or won't he *get caught*?"

The goal of a spy thriller writer is to track a secret from point A to point B, while the goal of the reader is to follow the twists and turns, holding his or her breath as the player character gets into (and hopefully out of) dangerous situations. Spy thrillers may contain international travel or gritty city settings. They can also take place in happy suburban towns, with a spy living next door.

Words that will help set the tone in a spy story: covert, drop point, espionage, intelligence, enigma, cloak-and-dagger, rival, dark, hushed, and winding.

TRY IT OUT: THE PARTY

You've managed to score an invitation to a party at a high-ranking official's house, and you've been assigned to plant a bug in her office.

Write a story about this scenario and determine how the player character should gain entrance to the locked room without raising suspicions. How can you use the (either:) macro to create random obstacles that pop up in the story to thwart your player character from his or her mission?

Exploring Adventure

Peril, excitement, and, most importantly, treasure—either monetary or sentimental in value—are like rapids in a river, sending the player character plummeting off cliffs, crawling through caves, and fighting off bad guys as they explore exotic locales and find what they're seeking. Danger is the overriding factor in an adventure story, with the player character defying the odds over and over again while taking tremendous risks.

The goal of an adventure writer is not only to get hearts pumping by penning inventive threats to drive the plot but to show how these adventures subtly change the player character. The goal of the reader is to feel as if he or she is bravely traveling alongside the player character without leaving home.

For adventure stories to succeed, the player needs to feel as if he or she is actually running from lions, jumping from planes, and diving into waterfalls, all while sitting still. Description, therefore, is key in creating a very vivid account of what the player would see, hear, smell, taste, and touch in that space.

Words that will help set the tone in an adventure story: muddy, khaki, ravishing, plummet, shining, jewel, forest, scaling, racing, and leaping.

TRY IT OUT: THE VALUABLE VAULT

You've gotten wind that there is a secret vault built underneath the Pelham mausoleum that can be accessed through Lady Pelham's coffin. It may be worth disturbing a few British skeletons because word is that there are five unpublished Shakespeare plays in the vault that Lady Pelham took to her grave. Are you daring enough to enter, and what will you encounter inside, especially in the twisty passages underneath the vault?

Write a story for this scenario, using the (either:) and (random:) macros to generate surprise.

Exploring Magical Realism

In magical realism, everything seems normal, but it's not. Wish-granting coins are found on city streets, tea is served by talking mice, and schools teach spell casting alongside reading, writing, and arithmetic. It's the world you know and love but with unbelievable elements that attempt to address what-ifs. By building on the recognizable world, a magical realism writer aims to point out the places where imaginations want to go, even outside the story.

The goal of a magical realism writer is to present wonder in the mundane, while the goal of the reader is to have his or her imagination stimulated. By taking the ordinary and making it extraordinary, the fantastical elements of the story polish up the dreary details of the real world and elevate everyday life to something magical. Mermaids hang out with swimmers, wizards work in boring offices, and time travelers turn out to be your next-door neighbor.

Words that will help set the tone in a magical realism story: conjure, wish, wonder, whimsical, floating, unbelievable, dream, enchanted, and flying.

TRY IT OUT: THE BLANK BOOK

You open your locker one day between classes and find a well-worn blank book tucked between your math textbook and bagged lunch. You flip through the pages and then toss the book into your backpack, wondering if it's a practical joke from one of your friends.

But as you're trying to track down your friends in the school, strange things start happening. Whatever you think inside your head starts happening in the world around you—sometimes with results you could have never predicted. You need to figure out how this book works so you can use it wisely, and you also want to learn who placed it in your locker and why.

Write a story for this scenario by using the (set:) macro in combination with the (either:) macro to create unique story paths based on the outcome of the player character's thoughts.

Exploring Historical

Jump back through history and visit monarchs, witness the construction of the world's most iconic buildings, and try your hand at life on the London streets in Victorian England with a historical fiction game.

Steampunk, which pulls elements from nineteenth-century industry and technology into the modern world, and time travel are both subgenres of historical fiction that have gained popularity in recent years as they also appeal to fantasy and science fiction lovers.

The goal of a historical writer is to explore the past, while the goal of the reader is to get a feel for living in a different time period. A keen eye for detail is of utmost importance to avoid inadvertently creating anachronisms, items that are out of place in the time period, such as light switches in colonial America.

Words that will help set the tone in a historical story: timepiece, monocle, time machine, petticoat, clockwork, kingdom, sail, decorum, and breathtaking.

TRY IT OUT: THE ROYAL DAUGHTERS

You are a maid at Livadia Palace, serving Tsar Nicholas II and three of his daughters, Tatiana, Maria, and Anastasia. Because you are close to their age, the daughters have befriended you, and they even include you in conversations while you help them prepare for the day or get ready for bed. Depict life in the Russian royal court during this tumultuous time. What topics would weigh on the hearts of the tsar's daughters?

Write a story for this scenario, using the (set:) macro in combination with the (random:) macro to track how the daughters react to the player character and whether she is in or out of favor with the Russian royal family.

Exploring Western

Visit the old frontier towns, witness a duel at high noon, and jump on your steadfast horse to ride into the Wild West. Western stories idealize a specific time in the expansion of the United States but also include stories set on farms and in other rural areas. Roles are sharply defined, with cowboys embodying the gender-based ideals of the time period.

The goal of the writer is to celebrate the beauty of rugged frontier life from the valleys to the mountains, while the goal of the reader is to find commonality with the characters' morality, especially when the black-and-white nature of sheriffs vs. outlaws is blurred in the anything-goes West.

Words that will help set the tone in a western story: mosey, horse, sheriff, six-shooter, spurs, saunter, dirt, dusty, outlaw, and saddle.

TRY IT OUT: DICE GAME

You walk into a saloon filled with cowboys, served by a tired old barkeep. You mosey up to the bar and immediately start playing a very important dice game with a random cowboy. Why is it important? Because finding the only exit out of the saloon requires that you roll a 10 or higher.

Write a story for this scenario, and as an extra challenge, try writing it using only two passages. Every piece of code you need to succeed has already been covered in this book.

So how can you write this game using only two passages? You have to create two conditional statements and use the (random:) macro, hiding the link to the second passage within a hook that is shown only if the condition set in the macro is met.

With these two paragraphs, you can create an infinite loop that releases the player only when he or she rolls a 10 or higher:

```
(if: (count: (history:), "Dice Game") is 0)[You step into the saloon. Your eyes
immediately travel to the cowboy in the 10-gallon hat, tossing the dice from hand
to hand. He lifts his eyebrows as if to ask if you want to play. "Roll a 10 or
over, and you can get into the room," he tells you. (set: $dice to (random: 2, 12))
You take the dice and toss them onto the table and look at the results: a (print:
$dice).](else:)[You pick up the dice again and toss them onto the table.
(set: $dice to (random: 2, 12))This time you get a (print: $dice).]

(if: $dice >=10)[The cowboy nods toward the door. "You can [[go in|Enter Room]],"
he says.](else:)["Can I try again?" you ask. The cowboy looks you up and down
[[and nods|Dice Game]].]
```

The first thing you do here is set a condition using the (history:) macro described in Chapter 6 for counting how many times the player has loaded the passage. If it's the first time the player has been in the passage, the program shows the opening of the story contained in the first hook. If not, the program skips to the text in the second hook, attached to the (else:) macro. Because the player is continuously looping through the passage until he or she rolls a 10 or higher, you need to account for two sets of text so the player character isn't entering the saloon over and over again.

Within each hook, you have the player character roll the dice, and the (set:) macro randomly assigns a value between 2 and 12 to that dice roll. The variable $dice tracks and prints out each value.

Finally, you create a second conditional with the second paragraph. If the value of the variable $dice is 10 or over, the text in the first hook is displayed, including a link to the second passage in the game called Enter Room: The cowboy nods toward the door. "You can [[go in|Enter Room]]," he says.

If the value of the variable $dice is under 10, the text in the second hook is displayed, including a link to the very same passage, Dice Game: "Can I try again?" you ask. The cowboy looks you up and down [[and nods|Dice Game]].

If the player clicks the link in the second hook, the screen refreshes. The player may need to try many times or he or she may get through on the first virtual dice roll because the value of the variable is at the mercy of the (random:) macro.

Exploring Nautical

Splash into the ocean, set sail into the sunset, or submerge in a submarine while exploring the high seas. Nautical tales are set in and near the water, and subgenres range from pirate adventures to submarine spy thrillers. The genre also moves from the realism of the navy to the magical realism of mermaids. Language should mirror the rocking of the ocean, with the plotline cresting in waves.

The goal of a nautical writer is to journey over the ocean, while the goal of the reader is to follow the player character embarking on a voyage and note the way nature interacts with human endeavor. A nautical tale may be man vs. sea, or humans vs. nature. A nautical tale may be about trying to tame nature, and, in time, may cover a person's heart in grief when nature gets the best of us.

Words that will help set the tone in a nautical story: maritime, anchor, wheel, lagoon, waves, hush, stormy, crash, and voyage.

TRY IT OUT: SKULL AND CROSSBONES

When you snuck onto the boat to find out if the rumors about it being a pirate ship were true, you didn't expect it to set sail with you still aboard. Do you come out of hiding and join the pirates in order to stay alive, or do you try to sabotage their plans by sinking the ship?

Write a story about this scenario, using the `(random:)` macro to decide whether the player character walks the plank.

Exploring Fairytale and Folklore

In fairytale and folklore stories, princesses fall into magically induced crying jags, flooding their kingdoms, while talking birds explain the endless chase of the sun and moon. Sometimes considered a subgenre of fantasy, fairytales and folklore are a category in their own right, sharing more in common with religion than with the quests of the fantasy world. Fairytales and folklore aim to explain observable facts such as why evil exists in the world or how the rain gets back into the sky after a storm.

The goal of a fairytale or folklore writer is to provide answers to life's difficult questions, and the goal of the reader is to be swayed into considering their own ethics through these fables. These stories explore both human instincts and forces in nature.

Words that will help set the tone in a fairytale or folklore story: crone, slink, roots, qualms, unease, harbinger, morals, gallop, squeal, and charming.

TRY IT OUT: THE FOREST OF WONDER

When the evil queen decrees that the long-standing trees of knowledge in the Forest of Wonder will be felled to make room for her new castle, it is your job to ensure that she doesn't succeed by using magic to transform the trees into indestructible towers of books that use their power to bring all the townspeople onto the side of knowledge instead of ignorance. Does the queen have a change of heart, or will she need to be removed from the kingdom in order to bring peace to her realm?

Write a story about this scenario, using the (either:) macro to randomize the conversations between the player character and the trees he or she is transforming.

Exploring Mythology

Gods throw lightning bolts from their mountain castles or shake up the oceans with violent storms as readers attempt to understand the world around them. Continuing in the vein of fairytales and folklore, mythology is a related category, defined by the inclusion of god families and mythological creatures such as sphinxes, centaurs, nymphs, and satyrs.

The goal of a mythology writer is to explain the world through origin, death, and nature stories, while the goal of the reader is to build a base of knowledge of the world around them. Subgenres include the Greek, Roman, Egyptian, and Norse mythology.

Words that will help set the tone in a mythology story: thunder, jealousy, greedy, endeavor, arise, descend, golden, shining, and nectar.

TRY IT OUT: UNHAPPY BIRTHDAY

Your best friend is one of Zeus's grandchildren, but unlike his siblings, he hasn't inherited any of the god's powers. He knows that and you know that, but the rest of his family and friends are about to discover this truth at his sixteenth birthday party, when society dictates that he must come of age and join his siblings in protecting your Greek town—that is, unless your friend has his way. He plans to conjure up a disaster of epic proportions that will move the town's focus from his birthday ceremony to dealing with the aftermath of the catastrophe.

Write a story about this scenario. Your friend's plan as well as whether you attempt to stop it is up to you. Use the (set:) macro in conjunction with the (random:) macro to track $creativity, $strength, and $persuasiveness.

Exploring Realistic Fiction

Traffic impedes you on your way to work, teachers pile on the homework, and you need to find a date to prom with the modern home—whether a suburban ranch house or an apartment in a city—serving as the setting in a realistic fiction game. Yes, this is plain, old reality, served up in a creative way that makes you want to read about someone else's triumphs and foibles as they make their way through an ordinary day.

The goal of a realistic fiction writer is to capture a moment in time and expose its truth, while the goal of the reader is to find elements of his or her own life reflected back in the storyline. Characters may grapple with a problem that plagues everyone—such as feeling left out—or give insight into a unique problem—such as dealing with a terminal illness. While these stories are fictitious, they *could* happen, which means the characters need to behave realistically, messy thoughts and all. No one is perfect, and that is abundantly clear in realistic fiction.

Words that will help set the tone in a realistic fiction story: bored, gorgeous, annoyed, moody, brick, bus, skateboard, aplomb, falter, and bluff.

TRY IT OUT: PROM DATE

Prom is one week away, and you don't have a date yet. What chance do you have of getting a date with the object of your affection? Will you get that person to say yes at the end of the game, or will you botch your chances for prom?

Write a story about this scenario, using the `(random:)` macro set with the `$promDatePossibility` variable at the beginning of the game. Have interactions with the person add or subtract from the base value of the variable.

Exploring Other Genres

The genres just described are just a few of the ones you'll encounter in the world of interactive fiction, though these descriptions don't do these genres justice. Each is more complex than can be encapsulated in a few paragraphs and using a handful of tone-setting terms. But that is the beauty of finding the genres that speak to your heart: They will turn you into a passionate defender of the distinctions of each type of story.

Of course, you've probably already noticed that there is plenty of crossover between genres, and maybe you will find a way to meld two or more of your favorite genres in order to leave the beaten path and create a whole new category of interactive fiction.

Think of these sections as just a starting point, ideas to pique your interest. Once you realize where you want to dive in, swim through the nuances of your chosen genre by playing games and reading more about that type of tale. There is nothing better than a good story.

Understanding Motivations

Cardboard characters are superficial, two-dimensional characters that don't seem real because they act without motivation. And yes, I know *real* is a funny word to apply to something fictional, but you need even your most fantastical fiction filled with dragons and mermaids to make sense.

People do things for a reason; they have motivation. There is always a purpose to human actions and meaning behind actions, even if it's secret.

Cardboard characters are predictable because you always know how they're going to behave. Examples would be a cheerleader who is cheerful even as zombies eat all the members of the football team, or an evil wizard who reduces every character he encounters into a toad, even his underlings who are trying to serve him, just because he's that evil. Simply put, the actions of cardboard characters don't make sense because these folks don't seem to react to their environment or have a reason for their actions.

A great example of a character who could have been cardboard but was guided firmly into three-dimensional territory is Harry Potter's Voldemort. He's an evil guy seemingly just for evil's sake, but over time, you get to know the reasons behind his actions and why he targets the particular people he targets. Those reasons don't make him any less evil, but knowing them certainly makes him more complex and unpredictable. The reader doesn't necessarily know when Voldemort will reward or punish his underlings, though you certainly want to keep reading because you know his motivations and want to know if he reaches his goals.

So plot twists are created when you don't get the answer you thought you'd get to that underlying question: Will he or won't he? The only caveat is that the character needs to twist and turn *for a reason*. There needs to be a reasonable explanation for why he or she is doing what he or she is doing.

For a writer, creating those plot twists takes three parts: Consider what you know about the character, consider what the character would usually do, and have the character impacted by his or her environment or have the character's past inform his or her present. Bring these three pieces together to make your characters make different choices. Let them be unpredictable for a good reason. Create choices in your story that allow your characters to do things they normally wouldn't do because there is something to be lost or gained by a particular choice. And keep in mind context; in a different time and place, the character may make a very different decision.

The point is to avoid creating cardboard characters, flimsy plots, and see-through storylines—anything that has the reader internally roll his or her eyes and wonder, "What is the point in continuing if I can already predict what happens next?"

People turn the page or, in this case, keep clicking, when they are intrigued and want to find out where the story goes—when you leave the well-beaten path of the genre and make it into something new.

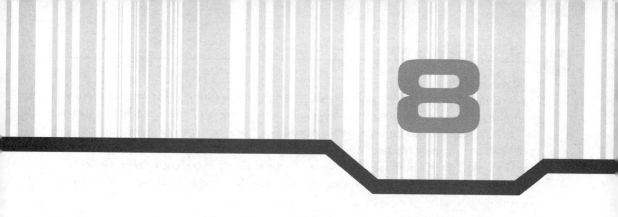

Constructing Believable Characters

One of the most beloved interactive fiction characters of all time is Floyd from *Planetfall*. This robot is so loved that ifMUD, an online hangout for interactive fiction enthusiasts, has a bot named Floyd as well as a group gameplay gathering called ClubFloyd. This chapter uses Floyd as a model for learning how to build a successful character—because, yes, there are steps you can take to ensure that people love *your* characters, too.

Floyd is a robot the player character encounters after crash landing on a distant planet. Floyd remains with the player character as he or she tries to help the inhabitants of the planet, who are all cryogenically frozen and awaiting a cure for the illness that is wiping out their population.

Recognizing the Traits of Successful Characters

So why is Floyd such a successful character? Well, first and foremost, there aren't many other competing characters in the game. The author, Steve Meretzky, focused on creating one main well-rounded non-player character rather than spread out his energy in creating lots of smaller non-player characters. In doing so, he also focused the player's attention exactly where he wanted it to go—like a literary spotlight.

Floyd is also successful because, like R2-D2 and WALL-E, he touches on our human longing for an android companion. Sure, robots aren't as cuddly as humans, but they have the distinct advantage of being customizable to fit our needs. Meretzky filled Floyd with a wide range of favored best friend traits to build the perfect sidekick. Floyd is as lovable and playful as a puppy, he says funny things, he's loyal to the core, and he's willing to sacrifice his life in order to help you reach your goals. He is fantasy best friend wish fulfillment, albeit in mechanical form.

But beyond all of Floyd's unique personality traits, you connect with Floyd because he also has a goal: to be the most helpful robot ever. Readers are drawn to characters that have a clearly defined goal and work to fulfill that goal.

Finally, Floyd is vulnerable, which means he's capable of being hurt, and it moves the reader to want to protect him. You feel sad when he goes into the Bio-Lab on the player character's behalf and returns torn apart. The player character is gutted by Floyd's death, and the player is, too, even though his sacrifice means that you can solve the puzzle at hand. Poor Floyd.

Anyone can create a Floyd-like character by following a few simple guidelines for creating believable, interesting characters. Start by limiting the number of characters you're throwing into a story. It's better to go deep with a handful of characters than to spread the story thinly over too many characters. After your first draft, look at whether there are characters that can be cut if their purpose is reassigned to a remaining character. Interactive fiction has more in common with short stories than with novels, so adjust the scope of the story accordingly.

Next, as the writer, have in mind a clear set of traits that define the character. If *you* don't know your character inside and out, readers cannot get a concrete sense of your character. You don't need to include everything you know about your characters. In fact, you shouldn't include it all, or it will come across as a laundry list of traits; rather, always keep these facts in the back of your mind and have them inform what the character says and does in the story.

You also need to give a character a goal and have him or her actively work to complete it. I spoke about this in Chapter 1, "The Nuts and Bolts: Getting Started with Twine," in regard to agency (that is, how much the character can affect his or her world), as well as in Chapter 7, "Exploring Interactive Fiction Genres," when I spoke about avoiding cardboard characters by having characters make choices off the beaten path for a good reason.

People cheer on characters who know what they want and are making things happen to get closer to their goals. People want to read about characters who do things rather than having things done to them. Make readers stick around because they want to know if a character succeeds. Your readers will only be as invested as the character is in reaching their goal, so make sure your character is highly invested, and the reader will mirror that level of emotional investment.

Finally, create characters that are vulnerable. The strongest characters reveal their foibles or let other characters help them—and you love them a little bit more when they do. Instead of looking weak, they come across as human, and this helps the reader to relate to them. So throw a few obstacles their way, have them admit that they're scared, and put them in a few dangerous situations that make the reader hold their breath until the character is back on stable ground.

Plug Floyd into this character-making rubric and see how he checks out. He isn't competing against a lot of other characters. He is constructed out of a clearly defined set of traits insofar as there are actions that are Floyd-like and actions that are decidedly un-Floyd-like. He has a goal of assisting the player character in obtaining the antidote, and he works to complete it. And he is definitely vulnerable since he gives up his life to save the day.

Of course, you don't want to replicate Floyd since each character is unique, just as each person is unique. Floyd's likable traits, such as his loyalty and sense of humor, are *Floyd's* positive traits. Your characters will have different, but no less likable, positive traits. Still, you can use Floyd as a model and plug *your* future characters into this rubric to see how they check out.

Take your time building characters. A big mistake that interactive fiction authors make is believing that their plot is so strong that they don't really need to build solid characters because the focus will always be on the action. And, yes, some plots are really exciting, but I would argue that you always benefit from having solid characters driving that action. After all, when you walk away from a story, it's rarely the setting or plot twists that remain with you. Hogwarts would just be a big, empty castle without the students and staff, and the fight scenes in *Star Wars* are exciting only because you're invested in Luke Skywalker and Princess Leia.

Because readers connect with a story through the characters, writing teachers always ask their students "Whose story is it?" to bring it back to character development. I want you to ask yourself that question every time you sit down to try one of the writing exercises in this book. In a cast of characters, whose story is it? (Hint: It may not always be the player character's story, despite the player seeing the tale from that point of view.)

So don't cut corners when it comes to characters. In this chapter you'll start with non-player characters because there's a little more distance from them, and you can therefore judge them more objectively.

But first you need to learn a few new macros that you'll practice in sample games. The (click:) and (mouseover:) macros can be combined with other macros, such as (click-replace:) and (mouseover-replace:), to have words appear or disappear on the screen, whereas the (prompt:) macro allows the player to name the characters, which creates even more investment in the story.

Using the (click:), (mouseover:), and (prompt:) Macros

You can use several macros in combination with other macros to create effects that show the personality quirks of characters. For example, you can combine the (click:) and (mouseover:) macros with the (replace:) macro to have words change on the screen—a perfect device for a character who frequently lies or is indecisive.

In addition, the (prompt:) macro allows the reader to enter unique text, such as a character name, into the game. First you'll look at the (click:) macro that you encountered in Chapter 4, "Designing Puzzles."

Using the (click:) Macro

You can use the (click:) macro to create a named hook. Remember that named hooks aren't attached to a macro, so there are no parentheses preceding them. A named hook utilizes a nametag that is then referenced elsewhere in the passage with a question mark placed in front of the name of the hook, similar to the way a dollar sign is placed in front of the name of a variable.

The `(click:)` macro is similar to the `(link:)` macro. You use it wherever you want clickable text to appear that the player can select to see more text. For instance, you could use it if you wanted the description of the character to come out in small pieces, as if eyes were traveling over the person's body.

To create a named hook, open a new story, call it Description, and write this in it:

```
You stare at the boy, your mouth slightly ajar.
There are his [ears. ]<ears|(click: ?ears)[They end in sharp points.]
There are his [eyes. ]<eyes|(click: ?eyes)[They are the pale blue of a robin's egg.]
His clothes look like they're constructed out of layers of leaves, and a small pan
pipe dangles from his fingers.
Your eyes finally rest on his [shoes. ]<shoes|(click: ?shoes)
[They curl at the tip, like smoke exiting a pipe.]
```

If the player sees only the text that begins on the screen, the character comes across as a normal, albeit strangely dressed, boy, as shown in Figure 8.1.

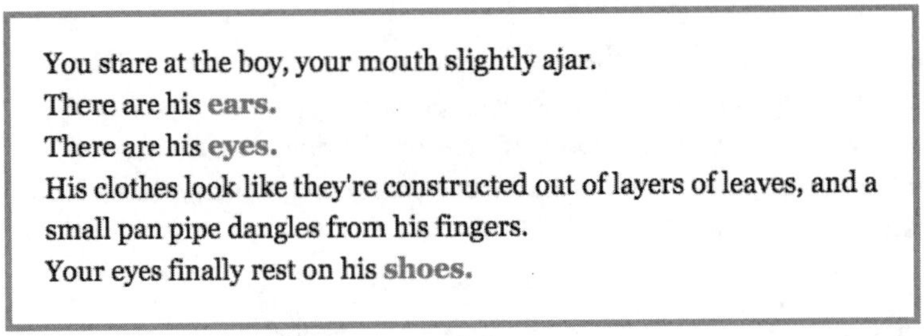

> You stare at the boy, your mouth slightly ajar.
> There are his **ears.**
> There are his **eyes.**
> His clothes look like they're constructed out of layers of leaves, and a small pan pipe dangles from his fingers.
> Your eyes finally rest on his **shoes.**

FIGURE 8.1 The text as it appears on the screen when the passage is opened.

There is plenty of plain text on the screen, but there are also three hyperlinked words (ears, eyes, and shoes). These words are connected to the `(click:)` macro, and when it is triggered because the reader selects one of those words, the rest of the sentence appears on the screen. Figure 8.2 shows what it looks like after all three words are clicked.

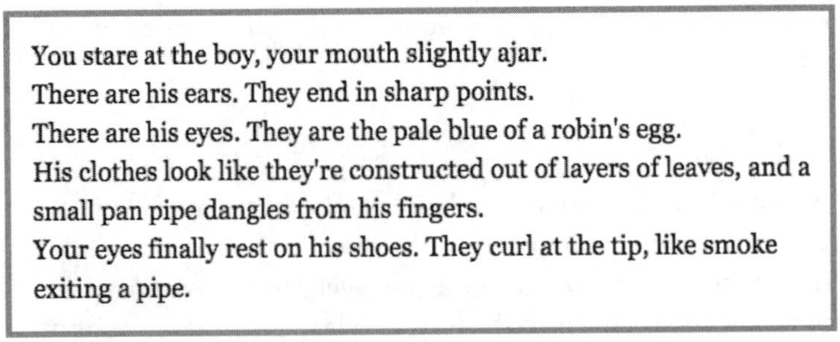

> You stare at the boy, your mouth slightly ajar.
> There are his ears. They end in sharp points.
> There are his eyes. They are the pale blue of a robin's egg.
> His clothes look like they're constructed out of layers of leaves, and a small pan pipe dangles from his fingers.
> Your eyes finally rest on his shoes. They curl at the tip, like smoke exiting a pipe.

FIGURE 8.2 The text as it appears on the screen after the `(click:)` macro is triggered.

Use this macro by placing the intended hyperlinked text inside a single set of square brackets and attaching a nametag to the named hook by combining an angled bracket, the name of the tag, and a pipe (<ears|). Afterward, the (click:) macro combines with an anonymous hook that contains the words that should appear on the screen after the hyperlink is clicked (They end in sharp points).

The hyperlinked text from the first hook remains on the screen as unlinked text after the word is clicked. If the hyperlinked text is not clicked, the words in the second, anonymous, hook do not appear.

TRY IT OUT: WARNING

Open a new story and call it Warning. The main character in this story is a clairvoyant person who has unfortunately predicted the fact that her teacher is about to lose her job. She is bound by the Clairvoyant Code not to reveal the future to non-clairvoyants, but she is miserable because she loves this teacher and knows how badly she needs her job. The character, of course, needs to keep attending class but can't say a word...or can she?

If she were merely to hint about the future, would it count as revealing the truth? Is her teacher bright enough to figure it out without having the future spelled out for her?

Use the (click:) macro to hide (and then reveal) the character's inner thoughts. Consider what it would be like to be a clairvoyant as well as unique traits this character possesses and use this knowledge to create a vibrant main character.

In addition, the (click:) macro can be combined with an additional changer macro, (replace:), to make clickable text that is exchanged on the screen for the text inside a second, anonymous hook. You can create another example inside the Description example to practice making a hyperlinked word disappear when clicked and have the words in the second hook appear in its place. Type the following inside Description:

```
[You turn on the light in the room.]<light|(click-replace: ?light)[There is only
a smooth expanse of wall where the light switch used to be.]
```

In this case, the words inside the named hook (You turn on the light in the room) appear on the screen as a hyperlink, as shown in Figure 8.3.

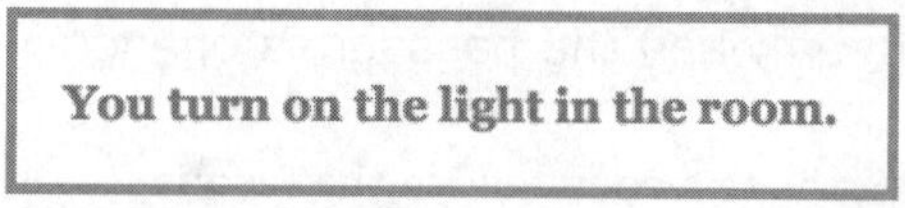

You turn on the light in the room.

FIGURE 8.3 The text as it appears on the screen when the passage is opened.

After the link is clicked, the words disappear from the screen and are replaced with the words inside the second, anonymous hook (There is only a smooth expanse of wall where the light switch used to be), as shown in Figure 8.4.

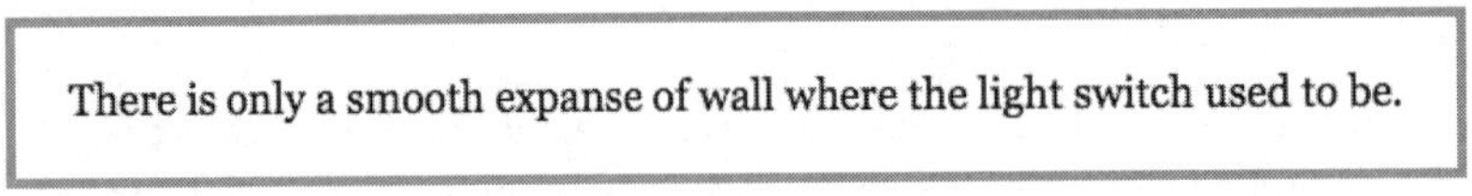

> There is only a smooth expanse of wall where the light switch used to be.

FIGURE 8.4 The text as it appears on the screen after the (click-replace:) macro is triggered.

Whether to use (click:) on its own or combine it with the (replace:) macro for (click-replace:) depends on whether you want the words in the named hook to remain on the screen after the macro is triggered.

Using the (mouseover:) Macro

Sometimes you want an effect to be triggered more subtly than by clicking hyperlinked text on the screen. The (mouseover:) macro triggers an event when the computer mouse passes over the designated text, which appears on the screen as plain text. In other words, the user doesn't know that something is going to happen on the screen until he or she moves the mouse over the chosen words.

Let's say that you want additional text to appear when the mouse moves over certain words on the screen. If the reader doesn't move the mouse over the words, he or she will not see the additional text. To get this effect, you can once again use a named hook in order to utilize the (mouseover:) macro. Start a new sample game called Magic to try out these examples.

In the first passage of Magic, write this:

```
There is a magician holding [an empty hat.]<trick|
(mouseover: ?trick)[Suddenly, a rabbit appears.]
```

What happens when you play this text in a game? You should see the passage open with both the plain text and the words inside the named hook (an empty hat) on the screen, as shown in Figure 8.5.

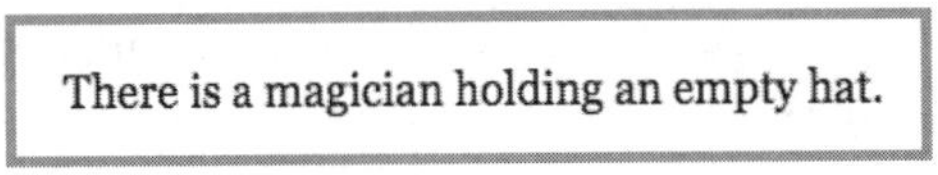

> There is a magician holding an empty hat.

FIGURE 8.5 The text as it appears on the screen when the passage is opened.

After the mouse moves over the words an empty hat, the text contained in the second, anonymous hook (Suddenly, a rabbit appears) pops onto the screen underneath the existing sentence, as shown in Figure 8.6.

> There is a magician holding an empty hat.
> Suddenly, a rabbit appears.

FIGURE 8.6 The text as it appears on the screen after the (mouseover:) macro is triggered.

The reader doesn't have a visual clue that there is changeable text on the screen as is the case with the (click:) macro that generates blue, hyperlinked text; therefore, you should use this trick sparingly or make sure the reader knows that there is something he or she needs to do on the screen. One easy way to achieve that is to hide the exit out of the room inside the second, anonymous hook. For example, change the text inside the first passage of Magic to read as follows:

```
The door out of the room was hidden behind the [bookcase.]<case|
(mouseover: ?case)[When he removed the book, he saw a small knob. Twisting it
brought him into the [[second library|Second Library]].]
```

Because the reader is accustomed to having something to click on the screen, he or she will likely move the mouse in confusion, trying to find the link. Finding the anonymous hook will teach the player to mouse over the words onscreen to look for hidden hooks.

This macro uses a named hook similar to the (click:) macro. Single square brackets are placed around the word (or words) that the writer would like to designate for triggering the macro—in this case, the word bookcase. The brackets can be placed around a unit as small as one letter or as large as a paragraph. You create a tag by combining an angled bracket, the name of the tag, and a pipe (<case|).

You can then use the tag by referencing it with the (mouseover:) macro, listing the tag with the macro preceded by a question mark (?case). When the (mouseover:) macro is triggered, the words inside the second, anonymous hook appear on the screen. Inside that hook is the hidden link to the next passage, Second Library.

So how does this appear for the reader on the screen when he or she opens the passage? The player is greeted solely by the words in the first, named hook, as shown in Figure 8.7.

> The door out of the room was hidden behind the bookcase.

FIGURE 8.7 The text as it appears on the screen when the passage is opened.

If the player doesn't move the mouse, he or she will never see the words in the second, anonymous hook and will therefore not see a link to click that will take them out of the passage. If the player moves the mouse over the word bookcase, the words contained in the second, anonymous hook that includes the link to the next passage will appear, as shown in Figure 8.8.

> The door out of the room was hidden behind the bookcase.
> When he removed the book, he saw a small knob. Twisting it brought
> him into the **second library**.

FIGURE 8.8 If the mouse moves over the designated word on the screen, the rest of the text is displayed.

You can also use a mouseover effect to transport the reader to a new passage by also utilizing the (goto:) macro you encountered in Chapter 6. Say that a person walks into a room with four colorful tiles embedded on the floor and no clear exit out of the room. When you give the reader the textual hint that the player character goes and stands on a tile, he or she will have a clue to follow suit and move the mouse onto a tile as well. When the player does this, he or she is transported into a new section of the story. To see how this works, begin a new sample story and call it Magical Creatures. In the first passage, type this:

```
You walk into the room and see four tiles embedded on the floor, each depicting a
different magical creature:
There is a [brown tile with a fierce-looking silver dragon,]<dragon|
A [blue tile with a beautiful mermaid,]<mermaid|
A [red tile with a golden phoenix,]<phoenix|
And a [green tile with a white unicorn.]<unicorn|
You go and stand on a tile.
(mouseover: ?dragon)[(goto: "Dragonland")]
(mouseover: ?mermaid)[(goto: "Ocean")]
(mouseover: ?phoenix)[(goto: "Forest")]
(mouseover: ?unicorn)[(goto: "Field")]
```

So how does the macro work? Single square brackets are placed around the designated text to create a named hook, and each hook is named with a tag corresponding to the animal on the tile; for instance, the tag <dragon| is created by combining an angled bracket, name, and pipe.

Toward the bottom of the passage is the (mouseover:) macro, along with its attached anonymous hook. Each (mouseover:) macro references one of the nametags by listing it preceded by a question mark (for example,?dragon). Each attached anonymous hook contains the (goto:) macro, which transports the reader to a corresponding passage, either the Dragonland, Ocean, Forest, or Field passage.

Even with a lot of spacing between the named hooks in the passage, it is very easy to accidentally mouse over a different named hook on the way to the one you want. You need to play around with the spacing and sizing of a hook in order to make it feasible for readers to access every hidden choice in the passage.

Remember, the (goto:) macro, unlike the [[link]] macro, does not create the passages for you. Before you play the story, you need to use the green +Passage button to create four passages and call them Dragonland, Ocean, Forest, and Field. Pay close attention to capitalization agreement between the link in the first passage and the second passage's title.

What happens when the player sees this passage on the screen? He or she encounters the opening text shown in Figure 8.9, ending with this direction: You go and stand on a tile.

> You walk into the room and see four tiles embedded on the floor, each depicting a different magical creature:
>
> There is a brown tile with a fierce-looking silver dragon,
>
> A blue tile with a beautiful mermaid,
>
> A red tile with a golden phoenix,
>
> And a green tile with a white unicorn.
>
> You go and stand on a tile.

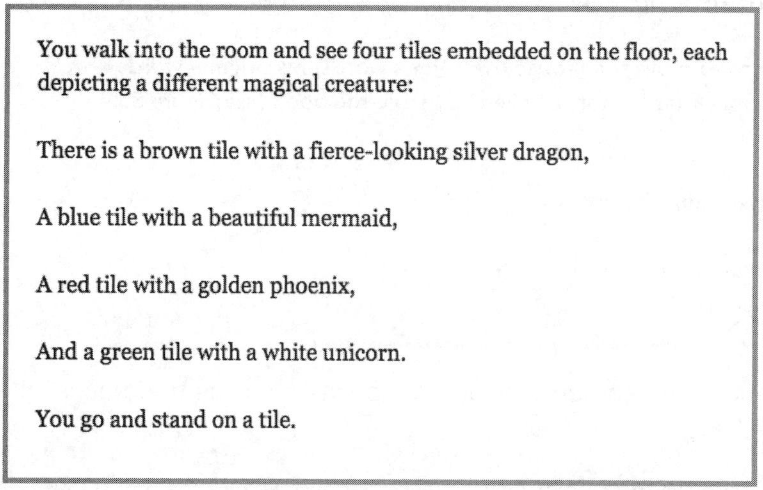

FIGURE 8.9 The text as it appears on the screen when the passage is opened.

When the player moves the mouse to one of the sentences, he or she is instantly transported to a new passage.

Finally, you can make a combination macro that brings together the (mouseover:) macro and the (replace:) macro, much as you did earlier with the (click-replace:) macro. The (mouseover-replace:) macro replaces the words on the screen when the mouse travels over the designated text. Begin another sample story and call it The Lie. In the first passage, type this:

```
["I placed the book back on the shelf,"]<lie| Alex admitted, biting his lip.

Maybe you should [[check the shelf|Check Shelf]] again, or you could
[[tell Mr. Dexter|Tell Dexter]] that the book is lost.
(mouseover-replace: ?lie)["I stole it,"]
```

This combination macro completely changes the text on the screen. The player opens the passage and finds a sympathetic Alex saying that he put the missing book back on the shelf (see Figure 8.10). The player can either check the shelf again or tell Mr. Dexter the book is missing.

> "I placed the book back on the shelf," Alex admitted, biting his lip.
>
> Maybe you should **check the shelf** again, or you could **tell Mr. Dexter** that the book is lost.

FIGURE 8.10 The text as it appears on the screen when the passage is opened.

But if the player happens to move the mouse over Alex's words, his original words are replaced by the admittance that he not only lied but stole the book (see Figure 8.11).

> "I stole it," Alex admitted, biting his lip.
>
> Maybe you should **check the shelf** again, or you could **tell Mr. Dexter** that the book is lost.

FIGURE 8.11 The text on the screen changes if the player moves the mouse over the original words.

The player may never get to see this side of Alex if he or she doesn't move the mouse over the words, so you should think twice about hiding important clues inside the (mouseover:) macro. If you do put crucial clues there, be sure to give the player instructions on how to best interact with the game. This type of warning makes the game more fun for the reader and makes it possible for him or her to encounter the cool things you coded into your game.

TRY IT OUT: STUCK

You're on an elevator that grinds to a sudden halt, and you're trapped inside with a seemingly nice and helpful elderly woman. She's a little dotty but has plenty of good suggestions as you work to get the elevator moving again. But is she as clueless or sweet as she seems?

Write a story for this scenario, using the (mouseover:) macro to make more words appear, hide links, and transport the player to new passages so that understanding slowly dawns on the reader that this kind little old lady is the last person you want to be trapped with between floors.

Using the (prompt:) Macro

Sometimes you want to give a player an opportunity to add words to a game, either to name a character or give an answer. Twine can remember such information if you assign it as a value for a variable, and it can recall the value at other points in the game.

The (prompt:) macro provides the reader with a text input box for entering any word or words. Open a new sample game and title it Name. In the first passage, write this:

```
(put: (prompt: "What is your name?") into $name)
```

What happens when you click the Play button? The player sees a hovering text box appear on the screen, along with the question What is your name? After entering text in the box, the reader gets a choice of two buttons: Cancel and OK (see Figure 8.12).

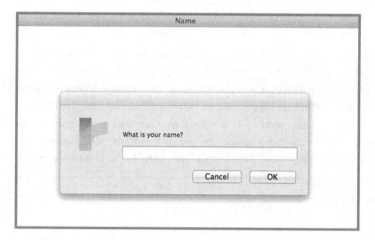

FIGURE 8.12   The text input box hovers on the screen, over the passage.

Unfortunately, if a player chooses not to enter a name and instead clicks Cancel, every time the game goes to print the value of the variable, the player will see an empty space. To try this out, reopen the passage and add the following text:

```
Your name is (print: $name).
```

Now play the game twice, one time entering a name and one time clicking the Cancel button. The first time, you see the name on the screen, as shown in Figure 8.13.

Your name is Melissa.

FIGURE 8.13   Twine prints out the value of the $name variable.

The second time, you see only a blank space where the name should have been entered (see Figure 8.14). Throughout the game, whenever Twine checks the value of the variable $name, it prints a blank space as it does here.

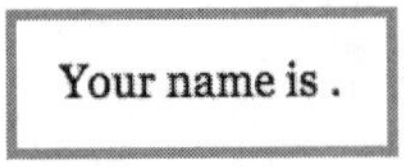

> **Your name is .**

FIGURE 8.14   Twine prints out a blank space because there is no value for the $name variable.

So how does the macro work? The (put:) macro works in a similar manner to the (set:) macro, placing a value inside a variable. In this example, the value of the (prompt:) macro is being put into the $name variable. The (prompt:) macro is merely an empty text box, so whatever is typed in that text box becomes the value for the variable $name.

It helps to think about the limitations of this macro when considering its usage. The macro returns the value of the variable exactly as it is typed, which means that if the reader doesn't capitalize the first letter in the name entered, it will be printed in lowercase letters every time it is used in the game. It also means that using conditionals becomes tricky because the (if:) and (else:) macros check the value exactly as it is written. Capitalization counts, and the game will not, for example, return the same results for red as it will for Red. However, it is always a nice touch to allow the player to name the player character, so just keep these limitations in mind.

So how can you use the macros you've just learned about to build memorable, interesting characters? I'll get to that shortly.

Distinguishing Types of Characters

Beware of anyone who tells you that a story needs to contain a certain *type* of character. While it's helpful to know what elements strong characters possess, avoid thinking that all detectives, elves, or princesses need to have certain characteristics in order to be recognizable for readers. Readers appreciate characters that don't fit the mold but subvert expectations.

You need to know about a few roles of characters before you begin character construction. For instance, the *protagonist* is the main character, the one who is working to solve the problem after the catalyst and bring the story to the point of climax. In interactive fiction, the protagonist is usually the player character, though the story could be structured so the protagonist is one of the non-player characters.

The *antagonist* is the character who works opposite the protagonist to keep him or her from solving the conflict. Think of the antagonist as the literary form of a human obstacle.

A *foil* is a character whose sole purpose is to serve as a contrast. For instance, in the Harry Potter series, Harry would be difficult to define if he were the only person in the book. But

Draco Malfoy serves as a foil by giving us more information about Harry. The contrast between the two characters shows us how they're different and how they are—much to Harry's chagrin—at times alike.

Finally, a *confidante* or *sidekick* is important because when the protagonist tells that person information, he or she is indirectly passing along that information to the reader, too. These characters are there to support the protagonist, to listen to the main character share their feelings, divulge their plans, or reveal their foibles. A solidly drawn confidante is interesting in his or her own right, meaning that he or she has a fascinating side story that adds to the enjoyment of the game instead of simply serving as a device so the reader can hear the protagonist's words in a less stilted way.

Limiting Characters

Building characters and getting the reader to care about them takes a lot of work. Remember that *you* know the characters because you've created them, but your readers are meeting them for the very first time.

Normally, writing a story with only a few characters sounds like it would be less work than writing one with lots of characters, but having fewer characters means that the characters you do have need to be complex and well fleshed out. It means you need to go deep and distinguish your characters with well-defined traits.

You are going to build three characters for the Try It Out that runs through the next three sections, which cover the three main steps to building believable characters. Two characters will be solid, well-crafted characters, and the third will remain a background character whose sole purpose is to highlight the main character's importance by remaining on the fringes of the action. Ready to try your hand at bringing a figurative person to life? You can start by listing traits.

Creating a Clear Set of Traits

To build a new character, begin by creating a list of character traits. Think of yourself as Dr. Frankenstein in the lab, piecing together a being on the table. What does the character look like, sound like, and act like? And, most importantly, what does he or she want, and how will the character's personality help or hinder on their way to that goal?

In this case, start with the outside of a character and then move inside the character's brain. Describe your character down to the smallest detail, including any visual quirks that you can use to help distinguish your character.

Start with a physical description. What is the first thing a person notices about the character? What is the person's hair color, style, and texture? What are the color and shape of the person's eyes? Describe the character's ears and nose, facial structure, and skin tone. Does the person have any distinguishing scars or piercings? What is his or her body type or body shape? Is this person tall or short?

Once you know what the character looks like, start jotting down some facts about your character, such as age, ethnicity, and nationality. Which languages does the person speak? What are his or her cultural practices?

Now it's time to go deep: What makes your character tick? How does this person process the world? How does the character's personality draw people in or repel them? Is the person smart? Kind? Does he or she miss the small details? Have a cruel streak?

It can be helpful to look at your character on the spectrum of what psychologists call the Big 5, or five consistent personality traits, which spell out the acronym CANOE:

Conscientiousness—Is the person dependable or unreliable? Is he or she highly organized, with clear systems in place so nothing slips through the cracks, or is the person more easygoing, approaching life in a carefree manner?

Agreeableness—Is the person friendly or standoffish? Are people attracted or repelled by his or her personality? Is the character easy to get along with, or is he or she very demanding or rude toward other people?

Neuroticism—Is this the type of person who worries about everything, or does he or she generally approach the world with confidence? Is the character nervous, or does he or she experience anxiety only in the face of actual danger?

Openness—Is the character willing to try new things, or is the person pretty set in his or her ways? Is the character able to give other people's opinions a chance, or does he or she refuse to budge from a particular stance? Does the person want to explore the world, or is he or she nervous to try new things? Does the person go for the new option or stick with what he or she already knows?

Extraversion/introversion—Where does the character draw energy? Is this person happier being part of a crowd, or does he or she need a lot of alone time to recharge? Is this person talkative and assertive or more likely to crave quiet and hold back his or her thoughts?

A special consideration for non-human characters is to think about which ways they're like humans and in which ways they are a totally different species. This is especially important for aliens, magical creatures, and personified animals.

Finish up by jotting down any personality traits you think might be important for your character, as well as any defining stories that have shaped him or her. Did something happen in the past that made the character who he or she is today? How did the character's family or circumstances influence the person in the story today? What are the person's hidden talents? Is this a truthful or deceptive person?

Once you've defined all these traits, use them. A big mistake many writers make in regard to their characters is to have them act in ways that don't ring true for them. Take, for instance, a game where the player character is a mousy scientist. Simply stating that the scientist is fearful isn't enough. The scientist should hesitate at doors or worry about the animals in the lab. You may need to make a character go where he or she wouldn't normally go for the sake of the story, and it's okay to do that, but have the character behave accordingly.

Make the character pause at the mouth of the cave before taking a deep breath, gathering courage, and stepping inside. That internal process reminds the reader that the character is timid, even if he or she now needs to go do something brave for the sake of the story.

Even if all the details you write for your character don't make it directly into your story, you, as the writer, need to know these things about your character so he or she is always behaving in character. With each passage, ask yourself whether the behavior is in or out of character, and if it is out of character, figure out if there is a clear reason the behavior is changing. If not, edit the passage so the character behaves more like himself or herself.

You will need to keep the personality of the character in mind and have it play out in all the choices so the player has agency while the character remains well-defined. For instance, returning to the example of the mousy scientist, you could give the choice whether or not the player character enters the cave. In both cases, the character needs to explain their reluctance—for instance, caves contain spiders—or their willingness—I'm terrified but I must save my friend. In both cases, the character remains true to their personality even though the control is in the hands of the player.

Of course, your character should change over the course of the story. Humans are affected by events and by newfound knowledge, so make your characters grow and change, too. When you finish writing your game, start playing it and note whether the characters are essentially the same at the beginning of the game as they are at the end of the game. If they are, you have some editing work to do.

TRY IT OUT: DINNER FOR TWO, PART I

You're going to build this practice story in three parts. For now, create three characters—the player character and two non-player characters—and set them at a restaurant. The player character and one of the non-player characters are having dinner together, and the other non-player character is a part of the wait staff.

Make sure the story opener quickly jumps into the work of introducing the reader to these characters. You want the reader to focus on the non-player character at the table and not on the waiter, so make sure the waiter remains part of the background.

The details you include will indirectly show the reader the character: What sort of restaurant is it? What do the characters order? How do they treat the waiter? Are they happy to be eating with one another? What is their relationship to one another?

These types of details tell the reader about the character. Pause the story after the characters order their meal.

You've now gone through the first part of building a character. Make each character your imaginary friend and think of them throughout the day, considering what they would do in every situation you encounter in order to get to them inside and out. Next you will give the character something to do.

Setting a Goal

Every character has something that he or she must do, and this goal helps define the type of story. This goal is nonnegotiable, and the whole story hinges upon whether the character does this task; the story falls apart without this obligation as a guide. Each character's own personal goal drives him or her in the story. Here are a few possible "musts" to get you started in brainstorming your character's goal:

Must get better—Does your character wish for self-improvement or want to get into a better station in life? This is a person seeking personal growth.

Must face fear—Does your character recognize that something is holding him or her back? This person must overcome fear and face the *something* head on.

Must do task—Does your character have a task to complete for another person, something that will help all the characters in the story if they're successful at their goal?

Must go and learn—Does your character have a life lesson to discover, some important truth that he or she needs to find in order to change his or her life's course?

Must find happy ending—Does your character aim to fall in love or win a huge prize? Does he or she need to convince another person to help in reaching that happy ending?

Must be free—Does your character feel imprisoned by circumstances in his or her life, or is the person actually being held in a restrictive situation? The person may be seeking literal and/or figurative freedom.

There are plenty of other possible "musts," but hopefully this list gets the wheels turning in your head so you can give each character something to do.

TRY IT OUT: DINNER FOR TWO, PART II

In the last Try It Out, the two main characters had just ordered their meal. Now you need to give each character a goal to accomplish. These goals may conflict, such as having one person want the other to be a vegetarian while the other character wants the first character to become a meat-eater. Or the goals may run parallel to one another. Of course, each character thinks his or her goal is the most important goal, and therefore each will try to steer the conversation to get what he or she wants.

Have the conversation happening on two levels. Using either the `(click:)` or `(mouseover:)` macro, have the words on the screen be replaced by a second set of words either when the player clicks on hyperlinked text or moves their mouse over the designated text. How do the additional words convey how the character feels about how well he or she is accomplishing the goal? Introduce the situation and then pause again when you feel both characters have made good first steps toward reaching their goals.

You now have characters with strongly defined personalities who know what they want. Now it's time to make them real by making them vulnerable and flawed.

Being Vulnerable

In the 1974 book *Origins of Marvel Comics*, Stan Lee asks whether you can name any of the attractive characters in the *Hunchback of Notre Dame*. He suspects that the only character you remember is the less-than-perfect Quasimodo. I found him to be right: I remembered Quasimodo, but I needed to look up the name Claude Frollo.

Our favorite characters are usually flawed in some way. Rather than being off-putting, such vulnerability makes characters seem real. You feel intimidated or bored by people who come across as too perfect. Flaws make people interesting.

Flaws are also what make goals harder to reach and slow down the pace of a story. Think about your character's goal and then think about what would be the largest obstacle in reaching that goal. That obstacle is your character's weakness, or Achilles' heel.

Say that your character's "must" is a special task: delivering a letter for the king. But the king doesn't know that your character, while seemingly fearless, has a secret phobia of the dark. Traveling to the neighboring kingdom means traveling through the Forest of Eternal Darkness.

Now the story is infinitely more interesting. After all, if the task were easy for the character, you wouldn't have a very long story. In the first passage, the character would be given the task, in the second passage the character would go to the other kingdom, and in the third passage, the character would deliver the letter. The end.

But if the character has to will himself to get on his horse or is going to try to invent a tool that to help light up the forest, readers start cheering on that character as he moves toward his goal because they realize that reaching the goal is not a given. The character may end up being too scared to deliver the letter. There is a possibility that he will fail at his task.

People like characters who need to overcome a few obstacles on the way to a goal. It makes readers feel that there is something at stake.

TRY IT OUT: DINNER FOR TWO, PART III

Return to the game you've been creating. You left the characters in the restaurant, starting to work toward fulfilling their goals. Now you need to make them vulnerable by having them internally admit their doubts about their ability to fulfill their goals. Look at their specific goals. What would be a weakness that would keep someone from fulfilling each of these goals?

Use the (click:) or (mouseover:) macro to hide each character's inner fears, making the words pop up on the screen as an aside that only the reader can see.

Finish creating your game. Which character achieves his or her goal? Do they work together or against one another?

I thought up a story involving a witch mother and her seemingly non-magical daughter meeting up for lunch in a fancy restaurant. It's the sort of place the mother assumes her daughter still loves, mostly because she hasn't noticed how much her daughter has changed over the years. But the daughter would be much more comfortable in a casual café than worrying about which fork to use in the current establishment.

The mother's goal is to have a heart-to-heart with her daughter about her suspicions that her daughter hasn't inherited her mother's magical powers. The daughter's goal is to convince her mother that she wants to leave the magical world behind and enroll in a science-focused boarding school with her best friend.

Both characters have weaknesses. The mother has always been worried that her daughter is too fragile to hear that she is non-magical and thinks the news will drive them further apart. The daughter doesn't want her mother to think that she is rejecting magic by studying science. In the end, the mother spills her opinion, and her daughter, hearing the words, realizes how much she really wanted to be magical. She goes into the bathroom to collect herself, and while she is washing her face in the mirror after a good, long cry, she sees a door in the mirror that isn't on the wall behind her. She reaches forward and finds herself tumbling toward an old fortress housing a magical school; she has passed the final test by admitting how badly she wants magical powers and has been granted admittance to the school.

So each of the two characters has unique character traits, clear goals, and secret weaknesses. I finished up the story by giving them each what they wanted, though they hadn't realized that they wanted the same thing at the beginning of the story.

Deepening Character Building

At this point, you have the basics for building a believable character. But maybe you want to dig deeper and really focus on making your characters come to life. Here are a few more tricks for introducing characters into your game.

Assigning Purpose

There should be a reason for every character in your game, even the small ones designated for the background. In my story, I had the characters' interactions with the waiter reveal a lot about their personalities; the mother was fretful, while the daughter acted bored, as if the whole meal was beneath her. The mother was overly polite, and the daughter was brusque to the point of rudeness.

See, the waiter gave more than just verisimilitude—that truthful quality which makes a scene more realistic—such as having wait staff in a restaurant. Without the waiter, the reader might not have seen the traits of the other characters.

So ask yourself what is the purpose of your character. Perhaps it's to provide contrast, to thwart, or to assist. Do you want to interact with the non-player character, or do you want to avoid him as you'd dodge perfume squirters in the makeup section of a department store?

Is the non-player character only there to act with the player character, or does she have her own rich side story? Some non-player characters will lead interesting lives separate from the player character, but others will pop out and fade back based on the player character's story.

After you examine the purpose of each character, ask yourself if you can consolidate characters and make one character do the work of two. Having fewer characters means that you can go deeper with each one.

In the end, cool coding doesn't matter if the non-player character doesn't add to the playing experience and the reader's understanding of the story. Don't just have them become cool obstacles; make them cool in and of themselves. Make them interesting or charming enough, and your readers will long to have those characters get their own spinoff games.

Providing Exposition

Sometimes a non-player character is there to provide *exposition*—the background details that explain what is happening at the present moment in the story. Of course, you don't want a big information dump in the story, and non-player characters allow you to provide exposition creatively.

Have your player character hide so he or she can overhear a conversation. Or have the non-player character be a mysterious figure that everyone discusses but who never appears. If everyone is terrified of this non-player character, it will be natural for them to talk about him and thereby provide details about what has taken place before the story begins. Think about how talking about Voldemort conveys a lot of information about the wizarding world before Harry Potter ever comes face to face with him.

Exploring Relationships

Stories and games need tension. When there is nothing at stake, there is nothing driving the story. The same is true for characters: When there is no tension, there is no space for the characters to grow and change. Games without non-player characters are difficult to write well because tension naturally grows within character relationships. If there are no non-player characters, there are, by extension, no relationships to explore in the game.

Imagine a string connecting all the players. That string needs to remain taut. When tension goes out of a string, it limply dangles. Similarly, interest goes out of the reader when everyone cheerily gets along. You need the characters to push and pull one another, shaping each other as they move through the story. Don't allow the relationship between characters to grow slack.

Tension naturally occurs when each character has his or her own goal. There is tension when goals conflict or when one character stands in judgment of (or, even worse, tries to thwart) another character's goal.

The way to keep things interesting is to keep the tension in balance. Just as a tug-of-war game isn't interesting when the two teams are obviously mismatched and one tugs the other forward in a matter of seconds, you want all the characters to stick up for themselves and tug back when they feel themselves being pulled by other characters. In other words, you want to take the reader on a gentle ride, not a roller coaster. Maintaining give and take keeps a story inching forward in an interesting manner.

You now have the building blocks for working interesting non-player characters into your story; people will think about them long after they've closed the story or game. It's time to go make your characters collect things once again, but this time, you'll build an inventory and give the characters an easier way to carry and use the items they collect in the game world.

Maintaining an Inventory

Back in Chapter 5, "Building Objects with Variables," I mentioned Infocom's first game, *Zork*, which was published in 1980. It's a traditional *dungeon crawl*, a type of game where the player character navigates a space—usually a series of underground rooms or a cave—in search of treasure. Thwarting the player on this scavenger hunt of riches are various dangers, such as a thief and a troll. Dungeon crawls like *Zork* are pretty straightforward: Pick up every object that isn't nailed down, kill the thief (but only after he has opened the egg for you!), and dump all the crystal tridents and chests of jewels you find into the trophy case. Every time you deposit a treasure in the trophy case, your score increases. When you hit the magical 350-point threshold, the game ends. Oh, and you win.

As much as I love *Zork*—and believe me, I really love *Zork*—there isn't a lot of story in that story. It's interactive *fiction*, but it's missing many of the storytelling elements I've talked about in this book so far, including a plot and character motivation.

Infocom quickly figured out that collecting items without a story frame is about as interesting as looking at someone else's vacation photos. It's not as if *you* get to keep the crystal tridents and chests of jewels.

By 1983, Infocom was putting out games like *Enchanter*, which has a clear plot line. You're a neophyte wizard, and you need to defeat a more powerful evil wizard named Krill. The way you do this is by using spells that you learn during the game. But remember that you start the game as a neophyte, so you don't know many spells to begin with. You need to collect them on scrolls during the game, transcribe them into a spell book, and then use them to solve puzzles. *That* is collection with a purpose.

Marc Blank and Dave Lebling wrote both *Zork* and *Enchanter*, but they're two very different games. Each is the first episode in a three-part trilogy (*Zork I, II, and III*—though the *Zork* series also had a bunch of related spin-offs—and *Enchanter, Sorcerer,* and *Spellbreaker*), so they're meant to get the player familiar with a new world. But that's where the similarities end.

In *Zork*, the dungeon crawl is underground, in what amounts to a dungeon. At the very least, you're locked inside the space until you can figure out how to get above ground again. In *Enchanter*, the exploration is also confined to a small space—in this case a castle—but most of it takes place above ground (despite the castle having a dungeon). Is *Enchanter* still technically a dungeon crawl? It certainly has a lot of hallmarks of the traditional dungeon crawl, but it no longer feels like it's resting on the work of a tired, overdone trope. In any case, regardless of whether you'd classify it as a type of dungeon crawl, the setting is infinitely more interesting in *Enchanter* than in *Zork*.

In addition, with *Enchanter*, you finally have a reason for picking up all those items in the game. Both the player and the player character are simultaneously collecting knowledge. The player learns the ins and outs of this new world, and the player character learns how to do magic. That is a lot more interesting than the player character picking up vague items such as a jade figurine or a sapphire necklace, without knowing anything about the figurine or necklace beyond the material made to create it!

But there's a larger reason I've chosen to pit *Zork* against *Enchanter*, and it all comes down to the spell book.

Managing Inventory with Arrays

Back in Chapter 5, I already talked about making object collection a purposeful extension of a story. But now I have to talk about two more facets of object collection: realism and organization.

Realism means a lot of different things when it comes to constructing games and stories. Unless new rules pertaining to weight, strength, and gravity are defined in the playing world, it's not very realistic to have the player character able to carry around a piano throughout the game (unless, of course, your player character is an always angry Incredible Hulk). So the characters—and, by extension, object collection—need to follow the rules of the game world. If a player character can tote around a piano, you definitely need to make it clear how the player character is able to do so.

But realism also pertains to how much a character can hold. Is it realistic to believe that the player character could carry 20 items in her hands and still be able to brandish a sword? Um...no.

The way you get around the difficulties of carrying many items at once in the real world is to place them inside a container—such as a bag or box or case—and then carry around the container. You can borrow that concept and organize a lot of game objects into a single list, called an *array*. Instead of writing out dozens of variables, each having a single value, you can write out one variable that has multiple values. To build and work with an array in Twine, you use the `(array:)` and `(count:)` macros.

An *array* is just a list of values, and it gives you a way of storing data neatly. With Twine you can use an array to create a list of string values. Remember that strings are what you call word-based values, such as `"gold"` or `"an enormous fish"`, in programming. The other types of possible values are numeric values or Booleans. But in this case you're going to use strings, with each string standing in place of an object in the game.

So the `(array:)` macro allows you to group related strings together in one place and then refer to all those strings by a single collection variable, such as `$bag`.

When I'm trying to figure out how to best use an array, it helps me to visualize an imaginary physical manifestation of the array inside my head. If a variable is like an empty box that you fill with a value, an array is like an infinite, expandable box that has unlimited compartments that can be filled with values. Each value gets its own compartment, called an *index*.

Say that you have an array in your game called $bag. The values you'll place inside $bag are all strings. You can pretend each string is standing in for an object in your game. Therefore, you can place the strings "sandwich", "chips", and "drink" inside $bag, and each string gets its own compartment as seen in Figure 9.1. If you add "apple" to $bag, a new compartment (or index) is formed after the original three compartments, and now your virtual bag has four compartments. Each time you add a value, the array expands by one index, which is one item on the numbered list.

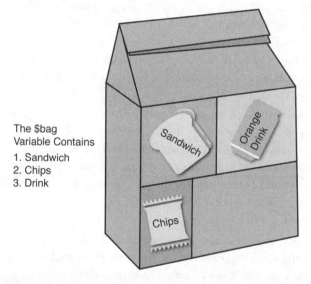

The $bag
Variable Contains

1. Sandwich
2. Chips
3. Drink

FIGURE 9.1 Imagine your array like a physical box or bag with multiple compartments and one item in each compartment.

Once you've built an array, you can check it in different ways. You can have Twine list everything inside the array, which is like peeking at an inventory in a role-playing game. For example, if you checked what's inside $bag at this point, Twine would list sandwich, chips, drink, and apple.

You can also check an array by using conditional text with the `(if:)` and `(else:)` macros, such as `(if: $bag contains "apple")[You place the apple on the teacher's desk.]` `(else:)[Your teacher sighs and says, "If you only had an apple, you would have passed this class.]` Ouch! What a terrible teacher.

You can also check the length of an array, which means you can check how many values are in the list (or how many indexes are in the array). You can then set conditional statements to have events occur when a certain threshold is met, such as having the front door to the school open when you have four items in your lunch bag (`$bag`). Or you can inversely set limits if a threshold is reached; for instance, if a person has five items in her lunch bag, she's carrying too large a load to fit through the door.

Aren't arrays fun?

You've hopefully seen how flexible arrays can be. They start out empty, and then you fill them with values. Your array doesn't need to be called `$bag`. It can be `$box` or `$suitcase`. Or, if you're feeling creative, you can make your array something like a `$spellbook`. Yes, the spell book in *Enchanter* functions like an array if you think of each spell as a string value. The player can add spells to the `$spellbook` array and also check the `$spellbook` to make sure certain spells are written inside. So get creative with your arrays.

Arrays are useful because they keep strings (which are standing in for objects inside a game) organized. Remember that a variable has only one value, whereas an array is a variable with a list of values. Even if you're tracking only a few variables, it can be tiresome to keep typing all those variables over and over again inside each conditional. An array allows you to neatly refer to a collection of values. It is much easier to check whether `$bag` contains an item than to constantly check whether the player character is carrying `$sandwich`, `$chips`, `$drink`, and `$apple` when constructing a conditional.

Plus, you can't check a variable's length. Well, you can, but Twine simply tells you the number of letters in the variable's string value. In other words, if you make a variable called `$bag` and give it the value `"apple"` and then ask Twine to print the length of the variable, it tells you 5 for the five letters that make up the word *apple*. That's not exactly helpful when you want to set things to happen when the player character is holding a certain number of items. So stick with arrays when you start making virtual collections of objects.

Oh, and just as you can create an unlimited number of variables, you can create an unlimited number of arrays. However, in this chapter, you'll create only one for each of the practice games to keep things simple.

Along with learning how to build and use an array, in this chapter you'll learn how to use literary techniques such as symbolism, allegory, metaphor, analogy, simile, allusion, irony, and hyperbole to say more with fewer words. And, hey, here's an analogy—a comparative statement—for you: Literary techniques are like arrays in that they help you streamline something complex for the reader's consumption. Okay, maybe it's not the best analogy, but you'll learn how to pepper these elements into your story to create a deeper reading experience.

While you're reading this chapter, think about playing with the traditional dungeon crawl form, perhaps moving it to unique locations or making the dangers and treasures an integral part of the story.

Using Variables to Work Around Arrays

Up until this point, if you wanted to create something akin to an inventory, such as pretending that the player has a bag and allowing the player to check which items are in the virtual bag, you could rig up a system of variables and links. This first example shows how to do that.

You can start out this sample game by giving the player a cauldron, a book of matches, and a spoon. Open up a new story in Twine, call it Magical Brew, and write this in the first passage:

```
(set: $haveCauldron to true)(set: $haveMatches to true)(set: $haveSpoon to true)
You come to the stream that Alden warned you about. It doesn't look particularly
wild, and the spot in front of you looks shallow. Do you want to risk [[crossing
the stream|Cross Stream]] or do you want to take the [[safer, longer path|Town]]
to the next town and see if you can cross at the Dilly Bridge?

[[Check Bag|Bag]]
```

So the game begins by setting a series of variables to true, giving some text as well as two choices, and ending with a strange link at the bottom: Check Bag.

If you put the Check Bag link at the bottom of every passage, the player can always check what is inside the bag. At any point, the player can click that link, see what is in the bag, and then return to the current passage in order to make a story choice, such as crossing the stream or taking the safer route into town.

Of course, you need to place something inside the newly created passage called Bag so that the player sees the variables that are true but doesn't see objects that are false—or haven't encountered yet.

Inside the Bag passage, write this:

```
Inside your bag, you see:

(if: $haveCauldron is true)[A small pewter cauldron]
(if: $haveMatches is true)[A box of matches]
(if: $haveSpoon is true)[A wooden spoon]
(if: $haveFeather is true)[A feather]
(if: $haveMarshmallow is true)[A puffy marshmallow]
(if: $haveWillow is true)[A willow branch]

(link-goto: "Return to Story", (history:)'s last)
```

When you click the Play button, the screen shows the two story choices as well as the option to check the bag at the bottom of the passage, as shown in Figure 9.2.

You come to the stream that Alden warned you about. It doesn't look particularly wild, and the spot in front of you looks shallow. Do you want to risk **crossing the stream** or do you want to take the **safer, longer path** to the next town and see if you can cross at the Dilly Bridge?

Check Bag

FIGURE 9.2   The text as it appears on the screen when the passage is opened.

In order to make the blue grid screen easier to navigate, you can drag the Bag passage to the far left, as shown in Figure 9.3. Every time you add a new variable in the future, you'll need to update this passage, so you want it to be easy to find.

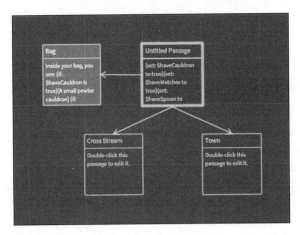

FIGURE 9.3   The important Bag passage has been dragged to the left side of the blue grid screen so it's easy to find.

The code checks the Boolean for each variable and displays the text inside the hook if the value is true. $haveCauldron, $haveMatches, and $haveSpoon are all set to true in the first passage, so when the player clicks the link to check the contents of the bag, he or she sees, as in Figure 9.4, the contents from three of the six possible hooks: a small pewter cauldron, a box of matches, and a wooden spoon.

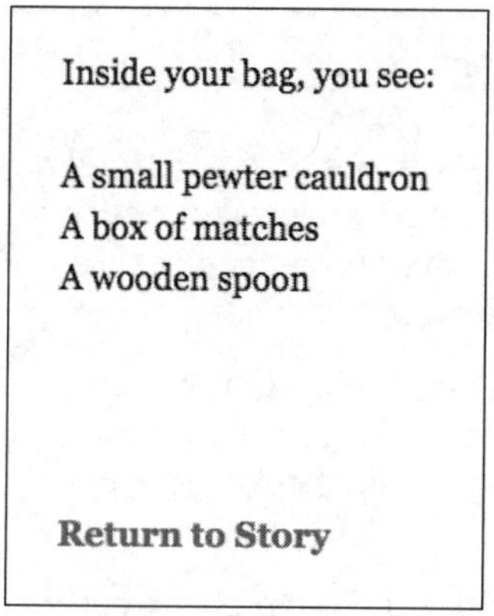

> Inside your bag, you see:
>
> A small pewter cauldron
> A box of matches
> A wooden spoon
>
>
>
> **Return to Story**

FIGURE 9.4 The contents of three out of six possible hooks are printed because their variables are set to `true`.

The player does not see the descriptions for the last three variables—a feather, a puffy marshmallow, or a willow branch—because those three variables are currently all `false`. Later in the game, when those objects are encountered and their associated variables are set to `true`, the descriptions will appear in the list when the player checks the bag by clicking the link.

At the bottom of the Bag passage is a small piece of code that sends the player back to the previous passage by utilizing the `(history:)` macro along with the combination `(link-goto:)` macro:

```
(link-goto: "Return to Story", (history:)'s last)
```

This code links the words at the bottom of the passage, `Return to Story`, to the last passage tracked by the `(history:)` macro. Remember that the `(history:)` macro checks a list of visited passages, though the current passage isn't yet part of that list. In this case, it notes the last passage the player visited and sends the reader back to that passage.

Actually, the `(history:)` and `(array:)` macros are similar in the sense that they are both numbered lists that can be checked using the `contains` operator. You can either specify a passage (or, in the case of an array, a value) or you can use the possessive operator (`'s last`). When you ask `(history:)` to check the list of passages and then use this specific operator (`'s last`) to list the last value, it always takes the player back exactly one passage from the current one.

TRY IT OUT: SHOPPING SHOWDOWN

It's Thanksgiving morning, and your mother has sent you to the store with a list of six items she needs to finish Thanksgiving dinner. The store is not only packed but seems (at least upon first glance) to be sold out of certain items. Customer service assures you that everything you need is in the store; you just need to keep looking.

Write a story for this scenario, and be sure to include a link at the bottom of every passage to allow the reader to check the shopping cart. Also make sure to include code to send the player back one passage when he or she finishes checking the contents of the cart so the player can continue the story.

Use (if:) and (else:) statements to stop the player from being able to check out whether he or she isn't holding all the items on their list, and make sure to throw in some annoying neighbors to serve as human obstacles.

This workaround clearly gets the job done, but it's not elegant, and it requires a lot of code. There are only six possible variables in the story, so the bottom of the passage is only about six lines down on the screen. But what if you have a much longer set of variables? Using the (if:) and (else:) macros for that many variables could become a typing nightmare. There's an easier way: Use an array.

Using the (array:) Macro

Variables are extremely useful, but nothing beats an array at keeping a long list of virtual objects organized. Have you ever tried carrying 40 marbles in your hands at once and then tried to tie your shoes? The marbles end up scuttling across the floor while you scramble to pick them up. But what if you tried carrying those marbles in a bag? Bet you can now tie your shoes without losing a marble because they're all contained.

In the following section, you will go back to the Magical Brew passage and build it again using an array. After you build it, you can add and subtract virtual items, display specific text in the story if the array contains a certain string, and even determine the number of virtual items in the array and have the story change when it hits a set threshold.

Building a Basic Array

In Twine, you have the choice about whether to write the macro as (array:) or abbreviate it to (a:). Personally, I prefer to use (array:) because it's easier for me to visually scan a passage for a word than for a single letter when I go to debug at the end of making a game, but both ways work, so you can decide on your own Twine style.

An array is a variable with a list of values, and you write an array using a dollar sign in front of the name, just as you do a variable. The array in this example will be called $bag. You need to let Twine know that $bag is an array, and you do that by setting the value of $bag to the (array:) macro:

```
(set: $bag to (array:) )
```

You now have an empty array because you used the (set:) macro to set $bag to the value of an array.

You could start off with an array containing certain items, since games often begin with the player character holding a few items they need to get started. Here's what that looks like:

```
(set: $bag to (array: "a small pewter cauldron", "a box of matches", "a wooden
spoon") )
```

In this case, you start with $bag already containing three items: a small pewter cauldron, a box of matches, and a wooden spoon. It's a good idea to write the items in this manner rather than as a single word (as you did when creating a variable for each item, such as $haveMatches instead of "a box of matches") because when you go to print the items in the array, Twine prints them as written. Of course, as with many other aspects of Twine, you need to pay attention to capitalization when referencing these items in the array later on. Figure 9.5 should help you visualize this abstract concept by comparing it to something tangible like an actual bag.

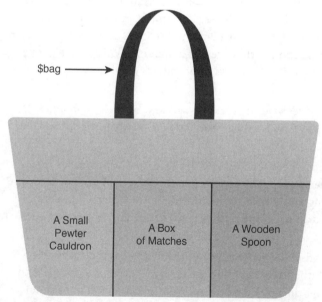

FIGURE 9.5 Visualize this array as a bag with three slots for items.

You now have a data structure that can hold all the string values (which are virtual objects in the game), making it easier to carry them from passage to passage and refer to them in the story. In the first case, the array is created but empty. In the second case, the array is created and filled with three starting items.

In the first passage of the Magical Brew example, swap out the variables for this new array:

```
(set: $bag to (array: "a small pewter cauldron", "a box of matches", "a wooden
spoon") )You come to the stream that Alden warned you about. It doesn't look
particularly wild, and the spot in front of you looks shallow. Do you want to risk
[[crossing the stream|Cross Stream]] or do you want to take the [[safer, longer
path|Town]] to the next town and see if you can cross at the Dilly Bridge?


[[Check Bag|Bag]]
```

You now have three new passages on your screen: Cross Stream, Town, and Bag. You'll fill the Bag passage in a moment, but first you need to add a new item that the player can find on the route into town.

Adding Items to an Array

An array is a numbered list. Even though you don't have to worry about the placement of a value (in other words, which number an item is on the list) when using Twine, it helps to understand the concept of indexes. Remember how I told you when I first introduced arrays that each new value is placed in its own compartment, called an index? Well the first value is nestled in the first slot, which is index 0. Why is this important to know? Because an empty array such as `(set: $bag to (array:) )` is very different from an array with the 0 slot filled because when the 0 slot is filled, the array contains one item. So the first item is in index 0, the second item is in index 1, and the third item is in index 2. When Twine goes to check the length of the array, it starts at 0 and counts three indexes (or three values) on the list.

Your `$bag` array is currently a list of three values: `"a small pewter cauldron"` is in index 0, `"a box of matches"` is in index 1, and `"a wooden spoon"` is in index 2. Now you want to add a fourth item and place it in index 3.

Luckily, you don't have to remember where each value is in the array. Twine pushes the new item to the end of the list. I use the term "push" here because it's the term used in programming (such as JavaScript) for adding an element to an array, and it will help you to visualize this concept. Imagine a new compartment being pushed onto the end of the list and a new value dropped inside like Figure 9.6.

To add another item to the array, you need to write the script so it keeps the current list in the array and adds a new item rather than rewriting the array. The way you do this is to make the value of the array whatever the array is at the moment plus the additional item or items.

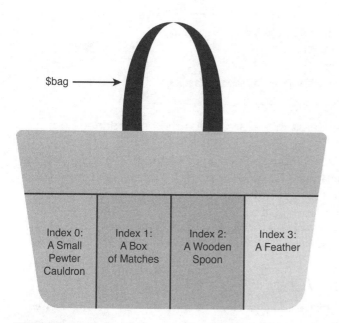

$bag ——→

| Index 0: A Small Pewter Cauldron | Index 1: A Box of Matches | Index 2: A Wooden Spoon | Index 3: A Feather |

FIGURE 9.6   Another item (and therefore, another slot) has been created in the bag array.

Say that the player starts walking into town and sees a feather on the ground. The player is given a choice: Do you want to take the feather or leave the feather? This choice creates two passages, Take Feather and Leave Feather. The script is placed in the Take Feather passage to push the new value, `"a feather"`, into the array, like this:

```
(set: $bag to $bag + (array: "a feather") )You pick up the feather and put it
in your bag. You continue walking into town and navigate to the
[[Dilly Bridge|Bridge]].
```

You don't need to place any code in the Leave Feather passage since the array remains the same (because nothing new has been added).

The (set:) macro is used to set the new value of $bag to be the old value of $bag plus this additional string value (`"a feather"`) pushed inside.

If you print out the array at the bottom of the passage by typing (print: $bag), you can see the items in the array listed out with commas between the items, as in Figure 9.7 (but no spaces between commas; you'll fix that in a moment):

```
a small pewter cauldron,a box of matches,a wooden spoon,a feather
```

You pick up the feather and put it in your bag. You continue walking into town and navigate to the **Dilly Bridge**.

a small pewter cauldron,a box of matches,a wooden spoon,a feather

FIGURE 9.7 The three original items in the array plus the newly added item.

Remember, of course, to keep your additions realistic. A piano cannot fit in a bag, and an open flame has no business being around fabric. Of course, it's okay to use realism as a consequence in your game. What if the player is given the option to add a torch to $bag, but in the process, everything inside the virtual bag catches fire, and the array is emptied? That would be a mean twist in the game, but it makes more sense than being able to carry around an open flame in a canvas bag.

Dropping Items from an Array

Remember how I used the term *push* for adding an item because it's the programming term for adding a new element to an array? It's also helpful to know the opposite term, *pop*, which refers to removing an element from an array. Again, you don't need to write the word "pop" in the code when you're using the Harlowe section of Twine, which is the current format, but it's helpful to visualize values pushing into or popping off a list to understand how adding items to or removing them from an array works.

Say that the player now gets to the Dilly Bridge, and there is a troll guarding the entrance. He demands his spoon toll because, in this world, wooden spoons are the most valuable items a person can own. Also, you happen to have a wooden spoon in your array, and you need to pop something off the list. Imagine the bag in Figure 9.8 and how an item and compartment can be removed from the bag.

After you give the player a choice to give the spoon toll or run away, you place the script to remove an item from an array at the top of the passage where the player character pays the toll, using the minus operator instead of the plus operator:

```
(set: $bag to $bag - (array: "a wooden spoon") )You sadly give your wooden spoon
to the troll, and he allows you to pass. Do you try to [[steal the spoon back|Steal
Spoon]] or just [[cross the bridge obediently|Cross Bridge]]?
```

Once again, the (set:) macro makes the new value for $bag be the value of $bag *minus* an item from the array—in this case, a wooden spoon. If you print out the value of $bag again, you see that the spoon is now missing from the list.

In addition, the length of the array is also one index shorter. You can check the number of items in an array by typing (print: $bag.length) anywhere in a passage. If you check the length before you give the spoon, you find that it is 4 for the four indexes in the array. If you check it after you've given the spoon to the troll, you find that it is 3 for the three indexes in the array.

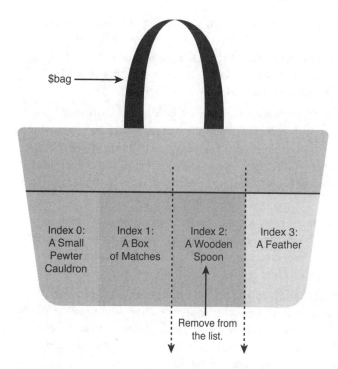

$bag

Index 0:
A Small
Pewter
Cauldron

Index 1:
A Box
of Matches

Index 2:
A Wooden
Spoon

Index 3:
A Feather

Remove from
the list.

FIGURE 9.8 Remove an item from an array.

Checking Strings in an Array

Okay, let's return to that Bag passage. At the bottom of every passage in the game, you want to give the player the ability to check the bag, so don't forget to add `[[Check Bag|Bag]]`.

In the workaround inventory (see, "Using Variables to Work Around Arrays," earlier in this chapter), you had to type a lot of code. Not only that, you needed to know all the variables that you wanted the player to encounter in the game and put in their bag, or you had to update the variable list every time a new item was added. Arrays make displaying an inventory (or, in this case, the contents of the virtual bag) easy. You just need to write two pieces of code in the passage:

```
(if: $bag's length is 0)[Your bag is empty.](else:)[Your bag contains the following:
(print: $bag.join ("\n"))]

(link-goto: "Return to Story", (history:)'s last)
```

The second part is familiar because it is the same code used in the workaround to return the player to the passage he or she was reading before checking the contents of the bag.

The first part is a little trickier. It begins with a conditional statement that uses the `(if:)` macro. If the length of the array is zero indexes, it prints the text inside the hook: Your bag is empty. Remember, an empty array doesn't contain any values and, therefore, doesn't contain any indexes. Each time a new value is added to the array, a new compartment or index is formed. Twine is counting the length of the list, or the number of indexes the array contains, and if the answer is none, it prints the first hook. You can skip this conditional statement entirely if you begin the game with items already in the array.

Next, you need to print the array. In this example, you place it inside an anonymous hook attached to the (else:) macro. Once there are indexes in the array, it prints out the text in the second hook, beginning with "Your bag contains the following". It also prints the list inside the array. Remember how when you wrote (print: $bag) earlier in the chapter, it printed the list with commas between each item and no space after each comma? It looked a little messy, right?

In this case, you first join the list, which means you ask Twine to print out every item in the list by using $bag.join. join is also a bit of JavaScript, and it pulls together the entire array as a single string (or group of words). When you ask Twine to print all the values in the array as a single string, it lists all the individual strings in the array.

But you follow the request to pull all the values into a single string with a second instruction, which might look familiar if you've done any other form of coding. You use "\n" to tell Twine to print out each item on a new line. It's a special character, often used with strings, which ensures that the list doesn't run together strangely. When you click the Play button, Twine prints the list in a more list-like form, as shown in Figure 9.9.

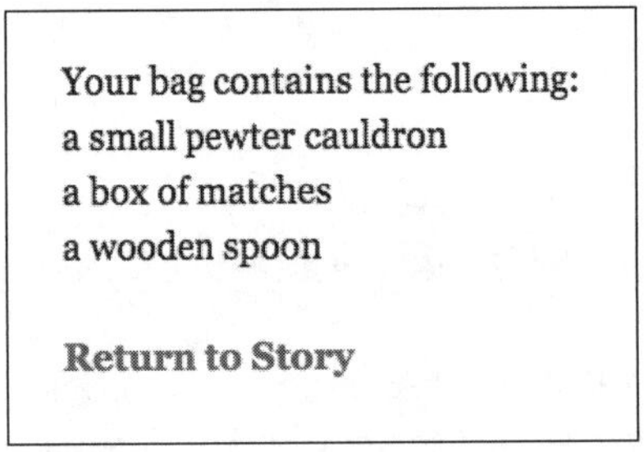

Your bag contains the following:
a small pewter cauldron
a box of matches
a wooden spoon

Return to Story

FIGURE 9.9 The array printed as a list.

Upon checking the bag, the reader sees a single, succinct list. Best of all, the writer doesn't need to keep returning to this passage to add new variables as they're introduced in the story. From this point forward, Twine always prints out the value of the array as it exists in the present moment.

Another reason to check an array is to display conditional text based on whether a character is holding an item. Let's say that you get to the bridge, and the troll asks you to pay the spoon toll. Earlier in the story, you may have made a choice to leave the spoon back in your house, or it may be in your bag.

You can have Twine check the array to see if the string, or value, appears in an index on the list. The way you do this is by using the keyword `contains`:

```
(if: $bag contains "a wooden spoon")[Luckily, you have a spoon. You sadly give your
wooden spoon to the troll, and he allows you to pass. Do you try to [[steal the
spoon back|Steal Spoon]] or just [[cross the bridge obediently|Cross
Bridge]]?](else:)[Unfortunately, you don't have a spoon. You left it in your house.
You tell the troll to wait a moment and [[jog home|Return Home]].]
```

If the array contains the string `"a wooden spoon"`, Twine runs the text in the first hook. If Twine checks the array and doesn't see that string, it runs the text in the second hook. Remember that capitalization matters. Make sure you have Twine look for `"a wooden spoon"` (how it was added to the array in the first place) and not `"A Wooden Spoon"`.

Checking the Array Size

You can check the size of an array by looking for the number of indexes. If you know that you will have four items in your game, you can set a conditional that runs a hook if the array is as long as or longer than four indexes. Let's say that if the player crosses the bridge and has four items, a special magical door opens that brings the player to the end point in the game, but if he or she crosses the bridge and has only three items, the player sees a tree trunk blocking the path, and the story continues until the player finds a different way to conjure the magical door.

Continue the story by having the player steal back the spoon (so he or she has four items; remember to add the string back into your array!) and cross the bridge. Also be sure to complete a passage that has the player calmly leave the spoon behind and cross the bridge. Type this for when the player reaches the other side:

```
(if: $bag's length >= 4)[A [[magical door|Magical Door]] appears shimmering on the
road before you.](else:)[When you get to the other side of the bridge, a large tree
trunk blocks your path. Do you want to try to [[go around|Around Tree]] the tree or
[[climb|Climb Tree]] the tree?]
```

In this case, you've set up a conditional statement. If the indexes are greater than or equal to four, Twine prints the text and links in the first hook, and the player sees the magical door. If the player didn't go back to steal the spoon and therefore has only three values in the array, the game prints out the text and links in the second hook.

Limiting the Array Size

You can use the same method you used to check the array size to create a limit, such as setting an item threshold that stops a player from being able to slide the bag through a narrow space or not allow the player to pick up an item because the load is already too heavy.

Let's say that the player gets to the bridge and decides to run away. The player happens upon a willow branch. If he or she has only three items in the bag, the player can add the branch to the array. But if he or she already has four items in the bag, the player will not be able to take the branch.

Open the passage titled Run Away and write this in it:

```
You see a willow branch on the ground. (if: $bag's length >= 4) [You can't pick up
the willow branch. Your bag is too full.](else:)[(set: $bag to $bag + (array: "a
willow branch"))You take the branch.]
```

Again, you've used checking the length of the array (in other words, checking the number of indexes in the array) to have one of two possible events occur. In this case, you've limited what can fit in the player's bag, but you could just as easily have used checking the length of the array to state that the player character couldn't pass through a certain room while carrying four items.

Notice that the second hook contains the (set:) macro, which adds the new value, "a willow branch", to the array if there is space in the player character's bag. If the conditions are met in the first (if:) macro, the array remains the same. But if the conditions aren't met with the (if:) macro and Twine moves to the (else:) macro, the array increases by a new string, "a willow branch", and another index is pushed onto the array, bringing it up to four items.

Troubleshooting Arrays

A particular issue may have occurred while you were building the array in the preceding section: Every time the player enters the passage that has the (array:) macro making a change to the array, it makes that change, even if it has already added that string to the array. This means that if the player starts at the first passage and checks the inventory by using the Check Bag link, he or she should see this text:

```
a small pewter cauldron
a box of matches
a wooden spoon
```

If the player returns to the story and then decides to check again, he or she now sees the list in duplicate, as shown in Figure 9.10.

Pop back and forth a few more times, and you end up with an array length of 12 and four pewter cauldrons in your bag.

Similarly, what if you have a game that is more map-based than story-based and allows the player character to explore a set area? This is a traditional dungeon crawl, and once the player has collected the one-of-a-kind, diamond-encrusted ring, you don't want him or her to be able to pick up the diamond-encrusted ring a second time or, heaven forbid, end up with a bag filled with diamond-encrusted rings.

There are three ways you can ensure that the player gets only one copy of the item in his or her inventory. The first is to limit access to the area after an item is taken. This, of course, only applies to a map-based games, but if you can cut off access to the area once the player has the item, you can prevent the player from reaching the passage that contains the item again.

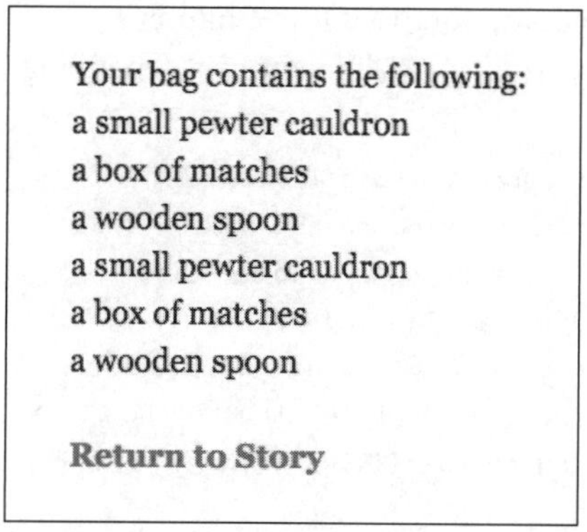

> Your bag contains the following:
> a small pewter cauldron
> a box of matches
> a wooden spoon
> a small pewter cauldron
> a box of matches
> a wooden spoon
>
> **Return to Story**

FIGURE 9.10   The strings are added to the array multiple times.

For instance, if the item is in a passage on the far eastern side of the map, and the player is traveling east again to return to the place, two or three passages beforehand, you need to add code that sends the player back in the opposite direction, like this:

```
(if: $bag contains "diamond ring")[You suddenly forget why you were traveling this
direction in the first place and (link-goto: "turn around.", (history:)'s last)]
(else:)[You can go [[east|Tunnel 2]] or [[west|Entrance to Tunnel]]]
```

This, of course, uses that handy operator (`'s last`) combined with the `(history:)` macro to check the list and send the player back one passage.

Similarly, you can use this trick to display different text on the screen depending on whether the player already has that item:

```
(if: $bag contains "diamond ring")[You fondly remember once finding a diamond ring
here. The rest of the room still looks the same down to the same door leading to
the [[living room|Living Room]] and the same door leading to the
[[kitchen|Kitchen]].](else:)[(set: $bag to $bag + (array: "diamond ring"))You walk
into the room and find a diamond ring on the table. You pick it up and slip it into
your bag. You look to see if anyone noticed. There's a door leading to the
[[living room|Living Room]] and a door leading to the [[kitchen|Kitchen]].]
```

So if the ring is already in the array, the text inside the first hook is shown, insinuating that this is the person's second (or even later) trip through this room. If the diamond ring is not in the array, Twine runs the text and links in the second hook, though it only runs this text a single time because the hook also uses the `(set:)` macro to add the value to the array. If the player checks the bag and then returns to the same passage, he or she sees the text in the first hook this time.

Finally, you can use the (history:) macro here the same way you used it in Chapter 6, "Stasis, Catalyst, and Climax: Understanding Story Arc," to display different text depending on how many times a player has entered a passage:

```
(if: (count: (history:), "Sitting Room") is 0)[(set: $bag to $bag + (array:
"diamond ring"))You walk into the room and find a diamond ring on the table. You
pick it up and slip it into your bag. You look to see if anyone noticed. There's a
door leading to the [[living room|Living Room]] and a door leading to the
[[kitchen|Kitchen]].](else:)[You fondly remember once finding a diamond ring here.
The rest of the room still looks the same down to the same door leading to the
[[living room|Living Room]] and the same door leading to the [[kitchen|Kitchen]].]
```

The first time the player encounters this passage, he or she sees the text in the first hook because Twine checks the number of passages and finds the count to be zero. (Remember that Twine doesn't count the current passage until you leave it.) Therefore, it displays the text and links in the first hook, but it also uses the (set:) macro contained in the first hook to change the array. If the player returns to this passage at any other point, he or she does not see the text in the first passage, nor is the array altered.

Using the (count:) Macro

You just saw (count:) used in combination with the (history:) macro to count the number of times a player has seen a passage, but you can also use it to count the number of a certain item inside an array.

For instance, what if you have a game with an array called $wallet, and throughout the game, the player can earn various amounts of money that are all placed in the wallet? Perhaps the point of the game is to reach a certain amount of money that's needed to buy a plane ticket and end the game.

The player can keep checking how many times "dollar" is in the $wallet by using the (count:) macro. If you want to display the amount on the screen, you can type this:

```
You have (count: $wallet, "dollar") dollars.
```

The (count:) macro counts the number of times this string appears in the array and then states the answer. Every time another "dollar" is added to the array—(set: $wallet to $wallet + (array: "dollar"))—the count increases by one.

This differs from finding the length of the array because $wallet may contain "dollar" five times and "coin" five times, which would be 10 indexes. The (count:) macro only counts the number of times a certain string appears in the array.

TRY IT OUT: BUS TICKET BLUES

You can't believe your car broke down in this strange town. The only way out is to hop on the 5 o'clock bus heading to the nearest city. The problem is that you don't have any money. You need $10 for the bus ticket.

Create a game for this scenario, building an array called `$wallet` and sending the player character through this strange town to find $10. Along the way, the player should be able to find other items to add to the wallet, such as a concert ticket which he or she can sell for cash, and others that are worthless. Also add thieves who are looking to drain a lost traveler's wallet of money.

Make sure you include a way to check the contents of the wallet and set a limit by allowing the player character to buy a bus ticket at the bus terminal only if he or she has $10 in the wallet.

So now that you're familiar with arrays, it's time to turn your eye to literary techniques that can help you create more vivid language choices.

Utilizing Literary Techniques

Most of what you write in a game or story is what I like to call flat text, meaning that the words don't stand out in the story, and they mean exactly what they say. Here's an example:

She was tired from staying up all night to finish her paper.

This text is okay. It tells the readers what they need to know. But it isn't very interesting. Of course, you need to write flat text to convey information, but if you have page after page of straightforward description, none of the details will stand out to the reader. You can use literary techniques to bring the ideas into sharp relief, such as using a *simile*:

She was as exhausted as a marathon runner crossing the finish line.

Well, now the reader knows a little more. Even someone who has never run a marathon can imagine how tiring it would be to run 26.2 miles. So readers get a sense of how tired this character is. They also get a sense of accomplishment: Finishing the paper, like running a marathon, required a lot of hard work. You can even take it a step further and use a *metaphor*, as shown here:

She was a wrung sponge, draped across the table.

Here you're making a comparison between a wrung sponge and the dear student. Is she actually a wrung sponge? No. But that's how she appears, sprawled across the table in exhaustion as if she is totally spent from her hard work.

These are literary techniques, and they're like cream in the same way that flat text is like skim milk. Both cream and skim milk are dairy drinks, but one is richer than the other and conveys more in the taste department. That said, just as you wouldn't really want to drink a full glass of cream (even though a dash of it is delicious in coffee), you wouldn't want a whole story that consists of nothing but similes and hyperbole. Literary devices should be splashed into a story, whereas the bulk of the words will be flat text. And this, by the way, is an *analogy*: a comparison between two unrelated things (milk and words) that helps you to understand the second thing based on what you know about the first thing.

Literary techniques are everywhere! In fact, you've probably been using them liberally without even realizing it. Let's take a look at some popular literary techniques to learn how you can pepper them throughout your stories to draw the reader's attention to important details.

Using Symbolism

Symbolism involves imbuing an object with more meaning than it naturally contains. For instance, ladybirds are a symbol of luck. If you had a ladybird appear in a story, you would expect the character who finds the ladybird to have good luck during the course of the story.

TRY IT OUT: EMOTION STONES

On the planet Donnu, children are born with flat personalities, unable to express any emotions. Before children can become adults, they must go on a journey and collect five different stones along the way. The red stone is for anger, the orange stone is for fear, the yellow stone is for happiness, the green stone is for calm, and the blue stone is for sadness.

Write a story for this scenario, and convey the meaning of the stones through symbolism. Have the game end when all the stones are added to the inventory (that is, the length of the array equals 5). At that point, your player character has collected an expressive personality.

Using Allegory

Allegory is similar to symbolism except that the symbol stretches over the whole story, and the point is usually to make a statement or teach a lesson. For instance, in a story where a dark cloud hangs over the town, making everyone feel ill with dread, that cloud becomes an allegory for the dark thoughts the townspeople are thinking about one another, or their impulse to do evil. It's more than just a cloud; it's an object standing in for a really big idea.

TRY IT OUT: FALLING STAR

A star-shaped rock crashes to Earth, disappearing somewhere in the nearby forest. Everyone in town wants this rock for a different reason: Some people want it to study it, some want to sell it so they can live a comfortable life, and some think that simply holding it will make them happy. For everyone, the star-shaped rock becomes a symbol of hope, that life can be better once it's found.

Write a story for this scenario, using an array called $bag to collect the items you need for your trip to find the rock, as well as a place to add items that you find along the way.

Using Simile

A *simile* is a comparison of two unrelated things which states that one of the things is *like* the other. *She is graceful like a wind-blown silk scarf.* Is the woman actually a scarf? No. But when I compare her to a scarf by making a simile, I give you a deeper understanding of the way she moves. You imagine a delicate scarf, the wind filling it as it trails from a person's hand, and you apply that understanding to the woman and the way she moves.

TRY IT OUT: THE FLYING POTION

The prince is locked at the top of the castle tower, and you need to make a flying potion to get him down. You need to go around the town, collecting the ingredients for the potion.

Write a story for this scenario. Create an array to hold each virtual item by making it a string value in the array. When the array hits an ingredient threshold, allow the player to brew the potion and save the prince. Of course, use a simile for each of the ingredients: as airy as a marshmallow, as graceful as a willow branch, as light as a feather....

Using Metaphor

A *metaphor* is a comparison of two unrelated things that does not use the word *like*. For example, *she is an angel* or *he is the black sheep of his family.* Is she really an angel? No, she's a human being. But calling her an angel evokes the understanding that she has angelic qualities. At the same time, is the boy really an ovine family member with black, curly wool covering his body? Of course not, but you use the black sheep as a metaphor for someone who is on the outskirts of the family circle due to their behavior, choices, or appearance.

TRY IT OUT: PILGRIMAGE

It's the year 2080, and you need to make the Pilgrimage of Four, a yearly walk between the far-reaching towns and the capital city. Along the way, you will find numerous objects that you can add to your bag (which, of course, is an array called $bag), each one a possible offering to make when you get to the gates of the city. Unfortunately, in this country, having certain items in your possession automatically bars you from entering the city gates.

Create a story for this scenario. Use conditional statements to check the array and determine whether the player character has collected a banned object. If the player character can't enter the city, use metaphors to convey how the player character is feeling as the story continues and he or she tries to solve the problem of how to get into the city. If the player character can enter the city, use metaphors to explain the wonder he or she encounters once inside.

Using Analogy

Think of two things that aren't the same but then think about what they share in common. For instance, being scared to attend your math class is not the same thing as drowning, but these two unrelated experiences are similar enough that your understanding of one experience helps you to connect with the other, unknown experience. For instance, the fear that comes from having to do an equation on the board can feel as heart-pounding as not being able to find the surface of the water. Just as an allegory is an overarching form of symbolism, an *analogy* is an overarching form of other comparative devices, such as similes and metaphors.

In interactive fiction, people sometimes structure whole games around an analogy in order to convey how they experience life, especially if they have special circumstances an outsider may have difficulty understanding.

TRY IT OUT: DEFINITION

You've traveled four light years and finally landed on the planet Honn-Do. But you must have somehow gotten off track because the aliens are definitely not speaking Honn-Doese. You would know; you've been studying the language six hours a day to prepare during this outbound trip, and you can't understand a single word the aliens are saying.

After such a long trip, there is no way to easily navigate your way off the planet. It's going to take years before there's a flight back home. In the meantime, you're going to have to figure out where you are, what the people are saying, and how to get by. And while you're there, you might as well collect some materials for research. Even if you're not on Honn-Do, you've landed somewhere four light years away, and scientists back home will want to see your collection when you return.

Of course, it you've ever felt like the odd man out, not understanding what is happening around you, this analogy will feel very familiar. Write a story for this scenario.

Using Allusion

An *allusion* refers to a well-known piece of writing or idea by either naming it directly or making it clear enough that the reader can draw a line between the two works. For instance, the name of a famous Shakespeare play is *Much Ado About Nothing*. If I were to name my game *Much Ado About Everything*, people would immediately understand that the game is going to be a comedy of errors (like Shakespeare's play) with a little romance thrown in for good measure. In fact, a popular way of using allusion is to retell a story while modernizing and changing it to highlight the ways the two stories are different or the same.

TRY IT OUT: SAM'S ADVENTURES IN... WONDERLAND?

Oh, my ears and whiskers, I am going to ask you to make an allusion to Lewis Carroll's *Alice's Adventures in Wonderland*, placing a new character in what will feel to the player character like a very familiar situation if they've read Alice's story. Both the reader and the player character think they know what to expect...or do they?

Have the player character move through the story, pointing out all the ways this Wonderland doesn't match the original. The queen is running a preschool, while the White Rabbit is howling for people's heads, and the Dormouse has become the prime minister by popular vote. The only way out of Wonderland seems to be to collect croquet balls for the Mad Hatter, who accepts them as payment for his back-to-the-real-world taxi service. Make sure you keep track of the number of croquet balls collected with the (array:) and (count:) macros.

Of course, if you haven't read *Alice's Adventures in Wonderland*, apply this idea to a book you have read that you can allude to in a game.

Using Irony

Irony is one of those literary techniques that is forever misunderstood as meaning a strange coincidence such as finding the winning lottery ticket that will save your home just as the bulldozer knocks it down. That is extremely sad, an unfortunate coincidence, but it *isn't* ironic.

What irony really means is that the intended meaning of the words differ greatly or are the opposite the actual meaning. Sarcasm is a form of irony, such as saying that someone looks fantastic when what you really mean is that they look awful. Situational irony would be buying you a clown lamp as a gift because I think that it will make you happy, but instead it freaks you out because you secretly are terrified of clowns. Additionally, you can have a non-player character make a statement that the player cringes upon hearing because they know that the words are wrong, such as NASA stating that the spaceship has had a great liftoff when the player knows the rocket will explode a passage later.

TRY IT OUT: THE BEST DAY OF MY LIFE

You accidently fry an entire computer lab, you're removed from your post as class president, and your prom date dumps you, all on a day that you ironically call the best day of your life when you wake up in the morning. You need to set everything right again by setting up the biggest all-school apology act ever, and you're going to have to collect a lot of supplies to make it happen.

Write a story for this scenario, using an array to keep track of everything you need to pull it off. Who knows? This may actually turn out to be the best day of your life.

Using Hyperbole

That spider is the size of a truck. No one really believes that there is a spider the size of a truck—unless you're talking about those acromantulas in the Forbidden Forest—but you understand from the exaggeration that the spider is really big, bigger than the speaker feels comfortable dealing with. To do *hyperbole* well, you have to make it obvious that you're exaggerating by making the statement over the top. If you talk about a spider the size of a fist, someone might believe that you are seeing a tarantula or another large spider that fits that description. So go big with your words but use this literary technique sparingly.

TRY IT OUT: CORAL REEF CRAWL

Your best friend has a tendency to speak in hyperbole, but maybe he wasn't exaggerating when he said that this is the greatest diving spot ever. Turn the traditional dungeon crawl into a coral reef crawl by having the player character and her best friend explore the ocean, leaving plenty of hyperbolic statements and bubbles in their wake.

Have eels dart out of the coral, and have other divers try to sabotage the player character's tank. And, of course, make the player collect a lot of sunken treasure. Give the player a bag for a waterproof camera, with plenty of space inside to store gold and jewels. Manage the player's treasure collection with an array.

The preceding sections describe just a few of the many literary techniques you can use to bring richness to your writing. I cover more of them later the book.

Achieving Proper Pacing

I've mentioned before that interactive fiction has more in common with short stories than with novels, even though interactive fiction games tend to have more words than the average book. A short story may consist of 5,000 words, whereas a novel is likely to have closer to 80,000 words. An interactive fiction game could have twice as many words as a novel. For example, *Sorcery!* by Inkle has about 150,000 words.

So how is an interactive fiction game more like a short story if it's longer than a novel?

First, remember that you're not encountering all 150,000 words as you play through the *Sorcery!* game. That game has 3,442 passages and 2,618 choices, which means that each time you play, you see only a fraction of the words that are written into the game.

Moreover, there are three elements that make interactive fiction games more like short stories than like novels, and these three elements will help you determine whether the story idea bouncing around in your brain is good game material or whether it would work better off the screen as a novel. Those three elements are character limits, scope, and pacing.

Interactive fiction authors and short story writers need to limit their character counts. Novel writers have the space to explore many different personalities, and they know that readers can flip back and forth in the book to review and keep all the characters straight. But interactive fiction writers and short story writers are limited in the number of characters they can reasonably introduce and fully explore in an abbreviated space. Both should stick to a small cast of characters and leave the long character lists to novelists.

Next, the scope of an interactive fiction game needs to be smaller because the writer cannot control how the story unfolds. By placing that task in the hands of the player, the writer relinquishes the ability to explore multiple storylines at the same time. Therefore, interactive fiction, like short stories, explores one plotline deeply rather than introducing multiple plotlines, as a novel does.

Finally, pacing in an interactive fiction story tends to be faster than in a novel. *Pacing* is the speed in which a story unfolds, based on the density of plot points and language choices.

Pacing is partially based on the action scenes in a story, such as fighting dragons and flying spaceships, but it's also focused on the balance between character introspection and character action. The faster pacing of interactive fiction means that the player character needs to keep busy making things happen, which means the writer needs to provide the player with plenty to do. Your player character won't spend a lot of time sitting around, thinking about life, like a novel character might do. Interactive fiction characters spend more time impacting their world with consequential choices, and these moments occur in greater density than they would in a novel.

In addition, an interactive fiction writer can play with language, phrasing each passage in a certain way so that the reader feels as if the game is moving faster than a novel. This chapter takes a deep look at how language impacts how a player senses time while reading a story.

Pacing is not only about moving the story along; it also involves making sure the reader can keep up. Have you ever gone running with another person? The goal of jogging with a partner is to keep the same pace so you can keep each other company. If the other person is too slow, you'll be itching to charge ahead and will end up leaving the other runner in the dust. And vice versa: If the other runner is too fast, you'll be left behind. Running together can't work when you're out of sync.

The same goes for pacing in a story. You don't want the story to become so laborious to read that the player "charges ahead" and leaves the game behind; in other words, you don't want the player to quit reading because the story's slow, plodding pace is boring.

At the same time, you don't want the story to move so quickly that you're blitzkrieging the player with action sequences or glossing over important details. When you do that, you lose the reader, too, by making the reader feel overwhelmed or confused.

Good pacing means keeping a balance between crisis and obstacles, with enough exposition in between so the reader understands what is at stake and cares about the characters and the situation. Crises make the story go faster, and obstacles make the story slow down.

Understanding Plot

Plot is another term for the *consequential* events that make up a story. "This happens so then this happens so then this happens" equals your plot line. In a strong story, the plot is driven by cause-and-effect events, and those events are called *plot points*.

For something to be a plot point rather than just one of the story's action moments, an event needs to cause something to happen or change the course of the story. There are lots of story moments but only a handful of plot points in a game.

What is the difference between a plot point and a story moment? Think about it in terms of an adventure story where an Indiana Jones–like character is trying to get a jewel hidden in a booby-trapped cave.

If the player character picks up a stone from a pedestal and that causes a hole to open so he can gain entrance to the cave, that's a plot point. The player does *X* (picks up a stone), so *Y* happens (hole opens). Through his actions, he has caused a new situation that he needs to deal with that moves him closer to or farther from his goal.

Now say that the player character is running through the cave, and an ill-timed earthquake shakes loose an avalanche of stones. That is certainly an action moment, but a choice the player character made didn't cause that event to occur, nor did the event change the course of the story. It is just one more thing that happens to the poor player character. Therefore, it's just one of many action moments in a story, but it's not a plot point.

So an event happens, which causes another event to happen, which causes another event to happen, until the story runs out of fuel and comes to a stopping point.

Back in Chapter 6, "Stasis, Catalyst, and Climax: Understanding Story Arc," you read about the story's structure, or *arc*. If the arc is the shape of the story, then plot is the movement that runs over that structure.

It may help to think about arc and plot in comparison to a roller coaster. Engineers build the roller coaster structure, pulling together the dips and steep climb to the final drop. That is like story arc. In Chapter 6, I drew a story arc as a smooth line, but in actuality, it's really more of a jagged course, as shown in Figure 10.1. The catalyst and climax are huge plot points, but there are also smaller drops and rises that indicate minor plot points.

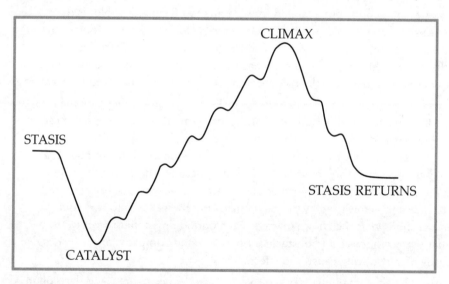

FIGURE 10.1   Arc is really a jagged line of tiny drops and rises amid the larger story's drop and rise.

But a roller coaster structure is not very exciting. It doesn't get your heart pounding until the engineers put cars along the track—cars that are chained together with one leading into the next one. That is the plot. Once the cars start moving over the track, you have yourself a wild ride.

The only problem with this analogy is that, unlike a roller coaster, arc and plot are built at the same time, with arc giving the story shape and plot making the story move forward and change.

So pacing is about determining how quickly the ride...I mean story...is moving. Are there lots of events linked together (remember that you need one event to cause the next one), dragging the reader quickly over the plunges and curves? In that case, you have a fast-moving plot in terms of events. On the other hand, if the character isn't doing a lot and there is little forward movement in the story, you have a slow-moving plot.

So how do you have all your plot points connect to one another into a chain of events? You simply let the choices in your game have consequences. This means that everything you have been doing up until this point—making sure your characters works toward a goal and have agency, building a vivid setting to place your characters, giving them the ability to pick up objects and have holding certain objects affect their ability to do things—are all a way to easily set the plot moving on that structure you built with story arc.

Ta-da!

Okay, so maybe it isn't simple, but a straightforward method for building plot is to introduce a crisis (cause) followed by an obstacle (effect). Not every choice you ask the player to make comes during a crisis—that would be too much conflict for a single story—but *some* of the choices will come after a crisis has been introduced into the story, and the path the player chooses introduces the complication or obstacle that needs to be overcome.

Say that you have a story where a player character picks up a sword during a moment of conflict with a bully (crisis), and because of that, he inadvertently becomes the nemesis of an evil sorcerer who was the former owner of the sword (complication or obstacle). If the player doesn't make the choice to pick up the sword, it introduces a different but equal complication that drives the story forward. For instance, because the player character isn't holding the sword when the evil sorcerer bursts into the museum, he runs into the next exhibit to hide and is thwarted by the class bully. One choice leads to two equal complications, ensuring that the choice matters. Each option drives the story forward by continuing that pattern of crisis and obstacle (or problem and complication), which is really just another way of introducing cause and effect.

With each crisis, the player character is asked to quickly act—make a quick gut decision in a charged moment. With each obstacle, the player character is asked to slow down and think, to solve his or her way out of the moment. In this way, a plot chain is created that moves at a decent clip: not so fast that the player can't keep up with the story but not so slow that the player grows bored due to a lack of action.

The pace of a story is also determined by how much things change—how much the player character changes, how much the events change the game world, how much the conflict in the story changes what happens next. When things are constantly in flux, the story moves quickly. When things stagnate and remain the same, the story slows down. So after every choice, you should determine whether something has changed in the story. If you see that you have too many choices in a row that don't create change, throw in a twist that gets things moving. That is the fuel driving the story over the story arc.

With a short story, the writer determines the plot. But with interactive fiction, that job is in the hands of the player. Therefore, you need to provide the tools, in the form of choices with consequences, to build a chain of cause-and-effect plot points.

Let's return to another idea from Chapter 6: the classic plot diagram. The terms used in a plot diagram can help you differentiate between the arc and the plot. In a plot diagram, the story begins with the non-movement of background information, also called *exposition*. Think of this point as the roller coaster turning on and the cars getting ready to move. Flipping the story into motion is a moment called the *conflict*. It turns on the plot. Now the story is moving and traveling up a ramp called the *rising action*. It's called rising action because the story needs to keep moving up and up toward a tension point, just like a roller coaster, by having events with steep consequences occur.

Finally, the story peaks with the *climax*, like a roller coaster reaching the top of the largest peak, and the story moves into a state of *falling action*. At this point, the pace is intense; the story has been building toward this moment, and the writer increases the action, changing the state of the game world and the characters themselves at a lightning pace. And then the story wraps up with a *resolution*. The conflict is solved. The ride is over.

The shape of a plot diagram is similar to the shape of the story arc, even though the terms have changed, as you can see in Figure 10.2.

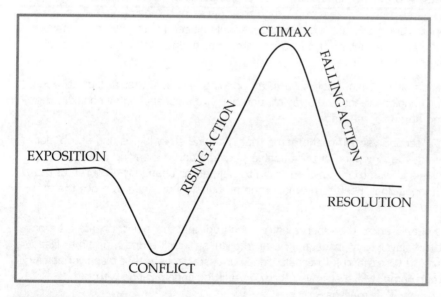

FIGURE 10.2 A plot diagram follows the same shape as a story arc.

Why do the story arc and plot diagram follow the same shape? Because the plot itself is shapeless: It takes the shape of the story arc. Plot without arc is an amorphous blob, and arc without plot is a non-moving structure. Arc is the frame over which you stretch the plot. Therefore, story arc and plot diagram look alike on paper, even though they are two separate entities in a story.

Of course, if you were to actually diagram plot, you would need to do more than write rising action or falling action along the line. You would need to list all the moments of cause and effect that move the story forward. Every choice the player makes that changes the course of the story needs to go on that diagram, creating tiny rises of crisis with equally tiny dips of obstacles.

TRY IT OUT: THE VANQUISHER

For this Try It Out you need to make two outlines offline before beginning to make sure that you have plot points moving the story forward.

Say that you're with your class at a museum, and the school bully dares you to pick up the Sword of Darkness from its accidentally unlocked display case. Doing so unfortunately marks you as the nemesis of the evil sorcerer, Vytrex. Not doing so makes you ill-prepared to fight Vytrex when he unexpectedly shows up at the museum to terrorize your class.

Create two versions of your game. In the first one, create three plot points. Remember that in order for something to be a plot point, it needs to cause something to happen and it needs to change the course of the game. In between those plot points, place at least two inconsequential choices for the player to make—in other words, choices that *don't* cause something to happen or change the course of the game.

This story needs *at least* nine story layers: an opening passage, first plot point, two inconsequential choices, second plot point, another two inconsequential choices, third plot point, and an ending passage.

Now, create a second version of the game that has nine story layers and seven plot points. Yes, with the exception of the opening passage and the ending passage, you need every single choice to cause something to happen or change the course of the story. The changes don't need to be monumental, but they do need to move the story forward toward the ending.

Both options should utilize the macros you've used up until this point. Create a timer to transport the player to a passage if he or she doesn't click a choice in time. Use the (if:) and (else:) macros to create conditional statements that track variables you add to your game. Make sure you throw in a little randomization with the (either:) or (random:) macros.

Have people play the two games and ask them to rate the pace of each version after game play. Which version appealed to the majority of players?

Setting the Pace with Language

Beyond the density of the plot, another way to determine pace is through language choice. You can slow down and speed up a story by choosing the end of the spectrum on which to construct your sentences in the following areas.

Determining Description Amount

Stories with brief descriptions move faster than stories that contain page after page of flowery description.

If you want a game to move faster, cut down on extraneous descriptive paragraphs, and if you want your game to slow down, bump up the level of detail in your descriptive paragraphs.

Employing Internal Thoughts

Stories with a dearth of internal thoughts move faster than stories that meander through a character's mind.

Do you think during a crisis? Of course, not: You *do*. When things are moving quickly, you act rather than pause to think. If you want a game to move faster, have your characters move without noticing all the small details and wondering about them. If you want your game to slow down, have the player character pause to rest and reflect.

Leaving Information Unknown

Stories with a lot of cliffhangers move faster than stories where the reader feels sure he or she knows what will happen next.

When a game contains a lot of unknowns, the player reads faster to find out what happens next. If you want your game to move faster, drop in intriguing details that the player will wonder about. If you want your game to slow down, have the outcome of a choice move on a clear, predictable path.

Setting the Danger Level

Stories with a lot of danger move faster than stories where the action calmly unfolds.

Danger builds tension, and tension makes the player read faster to get to a place where his or her stomach unknots. Danger doesn't have to be mortal danger; it can be tension between two friends or an uncomfortable exchange that threatens to end a relationship. If you want a game to move faster, drop in a little danger. If you want a game to slow down, write a few calm passages in a row to allow the player to catch his or her breath.

Varying Sentence Length

Stories with short sentences move faster than stories with long sentences.

Time speeds up when sentences are brief. It slows down when sentences unroll like a languid summer afternoon with plenty of commas and conjunctions making the words unfurl like an unspooled ribbon.

Back up and look at the last two sentences again. They each convey a simple idea, but the first sentence in this paragraph delivers the information in a clipped tone, whereas the second sentence extends the delivery time by adding multiple descriptive words and similes. If you want your game to move faster, make your sentences short and sweet. If you want your game to slow down, extend your sentences, packing as much imagery as possible in with the basic information you need to convey.

Regulating Passage Length

Stories with short passages move faster than stories with long passages.

The longer the passage, the more time it takes for the player to reach a place where it's possible to impact the story with a choice. In addition, seeing a lot of text on the screen may make a player slow down to read carefully, whereas brief passages allow the player to confidently scan the screen. If you want a game to move faster, break up long passages into multiple shorter passages by giving only one choice that takes the player to the next screen. If you want a game to slow down, combine many smaller passages into one longer passage and reduce the number of choices.

Limiting Word Count

Stories that use a minimal number of words move faster than stories that use a lot of extraneous words.

Write the first draft of a story without paying attention to the number of words you're using. When you're done with this draft, comb your game for places where you use more words than necessary to convey an idea. For example, say that you've written "You feel very sleepy and you barely want to do anything after you stay up well into the night playing games like the ones you have for your Xbox." How can you edit that so you don't lose the meaning of the sentence but you trim out any unnecessary words? How about, "You're lethargic after staying up all night playing video games." If you want a game to move faster, make fewer words do more work for you. If you want a game to slow down, bulk up your sentences with extra words that simply highlight an already present idea.

Using Sentence Fragments

Stories with sentence fragments move faster than stories that are all full sentences.

Stop! From now until later. Over there! Sentence fragments, or sentences that can't stand on their own because they are missing key parts needed in an independent clause (such as a subject), convey information faster than full sentences. This is because the missing pieces that would turn the fragment into an independent clause are tacitly understood, such as the missing "you need to look" that should come before the fragment "over there!" But be careful; sentence fragments can easily cause information confusion because they don't clearly state the whole message.

If you want a game to move faster, construct high-emotion moments with fragments. If you want a game to slow down, take the time to write out full sentences.

Moving with Vivid Verbs

Stories with vivid verbs move faster than stories with general verbs.

The more specific your verbs—action words—the faster the story will flow. *Racing* is a verb that conveys faster movement than the more general *running*, and when you're more specific with your language, the reader has an easier time creating a mental picture of the action. If you want a game to move faster, choose the most vivid, specific verbs. If you want a game to slow down, utilize general verbs and more *to be* verbs.

TRY IT OUT: SHERLOCK HOLMES AND THE LOCKED BOX MYSTERY

Murders are happening across modern-day London, but the killer has left a clue for Sherlock Holmes and John Watson about his or her identity and next victim. The clue is inside a locked box. Use all of the macros you know about at this point to construct a puzzle box that Holmes and Watson need to figure out how to open. Can you set a time limit on solving one of the puzzle locks? Or can you have the duo collect items that will help them break open the case?

Decide whether you want your story to move slowly or quickly and then follow all the advice you've read in this chapter to keep the same pace throughout your story. Ask some friends to play your game and give you feedback on the pacing.

Utilizing Setter Links

Up until this point, you've usually been setting the value of a variable by placing the value in the next passage whenever a choice is made. Sometimes this method can slow down the pace of a story because it means there are multiple passages that exist solely to provide a space to set the value of the variable.

The way you can get around this is to use *setter links*. With a setter link, the variable is set when the link is clicked rather than when the player passes into another passage. Open a new story and call it Personality. In the first passage, write this:

```
Whatever you decide will seal your fate. Do you choose the (link: "sword")
[(set: $personality to "warrior")(goto: "Start Journey")] or the (link: "feather")
[(set: $personality to "peacemaker")(goto: "Start Journey")]?
```

By using the (link:), (set:), and (goto:) macros in combination with one another, you can have the variable $personality set to a value of either "warrior" or "peacemaker", depending on which option is clicked.

The setter link opens with the (link:) macro creating a hyperlinked word. In the first option, the word is "sword", and in the second option, the word is "feather". The macro links however many words appear between the two quotation marks. The (link:) macro is attached to an anonymous hook that contains two additional macros. These two macros inside the hook are triggered when the (link:) macro is clicked.

The first macro inside the hook is the (set:) macro, which assigns a value to the variable $personality. The second macro inside the hook is the (goto:) macro, which takes the player to the next passage. Remember that the (goto:) macro doesn't automatically generate a new passage like the [[link]] macro does, and you therefore have to click the green +Passage button and add a passage. In this example, the new passage is called Start Journey. Remember to pay attention to capitalization so the two passages connect.

As shown in Figure 10.3, when the player clicks the Play button, the two links appear like hypertext on the screen.

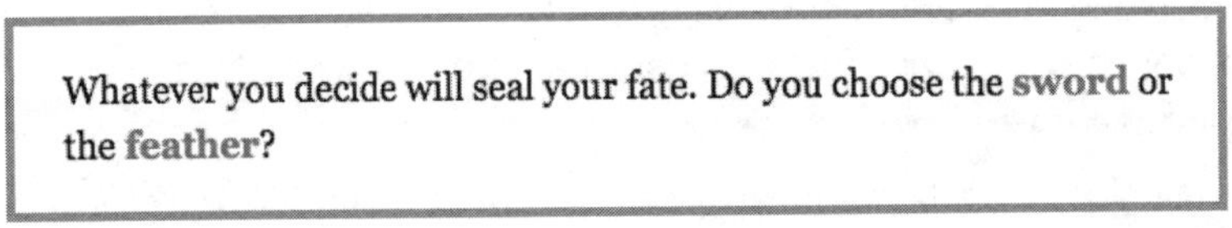

Whatever you decide will seal your fate. Do you choose the sword or the feather?

FIGURE 10.3 Two setter links appear as hyperlinked words to the reader.

Clicking either option sets the variable $personality with the corresponding string value. If you print the value in the Start Journey passage by typing (print: $personality), you see either the value "warrior" or "peacemaker" printed on the screen.

Similarly, you can use named hooks and the (click:) macro to achieve the same effect. Erase the example currently in the first passage and replace it with this version, utilizing the (click:) macro:

```
Whatever you decide will seal your fate. Which item do you choose?
[Take the sword]<personality1|
[Take the feather]<personality2|
(click: ?personality1)[(set: $personality to "warrior")(goto: "Start Journey")]
(click: ?personality2)[(set: $personality to "peacemaker")(goto: "Start Journey")]
```

This time, the two choices (take the sword and take the feather) are presented in two named hooks. These hooks each have a tag attached, constructed out of an angled bracket, name, and pipe, such as <personality1|.

At the bottom of the passage, each (click:) macro is attached to an anonymous hook containing the same (set:) and (goto:) macro options as the first example. In Figure 10.4, the two options appear on the screen as hyperlinked text.

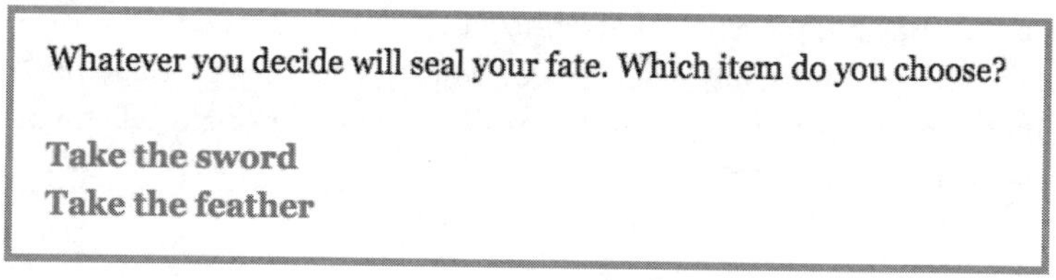

Whatever you decide will seal your fate. Which item do you choose?

Take the sword
Take the feather

FIGURE 10.4 You can also use named hooks to create setter links.

Once again, when one of the options is clicked, the value of the variable $personality is set, and the player is transported to a new passage via the (goto:) macro.

Setter links are handy when you're building a role-playing game and need to assign traits to each character, but you can use them any time you want to speed along game play by reducing the number of passages while still being able to place a value on each variable.

TRY IT OUT: UNDERWORLD

It's possible to use other characters as obstacles to slow down game play. To try this out, create a game in which both human and animal characters serve as obstacles. Use setter links to reduce the number of passages you need in order to set variables and tell the story.

Say that the player character isn't dead, but he or she needs to get into Hades to retrieve a magical sword a kinsman was using when he was killed in battle. Of course, Charon doesn't take too kindly to ferrying living souls across the River Styx (or Acheron, depending on which mythos you follow). Therefore, the player needs to move between the above-ground world, to collect items that are of use to Charon beyond the coin, and the underworld, where you'll have to find and retrieve the magical sword.

Along the way, the player should run into a series of obstacles beyond the river and Charon. Have Persephone show up if the player tries to return above ground from the underworld and keep the player from being able to collect what he or she needs from the living world. Also have Cerberus make an appearance and require the player to get past his three heads in order to retrieve a necessary item.

As a special challenge, can you build a system with conditionals where the player reads different text depending on his or her interactions with the character during the game? For example, if the player treats Charon well, Charon will treat the player well. On the other hand, if the player treats Charon brusquely, Charon won't take the player's coin or ferry him or her across.

Now that you know more about pacing, pay special attention to the cause-and-effect events as well as language choices you work into your games. Pacing becomes particularly important when you combine it in the next chapter with foreshadowing, especially when you want to slowly plod the reader toward a feeling of dread.

Foreshadowing Important Clues

In the Twine story *Beware the Faerie Food You Eat* by Astrid Dalmady, a huge clue about what sort of story this will be smacks you at the beginning of the title. *Beware*? Well that doesn't make it sound like a story about nice, helpful Tinkerbell-like faeries.

The game continues warning you over and over that interactions with faeries rarely end well. And because you're warned, you go into your choices with your defenses up. From the moment you step into the ring of mushrooms and smell the "ozone and petrichor" in the air to the abnormal brightness in the woods ("The leaves are tinged too green, the sun is a smidgen too bright.") to the strange silence as you begin to walk down the path, you get the sense that this isn't a place to relax and enjoy. This is a place to be on guard.

That smell of ozone and petrichor, the strange brightness, and the silence are all examples of *foreshadowing*, literary clues that nudge you to read or make choices carefully. Those three aren't the only clues in the game: Good foreshadowing is a little bit like Hansel and Gretel's dropped bread crumbs in the woods, marking the path. Each time you see a little bit of out-of-place oddness, like the rebuffed faerie whose teeth suddenly seem sharp like a shark's, you get a jolt to pay attention, read carefully, proceed with caution.

Chapter 2, "Using Choice to Create Agency," mentioned a famous quote from the playwright Anton Chekhov: "One must not put a loaded rifle on the stage if no one is thinking of firing it." Back then, I introduced Checkov's admonition to let you know not to put in extraneous details that will distract the audience, but now you can consider this quote from another angle: Placing a gun on stage is foreshadowing if at some point in the play, it's going to be used. This tactic builds tension because the reader is perpetually cringing, waiting for the gun to go off. Introducing it early instead of pulling it out at the moment of the shooting gets the reader thinking that danger is coming without knowing who, what, when, why, or where. Just knowing the "how"—the gun—is enough to set the reader on edge.

Foreshadowing can be used to set a tone. In the faerie game, the strange silences and sharp teeth are harbingers of the reader's ghastly end, which may be death by knives or death by dancing. In fact, there are 10 different ways to die in the game. Of course, foreshadowing doesn't always need to be terrible. You could just as easily give clues that something good is about to happen.

The second point of foreshadowing is to provide in literary form something you naturally do in everyday speech: draw attention to the important details for the listener.

What happens when you argue or you're passionately trying to convince another person to do something? You either slow down for certain words or make your voice louder when you reach the important point you're making. You do this because you want to draw the listener's attention to particular words. When you write a story, you can do the same thing by guiding the player to focus on certain characters and not others or pick up certain objects and not others. You do this by dropping clues—both subtle and direct—into the story. Think of these moments as the equivalent of slowing down or raising your voice.

Usually the point of foreshadowing is to help the reader make good decisions. But it can also be used to mislead the player, such as by dragging the reader's attention to *red herrings*—details that are meant to distract the player from figuring out the ending too soon. Red herrings can build suspense, leading the player to fret over whether he or she is following a real or false lead. Misleading details help keep the reader wondering about the ending. Red herrings done well are like a magician's sleight of hand trick, drawing the reader's attention away from what you don't want them to notice yet. Red herrings done poorly can make the reader distrust the writer. So use this trick sparingly.

So foreshadowing can set a tone, mentally prepare the player, or build suspense. In this chapter, you'll learn how to pepper clues into your story in order to give the player a "map" of how you want the story read. To do that, you'll need two new macros: (append:) and (prepend:).

Using the (append:) Macro

The (append:) macro is a changer macro, which adds text *after* the words in the hook. It works in combination with either the (click:) macro or the (mouseover:) macro. Just like the changer-sensor combination macros you saw in Chapter 8, "Constructing Believable Characters," this one also utilizes a named hook.

It's time to see this macro in action, weaving a bit of foreshadowing into a passage. Open a new story and call it The Curse. In the first passage, type this:

```
He stared at the object in horror. ["What is it?" he asked.]<whatIs|
```

```
(click-append: ?whatIs)[ (Of course, you know. It's the only thing she has
ever cared about.)]"I don't have the faintest idea," you reply.
```

This example starts out with some plain text before segueing into a named hook that contains a clickable question: "What is it?" he asked. This hook is attached to a nametag constructed out of an angled bracket, a name (whatIs), and a pipe character.

This tag is then utilized with the (click-append:) macro via a question mark preceding the name of the tag: ?whatIs. The (click-append:) macro is attached to an anonymous hook that contains the additional information you want to appear when the named hook is triggered because the words are clicked. Finally, more plain text appears after the second hook.

What happens when you play this passage? As you can see in Figure 11.1, all the plain text appears on the screen, in addition to the words in the named hook, which appears as blue hypertext.

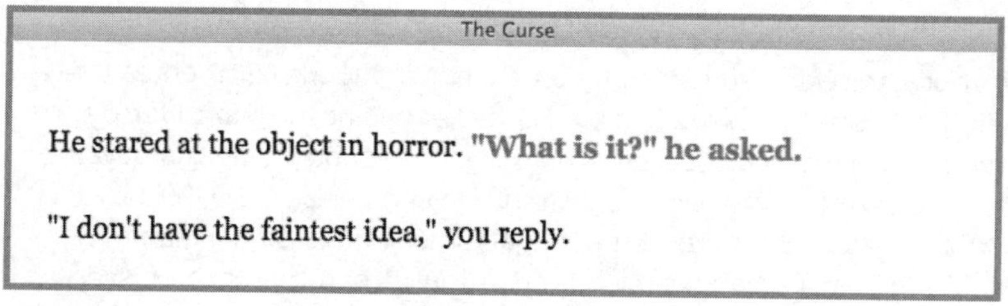

The Curse
He stared at the object in horror. "What is it?" he asked.
"I don't have the faintest idea," you reply.

FIGURE 11.1 The plain text and the words in the named hook appear on the screen when the passage opens.

If the words in the named hook are clicked, the words in the anonymous hook appear, and the hypertext of the named hook turns into plain text, as shown in Figure 11.2.

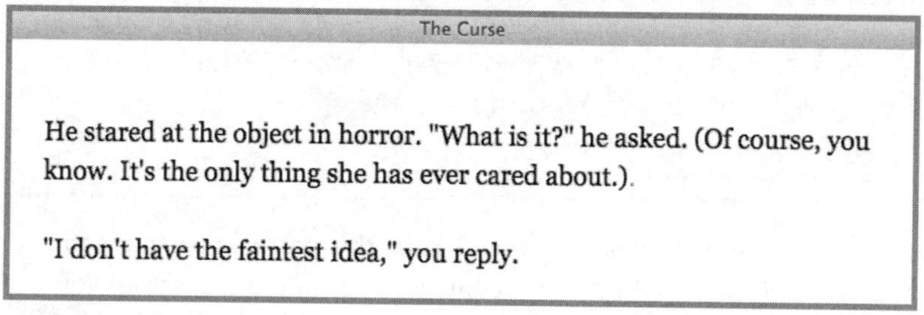

The Curse
He stared at the object in horror. "What is it?" he asked. (Of course, you know. It's the only thing she has ever cared about.).
"I don't have the faintest idea," you reply.

FIGURE 11.2 The plain text remains on the screen, while the hypertext turns into plain text and the words inside the anonymous hook appear.

You can achieve the same effect by combining the (mouseover:) and (append:) macros. Replace the text currently in the opening passage with a (mouseover-append:) version, like this:

```
He stared at the object in horror. ["What is it?" he asked.]<whatIs|

(mouseover-append: ?whatIs)[ (Of course, you know. It's the only thing she has
ever cared about.)]"I don't have the faintest idea," you reply.
```

Play the game again, and you see that the effect is much more subtle. The player now sees the text in the anonymous hook only if he or she moves the mouse over the question. If the mouse doesn't move over the question, the additional, parenthetical thought doesn't appear.

Both methods give the player clues about the player character and the object at hand, but one takes a direct approach, clearly wanting the player to see the words with the (click-append:) macro, and the other takes a more subtle approach, revealing the player character to be a liar only if the player moves the mouse over the seemingly unmarked words.

TRY IT OUT: USEFUL ITEMS

Use the direct foreshadowing technique just described to draw the reader's attention to certain objects that are necessary to complete a later, unknown task.

Say that the player character has been hired by an eccentric billionaire to enter the caves that have been unearthed on his property. He hints that according to family lore, dangers as well as enormous treasures are likely to be found inside the caves. The player needs to be up to the challenge: Unless he or she raises $10,000 by the end of the week, the player character is in danger of losing his or her home and everything in it. The billionaire has promised much more than that if the player character finds the treasures buried inside the cave.

Strangely, the billionaire disappears the night before the player character is planning to enter the caves. Was he dragged inside by something lurking in the twisty passages? Is this going to be a rescue mission in addition to a treasure hunt?

Using the (append:) macro, give the player clues about collecting items that will help with the task in the cave. (Of course, you first need to decide what the player may encounter and drop hints so he or she can mentally prepare.) Award points when the player picks up something that will be helpful and remove points when he or she takes something that will prevent doing the best job possible in the caves.

Yes, awarding points is a form of direct foreshadowing, letting the reader know in a game that he or she is completing tasks that will help in the future. So how did you set up your award system to hint to the reader that he or she is on the right track?

You could drop a lot of hints that the player is going to encounter vampires inside the cave by leaving clues in the house. There is plenty to pick up in the house, including a heavy case of silver bullets (helpful if you're hunting a werewolf but not a vampire) and a sword. Those two items will lower the score by a point because carrying them only serves to slow down the player. Hopefully after mistakenly taking a few of those useless items, the player will know what he or she is *not* up against.

On the other hand, if the player picks up anything useful for killing a vampire—such as a magnifying glass that you can use to capture a stream of sunlight and direct it at the vampire or a wooden stake—the reader will gain a point. Here's how you'd make this work:

```
The back corner of the yard is a mess of broken boards from a decomposing shed.
It doesn't look like there is anything particularly helpful out here, except perhaps
one of the sharp slivers of wood. [Do you want to take a sliver of wood?]<stake|

(click-append: ?stake)[ (set: $score to $score + 1)Your score goes up one point as
you take the wooden stake. You now have (print: $score) points.]
```

Now when the player character enters the cave, it won't be surprising when she encounters a blood-sucking vampire, though the player may be shocked to learn that the blood-sucking vampire is really the eccentric billionaire who has lured her into the cave to build his vampire army!

Oh well, foreshadowing can only take a reader so far.

Using the (prepend:) Macro

Upon first glance, the way you use the (prepend:) macro in a passage looks exactly like how you use the (append:) macro, only instead of the new words appearing after the words in the named hook, the new words appear *before* the words in the named hook. In a new story called Time Traveler, you can test out this script in the opening passage like this:

```
[He squints at you.]<timeTravel| "So weird that I haven't met you before if you've
lived on this street for years," he mentions.
```

```
(click-prepend: ?timeTravel)[The reality is that you've loved him forever. ]
"I know. So odd," you reply. This is the problem with being a time traveler.
```

Once again, there is a named hook inside single square brackets on the screen, attached to a tag constructed out of an angled bracket, a name (timeTravel), and a pipe. You later reference this tag with the (click-prepend:) macro by writing the name of the tag preceded by a question mark: ?timeTravel.

When the words in the named hook are clicked, the blue hypertext changes to plain text, and the words of the second, anonymous hook appear on the screen *before* the named hook.

If you play the game, you see that the passage opens with the words in the named hook in blue hypertext on the screen and the rest of the passage written in plain text, as shown in Figure 11.3.

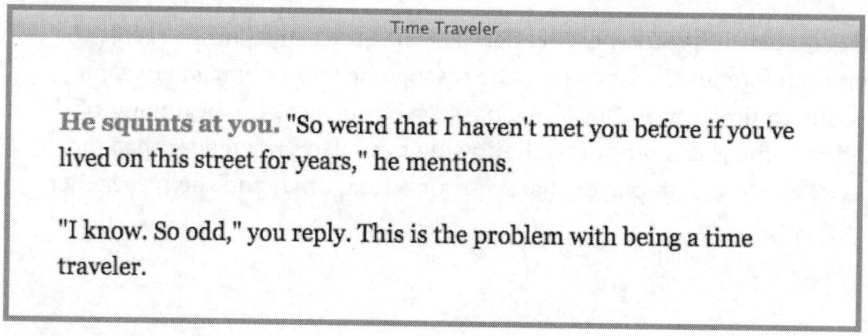

Time Traveler

He squints at you. "So weird that I haven't met you before if you've lived on this street for years," he mentions.

"I know. So odd," you reply. This is the problem with being a time traveler.

FIGURE 11.3 The plain text and the words in the named hook appear on the screen when the passage opens.

If the reader clicks the words in the named hook, the words in the anonymous hook appear, and the hypertext of the named hook turns into plain text, as shown in Figure 11.4.

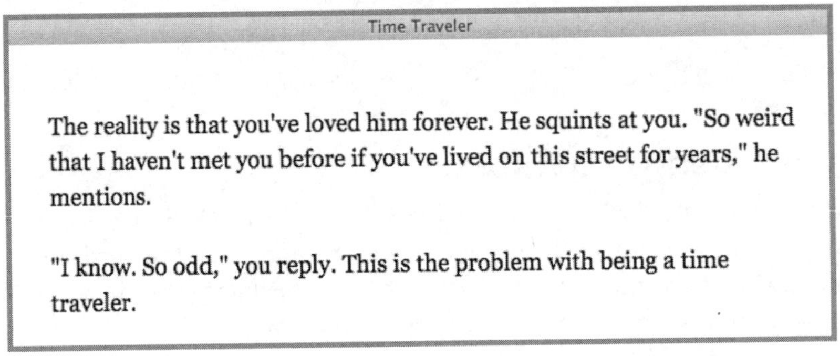

> **Time Traveler**
>
> The reality is that you've loved him forever. He squints at you. "So weird that I haven't met you before if you've lived on this street for years," he mentions.
>
> "I know. So odd," you reply. This is the problem with being a time traveler.

FIGURE 11.4 The plain text remains on the screen, while the hypertext turns into plain text, and the words inside the anonymous hook appear before the rest of the words in the passage.

Once again, you can achieve the same effect by combining the `(mouseover:)` and `(prepend:)` macros. Replace the text currently in the opening passage with this `(mouseover-prepend:)` version:

```
[He squints at you.]<timeTravel| "So weird that I haven't met you before if you've
lived on this street for years," he mentions.

(mouseover-prepend: ?timeTravel)[The reality is that you've loved him forever. ]
"I know. So odd," you reply. This is the problem with being a time traveler.
```

Once again, the triggering words look like plain text on the screen, but if the reader runs the mouse over the words in the named hook (`He squints at you`), the words in the second hook appear before the named hook does. It's a very subtle hint that is revealed only by chance.

If this passage appears later in the story, the reader likely has the same knowledge as the player character and therefore understands that the reason she knows him whereas he doesn't know her is due to time travel. But if this passage happens at the beginning of the story, the prepended statement is a bit of foreshadowing that alerts the reader that the player character has known this non-player character for a long time, and the player then wonders how this is possible.

TRY IT OUT: THE MISSING LETTER

Someone has stolen all the letter *T*s off the keyboards of the school's computers, and no one has a clue why. But your best friend, Dave, seems to be hiding something. You don't think he's the one who took the keys, but you know something is strange.

Using the (prepend:) macro, write a story for this scenario and subtly drop clues about Dave's strange behavior. Drop hints about his involvement in this strange prank and drop more hints about why someone would want all the letter *T*s. Feel free to include other non-player characters, especially if you use them to let slip clues that benefit the player character (and, by extension, the player).

An extra challenge: Can you use conditional statements to display *T*-less text if the keyboard in the room hasn't been fixed and regular text, with *T*s, if the keyboard in the room has been fixed?

Foreshadowing Clues

To review, you can use foreshadowing to help set the tone or allow a reader to make good decisions by embedding clues into the text. You can also use foreshadowing to keep the reader from noticing facts before you want them revealed and to build suspense. There are many different ways to work foreshadowing into a game or story.

Dropping Direct Clues

You've already encountered one very direct way of dropping clues for the reader: making the player's score go up or down. But direct foreshadowing also involves the introduction of important facts or objects that the reader is meant to notice now but not fully understand until later.

A perfect example is the Chekhovian gun. If the player character was invited to a weekend gathering at an English manor and hid a gun in his or her suitcase, the player would mentally note that this is something important to keep in mind—the player character is carrying a weapon—but would not understand what it is for until the danger is revealed later in the game at the manor.

Dropping Subtle Clues

Subtle clues, or indirect clues, influence the player's understanding or mood without obviously attempting to do so. These are the sort of clues that become apparent only in retrospect. If I were to ask you how you knew to trust a character or why you thought there was a monster in the closet, you would need to think deeply about the story.

Subtle clues might be a character who always mysteriously disappears when there is danger happening, or a character whose emotional reactions seem out of proportion. Such subtle clues make the reader subconsciously wonder if things aren't as they seem on the surface.

Dropping Dream Clues

Dream clues can be a bit heavy-handed, but using them is a common method for hinting about moments to come. With a dream clue, the character falls asleep and has a premonition; the dreamer usually wakes either not understanding what he's seen (though he will keep trying to interpret those dream moments while playing the rest of the game) or dismissing the dream as wishful thinking.

A form of dream clues is used in the game *Dreamhold* by Andrew Plotkin. The amnesia-stricken player character holds various masks to his or her face and, in doing so, gains access to snippets of memories. Pulling all these memories together gives the player a sense of what happened before the player character lost his or her memory.

Dropping Feeling Clues

Paying attention to descriptions of how the player character feels can give the reader a lot of clues about future moments. Is the player character described as anxious? Humming contently to herself? Wracked with guilt? Mentioning emotions is an indirect way of foreshadowing events.

In addition, you can drop clues about how things feel *outside* the body. Is there a chill in the air on a warm day that is meant to convey a feeling of apprehension? Is the room suddenly too warm for comfort when the cute girl walks into the dance? Again, as with emotions, what the player character senses often speaks volumes about things to come.

Dropping Red Herrings

Of course, sometimes you don't want the reader to pick up on the facts too soon, especially in a mystery story that ends with a big reveal. In such a case, you can use foreshadowing to mislead the reader with false clues. Make items appear to be more important than they actually are or have a non-player character's behavior seem untoward when he or she is actually going to come to the player character's rescue later in the story.

TRY IT OUT: THE SPELL BOOK

Your teacher at the Mylington School for Magical Studies has hinted that your final exam will be a dangerous feat. Um, can he actually do that to students?

You're not going to take your chances. You go to the library to prepare by copying important spells into your spell book (which, of course, is an array). Unfortunately, there is only room for five spells, so you'll have to choose wisely.

Write a story for this scenario, dropping in clues about the dangerous task ahead so the player can make choices as to which spells to write in the book.

Later in the game, present the impossible task. If the proper spell is in the spell book, the player is allowed to cast it. If not, he or she will have to solve the problem some other way.

Use various forms of foreshadowing—from direct clues to red herrings—to help the reader figure out how to best move through the story.

As an extra challenge, hide funny messages by using the (append:) and (prepend:) macros inside the library books.

Creating a Hint System

Hint systems in various forms have been present since the beginning of interactive fiction. The old Infocom games came with InvisiClue booklets—paper books written in invisible ink that was activated with a special accompanying pen. When the highlighter was dragged across the paper, a clue to a preprinted question was revealed, one step at a time. A player was supposed to reveal only as much information as needed to solve the puzzle.

By default, hint systems are a form of foreshadowing because the fact that a clue exists tells the reader that the moment is important. To get around this problem, Infocom dropped plenty of red herring questions into its InvisiClue books. If players revealed the answers underneath the question, they would discover that they had been duped and given a gentle admonition to not peek at clues that aren't needed.

Hint systems still have a place in interactive fiction games. Some people opt for a modern iteration of the InvisiClue model, while others post complete walkthroughs on websites.

An easy way for Twine users to introduce the concept of clues is to create a clue space similar to the way you created an inventory in Chapter 9, "Maintaining an Inventory": You can place a link, such as [[Clue Book|Clue Book]], at the bottom of each passage.

You could construct a clue page multiple ways, such as having the answers on the screen but in a code such as a ROT-13 system so the answers aren't easily readable until the player is ready to see them. ROT-13 stands for "rotate 13 spaces" and it swaps the first half of the alphabet with the second half. A, for instance, becomes N. B becomes O, and so on and so on. Each time you want to write a letter, you count 13 spaces ahead and write that letter instead. To decipher a ROT-13 message, you continue this trend, taking each letter on the screen and rotating it 13 spaces. ROT-13 messages look like gibberish, but they easily unravel into readable text simply by swapping every letter 13 spaces.

A more subtle way to have more text appear under the question would be to utilize the (append:) macro to add text with each additional click—sort of a computer version of the InvisiClue books. For instance, say that you want to add a clue page to the story you wrote in the last Try It Out. Use the green +Passage button to create a new passage and drag it to the far left of the screen. This new passage will serve as your clue book, separate from the actual story passages.

Start adding clues that will help the reader make decisions within the story. One of the questions on the clue page may look like this:

```
1. [Will the flying spell be useful?]<fly|
(click-append: ?fly)[
A lot of people dream about flying, don't they? [more]<fly2|]
(click-append: ?fly2)[
In fact, didn't you have a dream like that the other night? [more]<fly3|]
(click-append: ?fly3)[
I would pay attention to dreams, if I were you.]
(link-goto: "Return to Story", (history:)'s last)
```

You can achieve an InvisiClue slow reveal format by embedding the next named hook inside the previous anonymous hook. Initially, the question appears inside the single, square brackets of a named hook. This named hook has an attached tag constructed out of an angled bracket, a name (fly), and a pipe: <fly|.

Next, the (click-append:) macro connects to the named hook by using the nametag preceded by a question mark (?fly). When the words in the first hook are clicked, Twine prints all the words in the second hook, including the embedded second named hook. The player clicking the words in the next named hook (More) triggers the macro utilizing its nametag (<fly2|) and prints the next anonymous hook. This chain continues until the final anonymous hook contains only text without a link to another statement.

So how does this look if you click over to the Clue Book passage in the game? As shown in Figure 11.5, the first question appears as hypertext on the screen.

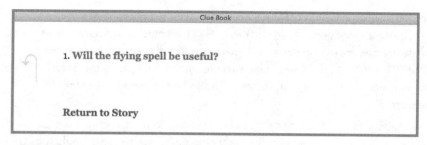

FIGURE 11.5 The passage opens with the question as a hypertext link and an additional link to return to the story.

When the question is clicked, the first statement appears, as shown in Figure 11.6.

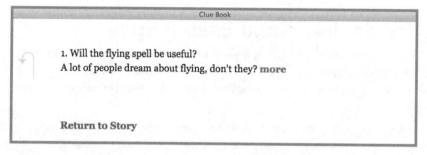

FIGURE 11.6 Clicking the question reveals the first statement as well as another link to see more of the answer.

This continues until all the additional "more" links are clicked and all the answers are revealed, as shown in Figure 11.7.

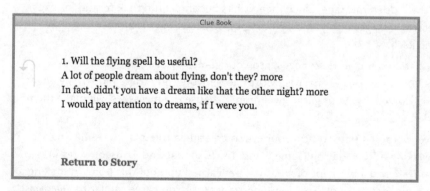

FIGURE 11.7 The entire answer is revealed, and the player can either return to the story or, if there were more questions on the page, click to see the next set of answers.

One important point to note is that you always need to make the tag unique to the question rather than use a more general tag such as `<clue1|` in multiple questions. The reason is that triggering one macro causes all the macros utilizing the same tag to reveal the text in the hook. Therefore, you should make each set of tags unique to the question at hand, as in the example above, where all the clues in the first question are names with variations on the word *fly*.

Of course, the clue page also has a link to take the reader back to the story: `(link-goto:` `"Return to Story", (history:)'s last)`. Each time the reader leaves the clue book, the exposed answers are reset, revealing only the hypertext questions the next time the player clicks over. Additionally, this snippet of code creates an error message if the Clue Book passage is the opening passage of your game. Therefore, set up this passage as a side passage, much in the same way you've set up inventory passages in other chapters.

Including Inside Jokes and Easter Eggs

I've already talked about InvisiClues, and this is a good place to mention that interactive fiction is riddled with in-jokes, especially allusions to old games or game creators. Sometimes these in-jokes are embedded into the game, and other times they appear as red herring questions on a clue page.

For example, *Adventure*, one of the first interactive fiction games, contained a magic word that would transport the player between two spaces, and you'll encounter this word—XYZZY—as an in-joke in many other games as homage to this early pioneer of interactive fiction.

It's fitting that the first known "Easter egg" to appear in a video game was in Atari's version of Will Crowther's game, also called *Adventure*, like its interactive fiction counterpart. The programmer, Warren Robinett, wrote his name into the game, though few found the location of the hidden message. Since then, it has become a fun trick to add in-joke references or secret messages into games. Finding these Easter eggs is almost as fun as playing the game itself.

So go ahead and add your own Easter eggs into your games by using the `(mouseover-` `append:)` or `(mouseover-prepend:)` macros. Most people won't find these hidden messages, but the ones who do will love your game even more because the messages will make them feel like an insider.

Speaking of adventures, it's time to turn your eye to creating a role-playing game. In Chapters 12, "Making a Role-Playing Game," and 13, "Combat and Consequences in Role-Playing Games," you'll use a lot of what you've learned up until this point in making a computer version of what amounts to a pen-and-paper tabletop game similar to *Dungeons & Dragons*.

12

Making a Role-Playing Game

In Choice of Games's *Choice of the Dragon*, you begin the game with a list of stats on the left side of the screen. Your brutality or finesse, cunning or honor, disdain or vigilance, and infamy are all set squarely in the middle at 50%. You have 5,000 gold coins, no injuries, and a lot of choices to make.

Welcome to the world of CRPGs—computer role-playing games—which are meant to bring the tabletop game experience to the screen.

In *Choice of the Dragon*, you're playing as the dragon, and the stats refer to your abilities as a princess-kidnapping beast. Choose not to harm the knight that charges at you at the opening of the game and watch your brutality score lower and your finesse score rise. The bar marking the balance between these two traits becomes more blue than red to indicate that favor has swung toward thoughtful decisions and away from mindless cruelty.

In this chapter, you're going to set up your own role-playing game. As the writer, you are leading the story in the sense that you are giving the players—yes, you're making a game that several people can play at the same time—a situation and setting. But the players will determine where the story goes based on unique attributes associated with their character, randomly assigned levels for certain traits, and skills and strength gained along the way.

You've already learned how to create several pieces of a role-playing game, such as tracking an inventory with an array. In this chapter you'll learn how to build characters. In Chapter 13, "Combat and Consequences in Role-Playing Games," you'll see how to place those characters in a brief adventure where they need to duel with a monster and open a tricky treasure box.

To begin, you need to set up a stat system that can track a multitude of information. This allows you to create one game that gives one or more players hours of game play since every time the game begins, new characters can be built, producing very different outcomes when they're thrown into the action.

In order to build a stat system, you need to learn another macro: the (datamap:) macro. Luckily, it functions in a similar manner to the (array:) macro, so you can apply a lot of what you know about the (array:) macro to the new macro.

Maybe swords and sorcery isn't really your thing, and that's okay. You can tweak the examples in the Try It Out sections to create your own role-playing game and apply the ideas to a completely different set of characters, such as astronauts on a distant planet, magical school students, or mermaids. Feel free to play with any of the stats or character-building elements; you'll know what you can tweak as the chapter unfolds.

First you're going to jump into the (datamap:) macro and see how, with a single variable, you can track an entire personality.

Using the (datamap:) Macro

Earlier in the book, I talked about visualizing an array as an expandable box, with a slot—called an index—for each individual value you put in the array. Now consider that a datamap is an expandable box, with a slot for each individual string value *and* a blank card inside each slot where you can give a fact about the item inside like Figure 12.1.

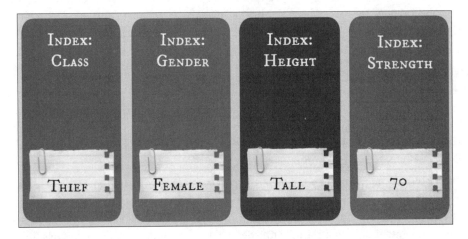

FIGURE 12.1 Datamaps allow you to organize values for strings.

That, of course, is an analogy. A datamap is not an actual box inside a game, but it functions like one. Although arrays are numbered lists, datamaps are *worded* lists. Instead of arranging the information as item 1, item 2, item 3 (a numbered list), a datamap creates the indexes out of strings, or words. It then allows you to assign a value to that string index. In Figure 12.1, the information isn't arranged as index 0, 1, and 2 as was done in Chapter 9, "Maintaining an Inventory." It's arranged as index Class, Gender, and Height. Underneath each index name (called a data name) is a value (called a data value): Thief, Female, and Tall.

Datamaps are helpful when creating a stat system because they allow the player to check *how much* strength the character has instead of just creating a binary state whether the player either has or doesn't have strength. The indexes are created out of words, and the assigned values can be in the form of words or numbers.

Which means that if you want strength to be a level that goes up and down, you make Strength the name of the index and you place a numeric value in that index, such as 70 in Figure 12.1. You could also have a string value for your string index, such as "very weak." Of course, once you have a value set, you can create conditional statements that check the value and display text accordingly.

To see how a datamap works, you'll place an empty one in the opening passage of a new story. This game will actually track three datamaps (one for each character), so name this first datamap $character1. Datamaps, like variables and arrays, are written with a dollar sign in front of the name.

Open a new Twine story and call it Role-Playing Game. In the first passage, place the datamap, like this:

```
(set: $character1 to (datamap:))You step into the circle and place your hand
on the promise stone. "I will go on the journey."
```

So the (datamap:) macro looks very similar to the (array:) macro. You use the (set:) macro to place the (datamap:) macro as the value of the variable $character1.

Adding Values to the Datamap

You assign values to the string indexes in the datamap much the same way you add values to an array. Here's an example:

```
(set: $character1 to it + (datamap: "Class", "Wizard"))
```

Later in this chapter, I'll teach you a second syntax you can use to add values to an index, but this first way should help you to see the fact that you have string indexes and string or numerical values assigned to those indexes.

The first word in the pair ("Class") is the *data name*. It is the name of the index. The second word in the pair ("Wizard") is the *data value*. It is the value assigned to that index. For each entry in the datamap, you have a data name and a data value. You cannot have a data name without a data value, and you cannot have a data value without a data name.

In this example, because the variable name—$character1—is so long, you may opt to use a Twine shortcut. I know, I know, I'm usually against Twine shortcuts like abbreviating the (array:) macro to (a:), but in this case, having to type a variable name that long twice every time you add a new value will take up a lot of space.

As a shortcut, you can use the keyword it to stand in for the second instance of the variable name. Because $character1 has already been set in the expression, you can refer to it with the keyword it other times *within the same operation*. You can't just throw it willy-nilly into a later operation, such as (set: it to 3). But if the object being changed is already defined *in* the operation, you can use it to refer to it rather than write out the variable a second time.

In other words, (set: $character1 to it + (datamap: "Class", "Wizard")) is the same as (set: $character1 to $character1 + (datamap: "Class", "Wizard")).

Removing Values from a Datamap

To remove indexes and their values from a datamap, you unfortunately can't use the array method because it gives you an error message in Twine. Instead, you use the `(move:)` macro to place the index (or data name) you no longer want to use in another variable. Here's how it looks:

```
(move: $character1's "Class" into $characterx)
```

In this case, you're telling Twine to move `"Class"` out of the `$character1` datamap and place it in a new variable, `$characterx`. The variable name you use should not be one you plan to use in the game, and you shouldn't reference it later in a conditional statement. This variable operates like a rubbish bin, a space to collect the data names you don't want to use anymore. You have to use the `(move:)` macro, and that means you need to move the data name somewhere else instead of just making it disappear from the game.

You will rarely want to dump a data name from a datamap after using it earlier in a game, but you need to know how to do it just in case.

Using a Datamap for a Stat System

So how can you use a datamap to track a role-playing game stat system, much as you used an array as the player character's bag for carrying inventory in Chapter 9, "Maintaining an Inventory"? In other words, how can you turn a piece of computer code into a usable system?

You can think of each data name as an element of the player character's personality—his or her class, name, gender, height, weight, strength, dexterity, intelligence, charm, or health. (Feel free, of course, to create different categories in your game for your data names.)

For each of those data names, you need to assign a data value. So the class may be wizard, thief, or knight. The name may be Melvin, Desdemona, or Buttercup. Gender may be male or female, and height may be a numeric value such as 46 for a 46-inch dwarf or a string value such as `"tall"`.

While data names remain the same throughout the game, data values assigned to those data names can change. To see how this works, change the `"Class"` data name to a different value.

This is the second syntax that you can use to set or change a data value for a data name. By using a possessive with the variable, you can refer to the data name and assign the value using the `to` operator with the `(set:)` macro:

```
(set: $character1's "Class" to "Thief")
```

So now, instead of being a wizard, the character is a thief. You can also check the value of a data name and display conditional text by using the `(if:)` and `(else:)` macros:

```
(if: $character1's "Class" is "Wizard")[You cast a spell!]
(elseif: $character1's "Class" is "Thief")[You steal the stone.]
```

Now that you know the basics of datamaps, you can start filling a datamap for each character.

Establishing Class

In tabletop games like *Dungeons & Dragons*, the classification influences the capabilities of the character. A knight, by default, is a better fighter than a healer. You can create a complex game that takes into account a multitude of characteristics assigned to a character's class. But for the sake of this sample game, you're going to keep it simple by creating six character classes, each with a dominant trait that influences the success of the character's endeavors based on this ability.

These classes will be wizard (magic), knight (combat), thief (stealth), healer (health), elf (nature), and dwarf (craft).

Becoming a Wizard

If the player chooses to be a wizard, the data name `"Class"` receives the data value `"Wizard"`. This means any time the player is given the choice to use magic to get out of a situation, success is based on whether he or she actually has magic as a wizard or whether the player is another type of character trying to cast a spell.

Becoming a Knight

If the player chooses to be a knight, the data name `"Class"` receives the data value `"Knight"`. This means that any time the player enters a fight, success is based on whether the player has combat skills as a knight or whether he or she is engaging in unskilled kicking and punching in hopes of slaying the beast.

Becoming a Thief

If the player chooses to be a thief, the data name `"Class"` receives the data value `"Thief"`. This means that any time the character needs to use slyness to complete a task, success is based on whether the player can silently creep into a space as a thief or whether his or her presence is known due to a noisy entrance.

Becoming a Healer

If the player chooses to be a healer, the data name `"Class"` receives the data value `"Healer"`. This means that any time the character needs to nurse another character back to health, success is based on whether the player has the skills of a healer.

Becoming an Elf

If the player chooses to be an elf, the data name `"Class"` receives the data value `"Elf"`. This means that any time the character needs to borrow supplies from nature, success is based on whether the player knows the ins and outs of nature, as an elf would.

Becoming a Dwarf

If the player chooses to be a dwarf, the data name `"Class"` receives the data value `"Dwarf"`. This means that any time the character needs to build a weapon or fashion a tool, success is based on whether he or she knows how to craft an instrument, as a dwarf would.

Coding Class Selection

Back in the sample game, open up the first passage and get ready to give the first player the opportunity to set his or her character's class. As shown here, you can use the `(link:)` macro to create clickable links, the `(set:)` macro to assign the data value to the data name, and the `(goto:)` macro to take the player to the next passage:

```
(set: $character1 to (datamap:))You step into the circle and place your hand on the
promise stone.  "I will go on the journey."
"What are you?" the king demands.
You bow your head in respect.  "I am a..."
(link: "wizard")[(set: $character1's "Class" to "Wizard")(goto: "Establish Name")]
(link: "knight")[(set: $character1's "Class" to "Knight")(goto: "Establish Name")]
(link: "thief")[(set: $character1's "Class" to "Thief")(goto: "Establish Name")]
(link: "healer")[(set: $character1's "Class" to "Healer")(goto: "Establish Name")]
(link: "elf")[(set: $character1's "Class" to "Elf")(goto: "Establish Name")]
(link: "dwarf")[(set: $character1's "Class" to "Dwarf")(goto: "Establish Name")]
```

The script in the first passage begins by setting up an empty datamap for the first character: `(set: $character1 to (datamap:))`.

Then, after some plain text, the six class choices are given to the player. The choice opens with the `(link:)` macro, so the accompanying word inside the quotation mark (such as `"wizard"`) is clickable. The `(link:)` macro is attached to an anonymous hook, and inside the single square brackets of the hook are two macros.

The first of the two macros is the `(set:)` macro. When the link is clicked and the macro is triggered, the `(set:)` macro in the hook creates the first entry in the datamap—the data name, `"Class"`—and assigns the accompanying value to the `"Class"` data name. In the first choice, the `(set:)` macro adds the value `"Wizard"` to the data name `"Class"`.

The second of the two macros is the `(goto:)` macro, which transports the player to the next passage, Establish Name. Of course, the `(goto:)` macro does not automatically generate a new passage like the `[[link]]` macro does; therefore, you have to click the green +Passage button in order to create the new passage.

So how does this look on the screen when you click the Play button? In Figure 12.2, you can see six options on the screen. Clicking one adds a data name and data value to the datamap and moves the player to the next passage.

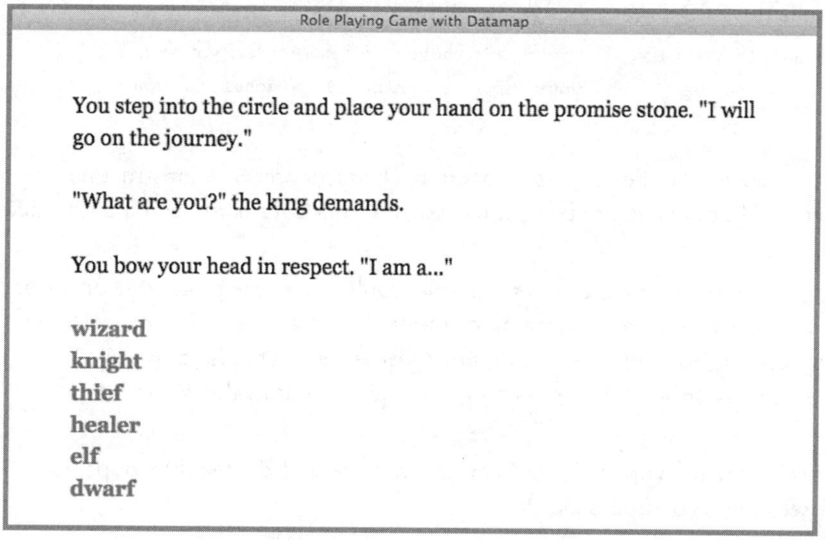

Role Playing Game with Datamap

You step into the circle and place your hand on the promise stone. "I will go on the journey."

"What are you?" the king demands.

You bow your head in respect. "I am a..."

wizard
knight
thief
healer
elf
dwarf

FIGURE 12.2   The passage opens with six options on the screen. Clicking one adds a data name (`"Class"`) and a data value to the datamap.

When the player reaches the next passage, you're going to add four more data names (and, subsequently, data values for those data names).

TRY IT OUT: ROLE-PLAYING GAME CLASS

You'll be building your own role-playing game over the course of many Try It Outs in this chapter and the next. At this point, consider the setting for your game and what sort of characters go with that setting. For instance, if the game is set in outer space, you may have a mix of humans and aliens working together on a quest, or you may have three astronauts who crash-landed on a distant planet.

Create a datamap for the first character as well as six possible positions or classes. Consider what special trait is associated with each individual class. Write a simple opening for your game.

Establishing Names

Using the (set:) macro isn't the only way to add a data value to a data name in a datamap. You can also use a text box with the (prompt:) macro in combination with the (put:) macro. At the top of the next passage, write this:

```
(put: (prompt: "What is your name?") into $character1's "Name")"So you are a
(print: $character1's "Class"), and your name is (print: $character1's "Name"),"
the king says.
```

You already learned how to use the (prompt:) macro back in Chapter 8, "Constructing Believable Characters," but now you're using it to assign both a data name and a data value at the same time.

Instead of putting the (prompt:) macro into a variable, you're using the possessive operator ('s) to put the (prompt:) macro into a data name inside the $character1 datamap. Doing so generates a pop-up text box with the accompanying question "What is your name?" When the player enters his or her name, the name becomes the data value for the data name, "Name".

How does this look on the screen? In Figure 12.3, you can see that the text box pops up before the player sees the second passage.

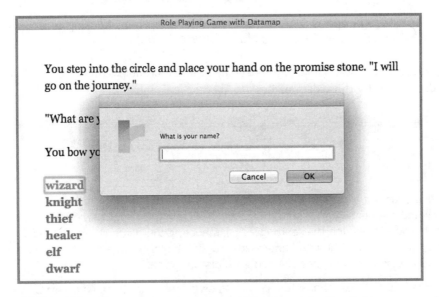

FIGURE 12.3 The text box hovers at the top while the first passage is still on the screen.

After the player fills out his or her name, the second passage appears on the screen, and via the (print:) macro, the king states the two pieces of information currently stored in the datamap: the character's class and name, as shown in Figure 12.4.

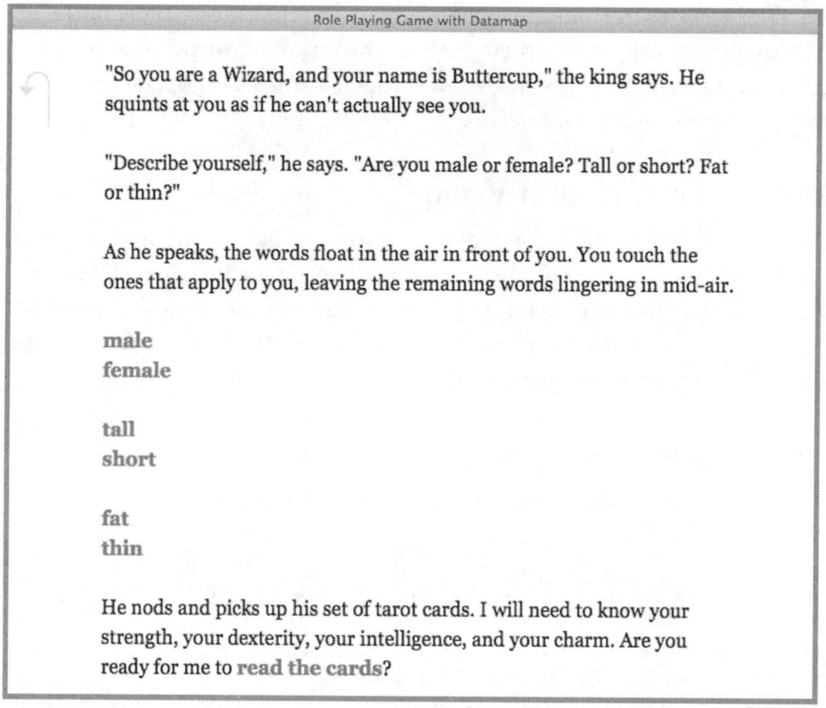

Role Playing Game with Datamap

"So you are a Wizard, and your name is Buttercup," the king says. He squints at you as if he can't actually see you.

"Describe yourself," he says. "Are you male or female? Tall or short? Fat or thin?"

As he speaks, the words float in the air in front of you. You touch the ones that apply to you, leaving the remaining words lingering in mid-air.

male
female

tall
short

fat
thin

He nods and picks up his set of tarot cards. I will need to know your strength, your dexterity, your intelligence, and your charm. Are you ready for me to read the cards?

FIGURE 12.4   The second passage prints the two data values stored in the datamap.

The passage continues adding values for three personal characteristics.

TRY IT OUT: ROLE-PLAYING GAME NAME

Continue your role-playing game by allowing the player to set his or her own character name or use the (prompt:) and (put:) macros to allow the player to input another piece of information into his or her datamap.

Establishing Personal Characteristics

This is a good time to remind you of that golden storytelling rule: Make sure that every detail you add serves a purpose. If you apply this advice to building a character, make sure there is a point to each of the details you're setting.

Sure, it's cool to allow the player to choose everything about the character's appearance, but unless the other characters will refer to these traits in the future or the traits complicate a plot point, such as having a character too tall to fit through a small cave opening, do yourself a favor and cut out the extraneous details.

Choosing Gender, Height, and Weight

In the sample story, you're going to allow the player to choose gender, height, and weight. All three choices will come into play in the story. Knowing the gender allows you to code the game to display the proper pronoun in future passages. You can use the height to make objects reachable or have certain characters notice objects close to the ground. You can use the weight to make characters strong enough to lift heavy objects or too large to fit into small spaces.

Here's how you continue allowing choices in the second passage:

```
He squints at you as if he can't actually see you.  "Describe yourself," he says.
"Are you male or female?  Tall or short?  Fat or thin?"
```

```
As he speaks, the words float in the air in front of you.  You touch the ones that
apply to you, leaving the remaining words lingering in mid-air.
(set: $character1's "Gender" to "Genderless")(set: $character1's "Height" to
"Heightless")(set: $character1's "Weight" to "Weightless")
(link: "male")[(set: $character1's "Gender" to "Male")]
(link: "female")[(set: $character1's "Gender" to "Female")]

(link: "tall")[(set: $character1's "Height" to "Tall")]
(link: "short")[(set: $character1's "Height" to "Short")]

(link: "fat")[(set: $character1's "Weight" to "Fat")]
(link: "thin")[(set: $character1's "Weight" to "Thin")]
```

```
He nods and picks up his set of tarot cards.  I will need to know your strength, your
dexterity, your intelligence, and your charm.  Are you ready for me to [[read the
cards|Stats]]?
```

All the links in this passage look very similar to the links that appeared in the first passage, except the anonymous hook contains only one macro, the (set:) macro. Clicking each choice sets the data value for that data name. Because you haven't included the (goto:) macro with these choices, the player can stay on the page and make multiple choices.

Troubleshooting User Play Decisions

Before the reader gets to the actual choices on the screen, you added some new data names to the datamap: "Gender", "Height", and "Weight". You set the value of "Gender" as `"Genderless"`, the value of `"Height"` as `"Heightless"`, and the value of `"Weight"` as `"Weightless"`. Why do all this if you are going to allow the player to set the data values one moment later?

The player can't move from the first passage without making a choice that adds a `"Class"` data name to the datamap. The player also needs to fill in a name upon receiving the text box, simultaneously adding a `"Name"` data name and data value to the datamap.

But on this page, it's possible for the player to move to the next passage without making any of the choices on the page. If the player tries to move on without making choices, the player will receive an error message in the future when the data name is referenced. Putting in a temporary placeholder value until the player clicks the link and changes the data value causes the data names to exist in the datamap regardless of how the player interacts with the page.

At the end of the passage, a link leads to the next passage, as shown in Figure 12.5.

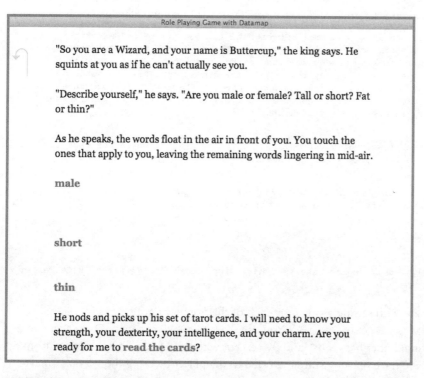

FIGURE 12.5 The player is given three choices in the middle of the passage before being given an outbound link at the bottom of the passage.

Establishing Traits

In the third passage, you will set five traits, using the (random:) macro, and pretend that the levels for each trait are determined by the king's tarot card reading. Here's what it looks like:

```
(set: $character1 to it + (datamap: "Strength", (random: 1, 99), "Dexterity", (ran-
dom: 1, 99), "Intelligence", (random: 1, 99), "Charm", (random: 1, 99), "Health",
(random: 50, 75)))The king places down the cards, shaking his head. "You are
an interesting one. The cards say that your strength is (print: $character1's
"Strength"), your dexterity is (print: $character1's "Dexterity"), your intelligence
is (print: $character1's "Intelligence"), and your charm is (print: $character1's
"Charm"). A very interesting set of traits."

You pause, unsure of whether you should say anything. "And I saved the best for last.
Your health is (print: $character1's "Health"). So how do you add up?"

The words of everything he knows about you burst into the air and hang before you;
the reality of your life boiled down to its most basic level:

(print: $character1)

He bows slightly, as if to indicate that he is impressed. You [[step back|Character
2]] from the stone.
```

The passage opens with setting a value for each of the five new data names (Strength, Dexterity, Intelligence, Charm, Health). You use the (random:) macro to set the value to a randomly chosen number between 1 and 99 (except with Health, which has a range from 50 to 75). Finally, you have the king state the value to the player by using the (print:) macro to display the randomly assigned value.

Deciding on Traits

Many role-playing games depend on tracking stats and having the outcomes of choices depend on the current levels of those stats. For the sample game, you need to track four traits:

■ **Strength**—The strength of the character determines how much the character can lift or carry. It also determines whether the character's battle jabs do damage or merely annoy the monster. A character's strength level mostly remains the same throughout the game, though you may choose to have a wizard capable of casting a strengthening spell or have strength points removed if the character gets injured.

■ **Dexterity**—The dexterity of the character determines how gracefully he or she moves, both in dodging an attack and delivering a blow. A character with a high dexterity score performs better in battle regardless of weapon than a character with a low dexterity score. A character's dexterity level remains the same throughout the game unless he or she is gravely injured and points need to be removed.

■ **Intelligence**—The intelligence of the character determines how knowledgeable he or she is when it comes to problem solving. A non-wizard character with a high intelligence score may also know a little magic, whereas a character with a low intelligence score may have his or her plans thwarted.

■ **Charm**—The charm of a character determines how other characters interact with him or her as well as how well the character can talk his or her way out of a situation. Characters with low charm may need to resort to sword play in a battle, whereas characters with high charm may be able to cleverly talk their way out of fights.

Determining Hit Points

Finally, you need to create a "Health" stat, which is sometimes known in role-playing games as the player's *hit points*. This stat tracks a player character's life level. 100 is perfect health, and 0 is...well...death. But in between are a range of numbers that indicate how capable a player is of performing a task. A player with a "Health" score of 3 may be too weak to cast a magic spell, while a player with a "Health" score of 88 should be strong enough to run quite a distance.

You end the passage by having all the stats printed on the screen at the same time, by using (print: $character1), as shown in Figure 12.6. This gives the first player one last chance to see the parameters he or she is working with in the game: strengths, weaknesses, and skills. Noting those numbers helps the player make good choices during the rest of the game.

At the very end of the passage, the link moves the player to a fourth passage that contains a message to pass the keyboard to Player 2: It's time to start building a new character.

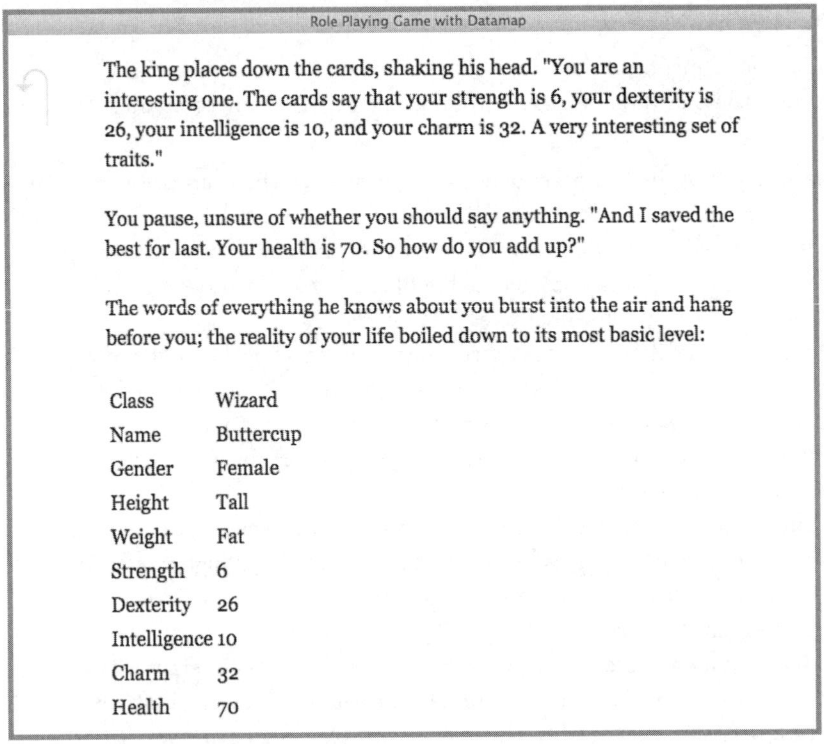

Role Playing Game with Datamap

The king places down the cards, shaking his head. "You are an interesting one. The cards say that your strength is 6, your dexterity is 26, your intelligence is 10, and your charm is 32. A very interesting set of traits."

You pause, unsure of whether you should say anything. "And I saved the best for last. Your health is 70. So how do you add up?"

The words of everything he knows about you burst into the air and hang before you; the reality of your life boiled down to its most basic level:

Class	Wizard
Name	Buttercup
Gender	Female
Height	Tall
Weight	Fat
Strength	6
Dexterity	26
Intelligence	10
Charm	32
Health	70

FIGURE 12.6 The player sees all of his or her stats in one place before the game continues.

TRY IT OUT: ROLE-PLAYING GAME TRAITS

Continue creating the game, tracking four or five traits that you will use in the game. Make sure the traits go with your story. Knowing a character's dexterity makes sense in a sword-and-sorcery role-playing game, but dexterity may be a meaningless trait if your characters are astronauts in bulky space suits. So think through what traits your characters will need to strategically fight or solve problems in the game.

Making the Next Character

This game is unique in the sense that it allows more than one player character. A player may choose to play alone, controlling three characters, or can pass-and-play with two friends, all working together to bring their characters through situations.

At the top of the next passage you place a note that it's time for the second player to build his or her character:

```
(text-color: "#CC0000")[(Pass the game to the second player)]
```

Using the (text-color:) changer macro, you list the hexadecimal code (a six-digit code for displaying colors online) for a bright shade of red: #CC0000. You then put the words that you want to display in that shade of red—(Pass the game to the second player)—inside the single square brackets of an anonymous hook. You are going to place a note like that, listing whether the passage should be read by the first, second, or third player, at the top of most passages. Once the names are set, you can personalize that message with the character's name and make the message read as follows:

```
(text-color: "#CC0000")[(Pass the game to (print: $character1's "Name")]
```

The passage continues to list most of the same text and all the same script from the first passage. It is easiest to simply copy and paste the first passage into the fourth passage and then tweak the text.

```
(text-color: "#CC0000")[(Pass the game to the second player)]

"Who will volunteer next?" the king asks.  It is now your turn.

(set: $character2 to (datamap:))You step into the circle and place your hand on the
promise stone.  "I will also go on the journey."

"What are you?" the king demands.

You cough and look around.  "I am a..."

(link: "wizard")[(set: $character2's "Class" to "Wizard")(goto: "Establish Name")]
(link: "knight")[(set: $character2's "Class" to "Knight")(goto: "Establish Name")]
(link: "thief")[(set: $character2's "Class" to "Thief")(goto: "Establish Name")]
(link: "healer")[(set: $character2's "Class" to "Healer")(goto: "Establish Name")]
(link: "elf")[(set: $character2's "Class" to "Elf")(goto: "Establish Name")]
(link: "dwarf")[(set: $character2's "Class" to "Dwarf")(goto: "Establish Name")]
```

Of course, the fifth passage is a repeat of the second passage, and the sixth passage is a repeat of the third passage.

I bet you can guess what happens with the third player. Yes, the process starts over again. It may help you to drag the three boxes that create each character into a row so you can easily see the passages that form each character. Figure 12.7 shows the three character-creating boxes in a column before being duplicated to the right into two more columns, each standing for one of the three characters.

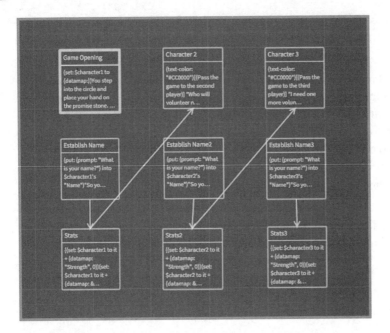

FIGURE 12.7 Three columns of passages, with each column creating a single character.

Wrapping Up the Opening

You are almost ready to send your brave adventurers on a journey. But first you want to tell your players their goal and allow them to pack their bags. At this point you could, for example, have the king deliver the goal to the player characters by telling them to bring back the stolen crown but not to bring anything else into the kingdom. Here's what it would look like:

```
(text-color: "#CC0000")[(Pass the game to the first player)]"So you will leave,
right now, and find the stolen crown. Do not bring anything else you find into
the kingdom because it is probably sabotaged. Only the crown."
```

```
(set: $bag to (array:))The king hands you a bag. "Everything you need for your
journey is in the next room. [[Pack your bag|Pack Bag]] and go."
```

There is a big foreshadowing clue in the passage: The readers should expect to see a lot of other items on this journey and should get the idea not to pick them up and bring them back, or they'll lose the game.

This passage also creates an empty array, `(set: $bag to (array:))`, which you'll fill in the next passage.

Limiting an Array

For the sake of this game, you may want to limit the number of items the player characters can take to three. It's a short journey, after all, and if you want players to think like their characters, you should make their characters realistic. That means setting a hold limit and ensuring that the player character can take only what a human could realistically carry.

Because the players can technically take more than three items each—there is nothing to stop them from continuing to take things from the list despite the instructions to take only three things—you can set up the passage to show two different options: one if it's the player's first time through the passage and the other if the person has been sent back to repack the bag after trying to take more than three items from the list. Here's how it looks:

```
(if: (count: (history:), "Pack Bag") is 0)[(print: $character2's "Name")
grumbles as you head into the next room. "I seriously hope we complete this
task by next Tuesday. I have other things to do."
"Be quiet," (print: $character3's "Name") says. (if: $character3's "Gender" is
"Male")[He](else:)[She] stares at the gear spread across the table. There is food,
tools, and a bunch of useless items. "What do you want to take?"
"The bag is awfully small," you say. "It will only fit three things."](else:)
[(set: $bag to (a:))You sigh and look at the stuff again. "I guess we really can
only take three things."]
You pack the bag:
(link: "Bread")[(set: $bag to $bag + (array: "Bread"))]
(link: "Water")[(set: $bag to $bag + (array: "Water"))]
(link: "Meat")[(set: $bag to $bag + (array: "Meat"))]
(link: "Ruby")[(set: $bag to $bag + (array: "Ruby"))]
(link: "Silver Key")[(set: $bag to $bag + (array: "Silver Key"))]
(link: "Yarn")[(set: $bag to $bag + (array: "Yarn"))]
(link: "Gold Coins")[(set: $bag to $bag + (array: "Gold Coins"))]
(link: "Wand")[(set: $bag to $bag + (array: "Wand"))]
(link: "Torch")[(set: $bag to $bag + (array: "Torch"))]
(link: "Shovel")[(set: $bag to $bag + (array: "Shovel"))]
(link: "Rope")[(set: $bag to $bag + (array: "Rope"))]
You hold up [[the bag|Contents of Bag]].
```

As you can see, you've learned a lot so far in the book, and this game is getting fairly complicated because you've been layering in everything you've learned so far. This passage begins by setting conditional text based on whether it's the player's first time through the passage: (if: (count: (history:), "Pack Bag") is 0).

It goes on to personalize the text displayed on the screen, including printing the character's names and using the proper pronoun in reference to the character's gender.

If the player has already been in this passage before, the (else:) macro resets the array with the piece of code in the hook attached to the (else:) macro: (set: $bag to (a:)). This ensures that all the earlier choices have been cleared out so the player can repack the bag. (More on that in the next passage!).

Finally, everyone gets an opportunity to pack (or repack) the bag after being given instructions to take only three things. When the player clicks the link at the bottom of the screen, he or she is taken into a final opening passage that checks the length of the $bag array. A player who has taken more than three items receives a message that sends her back to the previous passage to repack her bag.

But if the player has followed directions and taken three or fewer items, she is allowed to pass into the next part of the story. Here's the code to make this happen:

```
(if: $bag.length >=4)[You try to shove too many things in the bag, and you end up
dropping them all. You sigh and start over [[packing your bag.|Pack Bag]]](else:)
[You hoist your bag over your shoulder and nod to the others.
"This is what I've taken," you say.

(print: $bag.join ("\n"))
"I think we're ready to be on our way." You set out of the castle towards Elseworth.]
```

In this chapter, in a total of 12 passages, you've created three characters, allowed them to pack their bag, and set them on their journey. And with the exception of the (datamap:) macro, all other elements of this game were already in your Twine toolbox.

TRY IT OUT: ROLE-PLAYING GAME INVENTORY

Finish off your opening by allowing your characters to pack a bag of items that will come in handy during exploration, fighting, and problem solving in the next section of your game. Don't have your characters schlep around a bunch of stuff they'll never need. Make the items go with various puzzles, so different parts of the game will be accessible or solvable to the player based on what he or she is holding. If you are building an inventory and allowing the player to pick up more items during the game, make sure that you place a link to an inventory passage at the bottom of each screen, as discussed in Chapter 9.

In the next chapter, you're going to throw a lot of trouble at these characters and see how they get back (or not!) with the stolen crown.

13

Combat and Consequences in Role-Playing Games

In J.R.R. Tolkien's *Fellowship of the Ring*, Frodo and eight other characters volunteer during the Council of Elrond to destroy Sauron's ring in Mount Doom. All of them know that danger lurks ahead—after all, the Dark Lord isn't really the type to stand aside and let his ring be destroyed—but they go into the journey with a lot of hope and lembas.

That's the same conundrum your characters—the ones you created in Chapter 12, "Making a Role-Playing Game"—are currently in as they set out to retrieve the stolen crown. Sure, they suspect that they're going to run into danger, but they've chosen their class and rolled their trait levels, and they're ready to forge ahead, believing they will succeed in their quest.

Famous last words.

It's time to set your story into motion and give the players a chance to use the characters they've created. They may retrieve the crown, or they may have their head torn off by a monster. Of course, unlike in real life, where losing your head would be the end of the adventure, you may choose to give your players a second chance to reach the lost treasure. That's the beauty of battling beasts in a role-playing game.

In fact, that is the *point* of a role-playing game. People play these games because they want to be able to do things in the play world that they can't do in the real world either because it's too dangerous or impossible, such as casting spells, battling dragons, and hanging out with magical beings.

The same reasoning applies if you're leaving the well-worn sword-and-sorcery path. Give your players a chance to try on a different, incredible life. Maybe you're allowing the player to pretend that they live underwater in a limnad colony (yes, lake mermaids have their own name: limnads) that battles the Loch Ness Monster or go visit Mars and fight the elements. You can even have a time-traveling role-playing game, with the party moving through time and space, encountering monsters of historical and future existence.

Your game can be anything you want it to be, so get creative!

A solid role-playing game focuses on three main elements—exploration, strategic fighting, and puzzle solving—with one overarching goal informing every story choice: replayability.

Replayability is how many times the player can replay the game and experience a new situation or story. Remember back in Chapter 7, "Exploring Interactive Fiction Genres," when you made a *Clue*-like game called *Cooked*, using the (either:) macro? That game had high replayability because the weapon, room, and culprit were all randomly assigned by the game. Just like the board game *Clue*, a player could re-experience *Cooked* several times and each time encounter a different solution to the mystery.

Counter that with *Her Story*, a video interactive fiction game by Sam Barlow. The game is a lot of fun and takes a long time to play, but once you know the ending, there isn't a point to playing it a second time because the ending doesn't change. It's a mystery with a single solution.

Your role-playing game needs to fall somewhere between those two extremes. It will be hard to replicate the randomization that is possible with a very simple game like *Cooked* because you're now balancing the story for three players, but you can provide a basic level of replayability that is missing from *Her Story*.

You can achieve that replayability by keeping your goal front and center as you introduce those three important elements of a role-playing game: exploration, strategic fighting, and problem solving.

In terms of exploration, you'll be using the character traits set in Chapter 12 to create a multitude of routes to the battle scene. Then, when the players reach the monster, you can build replayability and chance into the game by utilizing the (either:) and (random:) macros during the fight. Finally, you'll set up a puzzle with multiple solutions to ensure that even the problem-solving portion of the game is enjoyable for several playthroughs.

While you work, your aim at all times is to create the highest level of replayability with the least number of passages. In other words, your job as the creator of the world is to figure out how to do a lot while using little. It is not to create a system so unwieldy that you can't finish making the game. Luckily, this chapter provides a lot of guidance on starting, working on, and finishing games by approaching them in manageable chunks.

Finally, tabletop role-playing games are led by a game master (GM). Of course you, brave writer, are the game master for this game, and your job is to provide the players with an immersive experience. Make the players believe they are inside the story, not sitting on their sofas, reading your game. They're in the forest, going after a stolen crown, positive that danger will lie in the path but unsure of what the journey holds.

One of the hallmarks of tabletop role-playing games is the game master's ability to respond to any action the players throw into the storyline. Moving the game to the screen removes some of the spontaneity and creativity that exists in a pen-and-paper role-playing game. The computer can only produce the results it is programmed to produce, which means the game master can't think on his or her feet, listening to the choices made by the players and reacting accordingly.

It's a trade-off, certainly, but it's one that I believe ultimately makes role-playing games so much fun to create. Your job as writer is to be a game master with mad premonitory skills.

Instead of waiting for the player to suggest a course of action, you need to implement creative problem-solving into the choices.

Give players straightforward options, such as "stab the beast" when fighting a monster, but also provide ideas off the beaten path, such as "bore the monster to death with a poetry slam" or "scare monster with fake snake in can" that would come up in a pen-and-paper role-playing game. In fact, a good way to gather ideas for your game is to beta test a copy and ask the players for other choices they wished had been included in the game. Sometimes making a good role-playing game takes a group effort.

If building the character back in Chapter 12 was the first "chapter" of your story game, exploration is the second "chapter." Let's take a close look now at the traits established at the beginning of the game.

Exploring the World

Right now, you're 12 passages or so into the game, and your characters are in the woods. You need to get them to the battle site. An easy way to build replayability into the exploration portion of your game is to create numerous paths that all converge in the monster's lair.

Exploration needs to be part of the story, and the exploration itself can tell a lot about the characters. Are they fearless or timid? Brilliant or dim? How do they interact with one another on the path? Do they have everything they need for their journey?

There are three built-in story elements you can use to set up "gates" that determine access to the various exploration paths that lead to the battle portion of the game: the personal characteristics, traits, and items you established in Chapter 12 while building the characters.

This chapter continues with the examples established in Chapter 12. Obviously, if you swapped out the characteristics, traits, or items I suggested for ones that fit your storyline, you should substitute your own options into the examples later in this chapter.

Using Personal Characteristics

Back in Chapter 12, you allowed the players to make two choices: whether they are tall or short and whether they are fat or thin. It's time to make those choices mean something.

You need a passage or two to establish the setting after the player characters leave the castle. Remember that you are not only a player's eyes and ears; you are his or her nose, tongue, and hands. So use all five senses to describe what the player characters are encountering along the route.

The player characters need to come to a physical space where their personal characteristics can either aid or hinder them from moving forward. By using conditional statements created with the (if:) and (else:) macros, set up four diverging story paths.

Call the current passage Crossroads and set up a scene where the first player needs to choose the direction the team will go:

```
(if: (count: (history:), "Crossroads") is 0)[As you turn the corner, the road you
are on abruptly splits into four paths. The first disappears down a gentle slope to
the west. The second trudges uphill to the north. The third snakes deep into the
fields to the east. And the fourth continues directly toward Elseworth, through the
heart of Creeping Forest to the south.](else:)[You return to the crossroads and
examine the remaining paths.]
Do you want to go [[west|West]], [[north|North]], [[east|East]], or [[south|South]]?
```

In this passage, you use the (count:) macro in combination with the (history:) macro in order to have different text display based on whether this is the player's first time through the passage. This Crossroads passage becomes a hub, giving the player the freedom to choose a direction, though his or her success with that path depends on the chosen physical characteristics of the second player.

Why does the first character's success depend on the second player specifically? There's no reason, really, except that *a* player needs to be chosen to serve as the "key" for getting through the "gate." There is not a literal key and gate, but the characteristic the player is carrying in his or her datamap is the key that unlocks the passage that is geared toward a specific characteristic. Because each player has two of the possible four characteristics in his or her datamap (tall, short, fat, and thin), the party will be successful in two directions and unsuccessful in two directions every time they play the game.

You can visually see this passage as a hub if the four attached passages are dragged into their corresponding positions, as shown in Figure 13.1.

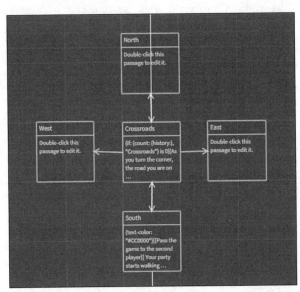

FIGURE 13.1 The Crossroads passage serves as a hub, with the four attached passages dragged into positions corresponding to their names.

This exploration section moves the game from a story focus to a space focus, and because of that, you may want to provide the player with a drawn map, such as the one in Figure 13.2, to accompany the game.

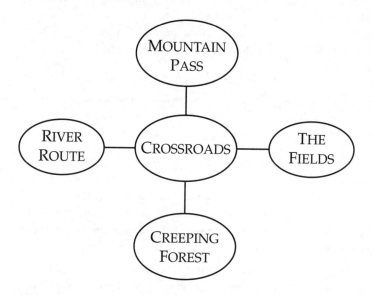

FIGURE 13.2   Include a map with your game if you want the game to move back and forth from a story focus to a space focus.

Making Consequences

What happens if the players go in the various directions? If they go west, they come to a river that they can cross only if they are tall enough to untie a rowboat's rope from a high-up branch on a nearby tree. If they are too short, they must backtrack to the Crossroads passage.

If they go east, they have to sneak by a magical scarecrow set up for surveillance in the field. If they're small enough, they can creep past. If they're too tall, they are encouraged to back-track to the Crossroads passage or risk dying if caught by the scarecrow.

If they go north, they need to have enough heft to move a boulder from the mountain path. On the other hand, if they go south, they need to be thin enough to slip into a hollow in the Endless Tree in order to pass. In both cases, if their body doesn't fit the needs of the space, they have to go back to the Crossroads passage.

Let's look at the South passage as an example:

```
(text-color: "#CC0000")[(Pass the game to the second player)]
Your party starts walking toward the Creeping Forest. Leaves crunch ominously
underfoot, sounding like grinding bones and snapping tendons. It isn't long before
```

```
you come to the fabled Endless Tree, an infinite trunk that stretches forever,
blocking access to the dangerous forest.
There is a very narrow slit in the wood, a hollow that you could squeeze into if
you're small enough. Your name, (print: $character2's "Name"), appears on a crude
wooden sign above the slit, almost like an invitation.
(if: $character2's "Weight" is "Fat")[You try to squeeze inside, but you are too
big to fit into the hollow. You nod to the others and head back to the
[[crossroads|Crossroads]].](elseif: $character2's "Weight" is "Thin")["I think I
can squeeze in there," you tell the others. You turn your body sideways and wedge
yourself into the tight space. You breathe out once you're on the other side.
There is a [[small door|Southern 1]] accessible from this side, and you open it to
allow the rest of your party to enter.]
```

In this passage, you describe the scene and ask Twine to check the datamap to see the data value for the data name `"Weight"`. If the data value is `"Fat"`, the player receives one set of text and a link, and if the data value is `"Thin"`, the player receives a different set of text and a link. The South passage serves as a gate to the southern area of the game, and the data value is the key that either allows the player to pass into that area or sends him or her back to the Crossroads passage to try a different path.

The passage begins by telling the players to pass the game to Player 2. After some plain text, you personalize the game by adding in Player 2's name, taken from the datamap where it was set back in Chapter 12: `(print: $character2's "Name")`.

Then there is a conditional statement created with the `(if:)` and `(elseif:)` macros that checks the data value in the datamap for the data name `"Weight"`. If the data value is `"Fat"`, the player sees the text and link in the first hook, as shown in Figure 13.3.

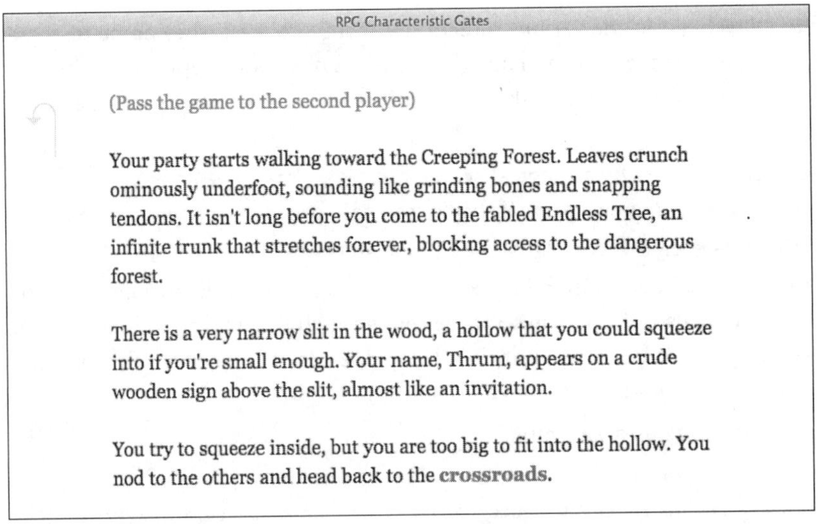

FIGURE 13.3   The text in the first hook displays if the data value for `"Weight"` is `"Fat"`.

If the data value is "Thin", the player sees the text and link in the second hook, as shown in Figure 13.4.

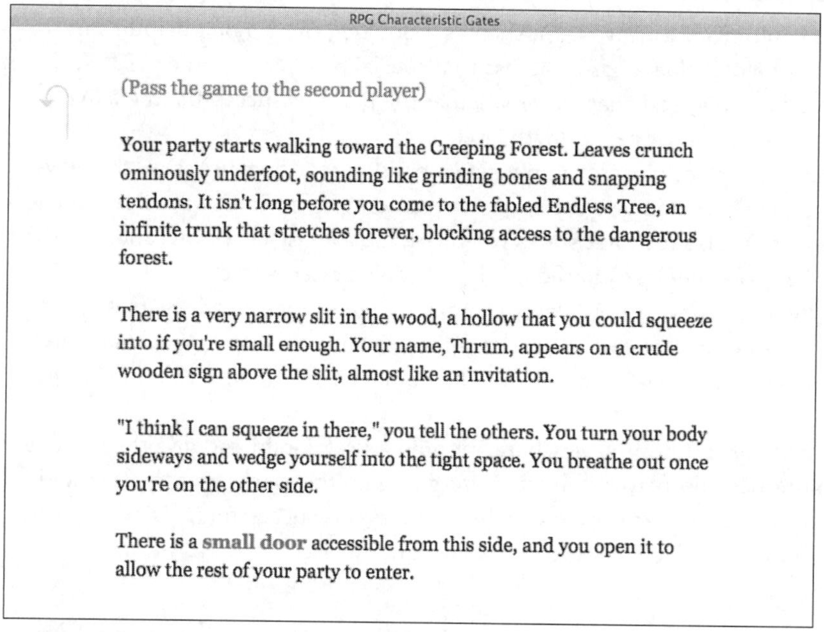

RPG Characteristic Gates

(Pass the game to the second player)

Your party starts walking toward the Creeping Forest. Leaves crunch ominously underfoot, sounding like grinding bones and snapping tendons. It isn't long before you come to the fabled Endless Tree, an infinite trunk that stretches forever, blocking access to the dangerous forest.

There is a very narrow slit in the wood, a hollow that you could squeeze into if you're small enough. Your name, Thrum, appears on a crude wooden sign above the slit, almost like an invitation.

"I think I can squeeze in there," you tell the others. You turn your body sideways and wedge yourself into the tight space. You breathe out once you're on the other side.

There is a **small door** accessible from this side, and you open it to allow the rest of your party to enter.

FIGURE 13.4 The text in the second hook displays if the data value for "Weight" is "Thin".

If the player is able to pass through the slit in the Endless Tree, he or she finds a door on the other side that can open to allow the rest of the party to enter the area.

On the other side, you stick with the spatial focus, giving Player 3 several sections of forest to access with directional choices, such as "go east" or "go west."

To make exploring the forest more interesting, you can hide some items the player can use for battle. Incorporate the lessons learned in Chapter 3, "Creating a Vivid Setting," to use the (link:) macro to hide [[links]], or use the (count:) and (history:) macros together to have the item appear only after the player has passed through the section several times. Also consider how found items change the game play. If a player picks up items, can she use them later in the game? What about that foreshadowing clue that the king gave at the beginning of the game? Should stuff be left on the ground, lest it harm the player when he tries to return to the kingdom?

Using Traits

You set a number of traits in Chapter 12—strength, dexterity, intelligence, and charm—and you can use them to add replayability to the exploration portion of the game. While these traits play a starring role in the battle section, determining the success of a player character's actions, they can also be used to create key-and-gate situations in the exploration section. Consider these examples:

- **Strength**—You could place a heavy item, such as a boulder, on top of a helpful clue. Having seen that helpful clue leads to access to a special passage. Use the (if:) and (else:) macros to display text that states whether the player is successful in reaching that passage, based on his or her strength level.

- **Dexterity**—You could place a useful item inside a balloon that floats past on the player's first visit to the space and give the player the option to grab it. Use the (if:) and (else:) macros to display text that states whether the player is successful (and add the item to his or her inventory if so) based on the person's dexterity level.

- **Intelligence**—You could have a non-player character who is blocking access to a special passage propose a riddle. Use the (if:) and (else:) macros to display text that states whether the player is successful in answering the riddle, based on his or her intelligence level.

- **Charm**—You could have a non-player character hold a useful item and give the player a chance to charm that non-player character into giving up the item. Use the (if:) and (else:) macros to display text stating whether the player is successful (and add the item to the player's inventory if so) based on his or her charm level.

Using Items

Remember how you had Player 1 pack the bag in Chapter 12? When you did this, you created an array holding three items. It's time to make those items mean something.

You can create a wandering non-player character and have him or her appear only the first time the player characters enter the passage. You can have the non-player character remain in the passage but ignore the characters on every encounter after the first one. To do this, you need to use the (history:) macro as you usually do to have different text appear on the first visit as opposed to subsequent visits.

To add more variation with fewer passages, use the (either:) macro to set a value to the newly created $visitor variable. Yes, this non-player character will be a variable! Here's how it looks:

```
(if: (count: (history:), "Clearing") is 0)[(set: $visitor to (either: "old woman",
"old man", "young woman", "young man"))You enter the clearing and see (if: $visitor
is "old woman")[an elderly woman wringing her hands. "Do you have any yarn?" she
asks. (if: $bag contains "Yarn")["[[Yes|Clue 1]]," you say, reaching into your bag.]
(else:)["No, I'm sorry. I don't."]](elseif: $visitor is "old man")[an elderly man
eyeing your bag. "Any chance you have a ruby?" he asks. (if: $bag contains "Ruby")
["[[Uh... yes, I do|Clue 1]]," you say, reaching into your bag.]
(else:)["No, I'm sorry. I don't."]](elseif: $visitor is "young woman")[a young
woman holding a box. "Any chance you have a key?" she asks. "A little silver key?"
```

```
(if: $bag contains "Silver Key")["[[Actually, I do have a key|Clue 1]]," you say,
reaching into your bag.]
(else:)["No, I'm sorry. I don't."]](elseif: $visitor is "young man")[a young man
eyeing your bag. "Any chance you have some coins?" he asks. "I'd trade you a clue
if you give me some money." (if: $bag contains "Gold Coins")["[[Sure, I'll trade you|
Clue 1]]," you say, reaching into your bag.]
(else:)["No, I'm sorry. I don't."]]](else:)[You return to the clearing where the
(print: $visitor) is leaning against a tree, ignoring you.]
[[East|Eastern Path]]
[[West|Western Path]]
```

With this single passage, you have created a plethora of variation. The first time the player enters the clearing, as set by the (count:) and (history:) macros at the beginning of the passage—(if: (count: (history:), "Clearing") is 0)—the variable $visitor is set with one of four string values using the (either:) macro.

It's important to assign the value for the variable inside this first enormous hook rather than in the second hook the player sees on all subsequent visits to this passage because you don't want the value for the variable to change once it has been set. It would be a little odd to have the player first encounter an old woman upon entering this passage and then see a young man on every other time through.

And it really is an enormous hook if it is the player's first time through the passage. In Figure 13.5, I've highlighted from the opening bracket to the closing bracket of the first hook.

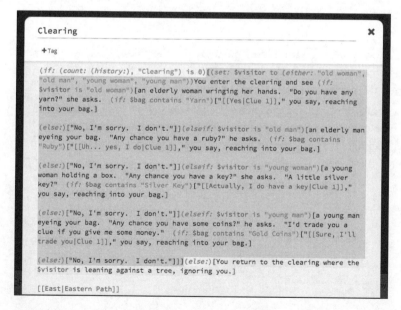

FIGURE 13.5 The opening and closing square brackets for the first hook are highlighted in this passage. Inside the first hook are numerous other hooks.

It is easy to get confused and leave out a bracket because there are so many hooks inside hooks in this passage, creating all that variation (and, by extension, replayability) in a very small space. Luckily, Twine highlights errors on the screen, though it does not tell you what punctuation is missing. Still, it is helpful to see that *something* is missing, even if it means you have to spend time combing the passage to find where you forgot a single square bracket.

So the value for the variable $visitor is randomly set, and then a series of possibilities play out in nested hooks inside the main first hook. If the value for $visitor is "old woman", the player character is asked if she has yarn in her bag. Twine then checks the array $bag and displays one of two responses, via the (if:) and (else:) macros. If the player has the yarn, she says yes and is provided a link to a special, secret passage. If the player doesn't have yarn, she apologizes and is given the two choices at the bottom of the passage: go east or go west.

Of course, if the value of $visitor is randomly set to one of the other options—the old man, young woman, or young man—the player is asked for a different item, which means the player can't predict while packing the bag in the beginning which item he or she might need on subsequent game plays since it depends on chance.

The second hook using the (else:) macro, which displays on all subsequent visits to the passage, has a simple message about the non-player character leaning against the tree, ignoring the player characters. Because the string used to set the value for the variable is also understandable as a description, you use the (print:) macro to state the value. Therefore, if the value of $visitor is "old woman", the player sees this:

```
You return to the clearing where the old woman is leaning against a tree, ignoring
you.
```

The point of the interaction is to get to the Clue 1 passage. In that passage, the non-player character gives the player character a clue about battling the monster, and that clue is an invaluable weapon when the player gets to the battle scene.

How does Twine know that the player has this clue? The option to kick the monster in its weak point, lessening its health by many points at a time, will be visible only if the player has been to the Clue 1 passage. If Twine checks its history and sees that the passage hasn't been visited, the player cannot see that option.

TRY IT OUT: ROLE-PLAYING GAME EXPLORATION

Open up your game and work on the exploration portion of the game, using the ideas given so far in this chapter. Make sure you have your characters quickly reach a hub-like space that you can use to send them in multiple directions.

Don't feel overwhelmed as you look in the four directions leading off from the hub that you'll need to fill. You can copy and paste the content of passages and change the plain text and details while keeping the same script. In other words, if the player encounters a dragon when he goes to the east, he may encounter a unicorn who does the opposite from the dragon when the player goes west. The script from the dragon passage can be brought over and tweaked for the unicorn passage to give the player a unique experience without a lot of extra work for you, the writer.

Take your time with this aspect of the game. It may take you several hours to get through this section of game creation. Therefore, you may want to break down the work into several sessions and tackle one direction at a time.

Remember that the point of the exploration passages is to set the scene and make the players feel as if they are there in the forest. Describe the sights, sounds, and smells and include as much detail as possible without going overboard with words. Your players don't just want to read; they want to do—and there is a lot they're going to do in the next phase, which you can think of as the third "chapter" of the role-playing game: battle!

Battling Monsters

All four directions need to lead to a single spot: the opening of the monster's lair. Tabletop games have plenty of monsters that behave according to a preset list of rules. This section shows how to make a disgusting, scaly-hide monster that reeks of rotting orange peels and singed hair.

A lot of the replayability for the battle scene comes from allowing Twine to decide whether the player character is successful or not in his or her attempt to harm the monster. You can make this happen in two ways: by using the (either:) and (random:) macros or by setting up the game to take the levels of various traits into account and assign success accordingly.

Either way, you need to build a turn-based system, which means that the first player chooses an action and learns whether the action was successful and, if it was, the effect it had on the creature. Then the second player chooses an action, and, again, learns whether it was a hit or a miss and how much damage was achieved. Finally, the third player goes, the beast gains or loses power, and then the whole process starts all over again. It's not very realistic if you think about it too much; after all, beasts don't generally hang out, patiently waiting for people to attack it, one at a time. Then again, you're battling a nameless beast that reeks of rotting orange peels and singed hair: You're already not in the most realistic of situations.

Turn-based battles tap into a favorite human pastime: gambling. In interactive fiction, though, instead of gambling with money, you're gambling with hit points. You get that gambling high because you are betting something of value (a character you love) against the action. You may win, or you may lose.

This sample game assumes that the third player has navigated the exploration area. If you had the players pass around the game, adjust the details in this example accordingly.

You need to have all the various paths lead to a single passage called Opening Battle and then write this in it:

```
(set: $beastHealth to 75)You smell the beast before you see the beast, a rank,
damp smell of rotting orange peels and singed hair. As you turn the corner, your
sword glows blue, and the beast lunges at you before you have a chance to get
your bearings.
To begin the battle, pass the game to [[Player 1|Options]].
```

Here you've set the scene using a lot of sensory information.

Starting the Fight

Here's how you can set up the options for the first player:

```
(text-color: "#CC0000")[Player 1, what do you want to do?]
Player 1's health is (print: $character1's "Health").
Player 2's health is (print: $character2's "Health").
Player 3's health is (print: $character3's "Health").
(if: $beastHealth <= 0)[(goto: "Beast Death")](else:)[The beast's health is
(print: $beastHealth).]
(if: (history:) contains "Clue 1")[You remember the words of the $visitor. Do you
want to [[kick the monster's knee|Kick]], [[stab the beast with the sword|Stab]],
[[cast a spell|Spell]], or [[punch the beast with your fist|Punch]]?](else:)[Do you
want to [[stab the beast with the sword|Stab]], [[cast a spell|Spell]], or [[punch
the beast with your fist|Punch]]?]
```

Here you start off the options by printing the health levels of the beast and each of the players. Though this example doesn't include the option, one variation would be to allow a player to not battle the monster and instead pass his or her turn to a player with a higher health score; in that case, printing the player's health would be invaluable. A player who sees that he or she is close to death could refrain from jumping into the battle and setting back the whole team. This example isn't so elaborate, though; the health levels are stated just to give the players a sense of how close they are to finishing the task...or being finished by the beast.

If Twine checks the beast's health level and it is above zero, it prints the current value for the variable $beastHealth. If Twine checks the beast's health level and it is at or below zero, the player is transported to an exit passage called Beast Death. This is the ultimate goal: to exit the battle area and enter the next "chapter," which is the puzzle-solving portion of the game.

A side note: Because you use the (goto:) macro in this example, the Beast Death passage is not automatically generated. Instead, you need to use the green +Passage button to add the passage and put some placeholder text in the passage:

```
The beast goes up in a puff of smoke. All three of you stand there, panting,
wiping down your swords.
```

Back in the Fight passage, the player is then given either three or four choices. All players get three basic choices: stab the beast with the sword, cast a spell, or punch the beast with your fist. If the player went to the Clue 1 passage during the exploration phase, she sees one additional option: [[kick the monster's knee|Kick]].

Moving on to the Kick passage, write this:

```
(set: $beastHealth to it - 25)You kick the beast's knee and he howls in pain.
[[You gauge your success|Options2]].
```

It's a simple, straightforward action: When the player who has the extra choice kicks the beast, she is guaranteed to do 25 hit points of damage without losing any health points herself; it's clearly a reward for getting the clue in the exploration portion of the game to be able to use this ability in the battle portion.

Of course, there are still three other possible battle options the player may choose (stab, cast a spell, or punch), and you have to fill the passages for those options. Here's what the Stab passage might look like this:

```
You stab your sword into the beast.
(if: $character1's "Strength" >= 60)[(set: $beastHealth to it - 20)(set:
$character1's "Health" to it + 5)You get a good hit to his soft underbelly.]
(elseif: $character1's "Strength" <= 59)[(set: $beastHealth to it + 5)(set:
$character1's "Health" to it - 20)You miss, enraging the beast, which seems to make
it draw strength from an unknown well of health.]
(if: $character1's "Health" <= 0)[You take your last breath, gasping as the life
leaves your body. All three of you are transported instantly to the
[[world beyond.|World Beyond]]](else:)[[[You gauge your success|Options2]].]
```

This option, as you'll see with the other options, uses the player's trait levels to determine success. It uses the (if:) and (else:) macros to see whether the player's strength levels are above or below 60 points. If the player's strength is equal to or above 60 points, the first hook is triggered, setting a new value for the $beastHealth variable (subtracting 20 hit points) as well as the player's health (adding 5 hit points). It also displays the accompanying text inside the hook.

On the other hand, if the player's strength is equal to or below 59, the opposite occurs: The `$beastHealth` variable increases in value by 5 hit points, the player's health decreases by 20 hit points, and the text reflects a very different outcome for the action.

In the last paragraph, Twine checks the player's health data value in the datamap. If it's at or below zero, the player sees that he or she has been transported to the world beyond. If the health data value is above zero, the player receives the instructions to "gauge your success," and the game moves to Player 2's set of options.

Similarly, the other two core choices—casting a spell and punching the beast—behave in a similar manner. In the Spell passage, you can use the player's class to determine success:

```
You attempt to cast a spell.
(if: $character1's "Class" is "Wizard")[(set: $beastHealth to it - 30)(set:
$character1's "Health" to it + 5)You feel the energy flow out your fingers and
watch a blue light hit the beast in the center of his chest. He howls with
rage.](else:)[(set: $beastHealth to it + 5)(set: $character1's "Health" to it - 10)
You've attempt to harness magic, but it drains you instead, filling the beast
with health.]
(if: $character1's "Health" <= 0)[You take your last breath, gasping as the life
leaves your body. All three of you are transported instantly to the
[[world beyond.|World Beyond]]](else:)[[[You gauge your success|Options2]].]
```

And in the Punch passage, you can return to checking the player's strength to determine the outcome of the action:

```
You pummel the beast with your fist and jump away.
(if: $character1's "Strength" >= 60)[(set: $beastHealth to it - 20)(set:
$character1's "Health" to it + 5)Your hit seems to have stunned him.](elseif:
$character1's "Strength" <= 59)[(set: $beastHealth to it + 5)(set: $character1's
"Health" to it - 20)You miss, enraging the beast, which seems to make it draw
strength from an unknown well of health.]
(if: $character1's "Health" <= 0)[You take your last breath, gasping as the life
leaves your body. All three of you are transported instantly to the
[[world beyond.|World Beyond]]](else:)[[[You gauge your success|Options2]].]
```

Each of the options accounts for the possibility that the player may be down to zero hit points. When that happens, the player is forced to continue to the World Beyond passage, which serves as a gentle end point, one that allows the players to restart the game or end the game entirely:

```
"Wait a second," you say, "only one of us died. Why are we all in the underworld?"
"When you entered the quest, your fates were tied to one another. If one dies, the
rest of you die, too," says a disembodied voice.
"That doesn't seem... fair," you say.
"That's the way it goes," the disembodied voice replies. "I will, on the other
hand, give you the option to return to the point where you made the decision. Would
```

you like to go back in time to the [[starting point|Game Opening]]? Or would you prefer to stay down here in the [[World Beyond|End Game]]?"

The player either chooses to end the game entirely with End Game, where you can bid your players farewell and tell them their ending point levels, or they can all return to the first passage, where the datamaps and array are reset and rebuilt and try again with newfound knowledge.

Continuing the Fight

If you've been following along with Chapter 12 and this chapter, you now have your first level of battle set with eight main passages: the battle opening, the battle options, the four action passages, the beast's death, and the players' deaths. You can see the opening for the battle section in Figure 13.6.

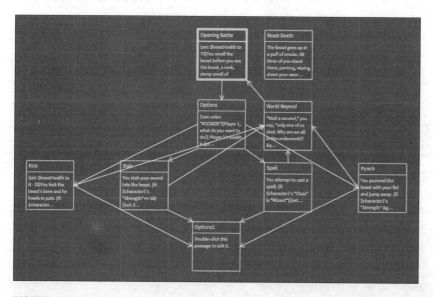

FIGURE 13.6 Eight passages construct the opening for the battle segment.

The hard work of writing the battle segment is done. The player only needs to repeat five of the passages, changing all the script to reflect $character2's datamap (instead of $character1's datamap). To do this, copy and paste the text from Options to Options2 and change the text and script for the new player:

```
(text-color: "#CC0000")[Player 2, what do you want to do?]
```

```
Player 1's health is (print: $character1's "Health").
Player 2's health is (print: $character2's "Health").
Player 3's health is (print: $character3's "Health").
```

```
(if: $beastHealth <= 0)[(goto: "Beast Death")](else:)[The beast's health is
(print: $beastHealth).]
```

```
(if: (history:) contains "Clue 1")[You remember the words of the $visitor. Do you
want to [[kick the monster's knee|Kick2]], [[stab the beast with the sword|Stab2]],
[[cast a spell|Spell2]], or [[punch the beast with your fist|Punch2]]?](else:)
[Do you want to [[stab the beast with the sword|Stab2]], [[cast a spell|Spell2]],
or [[punch the beast with your fist|Punch2]]?]
```

Similarly, you can copy and paste the text from the original Kick, Stab, Spell, and Punch passages into their second-round counterparts. Make sure you update the text and code to reflect the second player.

Finally, do the same thing one more time for $character3's datamap, taking care to lead back to the first player when his or her actions are complete. The three players can pass the game back and forth, taking turns stabbing or punching the monster until they are either killed or the monster is dead.

With 18 passages, you can construct a turn-based battle scene, as shown in Figure 13.7.

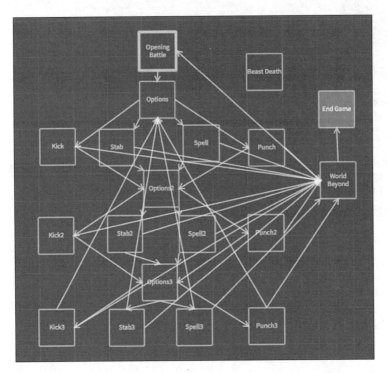

FIGURE 13.7 Nineteen passages construct the opening for the battle segment.

TRY IT OUT: ROLE-PLAYING GAME BATTLE

Build your own battle segment, using the ideas presented in this section. You need to decide whether to have the game base the success of the action on already established trait levels or whether to use what you know about the (either:) and (random:) macros from Chapter 7.

You should be able to write this section of the game in one sitting. The most time-consuming aspect is likely to be deciding how you want to reward or remove hit points.

Unless you are planning to move your players into multiple exploration segments and battle scenes, you've reached the final "chapter" of your game: the puzzle.

Solving Puzzles

Luckily, you've already had a lot of experience building challenging puzzles in other chapters in this book, but it's worth pausing for a moment to talk about how to build replayability into your puzzle segments.

If a puzzle has only one solution, this portion of the game will quickly become boring on subsequent playthroughs. Therefore, in the puzzle section you want to use randomness to make the playing experience unique each time the game is opened. For example, you can use the (either:) macro to have Twine randomly generate the solution.

In the sample game, once the monster disappears, the player characters see that it was guarding a wooden box. They're warned that the box could be booby-trapped and given a choice of whether to open it. If they open the box, it duplicates six times, each copy identical to the original, with one exception: the color of the box. At this point, the winning box is marked using the (set:) macro in conjunction with the (either:) macro, and the variable $box is given a string value of a color:

```
(set: $box to (either: "red", "orange", "yellow", "green", "blue", "purple"))
```

The player is then presented with a choice. This "Examine Boxes" passage is used in all subsequent passages with the (display:) macro, so you want to keep it simple:

```
You lean over and examine each box in turn. As you hover over [one]<magic| of the
boxes, you feel a strange twinge of magic.

Do you want to choose the [[red box|Red Box]], [[orange box|Orange Box]],
[[yellow box|Yellow Box]], [[green box|Green Box]], [[blue box|Blue Box]], or
[[purple box|Purple Box]]?

(mouseover-append: ?magic)[ (a flash of (print: $box)!) ]
```

Here you are being kind and giving the player a little clue. If a player happens to mouse over the word one onscreen, he or she receives a little message stating the color of the correct box. If the player does not mouse over one, it comes down to chance. In each color-based passage, you can use the same text and script but tweaked to state the appropriate color. Here is what one of the color passages (Red Box) would look like:

```
(if: $box is "red")[You pick up the red box and turn it over, examining the strange
concave glass in the lid and the four metal spikes protruding from its sides. You
notice a small button in one corner and [[press it|Magic Box]].](else:)[(set:
$character3's "Health" to it - 10)You pick up the red box and turn it over,
examining the strange concave glass in the lid and the four metal spikes protruding
from its sides. You feel energy drain out of your body, and when you check your
health, you can see that it's down to (print: $character3's "Health").

(if: $character3's "Health" <= 0)[You feel your [[life|Dead]] leave your
body.](else:)[(display: "Examine Boxes")]]
```

If the randomly assigned value of $box is "red", the player sees the text in the first hook, which includes a hidden link to the passage Magic Box. If the randomly assigned value of $box is not "red", the second hook is triggered, removing 10 hit points from $character3's health. When Player 3's hit points are gone, the trio is transported once again to an ending (with an offer to restart the game), but until then, the choices display again, and the player is given a second, third, or fourth chance to find the correct box. You can use the same text in the other passages, tweaking the color to reflect the value of the $box.

Of course, you may choose a completely different sort of puzzle for your game, such as a useful item puzzle based on something in the players' inventory. Just make sure that multiple routes lead to the solution or have the solution randomly generated in order to have the game change with each playthrough.

TRY IT OUT: ROLE-PLAYING GAME PUZZLE

It's time for you to build the final piece of your role-playing game—the puzzle—using the ideas described in this section. Decide whether you want your puzzle's solution to take into account a character's class, characteristics, or traits. In addition, decide whether you want to have consequences for wrong answers or allow a player to guess at the solution until he or she finds it.

You should be able to complete this section in one sitting.

Writing a Conclusion

It's time to write the final section, which is a brief conclusion. Do the players bring back the crown to the kingdom? Do they decide to steal it and set up their own principality on the other side of the Creeping Forest? Whatever conclusion you come up with, congratulations! You've written a complete role-playing game! Now go grab two friends and play it, or build and manage all three player characters and enjoy it on your own.

Taking Your Role-Playing Game to the Next Level

Now that you know the basic layout of a role-playing game, it's easy to apply this model to a much larger game. The key is to treat each of the core elements—exploration, strategic fighting, and problem solving—as equal ingredients, putting dashes of all three in the story. For instance, after the players get the crown from the magic box, they may steal it and travel to a new land (exploration), where they have to battle vampires to claim a castle (strategic fighting). Victorious, they may then trek down into the dungeon (exploration), which is infested with talking snakes (strategic fighting) that turn into water as they're killed, threatening to drown the players (problem solving).

Another aspect of tabletop role-playing games that you may want to incorporate into your own games is the idea of allowing players to level up after succeeding at a particularly difficult task. Of course, leveling up should mean something, such as a player obtaining new skills or a new weapon. Leveling up makes your game's difficulty trickier to manage as you must consider that not all players will reach an encounter at the same level.

In addition, you may want to consider printing out the final statistics at the end of the game and allowing players to input those numeric levels into the sequel to your game; you could enable this by using the (prompt:) macro. Once your players have fallen in love with the world you've created and the characters they've built, they'll want to be able to jump into another adventure with familiar friends.

If at any time you're struggling to come up with a good storyline or situation for your player characters, look back at Chapter 5, "Building Objects with Variables," and choose a quest. Remember, the point of a quest is to give the player a purpose, and agency is the key to an enjoyable quest in a role-playing game.

Breaking Down Game Writing into Manageable Chunks

Through the exercise in this chapter, you have learned an even more important skill than setting up role-playing games: You have learned how to break up large projects into small, manageable sections in order to make completion probable. It's easy to start a project, especially when the ideas are flowing and everything feels new and exciting. People tend to start projects when they have a window of time.

But that doesn't mean that the window of time remains open for as long as it takes to write a complex game. Life gets in the way, and writer's block and coding obstacles may throw the writing process further off-course. It may seem easier to give up than to power through and finish up a game.

Instead of thinking of your game as a single entity, consider it an amalgamation of chapters. Think of your goal as sitting down and writing each individual section, not worrying about all the sections at once and not going on to the next section until you've closed up the one before it.

Moreover, I always recommend not sitting down and starting a section if you don't have time to complete it. By keeping the sections small, you will associate writing time with working toward and completing a goal. This is much less scary than sitting down and feeling like you need to produce a whole game and failing when you can't do it in one fell swoop.

If you look at the sample game in this chapter, you'll notice that each "chapter" can be written to completion within an hour or two. First, the character-building section is constructed, then the exploration section is broken down into four manageable chunks, then the battle scene is written, and finally the puzzle is introduced and solved. Seven sections means seven writing sessions.

This shift in thinking is applicable to any game you make. You can make your load lighter by working with set stopping points and goals. Yes, you still end up doing the same amount of work, but it is much less daunting to think about writing seven small sections than it is to think about writing one large unwieldy game. Consider this your own personal Jedi mind trick.

I've spent a lot of time in this chapter focusing on words, but you got a small glimpse of another side of Twine in this chapter when you changed the color of the text to make it noticeable for the players. In the next chapter, you'll learn how to make your words wiggle, enlarge, change color, and fade out. It's time focus for a bit on the visual experience of a game.

Wiggling Words: Changing the Text Appearance

Star Wars: A New Hope opens with that iconic line: "A long time ago in a galaxy far, far away...." The words fade out, and the Star Wars icon bursts onto the screen as the music plays. The icon gets sucked backward, almost like a spaceship attempting to leave Earth's orbit, and as it disappears into the far distance, words begin scrolling onto the screen, telling the backstory of *A New Hope*.

The movie creators could have had the words move like movie credits, beginning as a straight line at the bottom of the screen and traveling upward at a slow pace. But that's not the way the words appear. Instead, the words take the same trajectory as the Star Wars icon, starting big to convey that they're close to the viewer and slowly getting smaller as they travel into the distance on the screen. They're heading toward an invisible central point somewhere in the infinite blackness of space. It makes the viewers, sitting comfortably in the movie theater, feel as if they're traveling among the stars, too. Just presenting the words at a different angle and making them move like a slow-traveling spaceship changes the way the viewer interacts with the movie.

Guess what? You can add cool effects like that with Twine.

In fact, a lot of interactive fiction authors borrow from comic book artists, who have long played with the presentation of words to convey extra meaning within simple phrasing. Writing the words "He punched him in the face, Bam!" feels very different when it's presented as it is in Figure 14.1.

He punched him in the face, ***Bam!***

FIGURE 14.1   A font change packs a big punch.

Changing the font, playing with letter size, and having the words appear (and disappear) on the screen in untraditional ways all add to game play. Matthias Conrady uses visual tweaks to great effect in his game *Alice Falling*, which is based on Lewis Carroll's book *Alice's Adventure in Wonderland*.

The game opens with blue words on a black screen and a single, salmon-colored word: "rabbit-hole." Click it, and the words slide off the screen to the left as if they're running away. A click or two later, and the words look as if they are falling down a hole. With each click, the words from the book travel up the screen, bringing the reader farther and farther down a dark tunnel, like Alice. It's only a transition effect, but it makes Carroll's words come alive. The reader feels as if he or she is falling, too, instead of just reading about it.

This chapter steps away from the logistics of writing compelling games and focuses on the presentation of words. By using simple changer macros, you can play with fonts, style, color, and transitions. Of course, you should use all of these visual elements sparingly so the appearance of the words doesn't distract the player from the meaning of the words. Nothing gives a reader a headache faster than having to navigate too many colors and text styles on the same screen.

Changing Fonts

A long time ago (in a galaxy far, far away!), a *font* was one element of a *typeface*, but today, in the digital age, people use the two terms interchangeably. What I mean when I talk about *font* in this book is the design of a letter.

Take a look at the letters making up the words in this book. They all have a similar look and feel. You may not have given this a lot of thought before right now, but someone needed to *design* these letters; they didn't just spring into being. An artist had to think about the height of each letter and the sizes of the counters (the enclosed spaces inside letters like *b* and *p*) and the tapered curves of the finials (like the part that hangs from the top of a lowercase *f*).

Each font has a personality. The font in this book is called ITC Legacy Sans. ITC Legacy Sans looks very different from other fonts, such as Times New Roman or **Comic Sans**. The artist who made the font wanted to mimic the feel of an old typeface used in a classic Roman text. It's pretty simple and straightforward, unadorned, and unfussy—a perfect font for a computer book that educates.

So think about it: What is the perfect font for *your* game?

Adding a New Font

The default font for the Harlowe format—which is the format you've been using in Twine—is Georgia. It's an elegant font with small embellishments, such as ball terminals (the little knobby dot hanging off the top of a lowercase *a*), but overall it's pretty simple. Maybe Georgia is perfect for your project, or maybe you want something different.

If you want to change the font in Twine, you use the `(font:)` macro combined with a string command, where the string is the name of the font:

```
(font: "courier new")[These words look as if they're written by a typewriter,]
and these words are written in the default font.
```

The font name goes inside quotation marks. Any words that appear inside the single square brackets are in the Courier New font. Any words outside the single square brackets are in the default font, Georgia, as shown in Figure 14.2.

> Text Appearance
>
> These words look as if they're written by a typewriter, and these words are written in the default font.

FIGURE 14.2   The words inside the single square brackets appear in a different font.

Be aware that you're limited to common Internet fonts when you use this method. Fonts that work on one machine may not work on another, but *web-safe fonts* work on a wide range of computers. Common fonts such as Palatino, Times New Roman, Arial, Lucida, Comic Sans, Tahoma, and Trebuchet should all work, but there are plenty of other, off-the-beaten-track web-safe fonts you can try out.

Designing Fonts

Fonts fall into a few main categories, such as serif, sans serif, cursive, and decorative. There is an example of each in Figure 14.3.

FIGURE 14.3   A sample of different font categories.

Serif fonts have little lines at the beginning and ending of each letter. For example, look at an uppercase A in Times New Roman. Small lines create a foot at the bottom of each diagonal stem. Those are serifs. Serif fonts tend to be more formal, and therefore they're perfect for a game set in a stuffy old mansion or an expensive boarding school.

Sans serif fonts do not have those little lines on the edges of letters. They are much more informal and are therefore fitting for stories set in the woods or at a beach. *Cursive fonts* mimic handwriting and are perfect for games that contain letters or invitations. Finally, *decorative fonts* are unique fonts that are meant to convey a time period or situation. Think about fonts that look like stitching or chalkboard writing or sticks stuck together. Sometimes these fonts can be difficult to read, but they can be used to great effect in small doses.

Picking a Font

When choosing to switch to a different font in your story, consider three things: the feeling the font conveys, how well it brings the reader into the moment, and how easily it can be read on the screen.

So what do you want to convey? Do you want the reader to jump like the characters when a door swings shut unexpectedly? If so, perhaps you should use a font like Impact to mimic the loud sound when the door hits the frame in Figure 14.4:

```
The door (font: "impact")[slammed!]
```

The door **slammed!**

FIGURE 14.4 *Fonts can convey a startling moment.*

Writing a mystery set in an English manor? Consider an elegant font, like Didot. Writing a story about fairies? Consider a playful font, like Candara.

Next, think about whether the font makes the readers feel as if they are there in the moment. What if you have a wizard find a long-lost scroll? You may want to use Papyrus for the words on the scroll to make the player feel as if he is holding an old scroll, too, as in Figure 14.5:

```
(font: "papyrus")[Beware anyone who reads this scroll.]
```

Beware anyone who reads this scroll.

FIGURE 14.5 *Fonts can make the reader feel as if they are in the story.*

Finally, consider how easy it is to read the font on the screen. You want your players to keep moving through your game, not pause because they have eyestrain. Use difficult-to-read fonts sparingly.

TRY IT OUT: FONT ADVENTURE

You're going through your brother's stuff (as you like to do whenever he leaves the house) and find three strange notes written in handwriting that you don't recognize. The notes make it sound like your brother is secretly the creator of the most popular video game of all time. Why wouldn't he tell you? And...um...why is he still living at your parents' house if he's a trillionaire?

Write a story for this scenario, using at least three additional fonts to present the writing in the notes or add special effects to the text.

Changing Text Style

The next thing you may want to change in your Twine story is the text style. The *text style* is the way the text appears on the screen. Is it in **boldface**? Or *italics*? Does it look blurred, as if tears have fallen on a piece of paper, washing away the words? Or are the words highlighted in yellow as if appearing in a student's notebook?

Like the font, the text style can be used to change the reader's understanding, draw the eye to certain words, and evoke feelings.

Adding Style

Twine comes with many built-in styles that can be referenced with a string command. For instance, the string `"italic"` in combination with the `(text-style:)` macro prints the words inside the accompanying hook in italics:

```
(text-style: "italic")[These words will appear in italics on the screen.]
```

If you click the Play button, you see the words inside the hook appear with slanted emphasis, as in Figure 14.6.

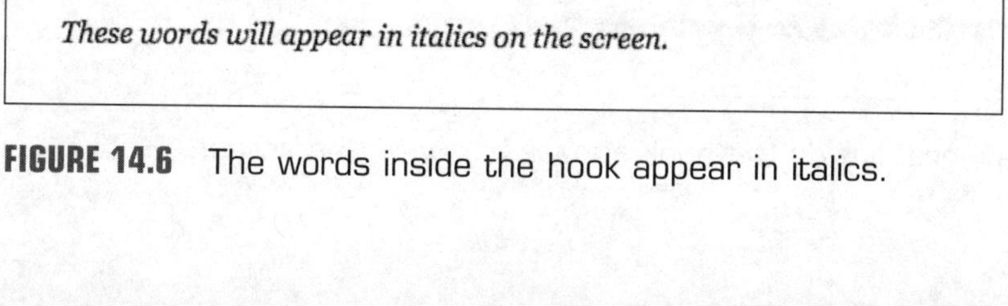

FIGURE 14.6 The words inside the hook appear in italics.

So what other styles can you use with Twine? You can bold (`"bold"`), underline (`"underline"`), and strike-through (`"strike"`), and you can highlight your words in yellow (`"mark"`).

You can also have your words blink (`"blink"`), rumble (`"rumble"`), fade in and out (`"fade-in-out"`), or shudder (`"shudder"`). You can have your words appear blurred (`"blur"` and `"blurrier"`) or smeared (`"smear"`). Or you can have your player character look at words in a mirror (`"mirror"`) or hanging upside-down (`"upside-down"`).

You can achieve all these effects and more with a simple macro, one of the above string commands, and a hook.

Changing Understanding

So why would you want to change the style of the words beyond creating something that looks super cool on the screen? Think of text style as the equivalent to stage notes in a play. The playwright provides stage notes for the actors because, in most cases, the playwright will not be on hand when the play is being performed, and he or she wants to let the actors know *how* the words should be read.

Stage notes are important because meaning can change depending on inflection. Say these two lines aloud:

Are you *angry* at me?

Are you angry at *me*?

In the first line, you are questioning whether the person is feeling anger or another emotion. In the second, you are questioning whether the person's anger is directed specifically at you. A playwright would tell the actor where he or she wants the emphasis placed so the meaning is clear. And, as you can see above, you can do the same thing with Twine simply by providing the emphasis in the form of italics.

You can also use text style to set a mood or evoke a feeling. Let's say that a player character is trying to peer through a smudged window to see inside a locked store. You can make the player feel as if he or she is really looking through filthy glass if you smear the words the player character is trying to read as in Figure 14.7:

```
(text-style: "smear")[You can barely make out the broken tables and smashed chairs
in the abandoned restaurant as you peer through the thick, dirty glass.]
```

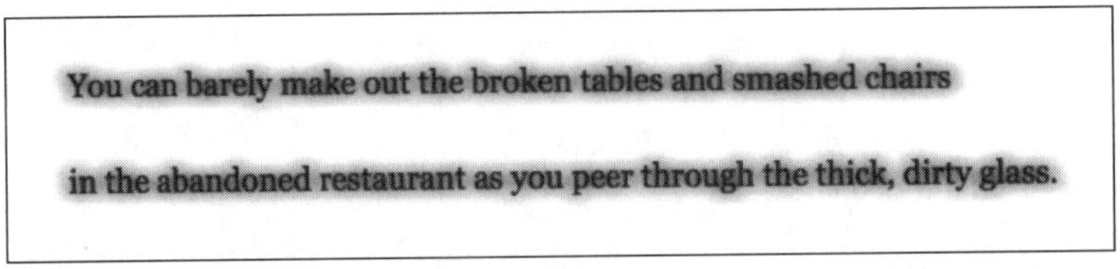

FIGURE 14.7 The words inside the hook appear blurry on the screen.

Or say that the player character finds himself or herself in an earthquake:

```
(text-style: "shudder")[Jodi gripped the wall and shrieked, "It's an earthquake!
Quickly, run for the [[door frame|Threshold]]!]
```

As the words shake on the screen, the player will feel like Jodi, scrambling for the door as the room shudders.

Changing Size

Regular HTML tags often work in Twine, too. You may want to change the size of certain words, such as having the words someone shouts appear larger than the other words on the screen. Or you might want to have words that are whispered appear smaller than the other words on the screen. You can do this by putting HTML tags around the words you want changed:

```
<span style="font-size: 200%">These words are very big.</span> These words are nor-
mal. <span style="font-size: 50%">And these words are very small.</span>
```

HTML places words between opening and closing tags instead of inside hooks and uses angled brackets around the tag. In the example above, the `<span style>` tag is utilized. This element allows you to set a new size for the text and apply that change to the words that appear between the opening and closing tag.

The opening tag begins with an angled bracket, the name of the element (`span style`), and an equal sign. Then the style you want to change (`font-size`) as well as the new style (`200%`) appear inside quotation marks. Finally, the opening tag ends with another angled bracket. The closing tag is an angled bracket, slash, element (`span`), and another angled bracket.

`200%` refers to how much larger the words will appear than the default font. It is two times the size of the default font. `50%` is half the size of the default font.

If you click the Play button now, you will see that the first sentence is very large, the second sentence is the normal size, and the third sentence is very small, as shown in Figure 14.8.

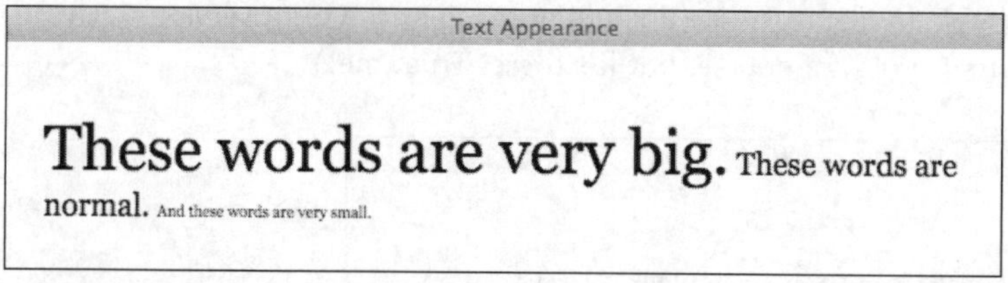

FIGURE 14.8 These three different font sizes display due to the HTML tags in the passage.

You can use this trick to convey that words are being shouted or whispered, and you can also use the size of the words to suggest that the size of the player character has changed.

Normal-sized words would look very large to someone who has been shrunken by aliens or very small to the giant in the fairytale *Jack and the Beanstalk*.

TRY IT OUT: TEXT STYLE ADVENTURE

Make a simple one-room exploration puzzle and use text style tricks to highlight different ideas. For instance, have the player peer out the window into the rain, describing the blurry world outside the room. Or have the player try to read a message reflected in a mirror. Make the player character pick up a vibrating object or have a digital clock blink the wrong time after a power outage.

For extra credit, turn the exploration into a great escape by hiding the exit out of the room.

Changing Text Color

You can change the *text color* in a game, as you know from Chapter 12, "Making a Role-Playing Game," where you wrote some words in red in order to make them stand out on the screen. But there are plenty of other reasons to change the word color. What if you want to describe the ocean in the exact shade of cerulean as the waves? Or have the player character drink a chartreuse poison? Or make the rust-colored shade of a non-player character's hair into an important clue? Color evokes feeling and adds understanding.

Colors online are coded with a *hexadecimal code*, a six-digit-or-letter code assigned to the color. Take, for instance, a good, standard red: #CC0000. Here's how you could use it in Twine:

```
(text-color: "#CC0000")[These words are in red.] These words appear in black.
```

The words inside the single square brackets are in red, while the words outside the hook are in the default black, as shown in Figure 14.9. (If you're looking at the print version of this book, you won't be able to see red, of course, but it's there. Trust me!)

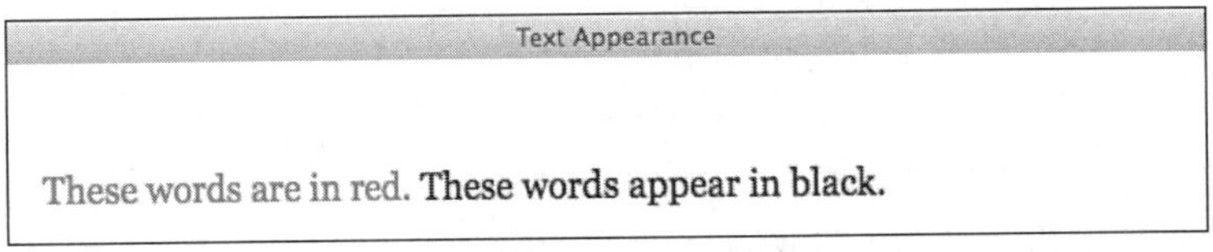

These words are in red. **These words appear in black.**

FIGURE 14.9 The words inside the hook appear in red, while the words outside the hook are black.

It is simple to look up hex codes online and get the perfect shade of blue for your story. To get you started, some common hex codes are #FFFFFF (white), #000000 (black), #CC0000 (red), #FF6600 (orange), #FFCC00 (yellow), #009900 (green), #0000FF (blue), and #6600CC (purple).

In some cases, you can also just write the color name instead of the hexadecimal code in order to use the color. As you'd suspect, you can use red, orange, or yellow, but you can also get very specific such as olive, aliceblue, or cornsilk. You can find a list of values online at https://developer.mozilla.org/en-US/docs/Web/CSS/color_value#Color_keywords.

TRY IT OUT: COLOR ADVENTURE

You are staring out at the ocean, remembering the time you watched a woman walk across the sand, dive into the ocean, and turn into a mermaid. Write a story for this scenario, using the (text-color:) macro to highlight important moments in the dream-tale in a wide range of colors.

Changing Text Transitions

You can change the way words come onto the screen by using the (transition:) macro. The default transition is for the words to subtly dissolve as you move to the next passage, but you can instead make them shudder or pulse for a moment.

Unlike the (text-style:) macro, which continues the shuddering or pulsing movement indefinitely (unless used in conjunction with the (live:) macro), the (transition:) macro does the effect for a moment right as the passage opens. Therefore, you can make the player feel as if he or she has just jumped into an earthquake or bounced against a force-field. And after that initial moment has passed, the words appear stable on the screen for easy reading.

Although Twine currently only recognizes two transitions, (transition:) is a macro worth learning because additional transitions may be added in the future. Any text that appears inside the hook will perform the effect (either pulsing or shuddering) only when the passage immediately opens:

```
(transition: "pulse")[This text will pulse when the passage opens.]
(transition: "shudder")[While this text will shudder when the passage opens.]
```

Click the Play button, and you'll see the first piece of text bounce for a moment, as if the words have landed on the surface of a big container of Jell-O, and you'll see the second piece of text shudder like a rocket at liftoff.

You can also have these transitions occur when text is clicked inside a passage (even if the player doesn't move to a new passage) by combining the transition macro with other macros, such as the (click-replace:) macro.

For instance, you can have the player character pick up an object, and provide a description of the way his skin feels when he holds the strange object.

```
He picks up the strange orb and instantly feels [his skin prickle.]<orb|
(click-replace: ?orb)[(transition: "pulse")[a pulsing spread through his joints.]]
```

When the player clicks on the hypertext words (his skin prickle), which are a named hook marked with a tag (<orb|), the (click-replace:) macro is triggered and the new words (a pulsing spread through his joints) pulse on the screen for a second before stopping.

TRY IT OUT: TRANSITION ADVENTURE

Your spaceship has landed on a distant planet, bouncing on its gelatinous surface. At first you have a lot of fun skipping around, bobbing over the reddish ground, until you notice that your spaceship is sinking! You can no longer access the door, though you may have some luck climbing in through an alternate entrance. Use the (transition:) macro to make the player feel as if he or she is also moving over the surface of the strange planet.

All the effects in this chapter apply only to the text inside the hooks. But what if you want to apply a new font to the entire game or have all the words print in a different color? For that, you need to dive into the story's stylesheet. In the next chapter, you'll learn a little bit about CSS.

Story Style: Changing the Game Appearance in Harlowe

There are certain games that you know you're going to love before you've read one word. For me, Emily Short's *Counterfeit Monkey* is one such game, and it has everything to do with the clever layout.

It's a parser-style game with the story and command line running down the right side of the screen. The left side of the screen is filled with a game map. The streets on the map (and, by extension, the sections you can explore) are constructed out of words. The map is not only useful but sets a tone for the game: You're going to play with, walk over, and twist around words.

Would going through the trapdoor in *Zork* feel as creepy if the screen wasn't black? Would you feel confident enough to explore Anna Anthropy's escape puzzle, *Afternoon in the House of Secrets*, if it weren't presented on a brightly lit white screen with magenta link accents?

In this chapter, you're going to dive into a new section of Twine and play with the stylesheet. Twine formats have a built-in stylesheet that tells the computer information such as the background screen color, the default font, and the width of the sidebar.

But Twine also gives you the ability to override those default settings by writing new ones on the stylesheet included with the individual game. You can access that stylesheet if you're on the blue grid screen.

Navigate to the menu (which is simply the title of your story) in the lower-left corner, next to the little house. If you click it open, you see a few options, including Edit Story Stylesheet. Click that, and you should be looking at a blank white screen that you're going to fill with all sorts of interesting things.

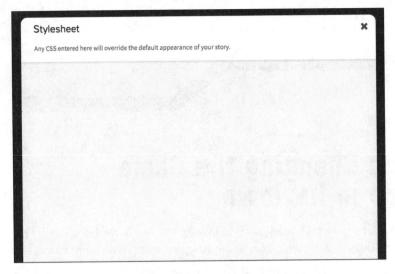

FIGURE 15.1 Edit the story stylesheet by writing new instructions.

Navigating the Stylesheet

The changer macros you learned about in Chapter 14, "Wiggling Words: Changing the Text Appearance," are perfect for making temporary changes, such as setting one line of text in red, as you did when you made the note to pass the game to another player.

But what if you want to apply a change to an entire game, such as using Garamond instead of Georgia for your font, or having the background color be blue instead of white? You do that with the stylesheet, writing up the new style choices in CSS.

CSS stands for Cascading Style Sheets, and it's a stylesheet language. Rather than set the style for each individual passage, you can write instructions in the stylesheet to tell the computer to apply particular design choices (such as font size, background color, and page layout) to the entire game or story, cascading the choices through every passage or page.

An easier way to think about CSS is with a website. Let's say you're shopping for video games on Amazon. Every time you click on a game to learn more about it, it loads in a new page. All these pages look somewhat alike: The same header runs across the top of the page, the same links appear on the right side of the screen, and the background and font colors are the same, page after page after page.

There are more than 200 million items on the Amazon site! If CSS didn't exist, someone would have to write the code on each individual page—200 million times. But because CSS *does* exist, no style decisions are made on the individual pages. Instead, the style code is set in the site's stylesheet, and that section of the site tells all the pages of the site how they should display.

The changes you make in the story stylesheet apply to every passage in the game. This is where you can change the formatting for anything you write, such as the paragraphs, the links, and the font, as well as the background.

The shared, consistent formatting is presented as a list of rules in the stylesheet, and the rules are broken down into two parts: a selector and a declaration.

Setting Up Selectors and Declarations

A *selector* is an element you want to change, such as tw-passage (which is the formatting in the body of the passage) or tw-sidebar (which is the formatting on the sidebar). The *declarations* are the property names (such as background-color) and value (black). Every declaration has two parts—sort of like how the datamap always has a data name and a data value—the property name and the property value. Declarations are always surrounded by curly brackets and end with a semicolon, like this:

```
tw-passage { background-color: #50A6C2; }
```

In this example, the selector is tw-passage. This means that whatever you put next is applied to every passage in the game. The declaration opens with a curly bracket. Then you state the property you want to change, which is background-color. You then type a colon and state the value, in this case #50A6C2, which is the hex code for a certain shade of blue. You finish the declaration with the always-needed semicolon and another curly bracket.

So how does the game now look on the screen? Open the first passage, write anything you want, and then click the Play button. You should see the words written within a blue box, as shown in Figure 15.2.

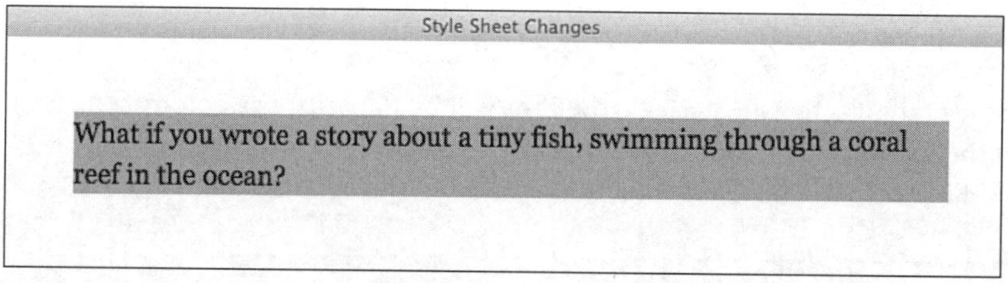

Style Sheet Changes

What if you wrote a story about a tiny fish, swimming through a coral reef in the ocean?

FIGURE 15.2 Change the background color of the passage by setting a new property and value in the stylesheet.

The blue section is small: only the length of the words in the passage. If you write three lines, it will be the length of three lines, whereas if you write three paragraphs, it will expand to house all three paragraphs. With this declaration, you make a change solely to the passage. What if you want that change to be everywhere on the screen, spanning the whole background so there aren't two colors on the screen? You do that by switching the selector to body so the style change is applied to every aspect of the layout.

Go back into the stylesheet and replace `tw-passage` with `body`:

`body { background-color: #50A6C2; }`

Now click the Play button again. You should see an entirely blue screen, as shown in Figure 15.3.

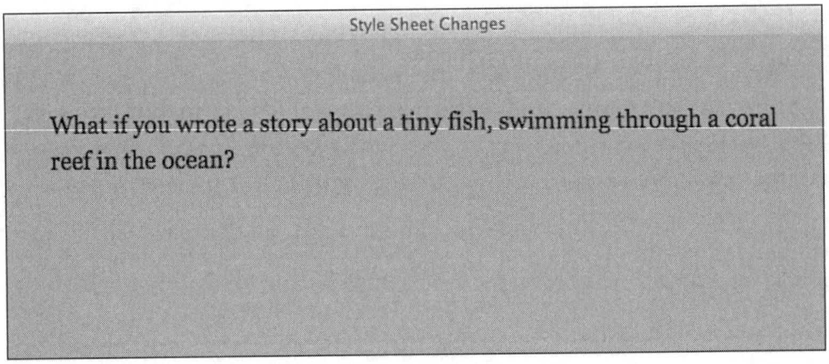

FIGURE 15.3 Change the background color of the entire game by setting a new property and value in the stylesheet.

The formatting is now applied to every space on the screen. Every time a player clicks on a link and opens a new passage, he or she will see a blue background.

By the way, let's say you want to make a bunch of changes to the same selector, such as setting the font color, the font size, and the font design all at the same time. You can either list the declarations each on a separate line or you can write them on a single line, separating the properties with semicolons:

`tw-passage { font-family: papyrus; color: white; font-weight: bold; }`

Now, in every passage (thanks to `tw-passage`), the font will be Papyrus, the color of the font will be white, and the weight of the font will be bold. If you now click the Play button, you see your words on the screen in your new font, color, and weight, as shown in Figure 15.4.

FIGURE 15.4 Change the font style and various font attributes by using the `tw-passage` selector and adding all the declarations, separated by semicolons.

With all CSS, your mileage may vary, as they say. How a site displays depends upon the browser. Therefore, some of the style elements you set in the stylesheet may not display for the player depending upon their computer and browser. This is something to keep in mind when designing your game.

Think you get the basics of CSS? Let's jump in and look at each element you may want to change in your game design.

Changing the Background

In Twine, the default background color is white, and it applies both to the space on the screen inside the passage and outside the passage, such as the sidebar. If you want to change the color of every part on the screen—the background inside and outside the passage area—use the body selector:

```
body { background-color: #278596; }
```

If you want to change the color only in the passage area of the screen and leave the rest of the screen in the default white, use the tw-passage selector:

```
tw-passage { background-color: #278596; }
```

You also don't need to have a solid background color. If gradient is more your style, you can make the screen a mixture of dark and light, blending two colors, like this:

```
body { background-image: linear-gradient(135deg, #FFFFFF, #50A6C2); }
```

In this example, the two colors are white (#FFFFFF), which is the starting point, and lake blue (#50A6C2), which is the end point. The left side of the screen is white, and it fades into blue toward the right, as shown in Figure 15.5. (The effect is harder to see in the print version of this book, but you should see a difference.)

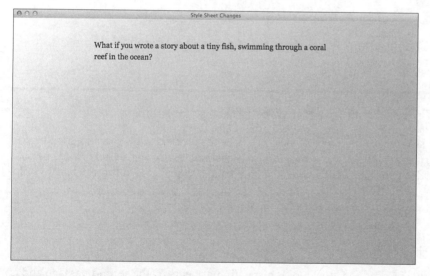

FIGURE 15.5 Change the background color to a gradient tone.

You can change where the fade begins by changing the number in front of the `deg` axis. If you think of the screen as a clock, the top center of the screen (or 12 o'clock) is `0deg`, and the bottom center of the screen (or 6 o'clock) is `180deg`. The left side of the screen (or 9 o'clock) is `270deg`, and the right side of the screen (or 3 o'clock) is `90deg`.

`135deg` is the lower-right corner of the screen (halfway between 3 o'clock and 6 o'clock, if the angles radiating out from the center were a timepiece). Look at where the fading occurs on the screen. Now change that number to the inverse, `315deg`. That is the top-left corner of the screen. In Figure 15.6, you can see that the blue is now in the top-left corner of the screen, and it fades to white in the lower-right corner.

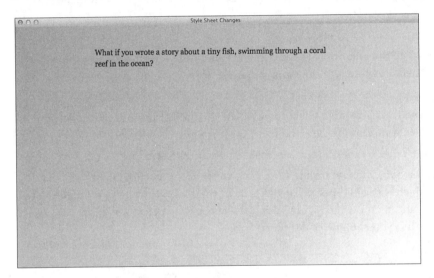

FIGURE 15.6   Change the gradient fade by changing the number on the `deg` axis.

TRY IT OUT: SWIMMING, PART I

Write a brief story from the point of view of a fish, describing what the fish sees while moving about the coral reef. How does the fish process his or her world? Change the background color to your favorite shade of blue to set the reader in the right frame of mind.

Changing the Sidebar

You have probably noticed the little curved arrow that appears by the second passage and is present throughout the game. Clicking this arrow allows you to go back one passage. Many game writers like to disable this undo button so they can have better control of their game. The easiest way to do this is to remove the sidebar display, like this:

```
tw-sidebar { display: none; }
```

Try adding this selector and declaration to the stylesheet and then create a second passage in your game. When you click the Play button and click your link, notice that the curved arrow is now missing from the game.

TRY IT OUT: NO ESCAPE

Being an escape artist was your father's idea, so he should be the one being lowered into this tank with his hands locked behind his back and chains snaking around both his legs. Unfortunately, you're the one taking one last deep breath before you sink under the surface.

Write a brief escape game that has many endings but only one that has the player breaking free. Remove the back button so the only way forward is...forward.

Changing the Font

In Twine, the default font is Georgia. You've already seen how you can use the tw-passage selector to change font properties in the declarations section of the rule. Here's another example:

```
tw-passage { font-family: papyrus; color: white; font-weight: bold; }
```

In the tw-passage selector, you can change the *font family* (font-family) to any web-safe font. You can change the *font color* (color) to a hex code (such as #FFFFFF) or to a color name (white). You can change the *font size* (font-size) by enlarging or shrinking the default size. For example, 25% would make it 4 times smaller than the current size, and 200% would make it twice as big as the current size. The following line would make it 50% larger than it currently is:

```
tw-passage { font-size: 150%; }
```

You can also change the way the words appear on the screen in terms of being flush left, flush right, or centered. To change the *text alignment* (text-align), add text-align as the declaration under the tw-passage selector:

```
tw-passage { text-align: center; }
```

The words should now be centered on the screen.

What if you want to import a new font to use with your story, and that font isn't a web-safe font that Twine already recognizes? The easiest way to add a new font is to use Google Fonts.

Go to Google Fonts (https://www.google.com/fonts) and choose your font. Click the Quick Use button shown in Figure 5.7, scroll down to the third section, and choose @import window. Copy the code that begins with @import url and ends with a semicolon.

FIGURE 15.7 Use the Quick Use button on the Google Font site to reach the code you'll need for your Twine stylesheet.

Return to Twine and open your stylesheet. Paste in the code at the very top, as shown in Figure 15.8.

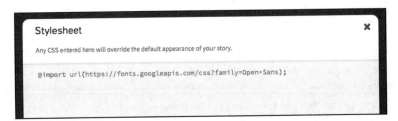

FIGURE 15.8 Paste the code from Google Fonts into the Twine stylesheet.

Go back to Google Fonts, scroll down to the fourth section, and grab the language that appears in that section (see Figure 15.9), beginning with font-family and ending with a semicolon.

Finally, in the Twine stylesheet, set up the selector as tw-passage and then paste in the language you just copied from the fourth section. This is what it might look like:

```
tw-passage { font-family: 'Open Sans', sans-serif; }
```

You now have a new list of fonts to play with for your story.

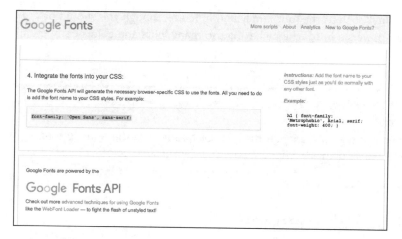

FIGURE 15.9 Grab the second piece of code from the Google Font site to complete the stylesheet.

TRY IT OUT: FONT TALE

There are currently more than 700 Google Fonts. Choose a number between 1 and 700. Count down the Google Font list until you get to your number. After you import the font, consider what sort of story that font would best complement. For instance, Russo One may lend itself well to a game about a girl locked inside a computer game, while Berkshire Swash may go well with a pirate adventure. Write a game using your new font to set a tone.

Changing the Links

In Twine, the default link color is blue. To change the link color, use the selector `tw-link` and change the color using your desired hex code, like this:

```
tw-link { color: #CC0000; }
```

Now all your links should appear in red. In addition, you can set a different color for when someone hovers over the link and touches the cursor to the words but doesn't click them. To do this, use the `tw-link:hover` selector as follows:

```
tw-link:hover { color: blue; }
```

Additionally, use the `tw-link:active` selector when you want to change the color that occurs when the player clicks on the link with their mouse or presses it with their finger when playing your game on a touch screen.

You can also change things such as the font family and font size, though you should be careful not to give your players a headache by having too many fonts and colors competing on the screen.

Getting Rid of Whitespace

You may have noticed that sometimes when you write code in a passage, you end up with unwanted white space on the screen when you play the game. You can remedy this by placing two curly brackets—yes, the same ones you've been using to write CSS—where you want the white space condensed. The curly brackets take all the possible white space that could occur between the brackets from line breaks, paragraph breaks, or code and reduce it to a single space. Take, for instance, this passage:

```
{The beast goes up in a puff of smoke. All three of you stand there, panting,
wiping down your swords.

(set: $character1 to (datamap: "Name", "Daria", "Health", 60))
(set: $character2 to (datamap: "Name", "Thrum", "Health", 72))
(set: $character3 to (datamap: "Name", "Grover", "Health", 50))

You look in the corner and realize that the monster was guarding a wooden box.}
```

When you put the brackets at the start and end of the passage, Twine reduces all that possible white space from the paragraphing and code to single spaces between sentences.

This chapter only scratches the surface of what you can do with CSS and HTML in Twine. Don't be afraid to play with the stylesheet or incorporate HTML into your passages.

By the way, this is the final chapter where you use the default Harlowe format. For the second half of the book, you'll be working with the other Twine format: SugarCube. Although this other format has many of the same capabilities as Harlowe, you'll write the macros in an entirely new way. To sweeten the deal, you'll learn next how to add images to your games.

Adding Images in a New Format

At the beginning of Lewis Carroll's *Alice's Adventures in Wonderland*, Alice muses when she peeks at the tome her sister is reading, "What is the use of a book without pictures or conversations?" Maybe you feel the same way. Maybe your favorite interactive fiction games blend words and pictures, like Inkle's *80 Days* or Simogo's *The Sailor's Dream*.

Learning how to add images to games may seem like an odd tangent since I've been approaching Twine as a medium for creating text-only games. But graphical interactive fiction (that is, interactive fiction games that include pictures or graphical games that include words) has a long history, extending back to the early 1980s.

Back then, the graphical interactive fiction games contained two-dimensional pictures akin to what you could draw today with Microsoft Paint. A good example is Sierra's first *King's Quest* game, which layered text into the image-driven story. The player used the cursor to make the character walk up to the castle's front door and then typed the words "open door" and received a chunk of text saying what was happening next. The words complemented the images.

Infocom went the other way, starting out making text-only games and expanding to include images after the company was sold to Activision. Back in 1987, Infocom started down this road with *Beyond Zork*, pairing the straight-text world of the *Zork* trilogy with a role-playing function and rudimentary map drawn on the screen. In 1997 Activision produced the very entertaining but text-light *Zork: Grand Inquisitor*.

By the late 1990s, the graphics capabilities of computer games were leaps and bounds ahead of where they had been back when Sierra first started putting together two-dimensional games. *Zork: Grand Inquisitor* went in the opposite direction of a text-based game. Clicking replaced typing, and pictures replaced words, giving *Zork: Grand Inquisitor* more in common with today's PlayStation and Xbox games than with the original text-only *Zork* trilogy.

There is, of course, a middle ground, and many Twine writers are using images to enhance games in the same way that illustrations scattered through text-heavy books can bring greater understanding to the words. For instance, *Secret Agent Cinder* by Emily Ryan has pictures at the top of a passage followed by words and choices below, while *Stars* by Lysander is a brief game that uses images to set a mood and advance the story.

So how can you add images to your games, and how do you know when a game can benefit from additional layers of media and when pictures are superfluous to the telling of the story? In this chapter, you'll tackle adding images to your games, and you'll do it using a new format, SugarCube.

Changing Over to SugarCube

SugarCube is a new format for *you*, but it's actually an older format than Harlowe, the format you've been working with up to this point. Thomas Michael Edwards created SugarCube as an additional format for an earlier version of Twine, and it quickly became a popular choice for game makers due to its flexibility.

Most of the macros you love from Harlowe are available in SugarCube as well, although they're written with a different syntax, and there are a few new ones to play with.

To switch over to the SugarCube format, navigate to the menu (which is simply the title of your story) in the lower-left corner, next to the little house icon. If you click it open, you see a few options, including Change Story Format. Click that, and you see the three options in Figure 16.1: Harlowe, Snowman, and SugarCube. Choose SugarCube and close the menu.

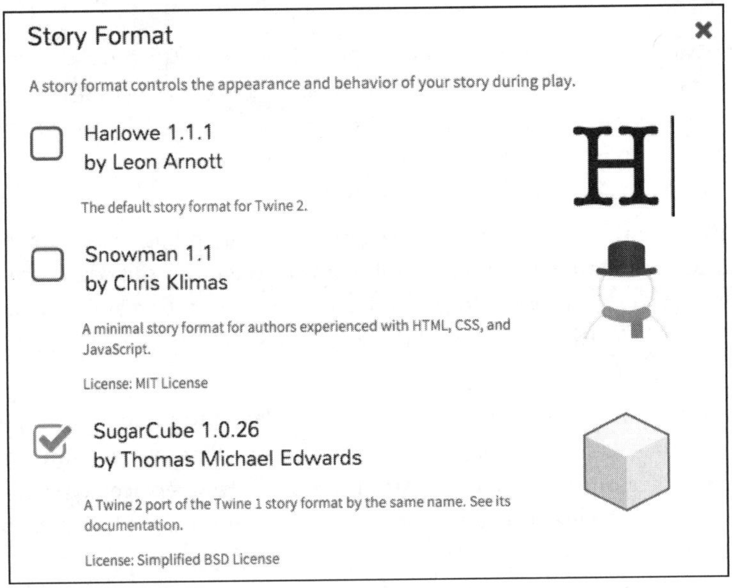

FIGURE 16.1 The format menu for Twine.

Because Harlowe is currently the default setting for new games, you need to switch over to SugarCube every time you start a new sample game for the rest of this book. A second option is to set SugarCube as the new default story format by going to the Stories screen, clicking Formats on the right sidebar, and clicking on the star next to SugarCube to change it from black to blue.

WHAT ABOUT SNOWMAN?

I mentioned Snowman in Chapter 4, "Designing Puzzles," and it's the third format option for Twine. Snowman is a bare bones version of Twine, made for people already comfortable with CSS and JavaScript. Unfortunately, it's not covered in this book, but I encourage you to play around with it as you start building a bridge between your understanding of Twine and other programming languages.

Learning a New Macro Format

SugarCube macros are written without hooks. Instead, you place the text you want to influence between an opener and closer for the macro. In addition, other macros are similar to their Harlowe counterparts in that they appear in the passage before the text to set a value for a variable but don't require a closing part to the macro in order to work.

Let's look at the `<<set>>` macro (equivalent to the Harlowe `(set:)` macro) as an example. It opens with double angled brackets, contains the name of the macro, and closes with two more double angled brackets:

```
<<set $key = "gold">>You pick up the key. The key you are holding is <<print $key>>.
```

In this example, the variable `$key` is set to a string value: `"gold"`. There are some similarities between how you write this macro in Harlowe and how you write it in SugarCube, though there are also clear differences. Let's look at these two macros side by side. Here is the Harlowe version:

```
(set: $key to "gold")You pick up the key. The key you are holding is (print: $key).
```

And here is the SugarCube version:

```
<<set $key = "gold">>You pick up the key. The key you are holding is <<print $key>>.
```

While the string value also appears inside quotation marks, this macro uses double angled brackets instead of parentheses, does not include a colon after the macro name, and uses an equal sign instead of the word operator `to`.

If you enter the SugarCube example in a new story in Twine and then click the Play button, you see two sentences on the screen, as shown in Figure 16.2.

FIGURE 16.2   The macro in action in the SugarCube format.

Of course, the most striking difference with SugarCube is the fact that the background is black and the text is white! There is also a sidebar that contains the title and a few more links.

I'm going to set aside macros in SugarCube for a moment in order to talk about adding images, especially since the main macro you'll use in this chapters is the `[[link]]` macro, which is written and works exactly the same way in both formats.

Deciding to Use Images

While you don't need images in a game—the human brain can do an excellent job of visualizing a scene if the writer provides a vivid description—images can definitely enhance the player's experience. You have five senses, after all, and it makes sense to use as many as possible in a story.

Knowing Which Image Files You Can Use

There is a tendency for people to go on the Internet and download pictures that they find via Google, but those media files are someone else's intellectual property. Just as you wouldn't want someone to take your writing and use it without permission, you shouldn't take any old image file that you find on the Internet, even if you give the original owner credit. This is especially true if other people are going to play your game or it will be uploaded to the web, but it's also true even if it's only going to remain unseen on your computer.

So where can you legally get images for a game? You can use any photograph that you take. Plot out the images you need and go on a photo-taking spree. You can also use other people's photographs if you've obtained written permission. When you get permission for a photo, make sure the owner of the photo knows how you'll be using the image.

There are plenty of photographs on the Internet offered under a Creative Commons license, usually abbreviated as a CC license. You can search large photo sites such as Flickr for images offered under a CC license or even use the Creative Commons site to search for images (http://search.creativecommons.org/), but you should make sure that the specific license fits how you'll use the image. For instance, if you're planning to charge money for your game, you'll need to find a license that offers the image for commercial purposes.

Of course, you can also make your own illustrations. Fire up your favorite iPad drawing program. Draw with a pencil in a sketchbook and then scan the image into the computer. Paint! Crayon! Doodle! Or use online software, such as PicMonkey or Canva, to create background images. Most programs have simple tutorials to help you get started.

Enhancing Understanding with Images

When deciding whether to include an image, ask yourself whether you can do a better job conveying the space, object, or character with words or with a picture. I call this my Diagon Alley rule, since I noticed this phenomenon when I saw the first Harry Potter film.

The Diagon Alley in my brain, courtesy of J.K. Rowling's descriptive writing, was more vivid and larger than the Diagon Alley on the screen. The Diagon Alley in my mind had twists and turns, stretching out in multiple directions, with many more stores to mentally wander. The Diagon Alley on the screen had to be smaller due to the limits of sound stage space. I still prefer the textual description of Diagon Alley over the visual creation of Diagon Alley.

Compare that to the DeLorean from *Back to the Future*. I could never have correctly imagined it if I had relied solely on words. It's so complicated that I would have needed many pages of text to accomplish the same understanding as gained from a single glance at Doc Brown's altered vehicle. In that case, a picture trumped words.

When you use an image, ask yourself if it benefits or detracts from the player's experience. Images should help reduce the amount of text needed rather than limit the player's imagination. Make sure your images give information or clarify a complicated idea, object, or place. You may be better off using words than pictures.

Enhancing Player Mood with Images

So you know you can use images to reduce the amount of descriptive text needed for a complicated place or object. There are also times when images set the mood. An image of waves about to crash on the sand transports the reader to a sunny beach. A picture of a moldering coffin can add to the level of terror in a horror game. And a cover image of a brooding old castle tells the reader what to expect before she starts reading the game.

Enhancing Game Play with Images

Some images, like maps, are not only useful but may be necessary for game play. By playing with the stylesheet in a game, you can alter the layout so the map is always visible on one side of the screen, or you can attach a map to a designated map passage and include a link at the bottom of every post, much the way you gave the reader access to checking his or her inventory in Chapter 9, "Maintaining an Inventory."

Also consider making the images you use integral to completing the game. Place a clue inside a picture and have the player character examine the image in the text of the game as the player examines the same image. Studying the picture can help the player figure out what to do to complete a later scene. When you use an image this way, the image does double-duty, setting a mood and elevating game play.

Adding Images to a Game

Twine supports all common image file types, from .jpg and .png to even moving .gif files. In order to add images to a game, you need to find somewhere online to host the pictures.

Dedicated image-hosting sites, such as Flickr, provide the URL that you need to place an image in a Twine game. You can also set up a free blogging space at Wordpress.com or Blogger that allows you to upload images so you can grab the URL.

Sizing Images Before Uploading

Wait! Before you upload that image to a hosting site such as Flickr or Wordpress, you need to size the image. Your image can be any size, although keep in mind that if a picture is too large, you will force the player to scroll left and right (or up and down) to see it.

You don't want the image to be too small, or the player will have to squint to see it, and you don't want the image to be too large, or the player will have to scroll to see it. 1,024 pixels by 768 pixels is a good size for an image that you want to have fill the screen without requiring the player to scroll up and down. Smaller images that you want centered in a passage may be sized closer to 500 pixels by 500 pixels. You can learn much more about image attributes from a Google Developers tutorial available at https://developers.google.com/web/fundamentals/performance/optimizing-content-efficiency/image-optimization?hl=en.

Writing Image Code in a Passage

Once you have an image uploaded to the web, you should be able to grab a dedicated URL that leads directly to that image. This is very straightforward with Wordpress.com. Simply upload the image into the media library, and Wordpress.com produces a URL beginning with `https://` or `http://` and ending with your image file suffix such as `.jpg` or `.png`.

Getting a dedicated URL for an image from Flickr requires a little additional navigation. After uploading an image to Flickr by following the instructions on the site, click on the image and navigate to the Share button. Choose the Embed option and grab all the code. Then look for the URL for your image buried inside that block of HTML:

```
<a data-flickr-embed="true"
href="https://www.flickr.com/photos/melissafordauthor/22909632532/in/datetaken/"
title="coffee"><img src="https://farm6.staticflickr.com/5800/
```

```
22909632532_11af304e82_z.jpg" width="480" height="640" alt="coffee"></a>
<script async src="//embedr.flickr.com/assets/client-code.js" charset="utf-8">
</script>
```

Remember that the URL for the image always begins with `https://` or `http://` and ends with an image file suffix such as `.jpg` or `.png`. Can you spot the URL you need? It's buried in the middle of the preceding code:

```
https://farm6.staticflickr.com/5800/22909632532_11af304e82_z.jpg
```

Once you have the URL, you can place it inside a passage by using standard HTML syntax, like this:

```
<img src="https://farm6.staticflickr.com/5800/22909632532_11af304e82_z.jpg"
alt="coffee" />
```

You can add some text and links below the image, too:

```
<img src="https://farm6.staticflickr.com/5800/22909632532_11af304e82_z.jpg"
alt="coffee">
The barista holds out the magic coffee cup. Do you [[take it|Take Cup]] or
[[run out|Leave Store]] of the store screaming?
```

Now when you click the Play button in Twine, you should see the image (in this example, a coffee cup) with the words below it, as shown in Figure 16.3.

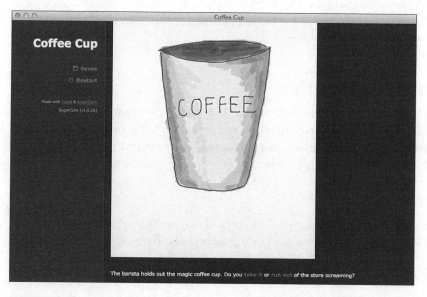

FIGURE 16.3 An image included in the passage, along with text and links.

SugarCube offers a second syntax for adding images, and it is commonly used to do more complicated things with images in Twine. Open the passage and place this code underneath the current image:

```
[img[https://farm6.staticflickr.com/5800/22909632532_11af304e82_z.jpg]]
```

The code opens with a single square bracket and `img`. Then a set of single square brackets surrounds the image URL. Finally, the opening single square bracket (the one before `img`) is closed with another single square bracket.

If you now click the Play button, you should see two copies of your coffee cup on the screen.

Both syntaxes work, and which you choose comes down to finding your Twine style. The first option will always work—even if Twine changes in the future—because it is written in HTML and doesn't depend on a Twine macro. The second option utilizes a Twine macro, and it also allows you to do a few more image tricks with Twine.

TRY IT OUT: PICTURE THIS

Draw or photograph five objects inside your home. Create a branching story using the standard `[[link]]` macro that you are already familiar with from Harlowe as you work now in the SugarCube format. Incorporate your five images into your story. How do the pictures influence the paths for the story or elevate the player's understanding of the words?

Using Images Creatively

So now you know how to add images to a passage, but what if you want to make an image link to another passage or use an image to set a value for a variable or even have word clues appear on the screen when the player moves the mouse over the image? You can do all those things in SugarCube by tweaking the second version of the image syntax.

Making Simple Links

You can use a picture to link to a passage. One way you can use this approach would be to set up multiple images on the screen—such as three doors—and have each lead to a different passage, much the same way you give a choice at the end of a block of text—but here you use pictures instead of words.

To turn a picture into a link, you first need to set up any additional passages. Begin a new sample story, make sure the format is set to SugarCube, and navigate to the green +Passage button at the bottom of the screen. Create a passage called Doorway.

I've set up a photograph of a door on Flickr that you can play with in this example: `https://farm6.staticflickr.com/5827/22956491301_361eb0361e_b.jpg`.

This is the syntax for turning an image into a link:

```
[img[https://imageURL.jpg][Passage Name]]
```

The code opens with the first single square bracket and `img`. A first set of single square brackets enclose the image URL, and a second set of single square brackets enclose the name of the next passage. Finally, the code closes with the last single square bracket. Add a bit of text above the image:

```
You take a deep breath and then knock on the door.
[img[https://farm6.staticflickr.com/5827/22956491301_361eb0361e_b.jpg][Doorway]]
```

When you now click the Play button, you should see the text followed by the image of the door, as shown in Figure 16.4.

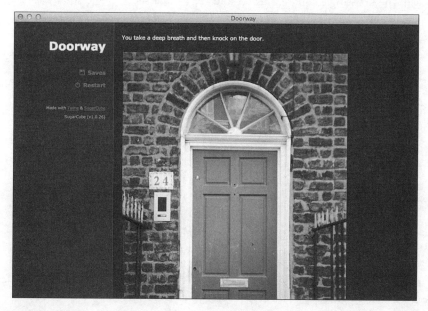

FIGURE 16.4 An image of a door becomes a link to the next passage.

If the player clicks the door, he or she goes to the Doorway passage, where the story continues.

TRY IT OUT: OBJECT PORTALS

Use the images you created for the last Try It Out in a new way. Instead of using the images to tell a story, use the images as portals to jump to new passages. For instance, if the player clicks a picture of a pair of glasses, Twine can transport the player to a passage called Eyeglass Store. Have the player move through the story by clicking on images. Extra credit: How can you use this image-linking method to work a visual maze into your game?

Making Setter Links

Not only can an image become a link to another passage, it can simultaneously become a setter link, placing a value into a variable. The setter link syntax nests another set of single square brackets into the straightforward image link code:

```
[img[https://imageURL.jpg][Passage Name][$variable to "value"]]
```

The code opens with the first single square bracket and `img`. A first set of single square brackets enclose the image URL, a second set of single square brackets enclose the name of the next passage, and a third set of single square brackets enclose the name of the variable and its value. (Remember that string values need to be enclosed in quotes, and numeric or Boolean values do not.) Finally, the code closes with the final closing single square bracket.

I've added a few images to Flickr that you can use for this example, and the URLs are included in the following code. You need to create a second passage called Checkout, using the +Passage button, before you enter this as the opening passage:

```
You walk into the store and grab a basket. "You can only choose one item,"
the wizard tells you. "What is it going to be?"


[img[https://farm1.staticflickr.com/756/22525688828_74841c72fb.jpg]]


What do you want to put in your basket?

[img[https://farm6.staticflickr.com/5722/22917992706_aa4f9b6f96_m.jpg]
[Checkout][$basket to "grapes"]]
[img[https://farm6.staticflickr.com/5719/22525688858_13f3011929_m.jpg]
[Checkout][$basket to "banana"]]
[img[https://farm6.staticflickr.com/5821/22917993066_aaacd721fb_m.jpg]
[Checkout][$basket to "apple"]]
```

When you now click the Play button, you should see the text along with the image of a basket plus the three pictures shown in Figure 16.5: grapes, bananas, and an apple.

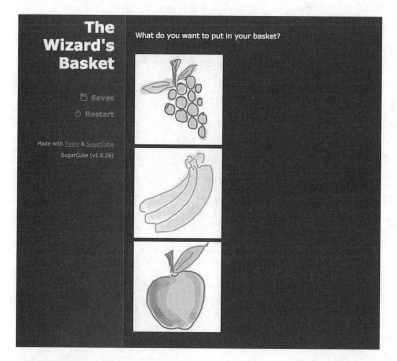

FIGURE 16.5 The images in the passage become links and set a value for the variable $basket when clicked.

When the player clicks on one of the fruit pictures at the bottom of the screen, the variable $basket is set to a string value that corresponds to the image: "grapes", "banana", or "apple". For the rest of the game, whenever the $basket value is checked, it returns the appropriate string.

TRY IT OUT: PACKING UP

Use the images from the preceding two Try It Outs in a new way. The player needs to choose one of the objects to help solve a puzzle. When the players clicks the picture, the variable $tool is set to the string value of the object. For instance, if you have a picture of a pair of eyeglasses, the variable is set by using $tool to "glasses". To state the value of the variable in the game, use the similarly written <<print>> macro wherever you want the value of the variable to appear: <<print $tool>>.

Making Mouseover Clues

Finally, you can have words hover on an image whenever the mouse is moved over the picture. You can use this trick to give the player additional clues. The syntax utilizes the pipe used with the `[[link]]` tool:

```
[img[Hover Words|https://imageURL.jpg]]
```

The code opens with the first single square bracket and `img`. A set of square brackets enclose two sections: To the left of the pipe are the words you want to appear when the mouse hovers over the picture, and to the right of the pipe is the image URL. Finally, the code closes with the last single closing square bracket.

What if you want to give the player a clue about what he or she will find by clicking the door image used earlier in this chapter? Open another sample story, make sure the format is set to SugarCube, and type the following example:

```
You pause for a moment by the door.

[img[Are you sure you want to go in there?
|https://farm6.staticflickr.com/5827/22956491301_361eb0361e_b.jpg]]

Do you want to go [[inside|Inside]] or try a [[different house|House 2]]?
```

What happens now when you click the Play button? You should see the door image as well as the text. When you mouse over the picture, the hover clue pops up as shown in Figure 16.6, giving the player a little more information before choosing one of the two links. Depending on the browser, it may take a moment for the words to show so keep this in mind when using this trick.

This trick can be invaluable for discreetly drawing the reader's attention to a tiny detail he or she may otherwise overlook in an image.

TRY IT OUT: ADDITIONAL CLUES

Using the images that you've used for the other Try It Outs in this section, give the player additional information that appears only if the player moves the mouse over the pictures.

It's time to dive into the rest of the macros used with the SugarCube format. Most will be familiar, albeit with different syntax. The first order of business is to learn a new way of writing conditional statements, and you'll do that by contemplating the three sections of a story: the pre-story, central story, and post-story. Ready to create a few cliff-hangers?

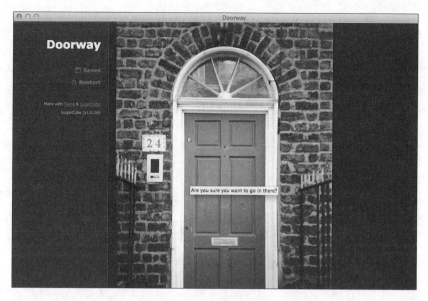

FIGURE 16.6 Additional words appear when the mouse moves over the image.

Setting Up the Pre-Story, Central Story, and Post-Story

All stories are imagined in three parts, though only one of those parts ends up on the page or screen. Take, for instance, Infocom's game *Moonmist*. You play the detective friend of Tamara Lynd, who has asked you to come to her estate in England to investigate a ghost that is haunting the castle.

The story begins *in medias res*, which is just a fancy literary term for noting that the story opens in the middle of the action. *In medias res* translates to "into the middle things," and that is the perfect way of understanding a tripartite story structure. The reader or player wants to get to the meat of the story, which is the action. But on either side of that middle section on the screen are the pre-story and the post-story off the screen.

The *pre-story*, often called the backstory, comprises the events that happen *off* the screen but inform the events *on* the screen. Before the game begins, the player character and Tamara meet and form a friendship, Tamara and Lord Jack Tresyllian start dating and get engaged, and the White Lady (the ghost haunting the castle) is murdered by Jack's ancestor.

You don't see any of those things occur, but you know they've happened based on things the characters say in the game. They are all part of the pre-story, events that occur before the action begins and that are important to the game. The events that aren't important to the game, such as Tamara's other friendships or prior relationships, are superfluous, but the ones I've listed help you understand the events currently unfolding on the screen. Therefore, those events are the pre-story. This literary device makes for a richer game; when the writer knows the pre-story and subtly conveys it to the player, both sides understand character intentions and motivations, as well as the weight of certain decisions.

The *post-story* comprises the events that take place after the action is over. Endings divide neatly into two main categories, *closed* or *cliff-hangers*, but both imply that life goes on after the action is over. Within the closed category are endings that wrap up the storyline neatly in a little bow and those that are open to player interpretation. In the cliff-hanger category, the ending is left dangling open, with the implication that the story will continue in a sequel.

Moonmist is designed as four stories within a game, and the ending depends on the color you choose when you reach the castle. By extension, the post-story also changes depending on the villain controlling the "ghost." But in all cases, the player is left with a sense of what comes next for all the characters in the game.

Throughout this book, you've been focusing on that central part of the story. If you imagine your game as a sandwich, you've been focused on creating the best possible filling. But sandwiches don't hold together without two slices of bread, right? It's time to turn your attention to the pre-story and post-story "bread" holding together the game.

You can approach pre-story and post-story through a few familiar macros written in the new-to-you SugarCube syntax. They will still accomplish the same tasks as the macros you already know in Harlowe; you'll just be writing them a little differently. Because you've encountered most of these before in their Harlowe form, I'm going to cover a lot of ground in this chapter, including the `<<set>>`, `<<unset>>`, `<<if>>`, `<<else>>`, `<<elseif>>`, `<<print>>`, `<<nobr>>`, and `<<silently>>` macros. So let's get started.

Learning New Macros

You already learned the general format for macros in SugarCube in Chapter 16, "Adding Images in a New Format," so you know that the words you want to influence either run after the macro, as is the case with the `<<set>>` macro, or are tucked between an opener macro and a closer macro. Don't forget to change your format to SugarCube before you begin trying out the information present in this chapter. If you try to write these macros in the Harlowe format, you will see your code highlighted in peach, indicating a problem.

Using the `<<set>>`, `<<unset>>`, and `<<print>>` Macros

You learned the basics of the `<<set>>` macro in Chapter 16, but here you will dive in a little deeper. Like the `(set:)` macro in Harlowe, the `<<set>>` macro in SugarCube is used to assign a value to a variable. You can use Harlowe's `to` operator, or you can use the equal sign (`=`), which is a JavaScript operator, with the SugarCube version of the macro. Both versions do the same thing, and I alternate between the two in this book, like this:

```
<<set $key to "gold">>
```

or this:

```
<<set $key = "gold">>
```

This is one of those cases where you get to find your Twine style, using either the common Harlowe operator (`to`) or the JavaScript operator (`=`) to assign the value.

As with the `(set:)` macro in Harlowe, you can also use the `<<set>>` macro to set three different types of values: a string (which is a word or words), a number, or a Boolean. String values always have quotation marks around them (for example, `"gold"`), whereas number and Boolean values are both written without quotation marks:

```
<<set $key = 1>>
```

or this:

```
<<set $key = true>>
```

But here's something SugarCube can do that may be helpful to one of your future games. While the <<set>> macro assigns a value, the <<unset>> macro unassigns a value and returns the variable to an unassigned state. Of course, the workaround in Harlowe is to continuously reassign a value to the variable each time you want it to change. But SugarCube gives you an intermediary step to unassign it. It helps to imagine this concept using an ice cream cone.

Say that you are holding an ice cream cone. If I put a scoop of chocolate ice cream in it, the cone would now be holding a scoop of chocolate. If you wanted to describe that in computer speak, you could say that the cone has a value of chocolate (or, writing it in macro form, $cone = "chocolate").

If you change your mind on the ice cream flavor, two things could happen: I could switch the ice cream to a different flavor, such as vanilla, *or* I could remove the ice cream altogether and leave you with an empty cone. See, two very different things!

Similarly, the <<unset>> macro returns the variable (for instance, $cone) to nothing instead of changing it to a different value. This could be helpful if you have a player character drop an object but then possibly (or not) find another copy of it later in the game. For instance, you could have the player find a gold key (<<set $key = "gold">>) and then drop it but have the possibility of finding a silver key later in the game. Once the player finds that silver key, the value of $key can be assigned as "silver", but if the player doesn't find it, it remains unassigned.

The <<unset>> macro is written with the variable inside the macro:

<<unset $key>>

Finally, you should become reacquainted with the <<print>> macro that you used in Chapter 16 without formally meeting it. The <<print>> macro in SugarCube does the same thing as the (print:) macro in Harlowe: It prints the value of the variable. If the variable does not have a value, it simply skips printing anything. The <<print>> macro is written without a colon, like all SugarCube macros:

<<print $key>>

To put it all together, try setting and unsetting the variable, using the <<print>> macro to check the value of the variable (and don't forget to switch to the SugarCube format):

<<set $key = "gold">>You pick up the <<print $key>> key. But then you drop it.
<<unset $key>>You aren't holding the <<print $key>> key anymore.

What happens now when you click the Play button in Twine? You should see the value of the key ("gold") the first time you check the variable using the <<print>> macro, but you should see nothing written on the screen despite the <<print>> macro being used again after the <<unset>> macro, as shown in Figure 17.1.

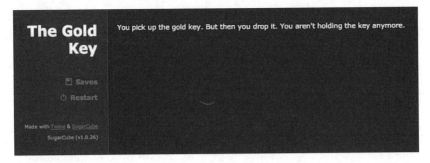

FIGURE 17.1   The `<<set>>` and `<<unset>>` macros at work in the SugarCube format.

All the same operators that worked with the `(set:)` macro in Chapter 5, "Building Objects with Variables," also work with the `<<set>>` macro in SugarCube. For instance, to add more to the value, you write out the macro as follows:

```
<<set $coins to $coins + 2>>
```

If you need to refresh your memory, return to Chapter 5 to review the various operators used with variables to set values.

TRY IT OUT: ROBIN HOOD RELAY

You are the Robin Hood of the high seas, stealing from rich merchant ships and distributing the wealth to lowly fisherfolk trying to eke out a life on the water. Your player character needs to jump aboard a lot of ships and collect items and then disseminate those items to other captains.

Use the `<<set>>`, `<<unset>>`, and `<<print>>` macros to simulate picking up and dropping off objects in the game, with the `<<print>>` macro keeping track of which variables are still in the player's possession. Don't forget to switch to the SugarCube format before you do all this!

Using the `<<if>>`, `<<else>>`, and `<<elseif>>` Macros

Remember I said that sometimes macros have an opener and a closer? The `<<if>>` macro is one such macro. The macro opens with the set of double angled brackets enclosing the name of the macro (the opener), followed by the words fulfilling the condition, and ending with the closer, which is the opener written with a slash, like this:

```
<<if $hitPoints gte 6>>You pick up your sword again.<</if>>
```

This conditional statement asks Twine to check whether the variable $hitPoints has a value greater than or equal to 6. You write that with the operator gte, which stands for "greater than or equal to." The opener is <<if $hitPoints gte 6>> and the closer is <</if>>. In between are the words that are printed if the conditions are met.

But wait, this is another place to find your Twine style because the closer can be written as <<endif>> or <</if>>. It may be clearer for you to use <<endif>> because *end* makes it sound like a closer. On the other hand, if you're familiar at all with HTML, you may be more comfortable ending the macro with a slash since that is the way it is written using HTML tags. The choice is up to you.

Before I continue to the companion <<else>> macro that is often used in conjunction with the <<if>> macro, let's take a look at a few of the operators you may use to make a conditional statement:

eq—Checks whether the two sides are equal.

is—Checks whether the two sides are equal.

gt—Checks whether the left side is greater than the right side.

gte—Checks whether the left side is greater than or equal to the right side.

lt—Checks whether the left side is less than the right side.

lte—Checks whether the left side is less than or equal to the right side.

and—Checks two variables and makes sure both are true.

or—Checks two variables and makes sure at least one is true.

So now that you know a few operators you can use to build conditional statements, let's take a look at the <<else>> and <<elseif>> macros.

The <<else>> or <<elseif>> macro immediately follows the if statement and comes before the end of the <<if>> macro with the closer. You do not close the <<if>> macro until all conditions have been stated. Therefore, all the other possible conditions contained in the else statements go before the <<if>> macro closer, as shown here:

```
<<if $hitPoints gte 6>>You pick up your sword again. <<else>>You breathe heavily
and kneel on the floor.<</if>>
```

In this case, if the hit points tracked by the $hitPoints variable are 6 or higher, you pick up your sword again. If the hit points are under 6, you breathe heavily and kneel on the floor. To test this conditional, you need to set a value for the variable $hitPoints. Begin by giving it a value of 7 by writing <<set $hitPoints to 7>> before the <<if>> macro.

Now click the Play button and check what appears on the screen. It should be the first statement, as shown in Figure 17.2—You pick up your sword again—since the variable $hitPoints has a value of 7.

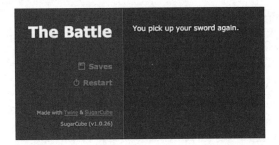

FIGURE 17.2 The `<<if>>` and `<<else>>` macros at work in the SugarCube format.

Of course, if you change the value of `$hitPoints` to 5, you should see the other sentence: `You breathe heavily and kneel on the floor.`

Just as in the Harlowe format, the `<<elseif>>` macro can be used to set a second (or third or fourth) condition, as shown here:

```
<<set $hitPoints = 4>><<if $hitPoints gte 6>>You pick up your sword again.
<<elseif $hitPoints eq 5>>You breathe heavily and kneel on the floor.
<<elseif $hitPoints eq 4>>You begin to feel dizzy, and the room tilts.
<<elseif $hitPoints lte 3>>You press your head to the floor, prepared to die.<</if>>
```

In this example, you need to set `$hitPoints` again in order to check the `<<elseif>>` statements. Four possible statements may run: one if the hit points are 6 or above, one if the hit points are 5, one if the hit points are 4, and one if the hit points are 3 or below. You can link together as many `elseif` statements as you want by using the `<<elseif>>` macro. When you click the Play button, you should see the statement shown in Figure 17.3 since the value for the `$hitPoints` variable is set to 4 in this example.

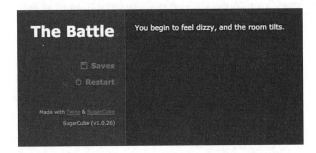

FIGURE 17.3 The `<<elseif>>` macro at work in the SugarCube format.

Now that you know how to use the `<<if>>`, `<<else>>`, and `<<elseif>>` macros, you can easily make those variables mean something. Go forth and create conditional statements based on the value of a variable and allow your player characters to pick up and drop objects once again.

TRY IT OUT: HAUNTED HOUSE ESCAPE

As the result of a Halloween dare, you have unfortunately gotten yourself locked inside a haunted house. Scattered about the house are objects that can either help you get out of the house and also objects that will unfortunately create new problems you need to deal with before you can leave. Using the `<<set>>`, `<<if>>`, `<<else>>`, and `<<elseif>>` macros, create a brief game that simulates picking up and using objects based on variables and conditional statements.

Using the `<<nobr>>` and `<<silently>>` Macros

Two macros you haven't seen yet accomplish a task similar to the curly brackets in Harlowe. In Harlowe, you place the curly brackets around large blocks of code in order to condense the white space. The `<<nobr>>` and `<<silently>>` macros accomplish the same task, in a different manner.

The `<<nobr>>` macro, which is written with the opener `<<nobr>>` and the closer `<</nobr>>` or `<<endnobr>>`, removes all the line breaks while still running the code that appears between the macro's opener and closer. Take, for instance, this example:

```
<<set $cone to "chocolate">>
"I would love an enormous scoop of
<<if $cone eq "vanilla">>
vanilla,"
<<else>>
chocolate,"
<<endif>> she said.
```

If you now click the Play button, you should see the words oddly spaced on the screen, as shown in Figure 17.4. Clearly, this way of writing the code makes it easier for the author to see how the if/else statement unfolds, but it won't work once the player sees it on the screen in the game.

FIGURE 17.4 Odd spacing on the screen due to Twine running every line break in the code.

This is where the `<<nobr>>` macro comes in handy. If you place it around the code, like this, it removes all the unnecessary line breaks:

```
<<nobr>><<set $cone to "chocolate">>
"I would love an enormous scoop of
<<if $cone eq "vanilla">>
vanilla,"
<<else>>
chocolate,"
<<endif>><<endnobr>> she said.
```

Now click the Play button again, and you should see the white space created by the unused portion of the `if/else` statement gone and the words run together as shown in Figure 17.5.

FIGURE 17.5 Odd spacing on the screen gone thanks to the `<<nobr>>` macro.

Similarly, what if you want to begin a passage by setting values to many variables? At the end of the long list of `<<set>>` macros, you start writing the text that begins the passage:

```
<<set $littleKey to "gold">>
<<set $mediumKey to "silver">>
<<set $largeKey to "iron">>
You pick up the keys and prepare to go.
```

When you click the Play button, you see that the plain text in the passage presents itself a few lines down the screen, as shown in Figure 17.6.

While the `<<nobr>>` macro removes line breaks, the `<<silently>>` macro hides the spacing created by the code. Now wrap the `<<set>>` macros inside a `<<silently>>` opener and `<<endsilently>>` or `<</silently>>` closer, like this:

```
<<silently>>
<<set $littleKey to "gold">>
<<set $mediumKey to "silver">>
<<set $largeKey to "iron">>
<<endsilently>>
You pick up the keys and prepare to go.
```

FIGURE 17.6 Odd spacing on the screen due to Twine leaving white space where code is written in the passage.

The unwanted spacing disappears, When you click the Play button again, the plain text now appears at the top of the screen, as shown in Figure 17.7.

FIGURE 17.7 Odd spacing removed due to the `<<silently>>` macro wrapped around the code.

The macros just described allow you to write code that is easy for you to read but that doesn't take up extra space on the player's screen.

Designing the Pre-Story

Unless your game begins with the player character's birth and ends with the player character's death (which would be a very long story), your game begins *in medias res*—in the middle things.

Take a look at Douglas Adams's *The Hitchhiker's Guide to the Galaxy*. Both the book and the interactive fiction game begin with Arthur Dent's house about to be demolished by a bulldozer. Talk about being in the middle of things.

Adams saves the reader from slogging through moments in Arthur's earlier life, such as moving into the house and working at the radio station. Those facts *are* important, but they belong to the unwritten pre-story. Adams begins with the action: the bulldozer parked outside Arthur's house and Arthur lying down in the mud to stop it. Of course, the house isn't long for this world since life on earth is ending in 12 minutes, and Arthur will hitch a ride on a spaceship, but still, it's a moment of high action.

Here's the deal: You would never get to the bulldozer part if Adams started with Arthur Dent's birth, continued through his many years of education, and then moved on to his interview for his job at the radio station. You would be bored stiff; you're living your own life, and you don't need to read about the mundane days of someone else's life. You would quit long before Arthur reached his 30s, when his world turned upside down.

But the last 12 minutes before earth ceases to exist and Arthur's subsequent hitchhiking aboard a spaceship form a *story*. Your eyes may glaze over if you have to hear about every breakfast Arthur ever ate, but you'll sit up and pay attention for Arthur's adventures in outer space.

Yet part of why a player relates to Arthur is his backstory. All the stuff that happened off the screen before the story begins made Arthur not quite at ease with himself and contributed to his inability to get the hang of Thursdays. Those things are important for Adams to know, even if they're not important for the reader to know directly.

So how do you go about creating the pre-story and subtly work it into the central story?

Telling or Not Telling

J.K. Rowling has a file cabinet filled with notes and unused ideas that helped her build her wizarding world but didn't make it onto the page. Some of these facts ended up on her site, Pottermore, or have been revealed in retrospect on Twitter, but they mostly live only in her office or wherever she keeps her writing notes. Similarly, J.R.R. Tolkien had hundreds of pages of notes and maps of Middle Earth that he left behind, some of which are simply unused ideas but others of which explain the connections of various characters in his novels or the earth counterparts to his fantasy locations.

Here's the thing: Take a hint from those authors and understand that you don't need to tell the reader everything. In fact, you shouldn't tell the reader everything because a big game of facts would be really boring. But you, as the writer, need to know the backstory.

Your readers are meeting your characters cold; that is, until they're deep into your game, they don't really know the non-player characters or even their own motivations. The characters are strangers they need to get familiar with.

But you, the writer, cannot *also* be meeting your characters cold without a clue as to what they'll do or why. You need to know whether an action is in or out of character, and the only way you can know from the first moment of the game is to construct the backstory.

Only tell what you need to tell to explain a character's behavior. For example, readers of Harry Potter books know that Ron is scared of spiders. That important fact comes up over and over again when it comes to the acromantulas. But the reader doesn't really need to know Ron's favorite candy, even though the author should know this sort of thing in order to be able to guide the characters well while writing.

Working the Backstory into the Game

There are plenty of ways to skillfully work the backstory into a game, and all of them have been done with great success by other interactive fiction writers.

Infocom was notorious for providing the backstory in additional materials that came with each game. Not only were those extra materials interesting, but they were usually necessary to read in order to solve a puzzle in the game. *Moonmist*, for instance, comes with two physical letters that Tamara asks the player character about when she arrives at the house. These letters give the player all the information she needs to know about the situation in order to jump into solving the mystery.

You, too, can provide the player with additional materials, such as a link to PDFs online or websites you construct in order to give additional information on each character. Twine supports connecting stories to external websites, and the syntax for doing this is similar to the syntax for a link between two passages:

```
[[Read more about the Wizarding World|http://www.pottermore.com/]]
```

In this example, the linked words—`Read more about the Wizarding World`—appear on the screen as a simple blue link with the external link icon shown in Figure 17.8.

FIGURE 17.8 An in-passage link to an external website.

You can create a free site on Wordpress.com or Blogger and fill it with necessary backstory information you want the player to know before he or she begins the game.

In addition, information can be revealed through recollections, flashbacks, dreams, or stories told between characters:

- *Recollections* have the player character or non-player character pausing to remember something important, such as an event that occurred earlier in the same space. For instance, as the player character enters the outer space saloon, she remembers the last time she was in that place, battling aliens. A physical space or object serves as a trigger for the memory.

- *Flashbacks* are longer stories inside stories that transport the player character (and, by extension, the reader) to an earlier point in time. For instance, the player character enters the dark woods and exclaims that she knows danger is near. She then recounts the last time these warning signs lined up before her and how she ended up battling a monster. After the flashback is over, the game or story returns to the present moment.

- *Dreams* are a literary device used to tell important information while the player character sleeps or goes into a daydreaming state. Dreams make sense in stories because humans often dream about important moments. Andrew Plotkin's game *The Dreamhold* utilizes this trick to give backstory information.

- *Stories* are sometimes told between characters, and they are meant to catch up not only the player character or the non-player character but the reader, too. Stories also serve to fill the time between point A and point B when you want to give the player the sense that time is passing. As characters talk about a point in time prior to the start of the game, in giving the information to each other, they also pass it to the player.

TRY IT OUT: A JOURNEY'S TALE

Practice using recollection, flashbacks, dreams, and stories to present the backstory in a new game about the kingdom the player character and non-player character are traveling to. Also create an external website on a free site such as Wordpress.com or Blogger and use it to provide the player with maps and other background materials that will help him or her understand the world.

Including Game Tutorials

Through this book, you've been focusing on the goals of the player character, but what are the goals of the player? Where does the game start, and where does the game end, and is it possible to win or lose the game? All this information can be contained inside a game tutorial.

Early interactive fiction games came with a how-to guide that informed the player not only how to play the game but the ultimate goal: to find all the items and put them in the trophy case; to defeat the evil wizard, Krill; or to save an entire outer space civilization from extinction due to an infection.

Opening a game with a tutorial that the player needs to read before reaching the actual story (or linking to a tutorial at the top of the first passage) can help the player immediately know his or her ultimate goal. Of course, if you do this, give the player the option to skip the tutorial during subsequent game play. Creating a tutorial helps the player understand why he or she has this goal in the first place. A tutorial is an easy place to introduce the backstory and make the player instantly care about helping the player character succeed.

Remember that people are drawn to characters who know what they want and who take action. Game tutorials are a perfect place to not only allow your player to feel grounded but to present motivations, too.

TRY IT OUT: GAME PLAY

Return to any game you've created so far in this book, especially a complicated one, and create a game tutorial for it. Explain to the player logistically how to play and provide any additional information the player needs to know in order to make good choices inside the story. Create a new passage using the +Passage button, set it as the opening passage, and link to the old opening passage at the bottom of the tutorial to get the game started.

Designing the Post-Story

Have you ever had a friend come to you for advice and then not return to tell you how things turned out with the situation? This can be frustrating because, in giving advice, you become invested in the other person's situation, especially if you care about her. After all, you want everything to turn out well for your friend.

Though your friend knows how everything turned out when she went to implement your advice, you are left wondering if all is well in her world. This common situation is mirrored in the frustration readers often experience with story endings, no matter how well written. Humans are designed to wonder what happens next.

Because humans have this built-in wonder system, you can encourage the reader to imagine what happens next by providing closure while simultaneously hinting that life continues on after the story ends. By doing a bit of careful writing, you don't need to spell out the character's world well into the future. You can sit back and allow the reader to imagine what he or she wishes, which is ultimately more satisfying for all involved.

Defining the Ending

Setting up the post-story begins by choosing the type of ending that best fits your story. As I said at the beginning of this chapter, there are two broad categories for endings: those that provide closure and those that end with a cliff-hanger. Within each of these broad categories are many subcategories that contain various types of endings.

You need to determine the amount of time you want the player to imagine into the future after the end of the game. Some stories trigger only a short-term interest on the part of the reader. For instance, readers are curious about how Dorothy copes with being back in Kansas at the end of L. Frank Baum's *The Wonderful Wizard of Oz* but aren't really interested in hearing about farm life years down the road. Counter that with the epilogue J.K. Rowling provides at the end of *Harry Potter and the Deathly Hallows*. She knows that people will want to know what becomes of Harry Potter well into adulthood since they have spent so much time watching him grow up.

The ending for *The Wonderful Wizard of Oz* provides explicit closure, neatly providing an explanation for everything that occurs in the book. This is true even though the series continues through many more novels. The ending for *Harry Potter and the Deathly Hallows* is more unresolved. The reader gets the sense that not only has life continued on but the events covered in the seven books continue to affect Harry Potter and his offspring.

Tight closure is used when the writer only wants the reader to imagine a brief distance into the future, and a lack of closure is used when the writer wants the reader to project many years down the road. So you need to decide how much you want to neatly wrap up the ending and explain everything that happens during the game.

Here are a few types of endings to help you figure out how you want to end your various games:

Concrete ending—This is a strong ending that clearly states what happened and why, leaving no room for questions. Every plot thread is neatly knotted, the characters are all accounted for, and the reader generally leaves the story feeling as if he or she understands everything encountered along the way.

Interpreted ending—This is a looser ending that leaves a lot of the understanding in the hands of the reader. Two players may walk away from the same game on divergent paths of understanding. These are the sorts of games that people like to talk about after they're over to see if other people understood them in the same way.

Open ending—This is an even looser ending, which may not feel like an ending at all, as it leaves the reader feeling as if there is more to come. Sometimes with cliff-hangers (where the writer leaves the reader dangling in the middle of the action), there actually will be another part of the story coming in the future. But other times, the story is left purposefully unfinished, implying that the story—like real life—does not have a neat end point.

Surprise ending—Everything is going in a certain direction and then...bam!...the writer throws in a surprising twist that changes the story right at the end. Make sure if you're going to write this type of ending that you've taken the time to plant plenty of foreshadowing clues so the ending makes sense in the moment. Poorly done surprise endings can feel as if they're coming out of nowhere.

Epilogue ending—This type of ending is actually a double ending, jumping the reader forward in time to tell what happens to all the characters years down the road. In other words, the action ends and then the reader is treated to a second ending that tells what happens to each character after the fact.

Ultimate ending—Death, of course, is the ultimate ending, and one that the player character cannot return from. The ultimate ending requires the player to restart the game and try again.

Of course, you may end up with more than one type of ending, and you can even mix several of these ending types to create a unique experience for your reader.

TRY IT OUT: END GAME

Take a look at the ending on your role-playing game from Chapters 12, "Making a Role-Playing Game," and 13, "Combat and Consequences in Role-Playing Games," and compare it to the list of ending types. What sort of ending did you give the reader with your role-playing game? Is there another way to structure the ending to provide more or less closure? Create for that game an epilogue that lets the reader know what happens to the three characters long after the game ends.

Moving Beyond Happily Ever After

Not every game will have a happy ending. In fact, many games benefit from having an unhappy ending, where the player character does not fulfill what he or she set out to do. The only type of ending to avoid is a wishy-washy conclusion that ends with the cliché that they all lived happily ever after—whatever that means.

Here are some of the various types of endings:

Happy ending—If the player character reaches his or her goal, it is usually thought to be a happy ending.

Sad ending—If the player character doesn't reach his or her goal, it is usually thought to be a sad ending.

Mixed ending—It is possible for the player character to reach his or her goal but lose so much along the way that the ending is bittersweet.

Completion ending—A long journey comes to an end, with the player character moving from point A to point B.

Understanding ending—The player character learns a valuable lesson based on his or her experiences inside the game.

TRY IT OUT: THE LONG JOURNEY

A young knight is sent on a journey to return a stolen artifact from a warring kingdom. Can he bring about peace between the two communities by righting this wrong, or will he be stopped before he can complete the task? Create five endings for this story, based on the five types of endings.

Making Sequels

Of course, if you leave your readers dangling in the action with a cliff-hanger, you may want to catch them with a sequel. This is especially useful if your game is becoming unmanageably long and you want to release a bit of it in order to gauge the reader's reaction before producing more.

Make sure you end the story at a recognizable pause point, the type of moment in the story that would be ripe for a commercial break if the game were a television show. In addition, make it clear that the story is to be continued, either by stating it outright or implying it within the ending. Many times this is done by introducing questions that may be tumbling through the readers' minds and telling them to stay tuned as if to indicate that you are aware of where they may be mentally and will help them in the future to find the answers to these questions.

Even if you don't end your first game in a cliff-hanger, you may want to return to the characters you've made and use them again in future stories. If you've gotten attached to your characters, chances are that readers have gotten attached, too. Brendan Patrick Hennessy does this well, bringing the main character from *Bell Park, Youth Detective* as a smaller character in his next story, *Birdland*.

Knowing how much to include of the pre-story and post-story is a balancing act, and it is usually smoothed over during the editing process. Ask friends and family members to beta test your game and let you know where there are narrative holes you need to fill with pre-story or post-story or whether those back details are weighing down the central story plot.

You focused in Chapter 8, "Constructing Believable Characters," on building believable non-player characters, but it's time to do the harder work of fleshing out the player character. Contemplating narrative voice, writing plausible dialogue, and deciding on whether your game benefits from a defined or blank player character are all elements of making a personality that the player longs to slip into to explore the world.

Developing a Strong Player Character

In Admiral Jota's game *Lost Pig*, you play an orc. As you can imagine, you don't speak in clear, lilting sentences. Your phrasing is fragmented, brief, and grammatically incorrect:

> Pig lost! Boss say that it Grunk fault. Say Grunk forget about closing gate. Maybe boss right. Grunk not remember forgetting, but maybe Grunk just forget. Boss say Grunk go find pig, bring it back.

Grunk the orc's speech has a clear cadence and rhythm, and it gives the game a distinct sound. That sound is the game's narrative voice. *Narrative voice* is *how* the narrator speaks and, by extension, how the storyteller presents the story. A lot of elements go into defining the narrative voice, including personality traits revealed through word choice and tone. But the voice also depends on whether the author uses breezy, lighthearted words or whether the author packs the game with dense, somber descriptions. It's even why two people can look at the same object and use completely different words to describe it. Narrative voice is the distinctive writing style of a particular game.

When the story is from the first person point of view, the narrative voice is the main character's voice. However that character "speaks" and what he or she chooses to focus on inform how the book sounds. Is this an anxious person? Then the language choice generally reflects that anxiety. Is this a serious academic, teaching at a university? Then the voice will be different, perhaps conveying that the person thoughtfully considers difficult topics.

When the story is from the third-person point of view, or in the case of Twine stories, the second-person point of view, setting the narrative voice requires more diligence. In a third-person story, the narrator is an omniscient presence, but in a second-person Twine game, the narrator is the player character. You have to think about the tone and information you're attempting to convey and then build a narrator who projects those qualities. Determining how you want the player to feel while moving through your story is imperative because the narrative voice plays a big role in setting the mood of the game.

Once you know that a story should have a distinct narrative voice, you'll miss it when it's not clearly defined. As much as I love the earliest Infocom games for their puzzles, they sadly lack a strong narrative voice. Compare these two descriptions, the first from the earliest Infocom game, *Zork*, and the second from a later Infocom game, *Wishbringer*:

> You are standing in an open field west of a white house, with a boarded front door. There is a small mailbox here.

> The seahorse looks at you with moist, frightened eyes. The seahorse opens and closes its little mouth pathetically.

The first narration is perfunctory: It tells you where you are and what you are seeing in the most basic of terms, devoid of personality. It's impossible to describe the narrator of *Zork*. On the other hand, the second narration is filled with emotion: The seahorse doesn't just have eyes; it has moist, frightened eyes. It doesn't just open and close its mouth; it does so pathetically. You know the second narrator is sentimental based on what he or she chooses to mention.

Because the narrator of a Twine story is usually the player character, voice extends to the dialogue, too. How the player character speaks, even more than what he or she says, will give the reader a lot of subtle clues about the character's personality.

This chapter focuses on ensuring that your game has a distinct narrative voice, realistic-sounding dialogue, and a purpose-driven player character. Back in Chapter 8, "Constructing Believable Characters," I covered non-player characters because they are easier to judge objectively. Everything you learned in Chapter 8 applies to building a strong player character, too, but this chapter adds another layer as the player's personality works with and against the personality of the player character.

As you learn about developing a strong player character, you'll also learn about many SugarCube macros, including `<<button>>`, `<<radiobutton>>`, `<<checkbox>>`, `<<textarea>>`, `<<textbox>>`, `<<click>>`, `<<append>>`, `<<prepend>>`, `<<replace>>`, and `<<remove>>`. This is a long list, but I think you're up for the challenge since you've already encountered the Harlowe versions of these macros earlier in the book. Let's dive in.

Using the `<<button>>`, `<<radiobutton>>`, and `<<checkbox>>` Macros

Buttons and check boxes allow you to leave the beaten path of linked text and enter a new realm of clicks. The `<<button>>` macro allows you to place an actual button on the screen instead of presenting linked text, the `<<radiobutton>>` macro gives the player a range of choices for assigning a value to a variable, and the `<<checkbox>>` macro allows the player to assign Boolean or numeric values to multiple variables at once.

Learning the `<<button>>` Macro

There is nothing very remarkable about the `<<button>>` macro in terms of what it can do: Click it, and it takes the player to the next passage, exactly in the same vein as the `[[link]]`

macro. The difference is that the <<button>> macro presents as a button on the screen, holding whatever text you want to place on its blue surface.

Let's say you want the player to run into a room and click a button to turn off an alarm:

```
You race into the room, trying to shut off the alarm. The only thing you see on the
dashboard is a big, blue button. <<button [[Panic Button|Next]]>><<endbutton>>
```

The macro opens with a set of double angled brackets and the macro name (button). Then the traditional [[link]] macro is nested inside: double square brackets, text that you want to have appear on the button itself, a pipe, the name of the next passage, and the closing double square brackets. After that, the <<button>> opener is closed by another set of double angled brackets.

This is a macro that also includes a closer for the macro. Immediately following the button, the macro is closed off with the <<endbutton>> or </button>> macro closer.

When you click the Play button in Twine, as you can see in Figure 18.1, the words appear on the screen along with a blue button labeled Panic Button.

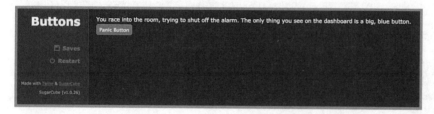

FIGURE 18.1 The <<button>> macro places a clickable blue button on the screen.

This macro is simple but useful when you want to include actual buttons in your game that the player can click to make things happen.

Learning the <<radiobutton>> Macro

You use the <<radiobutton>> macro to give the reader an interesting way to set a value to a variable. Multiple choices are provided, and the player can choose one by clicking a radio button and moving onto the next passage with the value for the variable set.

In other words, this macro behaves similarly to setter links in the sense that the player can make a choice in one passage and continue to the next passage with the value assigned to the variable rather than waiting to assign the value when entering the next passage. This, obviously, cuts down on the number of passages you need to create to do the same task.

Let's say you want to give the player the choice to leave the room, and you want the choice to be remembered in a variable called $choice. You could use this code to accomplish that:

```
Do you want to leave the room?
```

```
<<radiobutton "$choice" "yes">> Yes
<<radiobutton "$choice" "no">> No
<<radiobutton "$choice" "maybe">> Maybe
<<button [[What do you do?|Choice Made]] >><<endbutton>>
```

The macro opens with a set of double angled brackets, the name of the macro (`radiobutton`), and the variable inside quotation marks (`$choice`). This is unusual because variables usually don't appear inside quotation marks, but the quotation marks are necessary here in order to distinguish each part of the macro.

Next the macro states the checked value inside quotation marks—that is, the value that will be assigned to the variable if that choice is chosen. In the first choice in the example, the word is `"yes"`. Therefore, the value `"yes"` is assigned to the variable `$choice` if that circle is picked. Finally, the macro closes with another set of angled brackets. Outside the macro is the plain text that will appear on the screen next to the circle.

When you click the Play button, you see the three choices on the screen, as in Figure 18.2, where three empty circles to the left of the words are ready for the player to make a choice.

FIGURE 18.2 The `<<radiobutton>>` macro gives the player a unique way to make a choice and assign a value to a variable.

Because the player remains in the passage after making his choice and continues to the next passage only by clicking the hypertext included with the `[[link]]` macro, it's possible for the player to change the value of the variable while in the passage. If the player clicks one circle and then changes his mind and clicks another, the value for the variable resets to the new choice. Technically the player can keep changing their mind, reassigning the value to the variable, until they leave the passage.

Learning the `<<checkbox>>` Macro

The `<<radiobutton>>` macro is great when you have one variable and want to give the player a chance to assign one value to that variable. But what if you want to allow the player to set multiple variables at once? You need to use the `<<checkbox>>` macro.

The <<checkbox>> macro is structured in a similar way to the <<radiobutton>> macro. Let's say you want to allow the player to pack some clothes in a suitcase that he can wear later in the game. You could use this code to accomplish that:

```
What do you want to pack?
* <<checkbox "$shirt" false true>> A shirt?
* <<checkbox "$jeans" false true>> Jeans?
* <<checkbox "$hat" false true>> Hat?
[[You look in the suitcase.|Suitcase]]
```

The macro opens with a set of double angled brackets and the name of the macro (checkbox). It then places the variable inside quotation marks. Next, it tells Twine the unchecked value (false) and the checked value (true). It finally closes with another set of double angled brackets.

How does this look when you click the Play button? Three choices are presented to the player, as shown in Figure 18.3, and the player can choose one, two, or three of the options.

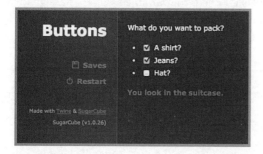

FIGURE 18.3   The <<checkbox>> macro allows the player to choose any of the choices offered.

Now you need to go over to the Suitcase passage and create a list:

```
Your suitcase holds
<<if $shirt is true>>a shirt<<endif>>
<<if $jeans is true>>jeans<<endif>>
<<if $hat is true>>a hat<<endif>>
```

What happens when the player clicks the check boxes in the first passage and then continues to the second passage? He should see a list of all the "true" choices from the check boxes in the Suitcase passage, as shown in Figure 18.4.

FIGURE 18.4 All the `true` choices appear on the next screen.

Inside the macro, for example `<<checkbox "$shirt" false true>>`, the unchecked value is always listed first (in this case, false), and the checked value is always listed second (in this case, true). You do not need to use Booleans. For instance, you can also assign a numeric value as your unchecked and checked values, like this:

`<<checkbox "$wallet" 0 50>> Wallet`

If the box is unchecked, the value is `0`. If the box is checked, the variable `$wallet` is assigned a value of `50`. You can have that amount of "money" increase and decrease throughout the game once the player assigns an initial value to the variable.

TRY IT OUT: CALM PANIC

You are Jim or Jane Smith, known for your calm exterior and interior. Nothing rattles you, including the end of the world. Yes, you are unfortunately on a field trip to NASA when word breaks that aliens are about to invade earth, and it's up to your class to help the scientists there protect the world. Make sure you convey calm through your character's word choices and actions. Even though chaos is happening on the screen, make sure you communicate tranquility through the narrative voice. Weave in the `<<button>>`, `<<radiobutton>>`, and `<<checkbox>>` macros to simulate pressing buttons or navigating NASA computer menus.

Using the `<<textarea>>` and `<<textbox>>` Macros

Like their counterparts in Harlowe, SugarCube's `<<textarea>>` and `<<textbox>>` macros allow the player to type in information and assign that information as a string value for a variable.

Learning the <<textarea>> Macro

The <<textarea>> macro provides an empty box for the player to fill with anything ranging from a single letter to an entire essay. Let's say that you want the player to be able to write a description that repeats throughout the game. You assign the description the player types as the value of the variable $description:

```
"Describe yourself," the voice commanded through the door.
You describe yourself:
<<textarea "$description" "">>
You [[nod your head|Door Opens]] as you finish, as if agreeing with yourself.
```

The macro opens with a set of double angled brackets and the macro name (textarea). The variable ($description) appears inside quotation marks—and, yes, it must have quotation marks around it—followed by a set of *empty* quotation marks ("") and the closing set of double angled brackets.

The empty quotation marks, by the way, are the string placeholder. Currently they are empty because the player hasn't typed anything yet. Of course, if you want to have words already in the box that the player needs to erase before typing, you can place them inside those empty quotation marks. If you want to leave the box empty, just make two quotation marks where the string will appear and close the macro.

When you click the Play button, you should see the plain text as well as the empty box on the screen, as shown in Figure 18.5.

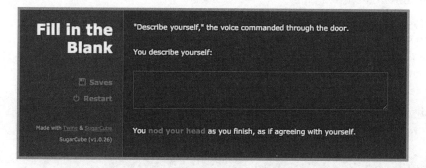

FIGURE 18.5 The <<textarea>> macro provides a space for the player to input his or her own words.

Fill in the box on the screen and then click over to the next passage, where you will use the <<textbox>> macro. Of course, if you want to check the description, type <<print $description>>, and you should see the string value you assigned to the variable based on what you typed in the box.

Learning the `<<textbox>>` Macro

The `<<textbox>>` macro in SugarCube is the counterpart to the `(prompt:)` macro in Harlowe. Say that you want to allow the player to enter a name for his or her character and then have the game recall that name throughout the game to personalize the story? You can do that with the `<<textbox>>` macro:

```
"So am I to understand this is how you describe yourself? <<print $description>>"
The door begins to swing open and then slams shut again. "Wait a second.
What is your name?"
You scrawl it into the air and press an imaginary enter key:
<<textbox "$name" "" "Door Fully Opens">>
```

The `<<textbox>>` macro does not automatically create a new passage for you. Therefore, you need to use the +Passage button to create a second passage called Door Fully Opens for this example.

The macro opens with a set of double angled brackets and the macro name (`textbox`). It then has the variable inside quotation marks (`$name`). Next is the empty set of quotation marks for creating an empty placeholder text box for whatever words the player types into the box. Again, if you want the box to initially contain words that the player needs to erase, place the words between that set of empty quotation marks.

The macro ends with the name of the next passage in quotation marks and a final set of double angled brackets. This is the passage the player goes to once he or she has entered words into the text box and pressed Enter.

Of course, the player may not know that you want her to fill in words and press Enter, so it's a good idea to write the story in such a way that the player knows what to do. If you are worried about this, you can provide a link to the next passage using the `[[link]]` macro, and the value assigned to the variable `$name` will be set as the player travels to the next passage, even if they didn't hit Enter.

When you click the Play button, you should see the plain text as well as the empty box on the screen, as shown in Figure 18.6.

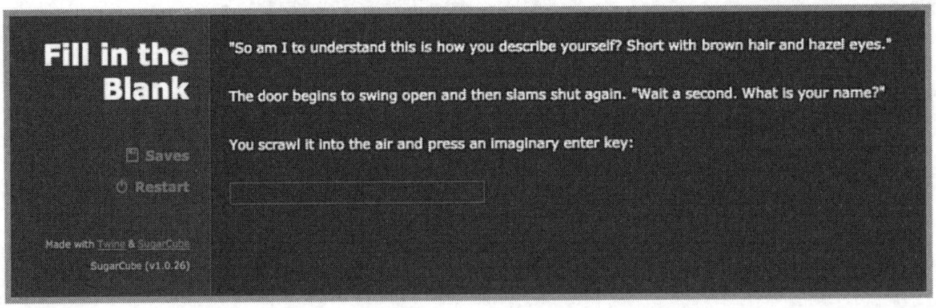

FIGURE 18.6 Write a name in the empty space provided by the `<<textbox>>` macro.

Fill in the box on the screen and then click over to the next passage (Door Fully Opens), where you can check the name by typing <<print $name>>. You should see the name that was typed into the box, which became a string value for the variable $name.

TRY IT OUT: SECRET AGENT

You're a thief hired by a rich old woman to steal back the priceless painting she lost in an unfair bet many years earlier. Your job is to infiltrate the fancy exhibit opening in disguise, somehow steal the painting when no one is looking, and get out of the museum to the rendezvous point. Of course, the moment you enter the museum, you bump into a very chatty museum patron who asks for your name. Consider how you can use the narrative voice to set a tone for this game.

Use the <<textarea>> and <<textbox>> macros to have the player assign a cover story and name that follow the player through the game. As an extra challenge, enable the player to make multiple cover stories and fake names and then navigate multiple non-player characters. If the player mixes up her cover story or name, she's busted, and the game ends.

Using the <<click>>, <<append>>, <<prepend>>, <<replace>>, and <<remove>> Macros

The <<click>>, <<append>>, <<prepend>>, <<replace>>, and <<remove>> macros work together much in the same way that their Harlowe counterparts modify the text on the screen. These macros allow you to add, replace, and remove text with a click.

Learning the <<click>> Macro

The <<click>> macro, like its Harlowe counterpart, turns text into a clickable link. In its simplest form, it can be used to create a link between two passages, like this:

You open the door and <<click "walk into the next room." "Next Room">><<endclick>>

The opener macro begins with a set of double angled brackets and the macro name (click). It then has the clickable text inside two quotation marks ("walk into the next room") followed by the name of the next passage inside two quotation marks ("Next Room"). The opener macro ends with the final set of double angled brackets. This macro also has a closer—either <<endclick>> or <</click>>. Once again, Twine does not automatically generate a new passage, so you need to use the +Passage button to create a passage called Next Room.

When you click the Play button, you should see the plain text and the clickable text on the screen as shown in Figure 18.7. If you click the text, it takes you to the next passage.

FIGURE 18.7 The `<<click>>` macro creates linked text on the screen.

The `<<click>>` macro doesn't do much on its own, but it combines with other macros to trigger them, much like the named hooks in Harlowe.

Learning the `<<append>>` and `<<prepend>>` Macros

The `<<append>>` and `<<prepend>>` macros work in the same way as their Harlowe counterparts, either adding text after (`append`) or before (`prepend`) the plain text on the screen.

In Harlowe, you achieved this with a named hook. In SugarCube, instead of using a nametag, you use the `<span class>` element. In HTML, elements are the smaller, individual components of a larger HTML document. Think of elements as the building blocks that construct a web page. This particular HTML element—the `<span class>` element—identifies the text you want to change when the element is referenced in a triggering macro, like the `<<click>>` macro. Classes, unlike IDs, can be used over and over again on the same page.

To use the `<span class>` element, place the opening `<span class>` and closing `</span>` tags around the words you want to change when the element is referenced with the `<<click>>` macro. Note that the element uses a single set (rather than a double set) of angled brackets:

```
You want to go to the <span class="place">zoo</span>. <<click "You look at the
ground.">><<append ".place">> and the movies<</append>><</click>>
```

Because this example uses the `<<append>>` macro, you can place the element around the word zoo. When the hypertext words are clicked, the new words appear directly after the word zoo.

The element opens with a single angled bracket and the name of the tag (`span class`) followed by an equal sign. The name you've given the class (`place`) appears inside quotation marks, and the opener ends with a single angled bracket. Afterward, the word or words you want to amend (`zoo`) appear before the tag closer (`</span>`). You now have a `<span>` element with a class attribute, similar to the named hooks in Harlowe.

Then it's time to use the element. The `<<click>>` macro opens with the double angled brackets and the macro name (`click`) followed by the words you want to be turned into hypertext inside quotation marks (`"You look at the ground."`). After the `<<click>>` macro opener is set, the `<<append>>` macro follows, opening with its own set of double angled brackets and macro name (`append`). It then references the element by writing the class name inside quotation marks, preceded by a period (`".place"`). The `<<append>>` opener ends with another set of double angled brackets. Next, the words that you want to add to the existing text on the screen when the hypertext is clicked (`and the movies`) appears before the closing `</append>>` macro. Finally, the `<<click>>` macro needs its closer, and it appears at the end of the code as `</click>>`.

When you now click the Play button, you should see the plain text as well as the hypertext on the screen, as shown in Figure 18.8.

FIGURE 18.8 The `<<click>>` and `<<append>>` macros create plain text and linked text on the screen.

When the hypertext is clicked, the text on the screen is modified to include the text contained in the `<<append>>` macro, as shown in Figure 18.9.

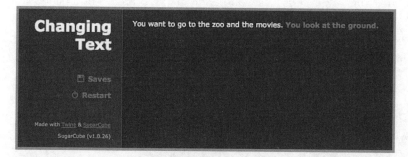

FIGURE 18.9 When the hypertext words are clicked, new words appear on the screen.

The hypertext remains on the screen and is still clickable. Each time the player clicks the link, the words are added.

The `<<prepend>>` macro works in exactly the same way, except that the placement of the element is different because the new words appear *before* the modified word:

```
<span class="reaction">You</span> run into the room <<click "crying.">>
<<prepend ".reaction">>You never wanted it to be like this. <</prepend>><</click>>
```

In this example, the `<<prepend>>` macro words—`You never wanted it to be like this`— appear before the first sentence when the hypertext word (`crying`) is clicked.

Learning the `<<replace>>` and `<<remove>>` Macros

The `<<replace>>` and `<<remove>>` macros also utilize an element to change the words on the screen. The `<<replace>>` macro switches the words inside the element with the words that appear inside the `<<replace>>` macro:

```
You run into the room, <span class="reaction">crying</span>. You snatch up the vase to
<<click "throw it.">><<replace ".reaction">>laughing<</replace>><</click>>
```

Once again, an element is created with a single angled bracket, the words `span class`, and an equal sign (that is, `<span class=`). Next, the name of the class you created appears as a word inside quotation marks, in this case, `"reaction"`, and the element is closed with the other angled bracket. Next, the word that you want to replace when the `<<replace>>` macro is triggered (`crying`) goes before the closer for the element (`</span>`).

The element is then used with the `<<click>>` and `<<replace>>` macros. The `<<click>>` macro opens with a set of double angled brackets and the macro name (`click`) as well as the hypertext words inside quotation marks (`"throw it."`). The opener ends with another set of double angled brackets.

Next, the `<<replace>>` macro opens with its set of double angled brackets, the macro name (`replace`), and the name of the class inside quotation marks, preceded by a period (`".reaction"`). That macro closes with its set of double angled brackets. And then both closers run, one after the other: `<</replace>><</click>>`.

So how does this look when you see it on the screen? If you click the Play button, you should see the plain text and hypertext as shown in Figure 18.10.

FIGURE 18.10 The `<<click>>` and `<<replace>>` macros work together to change the words on the screen.

When the hypertext words (throw it) are clicked, the word connected to the element (crying) disappears and is replaced with the word inside the <<replace>> macro (laughing), as shown in Figure 18.11.

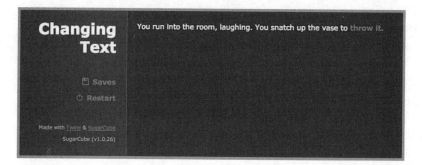

FIGURE 18.11 The word "crying" is replaced with the word "laughing" when the hypertext is clicked.

The <<remove>> macro works in a similar manner, except it removes text without replacing it. In addition, the <<remove>> macro does not have an opener and a closer. Like the <<set>> macro, it works on its own. Here's an example of how to use it:

```
<span class="theft">You steal the painting from the wall.</span> You look around the
room<span class="theft">, <<click "carefully">><<remove ".theft">><</click>></span>.
```

When you click the word carefully, the words in the element (You steal the painting from the wall) as well as the hypertext carefully are removed from the screen.

TRY IT OUT: A CASE OF MISCOMMUNICATION

Your spaceship has crash-landed on a distant planet, where the aliens are anything but friendly. They seem to be easily offended by the most innocuous statements. Navigating the conversation and getting them to help you repair your spaceship so you can leave feels like a tightrope act. You can hear the tension in the narrative voice.

Use the <<click>>, <<append>>, <<prepend>>, <<replace>>, and <<remove>> macros to build a verbal maze that the player needs to navigate in order to get off the planet.

Working with Narrative Voice

The narrative voice provides the personality for a story or game. Just as you would never want to hang out with a dull person, devoid of personality, people don't want to read interactive fiction that lacks a clear voice. The voice should convey the story's temperament and the emotions the voice dredges up for the reader. For instance, do you want the reader to feel nervous or confident? Do you want the reader to feel as if she is walking through a lovable or disagreeable world? Should he look at his surroundings as disorganized or highly structured?

In other words, it's time to go back to Chapter 8 and review how you create a character's personality and then take those concepts a step further to apply that personality to a game. Make the word choice convey the disposition of the game. Doing so sets your game apart and takes your writing to the next level. A strong narrative voice sets apart polished games and stories.

Setting the Narrator

Sometimes you walk into a house and immediately feel comfortable. The furniture is cozy, the host is warm, and you easily fall into the conversation. Other times, you walk into a house and feel like you're in a museum. You sit up straight and lower your voice because it seems like you should be whispering.

Transfer that understanding to interactive fiction, replacing the house with the story and the owner of the house with the narrator of the game.

Every story has a host—the narrator—that sets the tone and leads the reader from plot point to plot point. In a second-person interactive fiction story, the player character is usually the narrator.

You've probably picked up on the inherent problem that exists solely within interactive fiction. With a book, the reader isn't part of the story. There is either a first-person narrator, who is the main character in the book, or a third-person narrator, who operates like a ghost, relaying the story events. Interactive fiction breaks down that wall and places the reader in the story. But if the narrator is the player character, and the player character is the player, what happens with all those personalities vying for a single role?

This is where you, the writer, have to take the reins. It is *your* job to set the narrative voice. If you skip this step and come off as a wishy-washy narrator, you're foisting the job on the reader. The writer sets the personality of a story via the narrative voice that the reader experiences.

Look back at Grunk, the narrator of *Lost Pig*. His strong personality differs greatly from mine, which means, as the reader, that I have to slip into that "costume" and take on that persona when I play the game. Sure, my personality comes into play when I give the game instructions, but the game always talks back to me in that distinct orc-like Grunk voice created by the writer, Admiral Jota.

Before you begin working on a game, sketch out the narrator's personality because it will influence the tone of the game. Give the narrator executable goals and a demarcated exploration space.

Once you have a clearly defined player character personality, allow that personality to permeate the writing. If your character is brusque, make the sentences brief and clipped to convey that. If you character is brilliant, choose erudite words that express the person's educational achievements. If your character is cheerful, make the language ebullient.

TRY IT OUT: THE SNOBBY DETECTIVE, PART I

You've been summoned to Hangleton Manor to help solve the ghastly murder of the estate's gardener. Unfortunately, with Lady Hangleton overseas on holiday, your host is her clueless son, Ernest.

Choose your words carefully in order to build a narrative voice for this story. Think about how a snobby detective would speak. Would he purposefully speak as if he's carrying around a thesaurus? What would he notice and comment on in his description of a room? How would he interact with the other characters to convey the boredom he feels dealing with Ernest Hangleton?

You don't need to finish the game now because you'll be continuing the story in the next Try It Out, but pause after a few passages and ask your friends and family members to describe the voice of the narrator in three words. If one of those words isn't *snobby* (or a synonym of *snobby*), go back and tweak the writing to make your writing sound more condescending.

Being Consistent

Once you've set the voice, stick to it. Have you ever watched a movie where an American actor is speaking in a British accent, and suddenly a word or two comes out in a distinctly non-British accent? It's jarring because it conflicts with your understanding of the character. Of course, the actor didn't intend to break character, just as writers don't intend to accidentally drop their narrative voice. But it happens, and keeping that in mind will help stave off the possibility.

In *Lost Pig*, the reason Grunk's voice works is that he always speaks in the same, grammatically incorrect English. For instance, if you try to pick up an object that isn't useful for the game, you get a message in Grunk-ese: "That not thing that Grunk can carry around."

Imagine if the narrator responded, "Oh dear me, that seems to be something too heavy for my brittle arms to pick up." While a sentence like that may sound at home coming out of the mouth of an elderly grandmother, it doesn't sound like something Grunk would say. Grunk doesn't speak in complete sentences, he doesn't use exclamations like "oh dear me," and vivid terms like "brittle" aren't part of his vocabulary.

So how can you avoid breaking the narrative voice? Whenever you sit down to work on your game, take a few minutes to play the passages that you've already created. Hearing the voice will help you remember to use the voice.

TRY IT OUT: THE SNOBBY DETECTIVE, PART II

Continue the story from the previous Try It Out. Say that after the funeral for the gardener, Ernest holds a dinner for all the estate staff and the gardener's friends and family. It's the perfect time to interview a few of the suspects—except a problem arises! You know one of the guests.

Slip into a disguise and take special care to change the way you speak around this character. How different can you make the snobby detective sound when he encounters this dreaded guest?

Changing the Point of View

If you're finding it difficult to set the narrative voice, changing the identity of the player character and, by extension, the story's point of view, can make a big difference. For instance, let's say you're writing a story about an astronaut who has befriended an alien and is taking the alien back to earth with him.

If you find that you're having trouble finding the voice of the astronaut, start over and rewrite the story from the point of view of the alien. How would the alien speak and think? What would the alien notice? How would the alien feel, and do its emotions align with the feelings you're trying to invoke in the reader? Switching the character telling the story changes the way the story is told.

TRY IT OUT: THE SNOBBY DETECTIVE, PART III

Take the same storyline from the preceding two Try It Outs but start over. This time, write the game from the point of view of the cook, who was romantically involved with the deceased gardener. You'll need to decide beforehand whether the cook is the person who killed the gardener (and is therefore hiding information from the detective) or whether she is in mourning for her slain boyfriend.

The sound of the story should change because the narrator has changed. How does the cook process the world? Are her observations more perfunctory, her sentences more straightforward? Are you choosing more commonplace synonyms in place of the detective's most obscure terms? It's the same situation, but telling the story from the point of view of a different character will give it a completely different feel. Which version do you like better?

Playing for Research

Now that you know that a good part of the work of setting the narrative voice is allowing the narrator's speech patterns and personality to seep into every nook and cranny of the story, play some interactive fiction games and start noting which ones have a strong narrative voice and which ones ask the reader to do the hard work of defining the narrator's personality.

TRY IT OUT: GAME JOURNAL

This Try It Out is more about research than creation. Play 10 games, either ones listed in this book or ones chosen from the Interactive Fiction Database (ifdb.tads.org), and take note of their narrative voice. For each story, describe the personality of the game and state how you were able to discern the personality by pointing out wording that supports your ideas.

Communicating with Non-Player Characters

Your player character, or the narrator of the game, may have to communicate with the non-player characters. Writing dialogue can be tricky, especially when it comes to making it sound realistic without bogging down the story with the unnecessary (but realistic) tics of daily speech.

Handling Dialogue

I think dialogue is the benefit to the hard work of juggling multiple characters. You can drop important clues for the reader in a conversation without it sounding stilted and obvious. Plus you can convey information about the characters based on what they say...or don't say. Do they spill their secrets or keep information close to their heart?

Conversations can do double duty, by both moving the story forward and exploring a relationship at the same time. How the characters communicate with each other can tell the reader whether they're angry or loving, suspicious or trusting. Players notice when one character is hogging the conversation or if all characters are getting equal speaking time.

So how do you write dialogue that sounds realistic and serves a purpose?

First and foremost, know what you are trying to communicate to the reader. Just as you pause to think about what you need to say and the best way to say it in your daily conversations, you need to pause when you reach dialogue on the screen and think about what you want to get across to the reader.

Next, as you did when setting the narrative voice, consider the "sound" of the character. Have you ever read a conversation in a book and noticed that even though the sentence doesn't state which character has said the words, you know exactly which character is speaking? The sentences spoken by Draco Malfoy don't sound like sentences that would be spoken by Harry Potter. So think about the unique conversational traits of your characters and make sure that you don't break character by dropping those quirks.

Of course, the setting and action should affect the dialogue. People who are running from a bear are not going to speak using long, thoughtful declarations. They're going to shout out quick bursts of words to conserve oxygen. Similarly, people who are hiding a secret may give terse answers. Conversation, in such cases, helps set the scene.

Finally, dialogue should be used sparingly. The general rule is to use dialogue if it serves a purpose, moves the story along, or conveys information. Leave it out if it doesn't accomplish one of those three things.

TRY IT OUT: CONVERSATION JOURNAL

Here's another research task that will elevate your games to the next level. Go to a crowded place and listen in to conversations around you and note how people speak. Everyone has verbal quirks, such as phrases they constantly say or pauses they put into their sentences. Maybe they ask a lot of questions or don't sound very confident in their statements.

Jot down some notes that you can use later when building characters. In fact, take the traditional typing sentence—The quick brown fox jumps over the lazy dog— and imagine how each person around you would say it to reveal their personality. Someone who is angry might say it as, "Are you stupid? How do you not know that the quick brown fox jumped over that lazy, good-for-nothing, dog?" Someone who is anxious might say it as, "Oh no, I can't believe it happened again. That dangerous brown fox was jumping over the dog last night. One of them could have gotten hurt!"

Using Twine Tricks for Conversation

You can provide conversation for the reader as plain text in a scene, but you can also make conversation an interactive choice for the reader. Take, for instance, a detective game where the player character needs to interview dozens of suspects. Instead of giving physical action choices, give the reader choices based on what they want to ask, as shown here:

```
Ask the cook about the [[missing pan|Cook Pan]].
Ask the cook about the [[spilled salt|Cook Salt]].
Ask the cook about her [[brother, Max|Cook Brother]].
```

You can place all the options for all the characters at the bottom of every screen or nest conversation options inside other conversation options so that each nugget of information opens up a new line of questioning.

Consider dragging the passage boxes into position much as you would arrange a physical space, with the detective's opening centered in the middle and the other characters each having their own introductory passage attached to dozens of answers to the possible questions, as shown in Figure 18.12.

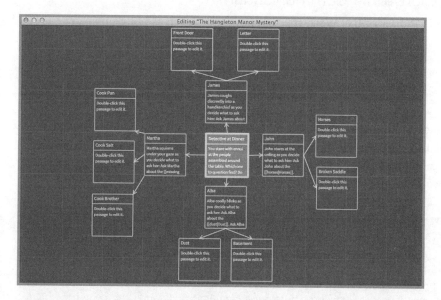

FIGURE 18.12 Arrange the passage boxes to make writing conversations easier when balancing multiple characters in the same scene.

Make sure to provide an exit from the conversation. Repeat this technique as often as necessary to make juggling multiple characters in the same conversation more manageable.

If you are going to make it possible for the player character to repeatedly encounter the same non-player character by returning to a passage, use the (history:) macro in a Harlowe game (or its SugarCube counterpart that you'll learn in Chapter 19, "Balancing

Pacing and Action") to ensure that the conversation sounds realistic. Characters would say a greeting to each other only once. After that point, they would mention that they had already seen each other.

TRY IT OUT: TRIAL

You are a lawyer, prosecuting an alleged criminal mastermind who is responsible for shutting off power to the city in order to conduct dozens of high-profile thefts under a cloak of darkness. You have the evidence connecting the suspect to the crime, and you have the motive....You just don't know how the person on trial managed to knock out the power grid. Write a story for this scenario. As you do, conduct questioning, calling forth witnesses. The correct line of questioning may unlock the information the player needs.

Conveying Nonverbal Communication

Not all communication is verbal. Wordless communication, such as body language descriptions (Is the character standing with her arms crossed? Does she hug the player character as he comes into the room?) or character reactions say just as much as the dialogue itself.

Become aware of how you hold your body when you're speaking to a person and transfer that knowledge to your characters. Characters who are lying may put distance between themselves and their conversation partners, positioning themselves on the opposite side of the room, whereas characters who have missed each other may stand very close to one another. Make sure you drop nonverbal clues so the player knows how the player character reacts to the people around him or her.

TRY IT OUT: SILENT CONVERSATION

The witch has removed your voice because you broke your promise. It's her punishment du jour. You're not the only voiceless victim. There's also the guy who tried to steal basil from her garden, the elderly lady who accidently ran over her cat, and a businessman who stole her idea for a wart-producing cream. Without using words—since you're all voiceless—work together to defeat the witch. How can you convey how this team works with one another without using one piece of conversation?

Employing Juxtaposition and Contrast

Sometimes what you know about a character is based on the traits of another character. By placing the characters next to one another, otherwise known as *juxtaposition*, you can see how they're alike and how they're different. At the same time, *contrast* can be used to point out the differences between two characters, such as making one character good and another one bad.

Consider defining the player character partially through comparison to other characters. Perhaps the player character looks better than he or she really is due to the non-player characters making terrible decisions. Or, inversely, maybe you start questioning the motives of the player character because the non-player characters seem more honest.

TRY IT OUT: QUICK COMPARISON

Create a mini story where what you know about the player character is based on the actions of the non-player characters. For instance, re-create a two-character relationship similar to that of Draco Malfoy and Harry Potter. Even though Harry does terrible things from time to time, the reader associates him with being "good" simply because he is a contrast to Draco, whom readers associate with "bad." Make your own good and bad characters interact with one another to highlight each other's traits.

Defining Goals and Assigning Purpose

Every character starts out a game with one big goal, but each one also has smaller goals from scene to scene. The big goal defines a character's purpose. The smaller goals help or hinder the character in fulfilling the overall objective.

Creating Blank or Defined Player Characters

Though this whole chapter has been about creating carefully defined player characters, there are times when you want to start a game with a blank hero for the player to use. A blank player character is one without definition, like the nameless adventurer in *Zork* that you know nothing about. When you start that game, you are...someone. It's like you've been bonked on the head and have no clue who you are or why you should wander into the house you're standing next to. As the game continues, you come no closer to understanding your backstory or what makes you tick.

On the other hand, a defined player character asks the player to slip into a role, one that has been carefully crafted to fit the story. The player is not just any nameless detective; she's the world's worst detective. Or he's an actor on a television show who has gotten mixed up in a diamond heist. Or she's a deep-sea diver who is looking for a treasure her father died trying to find the year before.

Still, there are times when you want piecing together the identity of the player character to be part of the story, as it is in Andrew Plotkin's *Dreamhold*, which is about discovering who you are and why you are in a wizard's home.

With careful writing, the reader can have fun discovering who he or she is throughout the course of the story. But remember: Strong characters can make a weak plot interesting, but weak characters can't hold up a strong plot. Even if your player character begins the game as a blank slate, by the final passage, he or she needs to have a clear, memorable personality.

Considering Gender

Handling gender in interactive fiction stories is tricky. If the gender of the character isn't set by the author, the player determines the gender of the player character. Take, for example, Taylor from *Lifeline* that I'll talk about more in Chapter 19. His or her gender is not clearly defined, and the player is allowed to mentally visualize Taylor as male or female, depending upon their preference.

Most of the time you'll be able to straddle both genders with your player character as long as you're careful about not making gender-based assumptions. Other times, you'll want to define the gender of the player character, such as a game set in an all-male boarding school or a game depicting the life of a princess.

Think about the story you want to tell. Do you want your player to experience a life unlike their own, or do you want the player to be able to find common ground with the player character? Is gender a big part of the story, or can the story be gender-neutral? If you write a strong character, the player will usually go along with the role and slip into seeing the world through a character's eyes.

Slipping Into Character

The easiest rule for making a memorable player character is to create a life that people want to try on. Imagine the most fascinating person you can and then put her in an interesting situation. Make creatures of routine who have odd quirks that make them unforgettable, like *Harriet the Spy* and her tomato sandwiches.

Make your player character creative, thinking outside the box, so the player is impressed with both the player character's imagination and his or her own puzzle-solving accomplishments. Give your player character a secret that is revealed a little bit at a time.

Make player characters who operate in shades of gray, sometimes making questionably ethical decisions. Contrast your player character with another character, making him more exciting by comparison than he would be on his own. Finally, make curious characters. Your players will be curious and want to explore if the characters they are playing are curious, too.

The most important advice I can end with is to find your own voice, no matter how wacky, long-winded, or poetic it seems. Don't try to emulate other writers or other games. By finding your own voice, you are certain to also find people who connect with that voice. Gamers are drawn to writers who have their own, distinct style.

It's time to turn your eyes to driving the story forward with risky and rewarding choices, as well as giving your player a redo after a mess-up. And you'll do that with a slew of SugarCube macros and functions in the next chapter.

19

Balancing Pacing and Action

Hello? Is this thing working? Can anyone read me? These are the opening words of *Lifeline*, an interactive fiction story by 3 Minute Games that consists of text messages back and forth with an astronaut named Taylor who is stranded on a distant moon after a spaceship crash. Taylor is counting on you to help her get through this crisis because you're the only person who answered her distress call. Of course, as you know from the last chapter, Taylor's gender is never defined in this game, but I like to think of her as a clever, brave woman doing her best to get through a very stressful situation. You may picture her...or him...otherwise.

The first time I played *Lifeline*, the story ended pretty quickly. I eagerly gave Taylor advice based on what *I* wanted to explore, and that sadly ended her life. Oops. But *Lifeline* kindly asked if I wanted to rewind and try again. I made better choices the second time, though I accidentally froze Taylor overnight. For my third try, I kept jumping off the game to research the choices (Would being exposed to 150 rads of radiation kill my new friend?) because by this point, I cared about this fictional character's well-being.

Part of that care comes from the pacing of the game. *Pacing* is how quickly the writer is moving the reader through the story. A lot of things go into pacing, including the spacing between action sequences, how often the reader gets to make meaningful choices, the lengths of the sentences, and the vividness of the language. Tell the reader too much too soon, and you risk having him repelled by rather than attracted to the character. Tell the reader too little too slowly, and you risk having the player grow bored.

So how does *Lifeline* achieve pacing success? It starts with its built-in timer. You enable notifications on your phone (or iPad or Apple Watch) when you start *Lifeline*, and then Taylor alternates between reaching out to you for advice and being busy implementing your ideas once you make a choice. I found myself checking my phone for new notifications, eager to see what happened to Taylor after each step, and I worried about her when she went silent for hours. Was she okay and just sleeping? Had my advice negatively affected Taylor?

It's possible to play the game on "fast mode," powering through the choices without the long pauses while you're waiting for Taylor to return, but those pauses elevated my emotional reaction to the game. The reality is that *Lifeline* itself is pretty thin in terms of text, and often the silence speaks more than the words. *Lifeline* needs its timer.

But you can achieve a similar level of emotional involvement without the use of timers, and there are plenty of tricks you'll learn in this chapter to get the reader to care about your characters.

It's time to turn your eye to the story's pacing. As the writer, you determine how quickly a story unfolds. There will be times when you want the reader to feel as if time is slowly plodding forward, especially if you're trying to build anxiety while the character waits for something to happen, and there will be times when you want the reader to feel as if time is whizzing by as they race into the action.

Ideally, your game will switch its speed from high to low and back again rather than keeping the same rate through the whole game. With such shifts, the action sequences make the reader *feel*, especially as the fast passages go by in a blur, and the descriptive passages make the reader *think*, slowing down to catch clues. This combination keeps moving the story forward and keeps the reader engaged while alternating between feeling and thinking.

More important than *how* is understanding *why* the pace needs to fluctuate, so you can fine-tune your game with purpose. The point to alternating the speed of the story is not just to allow the reader to catch his breath between moments of high excitement; it's to highlight the important points you want to convey to the reader, such as how the characters change over time due to events in the story. Those quieter, reflective moments allow the player to subconsciously note that the characters are different from how they were at the beginning of the story.

This means, yes, that your characters need to change. They need to be affected by events. They need to keep the same core personality but incorporate new traits that come from living life...or, in the case of fiction, living the story.

So turn that figurative dial, speeding up and slowing down the story in order to highlight the changes.

You do this by using a lot of new macros and functions. Functions are like macros, at least from the perspective of the writer, although the computer interacts with functions and macros in different ways and you can do math with functions. In this chapter, you'll learn about the `either()`, `random()`, `turns()`, and `visited()` functions. You'll also learn about the `<<back>>`, `<<return>>`, `<<display>>`, `<<actions>>`, and `<<choice>>` macros. Finally, you'll learn how to give your players the option to save the game before a critical choice and how to reload the game and try a different option if they don't like the outcome.

That's a lot of ground to cover, so open up a new SugarCube game (remember to change the story format!) and let's get started.

Using the `either()` and `random()` Functions

You already encountered these functions in Harlowe with the `(either:)` and `(random:)` macros. These functions effectively accomplish the same task, even though they're written with a different syntax.

Learning the either() Function

You use the either() function to print a randomly chosen number or string from a list. You can also use it to assign a randomly chosen value (number, string, or Boolean) to a variable or send a player to a randomly chosen passage.

For instance, you can use the either() function to print out a randomly chosen word from a list:

```
Every time you go to the zoo, you like to see the <<print either("monkeys",
"lions", "snakes")>>.
```

In this case, you're combining the either() function with the <<print>> macro in order to see the function in action. The macro opens with a set of double angled brackets and the name of the macro (print).

This example then segues into the either() function by writing the name of the function (either) and then putting in an open parenthesis. Inside the parentheses are three strings, each in quotation marks, separated by commas ("monkeys", "lions", "snakes"). There can be as many options as you want in the list, and the strings can be as many words as you prefer, as long as each string is contained inside its own set of quotation marks.

The function closes with the end parenthesis, and the macro closes with another set of double angled brackets. When you click the Play button, you see either the word monkeys, lions, or snakes on the screen, as shown in Figure 19.1.

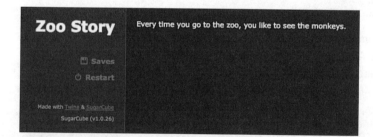

FIGURE 19.1 The <<print>> macro combines with the either() function to display one of the strings in a list.

You can also use the either() function in conjunction with the <<set>> macro to assign a random value to a variable. In the following example, I've assigned a numeric value, though you could also assign a string or Boolean value:

```
<<set $points to either(1, 2, 3)>>
```

The macro opens with a set of double angled brackets and the name of the macro (set). It then lists the name of the variable ($points) and the to operator before launching into the name of the function (either), an open parenthesis, the possible values separated by commas, the closing parenthesis, and the closing set of double angled brackets. In this case, a value of 1, 2, or 3 is assigned to the $points variable. Of course, those numbers could be any numeric value—such as 25, 50, 75, or 100—and you could have the numeric list be as many entries as you want. Remember to put quotation marks around the words if you go with a string value instead of a numeric value.

Finally, you can use the either() function to send the player to a randomly chosen passage, just as you can do in Harlowe with the (either:) macro. Here's an example of what you could type in this new passage:

```
You fall down the hole and end up in <<print either("[[a strange room|Red Room]]",
"[[a strange room|Yellow Room]]", "[[a strange room|Green Room]]")>>.
```

In this example, the <<print>> macro, either() function, and [[link]] macro work together. The macro opens with a set of double angled brackets and the name of the macro (print). It then segues into the either() function. Inside the parentheses are three options of hypertext words separated from passage names by a pipe (for example, "[[a strange room|Red Room]]"), each enclosed in quotation marks and separated by commas. The macro closes with another set of double angled brackets.

In this example, the either() function chooses to display one of three [[link]] macros listed with the function. The hyperlinked words are always the same—a strange room—but each set of hyperlinked words are attached to a different passage. The player doesn't know where the link leads until they click. As always, you can list as many options as you like; you don't have to stick with three as in the example.

Learning the random() Function

The random() function in SugarCube operates in the same way as the (random:) macro in Harlowe. It chooses a numeric value for a variable within a given range. It cannot be used with strings or Booleans. Here is an example of its use:

```
<<set $strength to random(1,99)>>You drink the purple concoction and instantly
feel stronger. You now have <<print $strength>> strength points.
```

This example uses the random() function in combination with the <<set>> macro. The macro opens with a set of double angled brackets and the macro name (set). Next, the variable is stated ($strength) with the operator to.

Then the random() function opens with its name (random) and an open parenthesis. A numeric range is given, in this case, 1 to 99 (1,99). You should give only two numbers here, but they can be any two numbers that you want to set for the range. Finally, the function closes with a parenthesis, and the macro closes with a set of double angled brackets.

When you check the value of the variable by using <<print $strength>>, it gives back a random number between 1 and 99, as you can see in Figure 19.2.

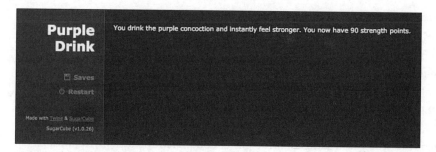

FIGURE 19.2 The random() function randomly assigns a numeric value within a given range.

So both functions operate in exactly the same manner as their Harlowe counterparts, even though they are written differently.

TRY IT OUT: ZOO ESCAPE

You thought it was a joke when the head of the zoo inquired about your services, claiming that the ghost of a disgruntled zoo employee was letting the animals out of the cages. Red pandas, boa constrictors, and emus have been found walking around the city, their enclosures open. Use the either() and random() functions to create a game where success in rounding up the animals and stopping the ghost is determined by a randomly assigned points system.

Using the turns() and visited() Functions

The turns() and visited() functions do the work of the (count:) and (history:) macros in Harlowe. You can use these functions to let the player know how many "moves" it took to get to the end of the game or display different text each time the player reopens a passage.

Learning the turns() Function

If you want to simulate counting moves in a game, an easy solution is to count each choice as one move, even if the player returns to the same passage over and over again. The turns() function handles this, keeping track of how many passages a player has read by logging them as a list. This function returns the number of passages in the history list, and the writer can use the result to tell the player how many "moves" he or she has taken to complete a task.

To see how many passages Twine has tracked and logged in the history list, combine the turns() function with the <<print>> macro to access the number:

```
You've used <<print turns()>> minutes.
```

The `<<print>>` macro opens with a set of double angled brackets and the macro name (`print`). Then the `turns()` function is written as is, and the macro closes with another set of double angled brackets.

How can you make the counting of turns an important part of the game? What if instead of tracking the real time used to play the game, you count each move as one minute within the game, similar to the clock used in the Infocom games of *Deadline* or *Wishbringer*.

Regardless of how many actual minutes it takes for the player to read those passages, if one passage has been read, the game states that the player completed the task in 1 minute. If three passages have been read, the game states that the player completed the task in 3 minutes, as shown in Figure 19.3.

FIGURE 19.3 The `turns()` function tells the reader how many moves he or she has made.

Of course, you can combine the `turns()` function with a conditional to limit the number of moves a player can make. Let's say that you want to give the player 10 tries to get out of the opening maze:

```
<<if turns() lte 9>>You can go [[left]] or [[right]].
<<else>>You've run [[out of time|End]].<<endif>>
```

The `<<if>>` macro opens with a set of double angled brackets and the macro name (`if`). It then contains the `turns()` function, written as is, along with the operator `lte`, which stands for "less than or equal to," and the number `9`. The macro closes with another set of double angled brackets followed by the text that appears if the condition is met (because the number of passages logged in the history list is 9 or fewer).

Next, the `<<else>>` portion of the conditional looks to see if the player has clicked on 10 passages and therefore made more than 9 moves. If that is the case, Twine displays the text in this second portion of the conditional statement. Finally, the `<<if>>` macro ends with its closer: `<<endif>>`.

This function can simulate the passing of time, lending a heightened sense of tension to the situation and forcing the player to pay close attention to the choices to avoid wasting any of the allotted moves.

Learning the `visited()` Function

The `(count:)` and `(history:)` macros worked together in Harlowe to check whether the player has already seen the current passage. In SugarCube, the `visited()` function accomplishes the same task. This is invaluable if you are treating passages like rooms and want different text to display on the first trip through the space than on all subsequent visits to the passage.

The most straightforward use of the `visited()` function is with the `<<print>>` macro, to have the game state how many times the player has accessed a passage and treat each click to the passage as a visit to the "room." Here is what this looks like:

```
It feels as if you have been here before. You have visited the kitchen
<<print visited()>> times.
```

After the plain text, the `<<print>>` macro opens with a set of double angled brackets and the name of the macro (`print`). Then the `visited()` function is written as is, and the macro is closed with another set of double angled brackets.

When you click the Play button, the game tells you how many times you have been in the Kitchen passage, as shown in Figure 19.4.

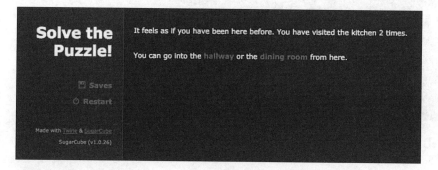

FIGURE 19.4 The `visited()` function tells the reader how many times he or she has seen a passage.

To use the `visited()` function to display different text, combine the function with the `<<if>>` macro to create a conditional statement:

```
<<if visited() == 1>>Are you new here?<<elseif visited() == 2>>I think you've been
here before.<<elseif visited() gte 3>>Don't you want to [[move on|Go]]?<<endif>>
```

Note the double equal sign used here to make a comparison inside an `if` statement, to ensure that two numbers match up. The first number used in this statement is the number of times the player has visited the passage. That number isn't listed directly, but it's contained in the `visited()` function since that function is returning a list of times the passage has been read. The other number is the condition-setting number: 1, 2, or greater than or equal to 3. If the two numbers match up, the text appears. Similarly, you could use the operator `eq` in place of the double equal signs for the same effect.

The macro opens with a set of double angled brackets and the macro name (`if`) as well as the `visited()` function, written as is. After a set of double equal signs, another number appears (1), and the macro ends with another set of double angled brackets. This code uses two more `<<elseif>>` options along with their specific text (and, in one case, a link) before the closer macro: `<<endif>>`. You can also use a simple `<<else>>` macro in place of the third `<<elseif>>`, both options accomplish the same task.

The first time the player visits the passage, the two numbers on either side of the double equal sign (`visited() == 1`) will match, so the first text option appears. The next time the player visits the passage, the two numbers on either side of the next double equal sign (`visited() == 2`) will match, so the second text option appears. Finally, on all subsequent visits to the passage, the third `elseif` statement will be `true`, so the third text option and link appear, as shown in Figure 19.5.

FIGURE 19.5 The `visited()` function can be combined with the `<<if>>` macro to make different text appear each time the passage is opened.

Again, this function behaves similarly to its Harlowe counterpart; it's just written differently.

TRY IT OUT: THE DISORIENTING MAZE

John Thurston, an eccentric billionaire who has built a maze to protect his safe, has hired you to see if the maze is navigable. He warns you that the maze will become progressively harder the more time you spend inside and that poisonous gas will be released into the maze after 20 minutes—a safeguard that allows him safe passage to the heart of the maze while knocking out criminals who try to steal his fortune.

Write a story for this scenario and set up a 12-passage maze and use the `turns()` function to limit the player to 20 moves. Use the `visited()` function to change the room description each time the player opens a passage, removing helpful clues each time the passage is accessed. You can use this trick in future games, since players will read carefully once they know that text may change each time a passage reopens. For extra points, also incorporate the `either()` function into one or two passages to send the player to a randomly chosen point in the maze.

Using the `<<back>>` and `<<return>>` Macros

The two simple macros `<<back>>` and `<<return>>` move the player backward, to the last passage read, using two different methods of return.

Learning the `<<back>>` Macro

You can put the `<<back>>` into any passage to send the player backward one passage. For instance, if you have an inventory passage that the player keeps accessing, you need to give the player an option to return to the story, like this:

```
You are carrying:
<<if $key is true>>A key<<endif>>
<<if $shovel is true>>A shovel<<endif>>
<<back>>
```

The macro is written as is, `<<back>>`, and it's important to understand how it works. It "rewinds" the history, erasing the passage just accessed from the list and therefore returning the player to the previous passage. This is helpful if you don't want to increase the visit count to the passage because it acts as if the jump to the inventory passage never happened. On the screen, this macro appears with a little arrow, as shown in Figure 19.6.

It is also possible to customize the message the player sees instead of the word back. For instance, what if you want the link to read, Return to the story? You put the words you want to appear as the hypertext inside quotation marks in the macro:

```
<<back "Return to the story">>
```

FIGURE 19.6 A little arrow appears on the screen next to the word `Back`.

You can play with the text that appears on the screen with the macro, though in all cases, the player returns to the last passage read.

Learning the `<<return>>` Macro

Though the `<<return>>` macro performs the same task as the `<<back>>` macro from the point of view of the reader, this macro actually moves the history list forward rather than rewinding it. In other words, it counts the return to the previous passage as a new visit, increasing the visit count by one.

If you are using the `visited()` function with an `<<if>>` macro, each time the player goes back to the passage, the game counts it as another visit and displays the appropriate text. Again, it is written as is, `<<return>>`, as shown here:

```
You are carrying:
<<if $key is true>>A key<<endif>>
<<if $shovel is true>>A shovel<<endif>>
<<return>>
```

This macro also displays the word `Return` with a little arrow, as shown in Figure 19.7. Or, like the `<<back>>` macro, the text that appears with the `<<return>>` macro can be customized in the exact same way.

FIGURE 19.7 A little arrow appears on the screen next to the word `Return`.

TRY IT OUT: CATASTROPHE!

Sparks are flying and alarms are ringing in the lab after an experiment explodes. Use the <<back>> or <<return>> macros to allow the player to teleport from the current point to two other locations in the lab and collect the objects needed to get the lab safe again. Use the visited() function to display new text each time there is a new visit to a passage.

Using the <<display>>, <<actions>>, and <<choice>> Macros

You've already encountered the <<display>> macro in its (display:) Harlowe form, but here you'll learn how to use the SugarCube version. In addition, you'll learn about the <<actions>> and <<choice>> macros, which add new functionality to your games.

Learning the <<display>> and <<actions>> Macros

Back in Harlowe, you used the (display:) macro to repeat the same text over and over again in other passages. You can do that with the <<display>> macro in SugarCube, and it becomes a more powerful tool when you pair it with the <<actions>> macro, which limits the number of times the player can access an option and removes it from the list once chosen.

This example requires you to create many passages using the green +Passage button because Twine does not automatically generate the new passages despite the fact that you are building a link in the macro. Begin by creating a new passage, named Tasks, so that there are two passages on the screen. Enter the following code in Tasks:

```
<<actions
"Pick up your suitcase"
"Kiss your mother"
"Give the note to Peter"
"Whisper the password to Michelle">>
```

In this example, the macro opens with a set of double angled brackets and the name of the macro (actions). It then gives four options inside quotation marks. These options appear on the screen as links when the passage opens, as shown in Figure 19.8.

It's now time to create four new passages and name them based on the words inside the quotation marks in your Tasks passage. For instance, "Pick up your suitcase" should be the name of one of the passages, and "Kiss your mother" should be another. Take special care with matching capitalization between the Tasks passage and the name of each new passage. You can see all four new passages as well as the Tasks passage and the Start passage in Figure 19.9.

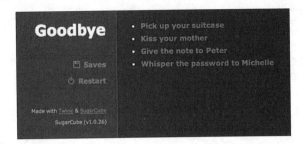

FIGURE 19.8 Four options are listed on the screen via the `<<actions>>` macro.

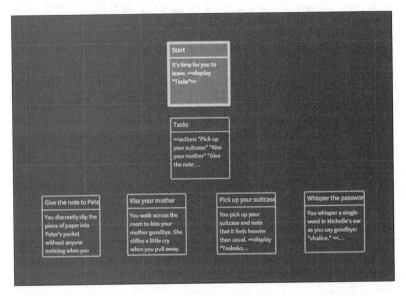

FIGURE 19.9 There are six passages on the blue grid screen in this example.

Next, fill in a few words in each of the four new passages and end each one with the same bit of code:

```
<<display "Tasks">>
```

This macro displays all the words from the Tasks passage at the bottom of the current passage. It opens with a set of double angled brackets and the name of the macro (`display`). It then has the name of the passage containing the options listed with the `<<actions>>` macro (`Tasks`). It closes with another set of double angled brackets.

Finally, open the Start passage and write a simple beginning along with the `<<display>>` macro:

```
It's time for you to leave.

<<display "Tasks">>
```

Now when you click the Play button, you should see the four options on the screen underneath the opening line, as shown in Figure 19.10. As each choice is made, the text from that passage appears, along with the remaining options in the list. A player cannot return to a choice once it has been made. Therefore, the player tells Michelle the password only once and slips Peter the note once, and this limitation adds an air of realism to the game.

FIGURE 19.10   The opening screen with all four choices listed via the <<actions>> macro.

Learning the <<choice>> Macro

Sometimes you want to give the player a choice that he or she can access only one time—unlike a link that can be clicked over and over again when the player enters the passage. Once a choice is made, it renders all other options using the <<choice>> macro in that passage as plain text, leaving only choices using the [[link]] macro.

Begin this example by clicking the +Passage button and making four new passages, named "The red room," "The blue room," "The yellow room," and "The green room." Then type the following in the opening passage:

```
Where do you want to go?
<<choice "The red room">>
<<choice "The blue room">>
<<choice "The yellow room">>
<<choice "The green room">>
[[Leave the house|Leave]]
```

Twine generates a new passage only for the fifth option: Leave the house. In each of the five option passages, write the <<return>> macro. Then click the Play button, and you see five options on the screen, as in Figure 19.11, but the choices don't perform equally.

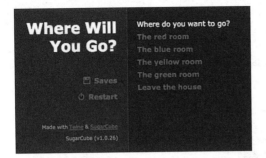

FIGURE 19.11 The opening screen with all five choices.

If you click on one of the first four links that all use the <<choice>> macro and then return to the passage, you see that the other choices have been turned into plain text and only the [[link]] macro option remains. If you choose Leave the house and then return to the passage, all the links are still on the screen because none of the <<choice>> macros were triggered. Remember that once you use one option connected to the <<choice>> macro, all other options disappear.

TRY IT OUT: CHOOSE THE RIGHT CARD

You are Alice, trying to get out of Wonderland. You encounter the Queen of Hearts, who promises you safe passage with the Four of Diamonds if you can find him in the deck. Of course, you can wander around Wonderland, trying to find another way out (and hopefully not meeting an untimely end in the jaws of the Jabberwocky).

Write a story for this scenario and give the player 13 card choices, using the <<choice>> macro as well as the option to walk away from the table using the [[link]] macro. Of course, 12 of those cards need to be dead ends for the player, but 1 should be the Four of Diamonds, which transports Alice home. If Alice finds a way out of Wonderland (either instantly or by moving through the rest of the game), use the <<actions>> and <<display>> macros to have her say goodbye to all the characters before she steps back to Oxford.

Saving Your Game

One of the reasons a lot of writers like the SugarCube format is that it has a built-in save feature for the game. Without doing any additional coding, you can allow your players to save their progress and restore to an earlier point in the story. This means you can give a player risky choices and let him or her go back to try for different results. So make the choices hard and make the consequences big: The Save button is the player's safety net.

Using the Save Feature

To use the save feature during a game, click the blue Save button on the left sidebar. This opens the pop-up window shown in Figure 19.12, with slots for eight save positions.

FIGURE 19.12 Eight save slots for each Twine game made with SugarCube.

To save the place in the game, the player can simply click the Save button and continue playing. If the player wants to save a new place but not lose the first place, he or she can simply choose the second, third, or fourth slot. To get rid of an existing save, the player can click the Delete button in the appropriate slot.

You can also allow the player to save to disk, placing a copy of the saved data on his or her computer so it can be opened in a different browser or even transferred to another machine. To enable this, the player clicks the Save to Disk button toward the bottom of the pop-up window. It prompts the player to save a copy to his or her machine.

Retrieving a Saved Game

If a player wants to rewind a story to a save point, he or she can click the blue Save button again and choose the Load button to restore. If the player used the Save to Disk button and now wants to reload that file, he or she can choose the Load from Disk option and navigate to the saved file.

TRY IT OUT: RISKY TRAVELS

The American Simulation Corporation is a virtual travel company that promises an immersive, life-changing experience...all in a tiny pill. Will you try the blue pill and explore the remains of a sunken ship, the green pill and shoot off into outer space, the red pill and wind your way through the dense foliage of the jungle, or the yellow pill and slide into an underground city?

Write a story for this scenario. Make sure the choices are risky and encourage the player to save his or her progress by using the Save button.

Playing with the Pacing

When you drive a car, you don't move at the same speed the whole trip. Pulling out of a drive-way at 60 miles per hour would be dangerous, though that speed is perfect for the highway. On the other hand, puttering around at 30 miles per hour is great on a country road, but you would probably have a lot of angry drivers behind you if you tried that on the interstate.

The same idea applies to an interactive story. Keeping the same speed throughout every pas-sage means that people will either race through parts where you need them to slow down and think or plod along through the action sequences. The solution is to vary the story speed by playing with the pacing. Turn back to Chapter 10, "Achieving Proper Pacing," for additional notes on the story speed.

Speeding Up the Story

When human beings are in danger, they don't pause to wonder about something they hap-pened to notice. In moments of panic, they *do*, they take action, they rely heavily on intu-ition and feelings, they experience heightened emotion.

To speed up your story, give your players plenty to do. Allow them to make frequent, high-stakes choices. You have the save feature at your disposal, so you might as well have players make life-or-death decisions.

During fast sections, avoid descriptive paragraphs because it isn't realistic for someone to notice ornate crown molding near the ceiling while fleeing the castle pursued by a vampire. Bring descriptions down to their bare bones in spaces where you want the reader to feel as if time is moving quickly. Give enough information to allow the player to orient himself or grab useful objects, but don't give the amount of information you would give if the player character were examining things closely.

Drop in an internal cliff-hanger or two. That's right: Cliff-hangers don't just happen at the ends of stories. You can have an evil non-player character plummet into a cavernous pit and disappear, leaving the player wondering if she'll encounter the evil one again. Such wonder drives the player to read faster to test his or her theory to see if it's right.

Play with the lengths of your sentences. Shorter sentences, especially fragments, make the player feel as if the story is speeding along. Increase the number of verbs and decrease the number of adjectives when you're focusing on doing, not describing.

Finally, games have a tendency to reach their top speed when the story hits the climax. Think of it like a roller coaster, with the triggering event sending the plot points careening down a steep drop. When the player sees that a lot of important moments are happening one after another, she knows she's getting close to the end of the game, like the explosive finale to a fireworks display, where the pyrotechnicians unload the most exciting fireworks all at once.

Look carefully at where you're speeding up the story and make sure it's a safe place to increase the pace. Make sure the player feels like he has a good grasp on the situation and world before you make him start racing through the passages.

Slowing Down the Story

But what about the quiet moments, the ones where you want the player to slow down and think? Your story is likely to start off slowly, like a car pulling carefully out of the driveway, because you want the player to grasp the facts and understand what is going on and who she is.

The same techniques you use to start the story this way—increasing the level of detail in the passage, giving a close examination to the contents of the given space or items the player is picking up—are the ones you return to in later passages to slow down the story after a burst of activity.

Include more sensory information, especially smell, taste, and touch. Readers may gloss over visual or auditory information, but they take notice when these three lesser-described senses are invoked.

Make your sentences longer, with plenty of clauses. You don't want run-on sentences, but you might try joining two related sentences into a compound sentence or starting off a sentence with a dependent clause. Choose highly descriptive language; this is the time to pull out vivid terms. Your passages can be longer, too, with more text between choices. This is a time for some lower-stakes decisions that can send the story ricocheting in new directions without bringing the plot to an untimely end.

This slower pace is like a valley between the spikes created by the high-action sequences. Think of these valleys as the figurative equivalent to dragging a highlighter across a page. These are times to draw the reader's attention to the important facts you don't want them to miss.

Striking a Pacing Balance

The best games alternate between fast and slow moments, perhaps not giving equal time to both ends of the spectrum but at least balancing between the two to use the momentum of the action sequences to propel the reader through the slower descriptive passages.

Remember that faster moments make readers *feel*, and slower moments make readers *think*. There will be times when you want the reader to feel as terrified as the characters, and in those moments, you should turn up the speed using the tricks above. At other times, you want the reader to think and solve problems, so slow down the text and give the player time to process what she's reading.

You don't want the reader to become overwhelmed or bored. A person can remain in a state of heightened emotions only so long before burning out, and you don't want to put the reader to sleep in the middle of the game by causing them to think too long and hard. So keep a decent balance between fast sequences and slow sequences to give the reader a chance to get moving or catch his or her breath.

TRY IT OUT: PIRATE ESCAPE

You're enjoying a lovely day on the king's yacht when pirates overtake the ship. What is a damsel or gentleman in distress to do? You will be forced to give up your fortune and walk the plank or choose to be fed to their pet sharks—it's your choice. With no possibility of rescue, your only chance for survival lies in your quick wits and ingenuity.

Create a story for this scenario. Play with the pacing to create a satisfying game that allows the player to ride the plotline. Be sure to carry the momentum of the action through the slower pace of the planning.

Managing Expectations

One last way to balance pacing is to manage reader expectations. Readers come into all games with certain expectations already in place and others that are born out of the events of the game. For instance, readers expect the characters to evolve over the course of the game because they'll be affected by the events in the game and change accordingly. At the same time, players try to guess what will happen next as the plot unfolds. As I said earlier, you can use cliff-hangers as great motivators for moving through the game.

Highlighting Change

People change. Things happen to us that give us new lenses through which to see the world. Our core personality remains the same, but we become, as an example, more confident or more anxious after a crisis. Similarly, our characters rub up against the fictional world, and that friction shapes who they are and their goals.

You can highlight such changes by slowing down the text after a crisis so the reader doesn't miss these moments. A simple way to do this is to have the character reflect after the high action is over. A character wouldn't pause to think while dodging bullets or swinging over crocodiles, but once she comes through the situation, she would internally consider what she just went through or describe the events to a non-player character.

These moments reveal insight into the character's personality. Return to Chapter 8, "Constructing Believable Characters," and look at the traits listed under the acronym CANOE. If your character starts out the story unreliable, does he become more dependable by the end? Does someone friendly become a little less warm and embracing of new people due to events in the game? Does someone who always worries become more laid back in her approach to life? Does a stubborn character become more open-minded? Does the character still love big crowds by the end of the story?

If you look at those traits as a spectrum, you can place each character on the line and mark his or her beginning point and end point. If a character doesn't budge at all, you may want to consider fine-tuning the story so changes occur.

In fact, check all of your major characters by describing them at the beginning of the game and then repeating the exercise at the end of the game. Make sure the two lists differ to reflect the change that occurs during the game.

Using the Rule of Three

You can play with the reader's expectations by exploiting or delivering on the *rule of three*. Think of it as the magic number of writing. The idea is that if you repeat something three times, the player is sure to notice or remember it. Two times, and it may just be a coincidence. Four times, and the player feels like you're beating her over the head with the information. But three times is perfect.

Perhaps trained by the repetition of three throughout literature from the *Three Little Pigs* to *The Three Musketeers* or, in the area of games, the three pieces of information in *Clue* or the bell, book, and candle for *Zork*, players have come to look for the third instance of an important event or item.

As the writer, you get to decide whether you give the reader what she is expecting and deliver that third part or whether to withhold that satisfaction. A word of caution: If the player's expectations aren't met, she may feel as if the story is left dangling at the end. For instance, if the player character encounters a terrible witch twice, the player mentally prepares for the third meeting. If that third meeting never takes place, the reader may walk away from the story feeling as if it was incomplete.

Either way, the rule of three definitely speeds up the story once the player notices the second instance because she is eagerly reading for the third occurrence.

Distracting the Player with MacGuffins

If the rule of three speeds up the game, MacGuffins slow it down. A *MacGuffin* is a plot device that serves as a distraction. The player character has a goal he is trying to fulfill or an object he's trying to obtain, but that motivation is actually distracting the reader from the real situation at the heart of the story.

For instance, the mayor of a town might implore a superhero to help rid the city of some evil entity by obtaining the serum that gives that evil entity his strength. The goal through the story is obtaining the serum, and the player is so distracted in helping the player character reach that goal that he's shocked when it turns out the mayor is evil and only wanted the serum for himself so he can wreak havoc in a new and terrible way. The reader is tricked because he is distracted by the MacGuffin and doesn't notice how oddly the mayor acts about the serum.

MacGuffins don't need to be a big shock for the player. For instance, the player may know that the player character's obsession with finding the chalice is beside the point because the real goal is to get the player character together with the prince in the neighboring kingdom. MacGuffins also don't need to be a long con. They can be short-term distractions, things that the player character gloms onto for a few passages and then drops when realizing those aren't important clues. In the meantime, each MacGuffin has served its purpose, distracting the reader and slowing down the game play.

TRY IT OUT: THE BUZZ

Try your hand at writing out the superhero situation described above. Mayor Jones is desperate to rid the town of The Buzz, an enormous, man-sized flying bee that drenches the buildings in honey and stings unsuspecting crowds of people, skewering them on his stinger. The Buzz is kept in business by a serum that he keeps in his secret lair.

Mayor Jones has asked the player character—Awe Girl or Awe Boy—to help her get the serum and put an end to The Buzz once and for all. The player character takes the case, not suspecting that it's actually Mayor Jones who wants to turn herself into the Queen Bee.

Employ the rule of three when having the player fight The Buzz and make sure to highlight how the player character changes based on this deception.

Pacing is necessary for maintaining interest in a game, but it's also important for the reader to feel engaged. Some of that engagement comes from giving the player meaningful choices and the ability to impact the story world, but you can elevate the reader's level of commitment by understanding the three types of players and the relationship between the writer and the unknown audience. You can do this by learning the SugarCube syntax for building an array so you can work collections into your future stories.

20

Keeping Players Engaged

80 Days won *Time*'s Best Game of the Year for 2014. Although that is wonderful for Inkle Studios, it's also great for writers in general because the game stands as an interesting case study for what makes a good game.

There are all the obvious things that Inkle did to make the game successful: It started with a text that is familiar but hasn't been overdone (*Around the World in 80 Days* by Jules Verne), created eye-catching graphics to supplement the storyline, and structured the whole game as a trip so the player feels as if he or she is always moving forward.

But what Inkle also did that is less obvious is write a single game that reaches three different types of players. For those who play games to win (or...to lose), they can win the game by beating the clock and making it around the world in 80 days. For those who like a good story, they can move their focus from the clock to the narrative, enjoying an interactive version of a classic tale. For those who play interactive fiction because they love to explore a world, they can pause in the markets or walk through the cities, spending time examining Paris, Istanbul, and Hong Kong.

One game, three very different ways to play it.

It's time to turn your eye toward bringing the audience into the equation. But wait! When you make a game, unless it is for a specific group of people, you have no clue who will end up playing it. So how can you make a game that appeals to your audience without knowing who is in your audience?

You can start with the three categories of text adventure players as defined by game theorists that Inkle focused on when making their game: those who play to win, those who play for the story, and those who seek the thrill of adventure from the comfort of their own living room.

If you want to make one game that engages a wide variety of readers, consider structuring a points system inside a strong narrative that allows the player to feel as if he or she is transported to a different space. That's no small feat, but you'll learn a few tricks in this chapter to make it possible. To focus on writing games with broad appeal, you'll return to using arrays, since object collection always lends itself well to ticking off the first task on that to-do list: Make the game "winnable." Object collection can also enhance the story when it helps the reader understand the world. Finally, object collection gives the player a reason to move around the landscape.

Arrays in SugarCube borrow elements from JavaScript rather than employing an (array:) macro, as in Harlowe. Luckily, though the syntax may be different, the usage will feel familiar.

Returning to Arrays

Remember arrays from Chapter 9, "Maintaining an Inventory"? An array allows you to use multiple values with a single variable. For instance, the value of the variable $bag may be a series of strings that simulate physical objects in the game, such as "sandwich", "chips", "drink", and "apple".

Just to review, an *array* is like an infinite, expandable box that has unlimited compartments. Each compartment is called an *index*, and every time you add a new item to an array, a new index is created. You can add items, drop items, or check an array, and you can even use an array with a conditional statement to display certain text if the condition is met. For instance, you can create a conditional statement which says that if an array contains a particular string, display particular text, and if the array doesn't contain that particular string, display some other text.

Got it? It's time to build a SugarCube array.

Building a New Array

Because Twine creates white space at the beginning of the passage where you build an array, you need to wrap an array inside the opening and closing <<silently>> macro from Chapter 17, "Setting Up the Pre-Story, Central Story, and Post-Story."

Open a new SugarCube game and type your empty array at the top of the first passage. While you're at it, you can set up a way to track points, too. Here's what all this looks like:

```
<<silently>><<set $bag = []>><<set $points = 0>><<endsilently>>
```

The <<set>> macros are enclosed inside the opening <<silently>> and closing <<endsilently>> macros for removing white space. The <<set>> macro opens with a set of double angled brackets and the name of the macro (set). Then the variable that you're setting a value to is stated ($bag), with an equal sign and an empty set of single square bracket ([]). The macro is then closed with another set of double angled brackets.

So let's talk about that empty set of single square brackets. That notation ([]) tells Twine that $bag is not going to be any old variable with a single value. The empty set of single square brackets indicates that this is going to be an array with multiple values. Of course, you can fill those empty brackets, putting values in your array from the get-go, like this:

```
<<set $bag = ["Sandwich", "Chips", "Drink"]>>
```

Or you can leave the brackets empty if you want to have an array waiting and then fill it as the game unfolds.

In addition, in the preceding example, a second variable—this time with a single value— follows the empty array with another set of double angled brackets and the name of the macro (set). Then the variable ($points) is listed, along with an equal sign. And then an initial value is set (0) and the macro is closed with another set of double angled brackets.

If you were to click the Play button right now, there would be nothing to see, but you can use the `<<print>>` macro to test whether your array and variable were created:

```
You are carrying <<print $bag.length>> items.
Your points: <<print $points>>.
```

If you click the Play button now, you should see that there are zero items in your bag, and you've earned zero points, as shown in Figure 20.1.

FIGURE 20.1 Use the `<<print>>` macro to check whether your array and variable have been created correctly.

Remember that adding `.length` to the name of the array tells Twine (well, really your web browser that is executing the code) to count how many indexes (compartments) are in the array. In this case, because nothing has been added yet to the array, the answer should be zero.

Adding Items to an Array

Okay, so your array is set up, and your player character is traveling through the story. Let's say that the player character enters a classroom and finds a shiny, red apple on the teacher's desk. The player has the option to take or leave the apple. You do not need to put any code in the passage where the player character *leaves* the apple, but in the passage where the player character *takes* the apple, you need to use the `<<set>>` macro to add an apple to the empty bag:

```
<<set $bag.push("Apple")>><<set $points = $points + 1>>You take the apple
and slip it into your bag.
```

So taking the apple places a figurative apple in the bag, in the form of a string. The macro opens with a set of double angled brackets and the macro name (`set`). Then the variable (`$bag`) is combined with JavaScript's `.push` (`$bag.push`), which adds the string contained inside quotation marks and surrounded by a single set of parentheses: (`"Apple"`). The macro closes with another set of double angled brackets.

If you check the array now by adding `You are carrying: <<print $bag>>`, you should see that you are carrying an apple, as shown in Figure 20.2.

FIGURE 20.2 Use the `<<print>>` macro to check whether you have pushed a new string into the array.

The *push method*—which is what it is called in JavaScript when you add `.push` to the variable name in order to add a new item to an array—should make you visualize an index being pushed onto the end of this infinite, expandable box.

Remember that arrays are actually numbered lists. The first compartment is index 0. The next compartment is index 1. And when you push a new item onto the list, which, in turn, creates a new compartment, it becomes index 2. Twine (and, for that matter, JavaScript) always pushes the new index to the end of the list. You don't need to remember the order of items in your array for Twine (unless you are using the order of items as part of the story, such as making something happen if you take one item before another), but it's still an interesting thing to know.

Dropping Items from an Array

There are two ways to remove an item from an array: the pop method and the splice method. The difference between these two methods circles back to the fact that an array is a numbered list. The *pop method* removes the last item added to the list by popping off the last index. But you can also use the more versatile *splice method*, which removes an item from any position in the list and then reorders the list so that each compartment shifts over by one slot:

```
<<set $bag.splice($bag.indexOf("Apple"), 1)>>
```

In the splice method, the macro opens with a set of double angled brackets and the name of the macro (`set`). Then the variable (`$bag`) is combined with JavaScript's `.splice` (`$bag.splice`), which removes the element listed in the next part of code.

Unpacking the next part of the code requires a bit of explanation so you can visualize what is happening inside Twine. You will probably notice that, like the push method, the `<<set>>`

macro with the splice method doesn't use an equal sign. The code is executed as it is written instead of doing an equation in real time.

After an opening parenthesis, the variable ($bag) is combined with JavaScript's .indexOf ($bag.indexOf). The .indexOf method is returning the position of a value in the array. In the preceding example, it's the position of the value "Apple." It is written in camelcase with the first letter of the second word capitalized for easy reading.

You use .indexOf any time you want to check that numbered list. In this case, you're checking it because you want it to find the string, which is contained inside quotation marks and surrounded by a single set of parentheses—("Apple")—and remove it along with one index. Splice is looking at both where to start removing values ("Apple") and how many values to remove (1). After a closing parenthesis to end the item that Twine is splicing from the list, the macro closes with another set of double angled brackets.

Now, if you use the <<print>> macro to check what is listed in the array, you should see a blank space as in Figure 20.3 because there is nothing to print.

FIGURE 20.3 Use the <<print>> macro to check whether you have dropped a string from the array.

You might prefer to use the pop method, which removes the last item you added to the array—but *only* the last item you added to the array:

```
<<set $bag.pop()>>
```

You don't need to specify an item with the pop method because it isn't searching the indexes to remove a certain item. It's just popping the last one off the list. So the macro opens with a double set of angled brackets and the name of the macro (set). Then the variable ($bag) combines with JavaScript's .pop ($bag.pop) followed by a set of empty parentheses: (). These should look familiar because you used them in Chapter 19, "Balancing Pacing and Action," with functions. And yes, you are once again calling a function as you remove the final index in the array. The macro ends with another set of double angled brackets.

You are likely to use the splice method more than the pop method—and you may decide to forgo the pop method entirely because it requires you to remember the order of the list.

Checking Strings in an Array

Okay, so you now have an array with a few items inside. It's time to check the strings in the array in order to build conditional statements in the game:

```
<<if $bag.indexOf("Apple") gte 0>>You are holding the apple.
<<else>>You do not have an apple.<<endif>>
```

In this example, if the string is present in the array, Twine displays one sentence, and if the string is not present in the array (because the player chose not to pick up the item or it hasn't been found yet), Twine displays a different sentence.

So you're back with your familiar friend, the <<if>> macro. The macro opens with a set of double angled brackets and the macro name (if). The variable ($bag) is then combined with JavaScript's .indexOf ($bag.indexOf), which checks the list for the string contained inside quotation marks and surrounded by a single set of parentheses: ("Apple"). After the gte operator states that the index number needs to be index 0 or above (meaning, at least one index exists), the macro closes with another set of double angled brackets.

I promised that you wouldn't need to remember the order of your array (and, in some cases, with different players encountering items in a different order), and with the gte operator (which stands for "greater than or equal to"), you don't.

When the web browser checks the list of elements in the array, it starts with index 0 and looks for the "Apple" string. Then it goes to index 1, index 2, and beyond. If it sees the string in any index in the list, it displays the first bit of text: You are holding the apple. But if Twine combs through every index and doesn't find that string, it displays the second bit of text: You do not have an apple. In other words, if "Apple" doesn't exist on the list, then indexOf() returns the number -1 (which means "not found"). Of course, the conditional is looking for a number greater than or equal to zero, so -1 doesn't fit the bill. Thus, it displays the text inside the <<else>> macro.

So the web browser isn't looking for the number of apples, in this case. It's calling the .indexOf method to comb through the list from beginning to end and seeing if the string is anywhere in that list. Pretty clever.

Because you dropped the apple using the .splice method, you should see the second text option, as in Figure 20.4.

FIGURE 20.4 The <<if>> and <<else>> macros are used to display conditional text.

Limiting the Array Size

You can use the length of the list—meaning, the number of indexes in the list—to set limits for your array size and how much the player character can hold. For instance, you may decide that you're going to limit the player character to four items at a time, like this:

```
<<if $bag.length gte 4>>You are carrying too many things! You cannot pick up the
cream pie.<<else>><<set $bag.push("Pie")>>You pick up the cream pie.<<endif>>
```

If she's carrying four items, she can't pick up anything new until she uses or drops one of the items she's holding. But if she's carrying only three objects, the player has enough strength to pick up one more object.

The macro opens with a set of double angled brackets and the macro name (`if`). Then the variable (`$bag`) is combined with JavaScript's `.length` (`$bag.length`), the operator `gte`, and the number `4`. The macro closes with another set of double angled brackets. If this condition is true and the player character is holding four or more things, Twine will let the player know that she can't pick up the cream pie: `You are carrying too many things! You cannot pick up the cream pie.`

Next, the `<<else>>` macro opens with the name of the macro (`else`) inside two sets of double angled brackets. Nested inside this conditional statement is another macro—the `<<set>>` macro. If this condition is met, a new item is pushed into the array.

That macro opens with another set of double angled brackets and the macro name (`set`). Then the variable (`$bag`) is combined with JavaScript's `.push` (`$bag.push`), which adds the string contained inside quotation marks and surrounded by a single set of parentheses: (`"Pie"`). That `<<set>>` macro is closed with another set of double angled brackets, conditional text is listed (`You pick up the cream pie`), and then the closing macro `<<endif>>` ends both the `<<if>>` and `<<else>>` macros.

When in doubt, read your code aloud and see if it makes sense. In this example, you could say: "If the number of values in the bag variable are greater than or equal to four, show this text. But if the number of values is something else, add the string 'Pie' to the array and display this text."

How does this look on the screen? If you click the Play button, you should see that you picked up the cream pie, as in Figure 20.5, because you weren't holding four or more items.

FIGURE 20.5 Setting a hold limit adds a new twist to a game.

Troubleshooting Arrays

You may run into problems when working with arrays. If you have the `<<set>>` macro pushing a new string into an array, it does so every time you open the passage. Let's say that you have a container of strawberries on the kitchen table that the player can pick up:

```
<<set $bag.push("Strawberries")>>You pick up the container of strawberries. The
refrigerator door is ajar. Do you want to look inside? [[Yes|Yes]] or [[No|No]].
```

Each time the player enters this passage, Twine adds another `"Strawberries"` string to the array. Jump back and forth into this passage a few times and then use the `<<print>>` macro to check your array. You should see multiple containers of strawberries in your bag, as shown in Figure 20.6.

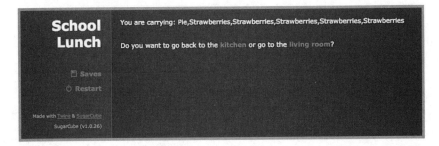

FIGURE 20.6   The same string gets added to the array each time you enter the passage.

The same workarounds for this problem listed in Chapter 9 work in SugarCube, too, but the easiest method is to nest the `<<set>>` macro inside the `visited()` function:

```
<<if visited() == 1>><<set $bag.push("Strawberries")>>You pick up the container of
strawberries.<<else>>You wander back into the kitchen.<<endif>> The refrigerator door
is ajar. Do you want to look inside? [[Yes|Yes]] or [[No|No]].
```

Now that the `<<set>>` macro is combined with the `visited()` function, the string `"Strawberries"` is added only the first time through the passage. Each subsequent visit to the passage does not create a new index in the array, so you don't have to worry about your bag getting stuffed with dozens of containers of virtual strawberries.

TRY IT OUT: OUTER SPACE EXCURSION

You've been sent to a distant, unexplored planet to collect useful information and samples and bring what you find back to earth so NASA can prepare astronauts for a future space mission that will leave them on the planet for months at a time. Obviously, you want to collect everything that isn't nailed down and place it in your bag. Less obvious is the fact that taking certain items may trigger the inhabitants of the planet to emerge and attack you.

Create a story for this scenario and build an array and chart the player character's encounters with the aliens, especially by checking strings in the array and displaying conditional text if the player character is holding certain items.

Checking Your Inventory

If you have an inventory in your story, obviously, you want to give the player the ability to check it. SugarCube has multiple ways to do so, but all utilize the same syntax for displaying the contents of the array. Back in Harlowe, you created a special passage called Bag and added a [[Check Bag|Bag]] link at the bottom of each story passage so you could reach it. Next you'll do that again in order to learn the SugarCube way of printing an array as a list.

Setting Up an Inventory Passage

You're about to see more code than text, but take a deep breath because you know every macro contained in this example. In the Bag passage, type this:

```
<<if $bag.length is 0>>You have nothing.<<else>>You are carrying:
<<print $bag.join('\n')>><<endif>>
Your points: <<print $points>>.
<<back>>
```

The <<if>> and <<else>> macros take into account that the player begins the game empty-handed. If this isn't the case and the player begins the game with a few useful items in his bag, you can skip straight to the "You are carrying" part. But let's pause for a moment to unpack everything that is happening in the Bag passage.

The <<if>> macro opens with a set of double angled brackets and the macro name (if). Then the variable ($bag) is combined with JavaScript's .length ($bag.length), the operator is, the number 0, and the closing set of double angled brackets. In other words, if there are no items in the array, this code says to display the following words: You have nothing.

Then the `<<else>>` macro opens with the name of the macro (`else`) inside two sets of double angled brackets. This is followed by everything that will happen if there is even one item in the array.

After displaying the words `You are carrying`, the `<<print>>` macro opens with a set of double angled brackets and the name of the macro (`print`). Then the variable (`$bag`) combines with JavaScript's `.join`, which brings together all the indexes on the list (`$bag.join`).

Before the `<<print>>` macro ends with its set of double angled brackets (and the `<<if>>` and `<<else>>` macros end with the `<<endif>>` closing macro), there's an argument for the `join()` method: (`'\n'`). An argument is a way to change the behavior of a function when you call it. And in JavaScript, `'\n'` is a shortcut for a line break. In other words, you're going to use this argument, (`'\n'`), to tell the function that you want it to place a line break between each item of the array.

Without that instruction, the array would be printed as one line, with all the items separated by commas. Instead, (`'\n'`) tells Twine to return the string with a line break, instead of a comma, between each item. When you click the Play button, Twine prints the list downward, as shown in Figure 20.7.

FIGURE 20.7 The array prints as a list due to the included character command.

The screen also now shows the other two parts of the example. Using the `<<print>>` macro, the points being tracked by the `$points` variable are also displayed underneath the contents of the bag. Finally, the `<<back>>` macro gives the player an easy way to get back to the passage he was reading before checking the bag.

This isn't the only way to give the player easy access to checking his inventory. You can also utilize SugarCube's special passages.

TRY IT OUT: BRAINS, PART I

The television network gives you a budget, drives you to the local grocery store, and lets you loose for 60 minutes to collect all the ingredients you need for your cooking competition show. You think you are about to perform on a straightforward, Food Network–like cooking show, but in this dystopia, there is another layer to the game. The network has planted zombies around the grocery store. And yes, this adventure of dodging and weaving brain-eaters is being televised.

Write a story for this scenario and create a variable called `$shoppingCart`, filled with items that you collect along the way, all the while avoiding the zombies that want to eat your brain in the cereal aisle.

Understanding Special Passages

SugarCube contains two special passages: StoryMenu and StoryCaption. They aren't preloaded with Twine, so you have to create them if you want to use them, but know that SugarCube is programmed to recognize these specific passages. Both allow you to utilize the sidebar in clever ways.

Using the StoryMenu Passage

The StoryMenu passage is for adding plain text and simple links. Anything typed in the StoryMenu passage goes above the Saves and Restart links on the left sidebar.

To utilize this special passage in SugarCube, click the +Passage button to create a new passage. Change the name of the passage from Untitled to StoryMenu. Capitalization matters here, so make sure that you capitalize both the *S* in Story and *M* in Menu. Then type the following in your new passage:

```
You are a student at Middlebrook High School.
[[Check Bag|Bag]]
```

When you now click the Play button, you should see the plain text and the link on the left sidebar as shown in Figure 20.8.

When you add a link to your Bag passage (or whatever inventory system you're using for your game) in the StoryMenu passage, you do not need to add a link at the bottom of every passage. The player will always be able to access it from the left sidebar.

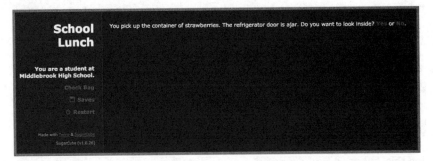

FIGURE 20.8 The StoryMenu passage allows you to add plain text and links to the left sidebar.

Using the StoryCaption Passage

Plain text and links are nice, but you can put code in the StoryCaption passage in order to forgo the Bag passage altogether and have the inventory or points system update in the left sidebar each time a new passage is displayed.

To utilize this special passage in SugarCube, click the +Passage button to create a new passage. Change the name of the passage from Untitled to StoryCaption. Again, capitalization matters. Add the text you would normally add to the Bag passage, removing the <<back>> macro because the information will be updating in the sidebar and visible throughout game play:

```
<<if $bag.length is 0>>You have nothing.<<else>>You are carrying:
<<print $bag.join('\n')>><<endif>>
Your points: <<print $points>>.
```

Now click the Play button and check your left sidebar as you play the game. Your items and points update as passages are opened and items are added to the inventory, as shown in Figure 20.9.

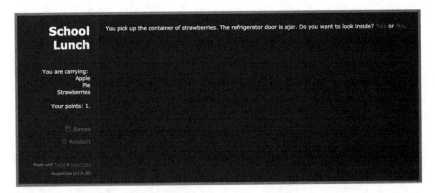

FIGURE 20.9 The StoryCaption passage allows you to have macros run on the left sidebar.

Other fun ideas are to show the player the number of moves she has made by using the turns() function and to display the character's traits in a role-playing game. There are many other possibilities as well. Any macro you can put in a regular passage you can also use in the StoryCaption special passage.

TRY IT OUT: BRAINS, PART II

Return to your zombie cooking adventure and use the two special passages to either give important instructions or links (StoryMenu passage) or update the contents of the $shoppingCart variable in real time (StoryCaption passage).

Knowing Your Audience

It's important to know your audience and write for your audience. This type of writing advice is doled out for everything from essays to fiction. But what does it actually mean, and how can you write for a group of people you don't even know? Quite soon, you'll be ready to upload your games to the Internet and release them to the world. Once that happens, anyone and everyone can play your games.

Rather than try to figure out the traits of the exact people who will play your game—an impossible task—you can go about knowing your audience in another way. You can create a game that will find the audience you want instead of trying to guess the audience that will find your game.

Aiming for a Niche

As you write, aim for a specific group of players. Rather than try to reach all people who play games or all people who like choice-based interactive fiction, aim to reach a niche audience.

It is impossible to make one game that satisfies all interactive fiction players in this world. Tastes vary from person to person, and a genre of story that appeals to one player is annoying to another. Even within genres there may be subgenres that appeal to some readers and not to others. Just because a person likes fantasy stories doesn't mean that she'll like *Lord of the Rings*, which is considered high fantasy, and *His Dark Materials*, which is low fantasy.

Pretend you have a player who loves science fiction stories but is bored to tears by sword and sorcery fantasy tales. You are not going to be able to reach that science fiction reader with your game about elves, no matter how cool you make the elf kingdom. So don't even try. Your goal when writing a fantasy story is to write the best fantasy story possible that appeals to fantasy story readers. Don't worry about the non-fantasy story readers; they don't factor into this equation. The same goes for other genres, and while we're at it, even subgenres.

You may not be able to make one game that appeals to all interactive fiction players, but you can make a game that appeals to all types of readers and players in a single genre. So mentally keep your audience small by trying to appeal to a single group instead of everyone in the world at the same time.

Speaking Broadly

Despite what you might think I've just said, aiming for a niche doesn't mean cutting off outsiders at the front door. You don't want to fill your game with inside jokes that will turn off people who feel excluded from the text or pack the game with obscure information that excites you, the writer, but would be of little interest to other people. Appeal to your core, absolutely, but leave the door open for newcomers to feel comfortable stepping in.

So once you've chosen your audience aim—for instance, all readers of science fiction—make your writing mirror the way you speak in the face-to-face world, going a more general route with a general group of people, and explaining the obscure references when it's necessary to mention them.

Rather than build a game that requires the player to have intimate knowledge of obscure facts, speak broadly and sprinkle lesser-known references into the game with plenty of explanation and support. In other words, while your average science fiction reader will be familiar with the general concept of rocket ships, you need to gently lead them into a puzzle involving ammonium perchlorate composite propellant. Especially if you're expecting the reader to know that the cured propellant is formed into a solid shape in production rather than produced as a powder.

See? Sort of boring unless you are super into rockets.

Assume that the average science fiction reader is *somewhat* into rockets instead of *super* into rockets. It's okay to include realistic details but make sure you support those details with explanation and make sure you include those details because they're necessary to the story and not just because you think they're cool facts that everyone should know. Remember, your reader wants to feel transported...not confused.

Writing for One Person

If you want a game that connects with a wide audience, imagine that you're writing a game for a single person. I know it's counterintuitive: How can writing for one person—whether that person is your parent, sibling, best friend, or spouse—translate into a game that lots of people want to play?

I don't mean you should flood your game with inside jokes and references that only one person will understand. What I mean is that a faceless audience can be a scary beast, full of unknowns. But writing for a friendly face, one that you know will support your writing efforts and be forgiving of a game that is in process rather than a completed, edited piece, can make a world of difference in how easily the words spill onto the screen.

So picture in your head one person. If he or she likes the genre you're using for your game, all the better. Your person can be anyone; the only requirement is that it be someone who would be supportive of your game. And write a game *for* that person. It will help you write better because you're writing for a safe person who has your back. And in writing better, you will ultimately end up making a better game that appeals to more people.

See, that's how writing for one person actually makes you write better for many.

Deciding on Length

When you think about audience, you need to know where people are playing your game. If they're playing from a mobile device, you'll want to make the "chapters" short so there are clear stopping points for game play, as is done in the game *Lifeline*. You can play that game while you wait in line and stop playing at any point without losing the thread of the story or where you are in the game. In other words, streamline the narrative and keep the plot simple for mobile device users.

If you're aiming for home users, you can make longer passages with a more convoluted plotline. Consider prompting the player to use the Saves button and marking the end of a chapter to give them the choice to keep going or stop playing for the day. Essentially, you want to make it easy for the reader to either move through the story in one sitting or go away and come back with good breaking points. Think of it like throwing in commercial breaks.

You also want to make it clear where you want people to play. *Lifeline* does this by setting up the game as a conversation in text messages. Obviously, you would play a game like that from your phone. Text-heavy games that require a lot of typing work better from a computer. The player may not always follow your gentle advice, but you should still structure the game so it's clear where the player will have the most enjoyable playing experience.

Piquing Interest with a Teaser

Take some time to pique the player's interest with a teaser. Steph Cherrywell did this to great effect before she released her game *Brain Guzzlers from Beyond!* She created a static image for the cover and released backstory details about the game, set in 1959 in Canyonville, New Mexico, during the town's Pine Nut Days festival.

Before I started the game, I was able to get a sense of time and place, and that made me look forward to playing. Steph found at least one member of her audience with that teaser (me!), and she delivered a great game to boot.

So give your readers a bit of backstory before they get started reading. You can link to a how-to-play tutorial or backstory information on the left sidebar, using the StoryMenu passage. Or you create an eye-catching image that goes with the story to catch a potential player's attention.

TRY IT OUT: THE WORST THING THAT HAS EVER HAPPENED IN THE KINGDOM

Before you begin writing this story, mentally choose one person to whom to direct your words. Keep that person in the forefront of your mind and write as if you are sitting across from him or her, telling the story.

Next create a fun drawing and some background information that you can slide across that figurative table to the player before he or she dives into reading through the game.

The tagline for your story is "The worst thing that has ever happened in the kingdom." Is your kingdom underwater, on a distant planet, or in a fairy-filled forest? The choice is up to you but build a vivid world with object collection as a key focus to solving the problem that is the worst thing that has every happened in the kingdom. Use an array to track the objects collected and have the list update in real time on the left sidebar by using the special StoryCaption passage.

Recognizing the Three Types of Players

Game designer Ron Edwards came up with what he calls the GNS theory, based on the Threefold Model for role-playing games. He believes that players engage with games for three different reasons. You can probably come up with more than three types of players, but three is a good starting point.

In his theory, the G stands for *gamist*. These are the people who play to win. The N stands for *narrativist*. These are the people who love a good story. The S stands for *simulationist*. These are the explorers who want to feel as if they're being transported into the story. The key is making one game that is enjoyable for all of these three types of players.

Making Games for Win Seekers

Win seekers are the most straightforward group to make happy. All you need to do is construct a game that has a winning threshold and make it challenging but not frustrating.

Keep win seekers happy by making sure the point of the game is apparent in the beginning. For instance, outline the goal in the first few passages so the reader can make decisions that she believes will help her reach her goal. In *80 Days*, the player knows immediately that she has to make it around the world in 80 days. She can see a tracker at the top of the screen that tells her how much time is left, so she always has a sense of how close she is to succeeding at the goal.

Don't just focus on the big goal. Win seekers also like to win at smaller goals. So pepper the game with smaller moments that have clear winners and losers, such as battles to obtain important objects. For instance, you could stage a battle with the Spider Queen to get her butterfly catcher, which will make capturing the butterfly later in the game easier, whereas players who don't have the butterfly catcher will face a random points system that determines their success.

Making Games for Story Seekers

If you're following the advice in this book, you shouldn't have a problem keeping the story seekers happy, too. Story seekers simply want a good story. They want character development, meaning that the characters are fully formed and change over the course of the story. They want a vivid setting that influences the narrative. They want story arc and plot points and a strong voice—in other words, everything you've been working on throughout this book.

You can turn up the volume by forcing the player to make difficult choices. In real life, you face decisions where you can see the pros and cons of both options and you struggle to decide which option is better. Those types of choices are interesting because you can see the story going in either direction. It's less interesting when one decision feels in character, such as asking if you want to give the apple to the starving princess, and the other decision feels out of place, such as asking if you want to pull the starving princess's hair. If the character isn't cruel, there is clearly one choice that makes sense and another that doesn't.

Also, make the choices have repercussions that echo through the rest of the story, with each decision contributing to a domino effect that culminates with resolution at the end.

Making Games for Realism Seekers

Realism seekers are the hardest to please, but that doesn't mean you shouldn't try. They want to feel as if they are there, one with the game. The way you do this is to help them mentally reach that space by providing vivid details and sensory information.

Have you ever read a story and felt as if you were physically there? Take a moment to consider how the author achieved that end. Chances are that the author provided information succinctly, using few but powerful words, to set the scene or convey the character's personality.

This level of writing takes a lot of practice, but it helps to mentally spend time in the world you're creating. Draw maps, write out character sketches for your non-player characters, keep notes. Don't just dive into writing the game. Take time beforehand to construct the world so it's stable when you enter your writing space and start to play with it.

TRY IT OUT: THE PERCIVALS' NANNY

Oh dear, you've taken a job as the nanny for the Percival children, who turn out to be pure evil. Your first day on the job, they glued their mother's collection of fake eyelashes all over the cat while you made lunch and informed you before bed that they had used your toothbrush to clean out the sink. Still, you're stuck at their rural estate, with havoc raging across the rest of the countryside. The children may be evil, but they're not as bad as the orcs roaming the woods or the magical trees that reach forward to strangle you whenever you try to leave the house. Yikes.

Create a game that appeals to all three types of players. Make the game winnable—either the player character charms and tames the children...or not. Create a story that is interesting and engaging. Finally, make the player feel as if he or she is in this countryside estate, caring for the Percival children.

Keeping Players Engaged

Once you've found your audience and hooked your audience, you need to continue to engage your audience. That is, you need to ensure that they stick with your game from beginning to end, regardless of why they started playing in the first place.

Having a Plan

Have you ever tried to follow someone who had no clue where he was going? It's pretty annoying, right? The same thing goes with stories. If you don't know where the game is going and you're fumbling through the plot, making it up as you go along with no sense of how the story will end, your reader is going to sense it and grow frustrated. You can easily fix this by having a plan in the first place. Create an outline and sketch out the story arc for your game before you begin writing.

Being Creative

A reader doesn't want to read a regurgitated plot or follow generic characters that feel as if they were all stamped out of the same mold. Be creative and give the player a new way of viewing the world or a new twist on an old trope. While this is easier said than done, consider whether your story feels new to *you*. If you're mimicking stories you've read and characters you've encountered in other places, step back and try again until the narrative feels fresh.

Giving a Purpose

You've heard this a lot of different ways in this book, but it keeps coming up because it's so important: Your player needs to feel as if he or she has a purpose. The player character needs to have agency and the ability to affect his or her world. The choices need to count and impact the story. Many parts of making a good game are tied together, with one (such as character development) depending on another (such as agency). Think of yourself as a weaver of the story and see how pulling all these threads together makes a strong narrative.

Rewarding Choices

Pepper the game with rewards, even if it's just a simple points system. Every time the player sees that number go up on the left sidebar, she'll be encouraged to continue the game to reach the next reward. Similarly, move the player up in ranking once she reaches various point thresholds. Maybe she starts out the game as a private first class. Next she moves up to corporal and then sergeant. Make sure the player knows how close she is to the highest rank and make it more difficult to achieve each rank once the player is hooked.

Leaving Them Dreaming

The best stories and games leave readers dreaming, and that should be your goal: to have the player thinking about your game long after he's closed the screen. If you love your story, other people will love it, too. That type of energy is infectious.

For instance, J.R.R. Tolkien clearly loved Middle Earth. The man kept hundreds of pages of notes, drew maps, and made character family trees that stretched back dozens of generations. You can feel that Tolkien loved Middle Earth, and the reader ends up loving it, too.

If you're not excited about the world you're building, scrap it and start anew. It's okay to start over. In fact, sometimes doing so saves you more time than pressing on with a project that hasn't grabbed your heart.

One way to make players think about your game long after the last word is to show, and not tell, the details. Doing so allows the player to utilize her own imagination and come to her own understanding rather than have the narrative spoon-fed. The next chapter tackles this idea of showing and not telling and also shows you the timer macros included with SugarCube.

21

Show, Don't Tell

Which of these openings is more interesting?

Villianhead is a very bad man, and he always does terrible things.

Villianhead stretched his lips coldly into something resembling a smile, though it didn't extend to his eyes. "Oh...the knife? I accidentally lost it in AmazingGirl's back."

Okay, so having a name like Villianhead probably tipped you off that this guy is evil before you got to the second word, but the point is that both of these openings convey something similar—that Villianhead is not someone you want to tangle with—but they do so in very different ways.

The first sentence states the information directly. It *tells* readers what they need to know about Villianhead, almost as if it's presenting the information as a list of facts. The second sentence states the information indirectly. It *shows* readers what they need to know about Villianhead, handing the reader the pieces of the figurative puzzle and allowing their imaginations to put it together.

There will be plenty of places in a story where you need to *tell*, but it is always a more powerful act to *show*. Showing engages readers and challenges them to read closely and think deeply.

"Show, don't tell" is quintessential writing advice, the slogan of every creative writing department around the world, but it's really difficult to do well. So why is it one of the first things that gets drilled into your head when you enter a writing workshop? It's important because it's the way that the writer shows respect for the reader. By showing instead of telling, you immediately convey to readers a silent message: I believe you are smart and that you will be able to pick up on what I'm trying to say. Such respect flowing from the writer to readers encourages readers to reciprocate by reading closely, considering deeply, and making choices they believe will lead them toward their desired ending.

So how do you show instead of tell? Begin by realizing that in the day-to-day world, you already show instead of tell. Humans are indirect creatures. Humans usually don't walk into a room and announce exactly what they're thinking or feeling. If you're angry with someone, you might snarl at her or try to pick a fight. If you have a crush on someone, you may avoid looking at the person or you might flirt. If you've missed someone, you don't stand in front of the person and woodenly say, "I have missed you." You throw your arms around the person and cry. Showing instead of telling just means that you're having your writing mimic real life.

Another way to approach this task is by thinking about showing instead of telling in terms of what's called the *iceberg effect* in writing. Icebergs are huge structures, big enough at times to sink a ship like the *Titanic*. What makes them dangerous (and interesting) is that only a small portion of the iceberg is visible at the surface of the water. The rest of the iceberg is hidden from view.

Now transfer that idea to writing. The philosopher Ludwig Wittgenstein (who inspired this idea of showing and not telling) famously said in 1919, "I wanted to write that my work consists of two parts: of the one which is here, and of everything which I have *not* written. And precisely this second part is the important one." The unspoken words, the ones that exist below the story's surface, speak volumes.

In your game, if you tell, you give the reader all the information. If you show, you give the reader the tip of the iceberg, so to speak, which means that their imagination needs to fill in the gaps. And everyone knows that imaginations have the ability to make the scary scarier, the funny funnier, and the sad sadder. Allow your readers to use their imagination and figure things out.

The way you do this is to write implicitly instead of explicitly. Explicit writing states facts directly. Everything is as it is. Implicit writing, the gold standard of fiction, uses narrative devices. Instead of saying things directly, the writer uses ambiguity to leave the exact meaning in the hands of the reader. Implicit writing is peppered with clues so the reader can infer the facts. It includes concepts like understatement, omission, and figurative language to jog the readers' imagination and allow them to fill in the blanks.

There are plenty of well-written interactive fiction stories that employ this idea of "show, don't tell" to great success, but the one that elevates it to an art form (no pun intended) is Emily Short's *Galatea*. This game consists of two characters, the player character and a speaking statue.

The statue states almost nothing outright. Instead, as the player character inquires about various aspects of the statue, the statue reveals the story, her views on art, and the relationship between the observer and the object. It's a gorgeous, brief story that lends itself to additional replaying in order to explore every nook and cranny of the statue's stone mind. In other words, what's not said becomes the powerful hook that draws the reader back to the game again and again.

A few SugarCube macros lend themselves to the world of "show, don't tell." Timers, in and of themselves, are a form of showing and not telling. Instead of saying to the reader that this is a very tense moment, a timer adds tension. Nothing gets hearts racing like the tick tick tick of a clock. In addition, delayed text mirrors the way a person takes in information slowly, like peeling back the skin of an onion to reveal the vegetable below the smooth, brown skin.

In this chapter, you'll use the `time()` function and the `<<timed>>` and `<<goto>>` macros to build time-related tension into a game. But first, you need to learn how to add additional formats to Twine since these macros exist only in a new version of SugarCube that you need to upload into Twine.

Learning About Other Formats

Twine is always changing, with new and better versions always in development. The Twine you've been using throughout this book is Twine 2.0. But there was an earlier version of Twine that you'll find if you read the forums or start poking around for more tutorials. That version, Twine 1.4.2, contained two other formats—Sugarcane (yes, Sugar*cane*, not Sugar*Cube*) and Jonah.

Sugarcane was the default format. It came with a plain black background, and it behaved similarly to both Harlowe and SugarCube in the sense that with each click, the old text of the previous passage disappeared as the new text of the next passage was appearing.

Jonah was the second format. It came with a plain white background, and operated with stretch text. With each click, the old text remained on the screen, and the new text of the next passage was added below. A reader could scroll up and see what he or she had done and where he or she had been.

A third format was constructed outside of Twine 1.4.2 by Thomas Michael Edwards and could be added to the Twine program as a third option. That format, SugarCube, enhanced and added to the vanilla Sugarcane format, making it possible to run additional macros.

SugarCube format was incorporated in the Twine 2.0 you know and love. The brand-new format, Harlowe, invented by Leon Arnott, became the default format for Twine 2.0, and SugarCube became the second option, giving Twine users two distinct ways to construct stories. By the way, there is actually a third format—Snowman, created by Chris Klimas—that's not covered in this book because it requires the user to know JavaScript and CSS.

It's entirely possible that by the time you read this book, additional, outside formats will exist that can be downloaded into Twine. As is, an updated version of SugarCube exists that isn't yet part of the standard download of Twine 2.0. So let's walk through the steps for adding a new format to your current version of Twine.

Adding New Formats in Twine

To add new formats to Twine, you need to first download the file. In the case of the new version of SugarCube that you need for the additional time-related macros covered in this chapter, you can find the file at http://www.motoslave.net/sugarcube/2/#downloads.

After you've downloaded the new format (SugarCube 2.x, though the x will be replaced by the number of the current version such as 2.3.1), unzip the file and move the folder somewhere on your computer—such as wherever you keep your documents—so you can easily find it in the future.

Next, open Twine and go to the Stories screen. On the right sidebar, in the middle of the list, is the menu option Formats, as shown in Figure 21.1.

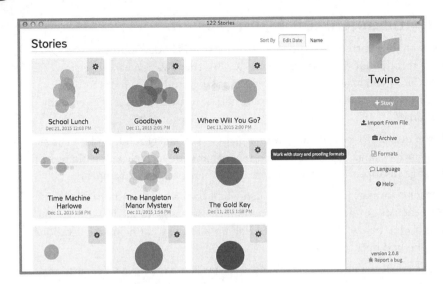

FIGURE 21.1   The Formats option on the right sidebar of the Story menu screen.

Click the Formats option and look at the top bar in the pop-up window. On the far right is the option Add a New Format. Click that option, and you see another pop-up window asking you for the file address for the format.js file.

The file address is the menu path for wherever the file is stored on your computer. If you don't know the file address, navigate to the folder and right-click on the format.js file to get more information on the file. Grab the file address and paste it into the pop-up window and click the +Add button.

Now, when you open a new story and navigate to the Formats menu, you should see a second SugarCube option, SugarCube 2. Choose that format so you can get started learning about the new time-related macros in Twine.

Utilizing the `time()` Function and `<<timed>>` and `<<goto>>` Macros

You've already played around with time in the Harlowe format. SugarCube 2 includes the ability to count the number of seconds the passage is open and display conditional text based on that amount of time. It can transport the player to another passage after a set amount of time or delay displaying the exit from a passage until after some time has passed. In other words, these macros are like a tiny clock ticking behind the scenes.

Counting Seconds

Let's say you want to have a single choice on the screen but have that link go to two different passages—one if the link is clicked quickly and the other if the link is clicked slowly.

Open a new game and type this in the first passage:

```
"I can read your mind," she says. "I know whether you want to go with me."
"Really?" you reply. "Then what is my <<click "answer">><<if time()
lt 3000>><<goto "Yes">><<else>><<goto "No">><<endif>><<endclick>>?"
```

The `time()` function kicks in and begins counting the seconds the moment the passage comes onto the screen. In this example, the player unknowingly has 3 seconds to click the hyperlinked text if he wants to move to a passage that will allow him to travel with the warrior queen. If he pauses for any reason, the warrior queen senses it, and the player is transported to a different passage that kicks him off the queen's trip. In this case, the `time()` function is combined with the `<<click>>` and `<<goto>>` macros to build a timer that allows real-life hesitation to influence the game.

Twine does not automatically generate these passages when you use the `<<goto>>` macro, so use the green +Passage button to create two new passages: one titled Yes and one titled No.

Let's break down the code in the example. The `<<click>>` macro opens with a set of double angled brackets and the macro name (`click`). It then presents the hypertext word in quotation marks (`"answer"`) and closes the macro with another set of double angled brackets.

Next, the `<<if>>` macro opens with its set of double angled brackets and the macro name (`if`). The `time()` function is listed along with the `lt` operator, which stands for "less than," and an amount of time: 3000 milliseconds, or 3 seconds. If the player clicks within 3 seconds, the `<<goto>>` macro, which is part of the conditional statement, is triggered, taking the player to a passage titled Yes.

But this `<<if>>` macro is followed by an `<<else>>` macro written as is and followed by its own `<<goto>>` macro that transports the player to the No passage if the player hesitates for more than 3 seconds. Both the `<<endif>>` closer and the `<<endclick>>` closer end the two open macros.

When the passage opens on the screen, as in Figure 21.2, the player can't tell that there is anything special about the link.

FIGURE 21.2 A seemingly simple hypertext link hides a SugarCube timer.

If the player clicks the link within 3 seconds, she's taken to a passage that allows her to join the warrior queen on her journey. If she pauses too long before clicking the button, the warrior queen notes the player's hesitation and bars her from the queen's trip. In that case, the player has a very different experience with the game, traveling alone through the wilderness.

TRY IT OUT: THE GREAT CLOCK ADVENTURE

You seem to have gotten yourself stuck inside the cogs of Mr. Tettlebaum's magical clock, but you're not the only one down here. Mr. Tettlebaum's tetchy assistant, Quinn, is skulking around the gears as well. He'll help you if he believes you, so you're going to have to do a good job convincing him.

Write a story for this scenario, using the `time()` function to have real-life hesitation or eagerness affect the outcome of this steampunk game.

Don't use this time trick solely as a punishment. You can just as easily reward the player for thinking deeply instead of rushing into a decision. Or you can have a character respond with suspicion if the player is too quick and therefore seems too eager. The point is that you can have time in the real world influence what happens in the game.

Building a Timer

You can have the player transported to a passage if he does nothing within a certain amount of time. For instance, you can tell the player that a box will explode if he doesn't choose one of the three buttons in time. If he makes a choice, the story continues to the designated passage, but if he sits staring at the screen, the box explodes, and the player is taken to a fourth passage that tells the player the game is over.

Although Twine automatically creates three passages for the links, use the green +Passage button to make a fourth passage called Boom. Set it aside for a moment and write this in the opening passage:

```
You can hear the fainting ticking of the timer that will destroy the box if you
don't choose the correct button in 3 seconds. Do you want to press the [[square
button|Square]], [[circle button|Circle]], or [[triangle button|Triangle]].
<<timed 3s>><<goto "Boom">><<endtimed>>
```

After choices are given, the `<<timed>>` macro is tacked on at the end of the passage. The macro opens with a set of double angled brackets and the name of the macro (`timed`) as well as the amount of time the player has once the passage opens before the macro is triggered. In this case, it's 3 seconds (`3s`). The macro closes with another set of double angled brackets.

Nested inside the `<<timed>>` macro is a `<<goto>>` macro. It opens with its own set of double angled brackets and the name of the macro (`goto`). Then it gives the passage name inside quotation marks (`"Boom"`) and closes with another set of double angled brackets. Finally, the `<<timed>>` macro has a closer: `<<endtimed>>` or `<</timed>>`.

This basic timer triggers the `<<goto>>` macro and transports the player to the Boom passage only if no choice is made within the allotted 3 seconds. While the player receives a textual clue in the passage ("choose the correct button in 3 seconds"), there is no evidence of the timer on the screen (see Figure 21.3), which only shows three choices.

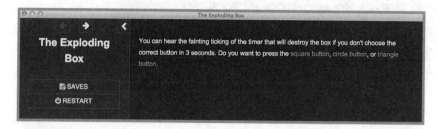

FIGURE 21.3 Three choices appear on the screen, along with a hidden SugarCube timer.

Make sure you give the player a fair amount of time to read the passage before you have the timer trigger. Once again, the timer doesn't need to be used as a punishment. You can also set up a situation where the player is rewarded for taking their time with a decision, only transporting to a special passage if they pause long enough in the current passage.

TRY IT OUT: RUNNING OUT OF TIME

Write a story about getting trapped inside a graveyard 20 minutes before zombies are supposed to start rising out of the graves. Use the `<<timed>>` macro to create a time-influenced maze-like horror game that has the player character trying to get out of a cemetery that has no easy exits and lots of surprises.

Delayed Text

Another way to use the `<<timed>>` macro is to delay text. In other words, the passage can open with a certain portion of the text already on the screen (though technically you also could have a completely blank passage) and then more text is added after a set amount of time. To see how this works, type the following in a new passage:

```
You look around the room but can't see an exit. Do you dare trust the old man's
advice? You blow out your candle and wait for a few seconds. <<timed 8s>>The
[[faint outline of a door|Exit]] appears on the far wall.<<endtimed>>
```

The passage opens with all the text that appears before the `<<timed>>` macro on the screen. This macro opens with a set of double angled brackets, the name of the macro (`timed`), and the amount of time that will pass once the passage opens until the next block of text appears on the screen: 8 seconds (`8s`). The macro closes with another set of double angled brackets. The text that will appear is placed before the closing macro: `<<endtimed>>`.

After 8 seconds pass, the additional text and link shown in Figure 21.4 are added to the text that appears on the screen at the opening of the passage.

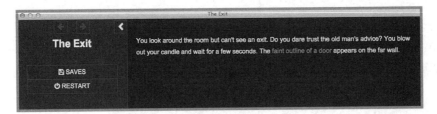

FIGURE 21.4 The extra text appears on the screen after 8 seconds.

This timer trick is wonderful for hiding links as well as simulating the passing of time inside the game.

TRY IT OUT: COLD FEET

You are a spy, meeting with a fellow agent who has cold feet about your current case. In the next few hours, you're supposed to infiltrate a party at the president's mansion and plant a bug in his office.

Write a story about this scenario. In it, use delayed text to simulate the conversational pauses between the player character and non-player character as well as the non-player character spy's reluctance to be involved in this field of work. Will you be able to convince the agent that the risks are worth the reward of information?

Practicing Showing, Not Telling

Showing instead of telling is an excellent way of engaging the reader with the text. Remember back in Chapter 5, "Building Objects with Variables," when I pointed out Edmund's obsession with Turkish delight in *The Lion, the Witch, and the Wardrobe*? If C.S. Lewis had written "Edmund is greedy," you may or may not have retained that fact, especially if it was stated one time toward the beginning of the book and never discussed again.

But C.S. Lewis never tells the reader what to think about Edmund. Instead, he has Edmund ask for a delicacy instead of an inexpensive, commonplace candy. He has Edmund stare at the empty box. He has Edmund wheedle the White Queen for a few extra pieces of Turkish delight, and he begs to be taken to her palace so she can fill his request now instead of later. And he stands, staring at her sledge after she drives away, filled with longing.

After a dozen or so clues, you start thinking to yourself, "Edmund is greedy," and because you've done the work of arriving at this knowledge, it's going to stick with you for the rest of the book.

Apply that concept to a game, and you can see how powerful a tool showing instead of telling can be in shaping how the player views the characters and retains important information.

Problems with Telling

Not only is telling boring, but writers who only tell have a terrible habit of saying that a character possesses a certain personality trait and then negating that fact later in the story. This is possibly because the lack of work in telling instead of showing means that the fact doesn't stick with the writer any more than it sticks with the reader.

For instance, a writer might tell the player that AmazingGirl is the bravest superhero at the beginning of the game and that's what makes her so amazing. Yet the writer might also give choices later in the game that show AmazingGirl hesitating in the face of danger. What's up with that?

You can safeguard against forgetting what you've told the reader by making sure that you show the player character's (or, for that matter, non-player character's) important traits. By letting the *reader* figure out who the character is and what makes her tick, you reduce the risk of not having your story match up as it unfolds. Every decision merely becomes one more clue in defining the character's personality.

In addition, one of the major problems with just doing information dumps (rather than delicately weaving the information into the fabric of the story) is that the writer lets out a figurative breath and thinks, "Okay, I've conveyed that point, so I don't need to mention it again."

Wrong! The character won't feel genuine if a trait is brought up once in the beginning of the game and never explored or experienced in the rest of the passages. What if you're told that AmazingGirl is cheerful, but you never see that cheerfulness coming out in the form of joyful action? Will you really believe that AmazingGirl is a jovial character?

An important step in avoiding telling is understanding the drawbacks of dumping information.

TRY IT OUT: HARRINGTON HIGH HAZE

You are scared of everything. Even things that aren't remotely dangerous fill you with a sense of dread. And life is about to become a lot worse because today is the start of the Harrington High Haze, a yearly tradition in which upperclassman make the new freshman run the gauntlet on their first day of school.

Write a story for this scenario, dreaming up obstacles to throw at this freshman player character to give her a nerve-wracking first day of school. Convey the player character's nervousness without ever telling the player how scared the character is of everyone and everything. Ask a friend to play your game and describe the player character. Does your friend pick up on the fact that the player character is anxious? Ask your friend to point to places where he or she definitely knew this side of the character's personality.

Describing Actions

An easy way to practice showing instead of telling is to pretend that you are on an ongoing game of *Password*. This game show from the 1960s had two players, one who knew the secret word and another who was trying to guess it. The one who knew the word couldn't use the word, though he or she could offer one-word clues. For instance, if the secret word was *ice*, player might have described it as *cold*, *water*, or *frozen*.

Here's how you can apply this idea to writing: Every time you're going to tell something, pause and consider how you can show it without using the word you have in mind. For instance, instead of saying the player character is nervous, you may have him bite his nails, check something many times, or huddle behind another character. All of these actions show nervousness, and telling the story this way is far more powerful than simply stating a trait. The showing becomes even more impressive if you never state the word, much as C.S. Lewis never uses the word *greedy* to describe Edmund.

TRY IT OUT: GAME SHOW

After years of trying, the player character is finally a contestant on his or her favorite game show. It would be a dream come true, but there's a small problem. The opponent is the player character's best friend, who told the player character backstage that he is going to cheat.

Without ever using the word *angry* (or any synonym for angry, like *infuriated* or *irate*), convey to the reader that the player character is furious. How would he behave if he had finally gotten this special opportunity to be on the show and then discovered that his best friend was prepared to cheat? Think about what you do when you are angry and use that base of knowledge to build an angry character. Which wins out—the player's friendship or love of the show? Or both?

Drawing Conclusions

With the iceberg effect, described earlier in this chapter, the writer withholds information *he or she knows* while letting the silence in the story speak volumes. In other words, the writer shows only the tip of the situation and implies that there is a lot more going on beneath the surface. What is not said is sometimes more important than what is said.

Did you catch those italicized words in the preceding paragraph? It doesn't count, and usually makes for a weaker story, when you leave out stuff that *you* don't know. Can't figure out how the magic the characters are doing works? When you leave out explanations or facts you don't know, that isn't the iceberg effect. That's just sloppy writing that you're hoping no one notices, like shoving your dirty pajamas under your blanket and pretending there isn't a lump in the bed.

No, with the iceberg effect, you leave out the obvious on purpose and allow the player to draw conclusions. The tension of not knowing and trying to figure out what characters are thinking or feeling, trying to discern what they know and what they've done...*that* is the iceberg effect because the hidden words have the ability to tear apart the reader emotionally as he or she crashes into a full understanding of the situation.

Like that analogy?

So think about what you can omit in order to strengthen your storytelling. Look at what you've said point blank and see where you can dial back the writing so that the same idea is conveyed though up to interpretation.

For instance, look at these two options, the first stated directly and the second full of insinuations:

> He walked into the room and thought, "I am guilty."

> He slinked into the room, his eyes trained on the floor. "I don't know what you're talking about," he murmured.

It's clear that the character is hiding something. In the first example, he tells us outright: He's guilty. In the second example, although he never comes out and says that he's guilty, his behavior points toward remorse twisting his stomach. He slinks, he looks only at the floor, he murmurs—all indicators that the character isn't feeling at ease. Maybe because he's guilty? Or maybe for some other reason? The interpretation is up to the reader.

This technique is wonderful for mysteries, when understated writing can be used for misdirection.

TRY IT OUT: BROKEN FRIENDSHIP

You, Sam, and Alex were all best friends until one day you borrowed Sam's jacket without asking, and everything fell apart. You still have no clue why Sam stopped speaking to you, and you also don't know why Sam dropped Alex from his/her life, too—or why Alex won't even look at you.

An incident has brought you and Sam together for a single day. Will you walk away, understanding what happened, and be able to fix your broken friendship?

Keep the iceberg effect in the forefront of your mind as you describe how the characters interact with one another. Use the `time()` function to have pauses in the real world affect game play.

Demonstrating Behavior

Have you ever tried to change another person's behavior? There are two routes you can take: telling them what to do or modeling what to do. I'll give you a hint as to which option is more effective in actually affecting change. It's the one that bears resemblance to good writing.

Let's say that you want someone to write thank-you notes after he receives a gift. You can remind him every time he receives a gift that he should write a note. This may work, but you'll probably also receive a healthy dose of grumbling along the way.

On the other hand, if the person always receives a thank-you note for gifts he gives, he will be much more likely to respond in kind and write thank-you notes himself. He won't even need to be told to do that writing because he will have subconsciously picked up on the idea that thank-you notes are not only well received but tend to lead to more gifts in the future. Moreover, the action will be grumble-free because the impulse will be internal rather than external. People are more likely to do, believe, or feel things if they come to a conclusion internally than if they have the idea fed to them externally by another person.

So how does this apply to writing? Rather than telling the reader exactly how you want him or her to view the character, show the character's personality through actions and choices. You'll still need to decide on the character's personality beforehand, but then you reveal that personality through the character's words, actions, and feelings.

By showing the player what you want him or her to see instead of telling the player exactly how to view the character, you create a stronger impression that sticks with the reader because he or she figured out the character. Remember how the hypothetical thank-you card writer doesn't feel put out when he comes to the idea to write thank-you cards on his own? The same goes for readers, who feel more attached to your characters when they get to form their own opinions.

So demonstrate a character's personality through words, actions, and feelings and allow players to connect the dots and come to their own understanding. They'll appreciate knowing that they've come to an idea all on their own.

TRY IT OUT: SAVE CAPITAL CITY

Capital City is in trouble, and it's going to take all the superheroes in this town to save it. The only problem is that this is the first time you're all meeting in one space, and you need to work together to fight against Evil Corporation, but you don't know which supernatural tools your fellow superheroes are bringing to the task. If you take five minutes to catch each other up on your capabilities, Evil Corporation will use that time to melt Capital City to the ground.

Write a story for this scenario. Because of the time limitation, you're going to have to dive into the action and have the capabilities revealed in the moment through action and choice. Instead of having a character insist he can fly, have him float between buildings. Instead of having a character state that she has amazing climbing abilities, have her scurry up the wall and grab an object that's out of reach. Give each superhero a distinct personality.

Use the `<<timed>>` macro to build timers into the task that transport the players to an end point if they don't solve the puzzles in time.

Transporting the Reader

Showing instead of telling is as much about conveying information as it is about transporting the reader. It is so much more powerful to have all the pieces of a puzzle and form the picture yourself than it is to have an image handed to you.

So be mindful that there are two ways to describe a scene. One way is to tell the reader everything he or she would see, hear, smell, taste, or touch while in the space. The other is to tell the reader everything he or she would see, hear, smell, taste, or touch while in the space *and* how to process all that sensory information. For instance, "The boy keeps his eyes glued to the floor" tells the reader where the boy is looking. But "The boy stares at the floor, which means he feels guilty" not only tells the player where the boy is looking but how to process that action.

The first option triggers the imagination to begin guessing what will come next, how the environment can be manipulated, or how the current situation may influence future events. The second option distracts the player, turning off the imagination until the player is mindlessly clicking around on the screen instead of making meaningful choices.

When you describe a scene, pretend that you are the player's eyes, ears, nose, mouth, and skin. Give the player as much information as needed in as succinct a way as possible. But once you've done that, stop. You're not a mother bird chewing up the story for the reader and depositing in the baby bird player's mouth! Let the player devour the story in peace.

TRY IT OUT: THE DEFACED FACE

Lady Ascot has always been able to solve a mystery the moment she steps into a room. Someone has scrawled an ominous message over the portrait of the Duke of Abbington, and the family needs to figure out who did it before anyone leaves the sitting room. Unfortunately, Lady Ascot is on the other side of the world, but she has sent you in her place to be her eyes and ears and describe what is happening in the room through text messages.

Describe the actions of the various non-player characters, their tone of voice, and how they appear in order to subtly indicate the guilty party through his or her behavior. Use the <<timed>> macro to have the text delayed on the screen to mimic real pauses in the conversation.

Trusting the Reader

Remember that the whole point of showing instead of telling is to demonstrate trust in your reader. It can be difficult to believe that a scene can stand on its own and convey everything the writer needs it to convey without explanation. The fear that the reader won't understand but the writer won't be there to answer a question is what causes countless game developers to overwrite their Twine pieces, feeding answers to readers *just in case*. They show but then they quickly follow up each show with a tell.

Throw away the idea of "just in case" and let your story jump out of your hands. Trust that its figurative parachute will open and that it will coast gently into the brain of the player.

Start from a place of trust. You'll learn from players what doesn't work during the beta testing portion of the writing process, and you can tweak the story at that point. But just as health care professionals live by the adage to "first, do no harm," writers should adhere to the adage "always trust the reader."

To convey trust, say an idea once, in showing form, and then let it be.

TRY IT OUT: PLUMMETING HEART

The player character is terrified to jump out of the airplane and skydive down to the ground, but it's not because he or she is scared of heights or has fears of falling. No, the player character has a much more creative reason for not wanting to leave the plane, and determining that reason will help you to build a game where the answer is unspoken but in plain sight.

Convey to the player how much the player character doesn't want to leave the airplane and try to find the magical combination of words or actions that not only allows the player character to remain in the plane until it lands back on the ground but clues the player in to why the player character doesn't want to go sailing through the sky.

Telling, Not Showing

Of course there are times when you need to tell and you can't show, and there are other times when telling belies the truth. Take, for example, Voldemort. The reader is told in the first book that he's evil. You don't get to see him in action, being evil all over town. Instead, you're told that he's the worst wizard in the history of the world.

But this telling is its own iceberg effect, and J.K. Rowling reveals what lurks beneath the surface in the sixth book, when she goes back in time and explores what made Voldemort such a horrific person. The telling, in this case, hides the truth and gives the reveal that much more impact.

Moreover, if you write a game that is all showing and no telling, you don't create footholds for players to use as they climb the figurative mountain. How can they keep climbing if there is nothing solid to hold onto? So give key facts that a player needs to have to understand and use showing to convey feelings and motivation. In other words, *tell* the incontrovertible facts and *show* the ever-changing internal struggle.

Use the pace of the story to determine when its best to show and when it works better to tell. The faster the action, the more you should be telling, and the slower the action, the more you should be showing. Remember that when the tension is high, the reader may be reading faster and might miss subtle clues, whereas when the tension relaxes, the reader slows down, too, and catches his or her breath. During slow parts, the player is then more inclined to read carefully and pick up on inferences in the text.

At this point, you're transitioning out of first-draft land and learning how to polish your writing. In fact, it may be helpful to think about showing and not telling as part of the editing process—as a last step where you look at ways to pare down what is said in order to invite the reader in as an equal partner in processing the story.

Showing, not telling can be difficult. Perhaps that's the real reason it's the motto of writing departments. Presenting this idea on the first day of a class gives the writer a lot of time to practice it. Because that's what you are: a writer.

Congratulations! You now know the basics of what makes a strong Twine game. But you still need to learn about manipulating the stylesheet as well as using CSS and HTML to change the look of your game. Carry on to the next chapter, where you'll learn about these aspects of game making.

Story Style: Changing the Game Appearance in SugarCube

Spunky Spelunky by Puck Saint makes you feel like you're climbing inside an arcade cabinet. It's a text adventure set in a cave, fashioned to look like a video game from the 1980s. The text is in that familiar pixelated font of yesteryear, and the story scrolls onto the screen in blocky declarations, reminiscent of old text-and-image games like the original *King's Quest*.

By manipulating the stylesheet, playing with transitions, and tweaking the appearance of the text in the passage, Saint takes a simple game about collecting ore and exploring caves and turns it into an adventure that looks more like *Legend of Zelda* than *Zork*. Saint used SugarCube as the base for the game, and you, too, can learn how to play with CSS and HTML in SugarCube in order to change the look of a game. Even small tweaks to the default font or the background color can change the feel of a game.

You're once again diving into the stylesheet. So navigate back to the menu in the lower-left corner, where you've been changing the story format. When you choose Edit Story Stylesheet, you find yourself with a blank white box.

The concepts involved in changing the default style settings are the same ones you used when tweaking the look of a story in the Harlowe format, even if the syntax is different with SugarCube. This chapter teaches you how to use color, fonts, and layout to enhance a story.

Navigating the Stylesheet

Remember back in Chapter 15, "Story Style: Changing the Game Appearance in Harlowe," when you learned about Cascading Style Sheets? By creating a single stylesheet for a game and cascading those decisions through every screen, you save yourself time because you don't need to make those style decisions over and over again for each passage.

Like Harlowe, SugarCube has its own settings that determine the default font, text size, background color, and page layout. Each instruction in CSS is called a *rule*. You alter the formatting for a story by writing a new rule. Each rule is made up of a *selector* and a *declaration*. These new selectors and declarations overwrite the settings that Twine established on the main stylesheet.

Reviewing Selectors and Declarations

A *selector* is an element you want to change. In Harlowe, a selector is written as `tw-passage` or `tw-sidebar`. In SugarCube, you write it as `.passage` or `#sidebar`. Every class is preceded by a period, and every ID is preceded by a hash symbol.

Wait a second. What are classes and IDs?

A *class* is one category of selector, and it's used with a style element that you're going to use over and over again in a single passage. One example might be the font. You're going to have lots of words in the passage, correct? And because you want the same style element to be applied to *all* the words, you use a class selector, such as `.passage`, to use the new font in every passage.

An *ID* is another category of selector, and it's used for unique style elements. For instance, maybe every time a certain character speaks, you want her words to appear in a special font. You can create an ID element that applies this special style rule any time you refer to that ID tag in the passage.

A class can be used multiple times within a page. An ID can be used only once within a page. Use a class if you want to style a lot of things the same way. Use an ID if you want to take a single element of the layout—like the sidebar—and display it in a unique way.

A *declaration* in SugarCube looks similar to a declaration in Harlowe:

```
.passage { font-size: 12px; }
```

This is the name of the element you want changed (such as `font-size`) followed by the value (for example, `12px`). Remember that every declaration has two parts: a *property name* and a *property value*. A declaration in SugarCube is also surrounded by curly brackets and ends with a semicolon.

To see how these elements work, let's return to an example you tried in Chapter 15. Open a new story and call it Something Weird Is Going On. Switch to the SugarCube format, type a few sentences in the first passage, and then open the blank stylesheet and enter the following selector and declaration:

```
.passage { background-color: #50A6C2; }
```

`.passage` is a class selector. The declaration opens with a curly bracket, the property name (`background-color`), and a colon. Next comes the hexadecimal code for a shade of blue, preceded by a hash symbol (`#50A6C2`). The declaration ends with a semicolon and a closing curly bracket. When you click the Play button, you should see the familiar black background of a SugarCube game, with the words inside a blue box, as shown in Figure 22.1.

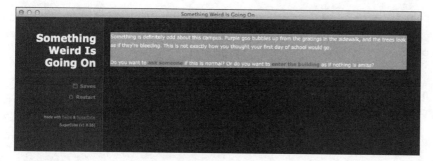

FIGURE 22.1 Change the background color of all passages by setting a new property name and property value in the stylesheet.

As in Chapter 15, the blue section is small, only wrapping around the words in the paragraph. If you want the blue to be applied everywhere in the background—inside the passage and out—you need to use the body selector. Because the body applies to every space on the page rather than an element of the page, it is neither a class nor an ID. Therefore, you don't see a period or a hash symbol in front of the word body.

Remember back in Chapter 15 when you replaced tw-passage with body to make the blue background fill every part of the screen? If you replace .passage with body in the stylesheet, like this, you see a very different screen when you click the Play button again:

```
body { background-color: #50A6C2; }
```

You should now see blue everywhere in the passage area, as in Figure 22.2, though the background of the sidebar is still black.

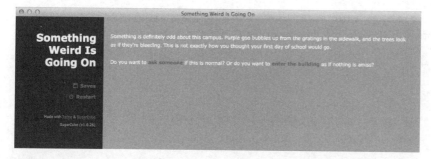

FIGURE 22.2 Spread the color through the whole passage area by using the body selector.

#ui-bar is an ID selector that refers to the sidebar on the left side of the screen. This is the space that contains the title of your story as well as the Saves and Restart menus, any links added to the StoryMenu passage, and any code added to the StoryCaption passage.

If you want the color to spread into the sidebar, too, you can add the ID selector `#ui-bar` to body, separated by a comma, so that both selectors share the same declaration. Add this new selector to the existing declaration:

```
body, #ui-bar { background-color: #50A6C2; }
```

The selectors run one after the other, separated by a comma (`body, #ui-bar`). The declaration opens with a curly bracket, the property name (`background-color`), and a colon. Next is the hexadecimal code for a shade of blue, preceded by a hash symbol (`#50A6C2`). The declaration ends with a semicolon and a closing curly bracket.

Now when you click the Play button, you see the blue background on every part of the screen, as in Figure 22.3.

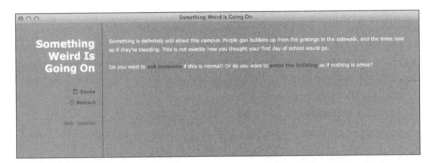

FIGURE 22.3 The background color now permeates both the passage area and the sidebar area.

SugarCube is similar to Harlowe in that you can make a bunch of changes to the same selector, such as changing the font and its size, at the same time. Using a similar example as the one in Chapter 15, you can change the syntax to use the `.passage` class for SugarCube's stylesheet:

```
.passage { font-family: papyrus; color: #000080; font-weight: bold;
font-size: 20px; }
```

Add this to the stylesheet, as shown in Figure 22.4, and you end up with all the words in a bold, 20-pixel, navy blue Papyrus font.

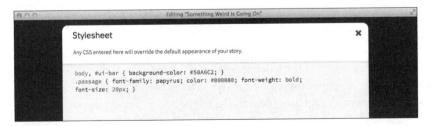

FIGURE 22.4 Change the font style and various font attributes by using the `.passage` selector and adding all the declarations, separated by semicolons.

Think you're ready to jump back into CSS? Let's take a look at what you can change about your game.

Changing the Background

You're already familiar with how to change the background color in a passage only, through the whole background, or even extending to the sidebar. But can you use a gradient background, as you did in Chapter 15?

Let's dive a little deeper into CSS. Twine is not producing the gradient on the screen; the browser is. That is true whether you're using Firefox, Internet Explorer, Safari, or Chrome. All Twine is doing is giving the browser a set of instructions about how it wants the page to display. The browser then complies, displaying the background color as Twine tells it to do.

Except when it doesn't.

Each browser reads CSS a little differently, and there isn't one universal way of writing CSS that makes the same project display *exactly* the same across every browser. Instead, the programmer sometimes provides multiple ways of stating the same instruction in the stylesheet, and the browser chooses the instructions it recognizes. All the examples in this book were made with the Firefox web browser, and what you see on your screen may vary depending on the browser you use.

Flat background colors are fairly simple, and browsers read commands to use them the same way. Gradient colors are a little more complicated, though almost all current browsers can handle gradient backgrounds.

To include the sidebar in this example, you can have the gradient move from left to right, so the sidebar is a solid blue and the screen finishes in white on the far right side. Open the stylesheet and type the following:

```
body { background-image: linear-gradient(to right, #50A6C2, #FFFFFF); }
#ui-bar { background-color: #50A6C2; }
.passage { color: #000000; }
```

This time I've separated out the `body` and `#ui-bar` rather than writing them within the same rule, separated by a comma. I want the sidebar to be a solid blue and the body to fade from blue to white.

Now click the Play button and look at what happens. In Figure 22.5, you can see that the sidebar is a solid blue, while the color fades across the screen, ending in white on the right side of the screen. (If you're reading the print version of this book, you should still be able to discern the change in shade, even though you can't see the blue.) Because the default white text would be difficult to read, I also changed the font color to black.

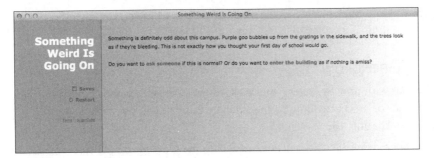

FIGURE 22.5 Gradient color spreads across the screen from left to right.

Although the gradient looks lovely now, this may (or may not) be the case once you upload the game and make it available online. Be mindful of this when using a gradient background for your game.

TRY IT OUT: FADE

You are studying physical magic, but it's not going too well. You can make yourself fade but not disappear, and this is problematic because the Nottingham School of Magic will never allow you to graduate with such a poor demonstration of your chosen area of study. Your friend has an idea: Throw you into an incredibly dangerous situation and see if the weight of the moment gives you the energy and power to master invisibility. Of course, that isn't exactly what happens.

Create a story with a gradient background that sets a tone for the game.

Changing the Sidebar

The selector for the SugarCube sidebar is #ui-bar. Of course, it isn't a requirement that you have a sidebar at all. Still playing with the Something Weird Is Going On example, you can remove the sidebar by deleting this line:

```
#ui-bar { background-color: #50A6C2; }
```

and replacing it with the following line of code:

```
#ui-bar { display: none; }
```

When you click the Play button, you see the gradient color spread across the whole screen and all the elements of the sidebar disappear, as in Figure 22.6.

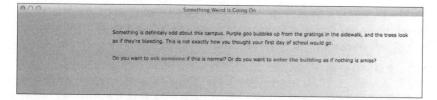

FIGURE 22.6   The sidebar disappears, and the gradient color spreads across the whole screen.

Remove that #ui-bar selector from the stylesheet, and the sidebar returns, which is good because you need to practice tweaking the text. In fact, add back in that original #ui-bar selector with the background color declaration so the screen returns to its gradient form.

There are multiple ID selectors that can change the way the text looks on the sidebar. To get a glimpse of some, add three elements to the sidebar: an author byline, a subtitle, and a banner. The title, of course, is set when you open a new story and name it. But you have to add these other aspects of the sidebar by creating new passages.

Click the +Passage button to create a new passage and call it StoryAuthor. Remember, capitalization matters in the passage name. In the body of that passage, fill in your name, as I've filled in mine in Figure 22.7.

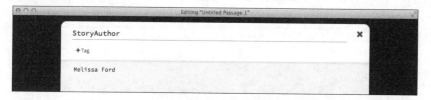

FIGURE 22.7   Fill in your name in the new StoryAuthor passage.

Now, when you click the Play button, your name appears on the left sidebar, underneath the title, as mine does in Figure 22.8.

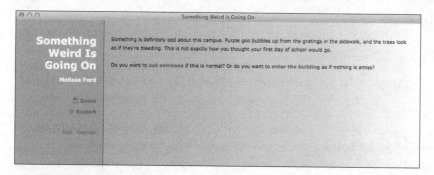

FIGURE 22.8   The author's name appears on the left sidebar.

Now add a subtitle for the story: "The Strangest Tale Ever Told." Again, use the +Passage button to create a new passage and call it StorySubtitle. Write your subtitle (The Strangest Tale Ever Told) in the body of the StorySubtitle passage.

Click the Play button, and you see the subtitle on the left sidebar, as shown in Figure 22.9.

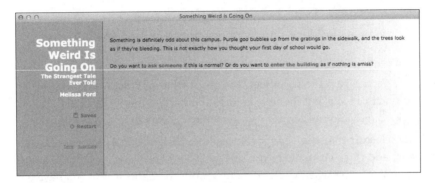

FIGURE 22.9 A subtitle now appears on the left sidebar.

Finally, you can add text above the title to create a banner that says `Oddities Abound`. Click the +Passage button to create a new passage and call it StoryBanner. Write the banner text (`Oddities Abound`) in the body of the StoryBanner passage.

Click the Play button again, and you see the banner appear above the title on the left sidebar, as shown in Figure 22.10.

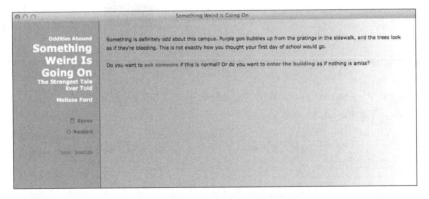

FIGURE 22.10 A banner now joins the title, subtitle, and author listed on the left sidebar.

Now it's time to play with the text on the left sidebar. Each of those elements—title, author, subtitle, and banner—as well as the caption and menu text if you're using the special StoryMenu or StoryCaption passages from Chapter 20, "Keeping Players Engaged," has an ID selector for the stylesheet.

For instance, to change anything about the way the title appears, use the `#story-title` ID. Begin with `#story-title` as the selector and then write your declarations, such as changing the font:

```
#story-title { font-family: courier; }
```

You can also change the color or size of the text:

```
#story-title { font-family: courier; color: #000080; font-size: 30px; }
```

Check these changes by clicking the Play button. If you made the changes shown previously, you now see the rest of the text in white, but the text for the title, as you can see in Figure 22.11, appears much larger and navy blue, in the Courier font.

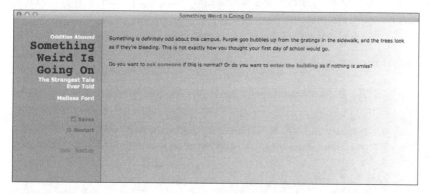

FIGURE 22.11   The title is a different color, font, and size from the other text in the sidebar.

The selector for the author (`#story-author`), subtitle (`#story-subtitle`), banner (`#story-ban-ner`), menu (`#story-menu`), and caption (`#story-caption`) text can all be used in the stylesheet with various declarations to change the way the text appears on the sidebar. Simply use the appropriate selector for the element you want to change and list the declarations afterward, within curly brackets.

TRY IT OUT: PLANET QUEST

The Universal Council, the governing body of outer space, has sent you on a special mission. There are 10 artifacts still missing from the incomplete planetary collection. Until those 10 artifacts are obtained, the time capsule can't be sent into the next dimension. Create an array to track the items and have that array update in the sidebar by using the StoryCaption passage to list the inventory.

Use all the special passages (StoryAuthor, StorySubtitle, StoryBanner, StoryMenu, and StoryCaption) to add information to the sidebar and then change the way the text displays using the stylesheet. Make sure it is easy for the reader to distinguish between the banner, title, subtitle, and author credit by using different fonts, text colors, or text sizes. Make sure the links and code are also easy to read.

Changing the Font

You've been playing with changing the font in the sidebar, but you can also use the .passage selector to change the font in all the passages. Return, once again, to the story Something Weird Is Going On. Open the stylesheet and change the overall font by using the .passage selector, like so:

```
.passage { font-family: courier; }
```

The default font in SugarCube is Verdana, but you can change it to any web-safe font. With this statement, you've now changed the font to Courier, which is a fairly small font. You may want to increase the size of the font on the screen and change the color to black so it is easier to read. Here's how you do that:

```
.passage { font-family: courier; font-size: 20px; color: #000000; }
```

Figure 22.12 shows that the text is, indeed, easier to read now.

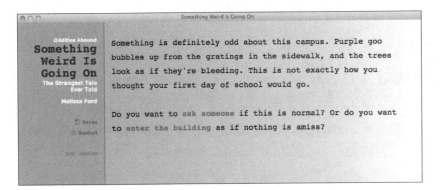

FIGURE 22.12 You can change the font face and size in the stylesheet.

Once again, as you did in Chapter 15, you can change the *font family* (font-family), *font color* (color), *font size* (font-size), *font style* (font-style), *font weight* (font-weight), and *text alignment* (text-align) by using the correct declarations. For instance, what if you want the font to be large, italic, and bold, with the text centered on the screen? Remove all .passage rules currently on the stylesheet and add the following:

```
.passage { font-size: 20px; font-style: italic; font-weight: bold;
text-align: center; color: #000000; }
```

Check the style elements of your game by clicking the Play button. In Figure 22.13, you can see the text in a larger type, italicized and bold, and centered in the middle of the screen.

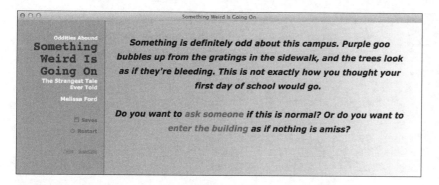

FIGURE 22.13 Change multiple facets of the way the text displays on the screen by listing the proper declarations with the `.passage` selector.

You can add Google fonts to SugarCube in the same way you add them in Harlowe (see Chapter 15); this gives you over 700 additional font options for your story. Navigate to the Google Fonts site (https://www.google.com/fonts) and choose a font that enhances your story.

For instance, find the font named Shadows Into Light and click the Quick Use button, which is a small arrow on the lower-right side of the screen, next to the blue Add to Collection button. Scroll down to the third section on the new screen and choose the `@import` window. Copy this code from that window:

```
@import url(https://fonts.googleapis.com/css?family=Shadows+Into+Light);
```

Return to the SugarCube stylesheet and paste the code at the top of the stylesheet. Now go back to the Google Font web page and move down to the fourth section. Grab the wording that appears in that box (`font-family: 'Shadows Into Light', cursive;`) and go back to the SugarCube stylesheet. Remove all `.passage` rules currently on the stylesheet and add the following wording:

```
.passage { font-family: 'Shadows Into Light', cursive; }
```

Although Shadows Into Light is the font family name, *cursive* is a keyword that connotes the generic family—the umbrella category that font belongs to, such as serif, sans-serif, or monospace.

Because this is another small font, you may want to increase the size by adding the font size declaration and change the color to black:

```
.passage { font-family: 'Shadows Into Light', cursive; font-size: 20px;
color: #000000; }
```

Click the Play button, and you see the new font on the screen, as in Figure 22.14.

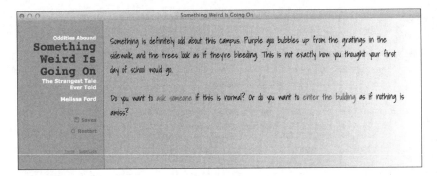

FIGURE 22.14 Add a new Google font—or 700 of them—to your SugarCube stylesheet.

You now have many more options to play with, so you can choose a font that complements your story and set a tone for the player before he or she has even read the first word. (Just make sure it's not difficult to read on the screen.)

TRY IT OUT: HISTORICAL TROUBLES

Choose a period of history and a situation that defines the time period and set your game in that world. Who are the key players? What is the situation? How is the problem solved? Are you going to place your players straight in the heart of the battlefield? Bring them into the remorseful mind of a guillotine executioner? Set them near the top of the structure on the final days of building the pyramids?

Choose a Google font that enhances the story, setting the mood. Use the instructions in this section to add a new font to your stylesheet and set the font family as a declaration under the `.passage` selector.

Changing Links

You can change the color of the hypertext links in a game. By default, clickable text appears in blue (#4466dd), but you can change that to any color by listing a different hexadecimal code on the stylesheet. The selector for links is a lowercase letter a. Make sure you've offered some choices in your first passage and then open the stylesheet again and type the following code:

```
a { color: #5C3317; }
```

Though it will be difficult to see in the pages of the book, when you click the Play button, instead of seeing the links in deep blue, you now see an elegant brown (see Figure 22.15).

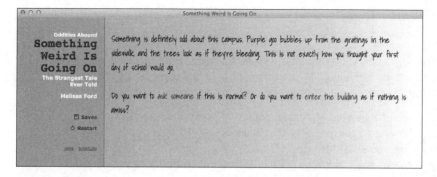

FIGURE 22.15 Change the color of links in the game by using the link selector in the stylesheet.

If you hold your mouse over the links, you'll notice that the words change color. This is the "hover" color, and you can change that, too. Currently, it is set as a pale bluish purple (#7799FF), but you can change it to orange to complement the brown used for the links. Open the stylesheet and type the following code to use the a:hover selector to make any changes to the text when the mouse moves over a link:

```
a:hover { color: #FF7722; }
```

So this looks different from anything you've seen so far. That selector :hover is a pseudo-class, which begins with a colon instead of a dot like other classes. It works like a class and represents a special state, in this case, when the mouse is hovering over the words.

Click the Play button and move the mouse so it hovers over your choices. You should see the words turn orange (I promise, they're orange even if you can't see it in this black-and-white book) and become underlined, as in Figure 22.16.

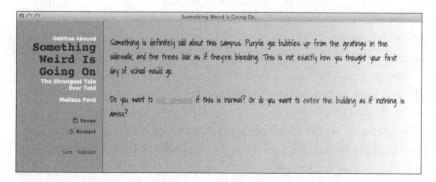

FIGURE 22.16 Change the color of links when you hover over hypertext with your mouse.

All other font traits, such as font family, size, weight, and style apply to links, too. You can use clever tricks such as having words enlarge or links turn bold when you hover over them. Just be careful not to go too far because your readers may get queasy if the words are constantly changing on the screen.

TRY IT OUT: ROBOROVER

You've been grieving since your dog died, but now you're ready to complete your greatest project yet: combining DNA with a robot to create sentient AI. In fact, in honor of your dog, you used his DNA in your robotic canine companion.

You bring RoboRover to life, but your celebration is short-lived once when you realize your new robot is trying to tell you something urgent. In fact, your robot is so much like your old pet that you keep forgetting that it's made of metal and wires. What is your robot trying to tell you? Is it trying to keep you out of danger or lead you into it?

Play with the way links display in the game, especially as you hover over them, to visually convey the duality of the outer barks of the robot and the inner thoughts of your old dog companion.

Creating a Class on the Stylesheet

As you build a game, you may decide that you want the words of certain characters to display differently from the main text on the screen. While I caution against mixing too many colors or font styles on the screen at the same time, in some games, you need it to be clear to the reader which character is in the scene, especially when you've purposefully written very similar characters.

For example, say that you enter a mansion and have five different robots take care of you. Their only distinguishing characteristic is the color of a button on each one's chest. Instead of writing "the red robot" or "the blue robot" over and over, you can simply use the correct color to display the word *robot* as well as the words the robot speaks in the game. You do this by setting up your own unique class on the stylesheet. Although many selectors have been created for you by the default formatting of SugarCube, you have the ability to create and use your own IDs and classes.

You've already encountered the `<span class>` element in Chapter 18, "Developing a Strong Player Character," with the `<<append>>` and `<<prepend>>` macros. Remember that elements are the individual building blocks that construct a web page, and in this case you want an element to apply a set of CSS rules to text on the screen when you use the `<span class>` tag.

You need to set those CSS rules on the stylesheet, so start a new game called Identical Robots, change the format to SugarCube, and open the stylesheet. A class is always preceded by a period, and it is easiest if you name your class so you can easily recall it in the passage. For this example, you can give each robot its own class and name the class after the color of the robot. For instance, the red robot will have the class `.Red`, and the orange (`.Orange`), yellow (`.Yellow`), green (`.Green`), and blue (`.Blue`) robots will be similarly named.

Once you've created the names of the classes, you can use them as selectors and start listing declarations for rules. For instance, use this to have the words of the red robot written in red:

```
.Red { color: #CC0000; }
```

You've now set the text color as red, and whenever you reference that class in the passage, it will print the words inside the opening and closing `<span class>` tags in red, while the rest of the words on the screen appear in the default white. To test this, open a passage and type in the following:

```
The <span class="Red">robot</span> moves across the room, silently. It notices you
just as it's about to turn off the lights. "<span class="Red">Can I help you with
anything?
Would you like me to [[prepare your bed|Bed]] or [[fetch you a book|Book]] from the
library?</span>" it asks in a mechanical voice.
```

The rule has been set in the stylesheet, but it's put to use in the passage. The element opens with a single angled bracket, the name of the tag (`span class`), an equal sign, the name of the class inside quotation marks (`"Red"`), and another single angled bracket. The word that appears after the element's opening tag, robot, appears in red on the screen instead of in the default text color. Finally, a closing tag is made up of a single angled bracket, a slash, the word `span`, and a single angled bracket.

The first use of the style rule is applied to a single word to indicate which robot is in the room. The second use of the style rule, later in the passage, is wrapped around the words spoken by the robot to the player. If you click the Play button, you should see the text in three colors on the screen, as in Figure 22.17: red for the text pertaining to the robot, blue for the clickable links on the screen, and white for the default text color. (If you're reading the printed book, which is in black and white, it may be challenging to see the differences here.)

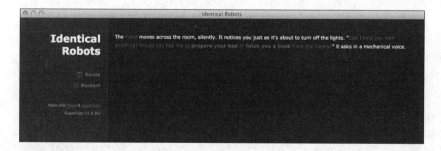

FIGURE 22.17 A class set in the stylesheet can be applied to certain text in a passage.

You can choose to set more than one declaration in the rule. For instance, maybe the red robot also happens to be the largest robot, and the blue robot is the smallest robot, so you want to apply different font sizes as well as color to the text. Or maybe you want each robot to use a different font. The options are endless. Classes are useful when you want to create a rule and apply it to certain text in the passage but not to all the text in the passage.

TRY IT OUT: IDENTICAL ROBOTS

You were thrilled to be invited to spend a night at Professor Eltron's estate. In the morning, you're going to interview him about his latest inventions for your magazine. You've heard a lot about his home and the staff of nearly identical robots the professor uses to keep the enormous mansion running smoothly.

But once you set your suitcase down, you realize that Professor Eltron's home is in a strange state of decay, falling apart before your eyes. And the professor himself is nowhere to be found. While the robots appear wonderful on the surface, they seem reluctant to tell you their owner's whereabouts. Will you ever find him to write your article, or will you be publishing a very different story than you thought?

Write a story that uses the `<span class>` tag to differentiate between the nearly identical robots. Give each a unique font or text color to make it clear which robot the player character is interacting with in the passage. Make sure you set the CSS rules on the stylesheet.

Using HTML in a Passage

While using a class is helpful when you want the same style elements to be applied over and over again, other times, you want a single word to appear italicized for emphasis or you want a single word to loom enormous on the screen. In Harlowe, you can use macros to apply such effects within a passage. In SugarCube, you use straight-up HTML in the passage.

HTML stands for Hypertext Markup Language, and it's one way instructions are given on a web page to tell the browser how to display the text and images on the screen. The CSS on the stylesheet cascades through your whole game, but you can use HTML in a passage to apply a style element on an individual basis.

To use HTML, you need to wrap the text you want to change inside opening and closing tags. The opening and closing tags look almost the same, but the closing tag always starts with a slash. Anything written between the opening and closing tags is affected by that style element.

The following sections show examples that you need to add to a single passage in a new story. Then, when you click the Play button, you can see how the words appear on the screen, with different text weight, style, size, and color.

Bolding Words

To bold words within a passage, enclose the words between `<b>` and `</b>` tags, like so:

```
"<b>Help!</b>" she screams as the finds herself trapped in the spider's web.
```

A single word (Help!) appears in boldface on the screen because you enclosed it in the opening and closing tags that apply boldface.

Italicizing Words

To italicize words within a passage, enclose the words between `<i>` and `</i>` tags:

```
<i>What?</i> you wonder. It sounds like your friend is screaming nearby, but there
is no way that she can be in the forest.
```

This causes the single word What? to appear italicized on the screen because you enclosed it in the opening and closing tags that apply italic style.

Underlining Words

To underline words within a passage, enclose the words between `<u>` and `</u>` tags:

```
She has been trapped inside a copy of <u>The Lion, the Witch, and the Wardrobe</u>
for the last three months. Unless… is it possible that she has gotten free?
```

This causes the title The Lion, the Witch, and the Wardrobe to appear underlined on the screen because you enclosed it in the opening and closing tags that apply underlining.

Resizing Words

You can use opening and closing tags to make text larger or smaller, once again using the `<span style>` tags you used in Chapter 14, "Wiggling Words: Changing the Text Appearance."

```
<span style="font-size: 200%">"Help!"</span> she shouts again. This time you're posi-
tive it's her.
You race deeper into the forest.
```

This causes the single word Help! to appear much larger than the text around it on the screen because you enclosed it in the opening and closing tags that apply a new font size (in this case, words that are double the size of the default font).

Changing the Color of Words

Similarly, you can change the color of text by using the `<span style>` tag, including the hexadecimal code for the color you want to use. Here is how you change the text in your passage to a lovely shade of red:

```
"Watch out," she shouts as you round the corner. But it's too late.
You see the <span style="color:#CC0000">blood</span> before you feel the spider's
pincers in your neck.
```

This causes the single word blood to appear in red on the screen because you enclosed it in the opening and closing `<span style>` tags and specified the color `"#CC0000"`.

Putting It All Together

After you have all the previously shown HTML samples together in a single passage, click the Play button and see how the text appears on the screen. As you can see in Figure 22.18, although there is still be plenty of plain text in the default font, words in the passage are now bold, italicized, underlined, large, or red thanks to HTML tags.

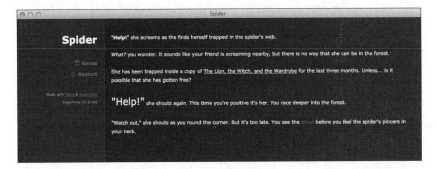

FIGURE 22.18 A variety of text options are created thanks to HTML tags.

TRY IT OUT: GHOST SHIP

Everyone has been curious about the empty ship bobbing in the harbor, but you're the only one brave enough to accept a dare that you can last a whole night along on the boat.

Write a story for this scenario, and in it, keep track of the supplies you bring and the supplies you collect by using an array that displays on the sidebar using the StoryCaption passage. Pepper your text with HTML to set the mood.

This is it: the home stretch. Your story is written, your style elements have been applied, and you're ready to reveal your game to the world. The last chapter takes you through the editing and debugging process, teaches you how to upload your game to make it available online, and helps you find your audience. Ready to release your creativity on the world? Turn the page and get started with the game release process.

Finishing Up and Clicking Publish

The writing process always ends twice. The first ending comes when you write the last words of your game, click the X in the top-right corner of the passage, and stare at the screen, realizing that your story is finally finished.

The second ending comes *after* you edit your game. It happens after combing the passages for grammatical and mechanical errors, checking the pace of the story while making sure an arc exists, and fixing all the bugs your beta testers find while playing the game.

The editing process can be a little tedious because it isn't like the initial period of creation, where the story is moving forward. Writing is exciting because you're always working on something new. Editing doesn't have the same energy because you're looping back into the same passages over and over again, tweaking aspects of the story and sometimes creating new problems you need to solve as you fix other issues.

Even so, stick with it: The editing process is worth it. It's what separates the good from the great, and you should always be striving for greatness with your writing.

Editing games has more in common with doing jigsaw puzzles than with reading books. You're not just making sure the story fits together; you're also confirming that the code works together. You need to ensure that the variables and conditional statements work in tandem and that you don't set up paths that make completing the game impossible.

Spend long enough working on making your story the best game it can be, and I promise you will feel a few things. You will doubt whether the story is any good. You will wonder if you will be able to fix all the problems. And you will feel an enormous sense of pride because you've not only created this beast, but you're now working to tame it.

The editing and publication process is a roller coaster of ups and downs, so put on your seat belt and get ready to tackle editing your story. In this chapter you'll learn how to get your story cleaned up, published, and in front of the right audience.

Editing Techniques

Editing involves looking at your story with a critical eye. For a moment, you take yourself out of the mind of the writer and put yourself into the mind of the reader. How will readers interact with your story? Will they understand what you're trying to say? Will they find all the possible endings?

Because you are so close to your story, you need to put a little distance between yourself and the words as you edit. Once you complete a game, let it sit for a day or two before you play it for the first time. I know this is not exactly the advice you want to hear when you're champing at the bit, excited to see how it unfolds on the screen. But even a 24-hour pause can help you see your story with fresh eyes similar to those that the reader will use when encountering your game for the first time.

Of course, sometimes it's difficult to edit your own work. Your eye may travel over errors that you would notice if this were another person's game, and you may not see problems with the story because your brain is mentally filling in the plot holes. So use this time away from the game to secure a few friends or family members to edit your game, too.

Tackling Different Types of Edits

Rather than trying to fix everything at once, approach your game with a series of edits, each serving a different purpose.

After your initial break from your text, you can complete all your edits back-to-back. But if you find yourself stuck or frustrated, give yourself another 24-hour period away from the game. Sometimes distance is all you need to find the way forward.

While working on one type of edit, you may find information that applies to a different edit. For instance, when you're editing for structure, you may find broken links. Instead of fixing them in the moment and taking yourself mentally out of the task at hand, note these errors on a sheet of paper or a digital tool such as Evernote and move back to the current edit. If you write down those problems, you won't forget to address them when you get to their turn. You also won't lose your momentum and focus with the current edit.

Editing for Structure

Start out easy by looking at the big picture. It may help to stand back from your game after you play it once or twice and see if it contains all the necessary story components.

Take out a piece of paper and draw the story arc, as described in Chapter 6, "Stasis, Catalyst, and Climax: Understanding Story Arc," and shown again in Figure 23.1. Don't draw it as it exists in your head but as it unfolds on the screen. In other words, does your story actually have a strong arc, or did you, say, forget to provide a clear catalyst and climax?

Similarly, take a look at your pacing, as described in Chapter 10, "Achieving Proper Pacing," and draw your plot movement, as shown in Figure 23.2. Remember that arc gives a story shape, and plot moves the story forward. Is your story moving at a good clip, or do you have long stretches where little happens? Does every story thread serve a purpose? Does every plot point move the story forward? Do you have a good balance of crisis and obstacles? Is there enough exposition that the reader won't be confused, and is there enough action to keep the reader engaged?

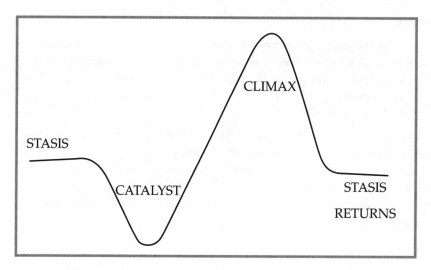

FIGURE 23.1 Reviewing the story arc.

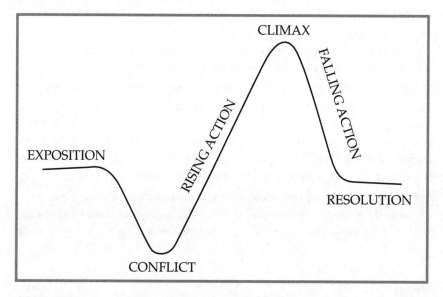

FIGURE 23.2 Reviewing the movement of the plot.

Of course, you don't want to find problems with your story—especially not at this point—but answer these questions honestly and smooth over any structural issues before you continue to the next edit.

Editing for Details

Now it's time to zoom in and look closely at all the smaller components of a story, such as the characters and setting. Ask yourself if every character serves a purpose and whether the characters are always working toward a goal. Do your characters know what they want? Are they working to get it? Do your characters remain "in character"—that is, always showing their personality through their actions?

How does the setting influence the story? Is your setting indispensable, or could your story be moved to another space and work equally as well? Do you give enough description so the reader can imagine the place? If you asked readers to draw your story's setting, would their pictures look mostly alike, or would every single picture be different? If the pictures would be different, you're placing the burden of building the setting on the reader's imagination rather than delivering the world.

Editing for Sound

Now play your story a few times (taking a different route each time) and read it aloud as you go. If you really listen to your story, you will start to hear any unnecessary turns of phrase, any redundant descriptions that slow down the story, and any weird transitions.

You want to delve down deep into the language and make every word count. Okay, maybe not *every* word because that will drive you crazy. But pay attention to the tone and the descriptions and note what you do well and what could use improvement.

If you bend or break any grammar rules, make sure there is a reason. For instance, J.K. Rowling does this to great effect with Hagrid, having him make grammatical errors in his speech to convey an aspect of his personality. Do you have a character who speaks in sentence fragments because their mind is always going a mile a minute? That would be a good reason to have a piece of a sentence dangling on its own. But sentence fragments that exist just because you forgot to put in a subject and verb need to be corrected.

While you're in each passage, improve it. Choose a better word or delete an adjective. Plump up the vividness of the language while paring down the number of words you're asking the reader to contemplate. And be sure to also pat yourself on the back when you string words together well.

Editing for Coding Errors

You need to make a pass at your story, looking for broken links that don't work, passages you forgot to fill out, and code that displays an error message when you enter the passage. In other words, you want to find and fix anything technical that is wrong with the game.

Now is also the time to look for errors that occur because you haven't accounted for every possibility, such as a player returning to a passage a second time but going through the same conversation with the same character because you didn't use the `(history:)` macro, or times when it becomes impossible to finish a game because there is no way to return to pick up a necessary item.

Fix bugs that require a quick tweak as you go along (such as adding a missing bracket or colon) and make a running list of bigger errors that require more writing once you've uncovered all the errors.

Editing for Mechanical and Grammatical Errors

Finally, go through your game looking for mechanical and grammatical errors. Make sure your commas are in the right places, words are spelled correctly, and tenses make sense (for example, don't move from present tense to past tense to present tense again).

If you struggle with this type of edit, grab a style manual, which is a book that answers all your punctuation and grammatical questions.

Navigating to the Proofing Copy

Many people like to open each passage and edit in the game. But you can also create a proofing copy, which is a document that lists all your passages and their contents.

Navigate to the menu in the lower-left corner of the screen that lists the story name and look at two options in the list. Click the first link, Story Statistics, to see a breakdown of your story, as shown in Figure 23.3, that provides useful information such as the word count and the number of passages. This section also tells you if there are any broken links. Of course, you want this number to be zero.

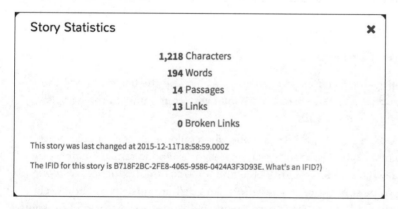

Story Statistics ✖

1,218 Characters

194 Words

14 Passages

13 Links

0 Broken Links

This story was last changed at 2015-12-11T18:58:59.000Z

The IFID for this story is B718F2BC-2FE8-4065-9586-0424A3F3D93E. What's an IFID?)

FIGURE 23.3 Story statistics from the menu.

Click the other link, View Proofing Copy, and you see a plain-text version of your story, as in Figure 23.4.

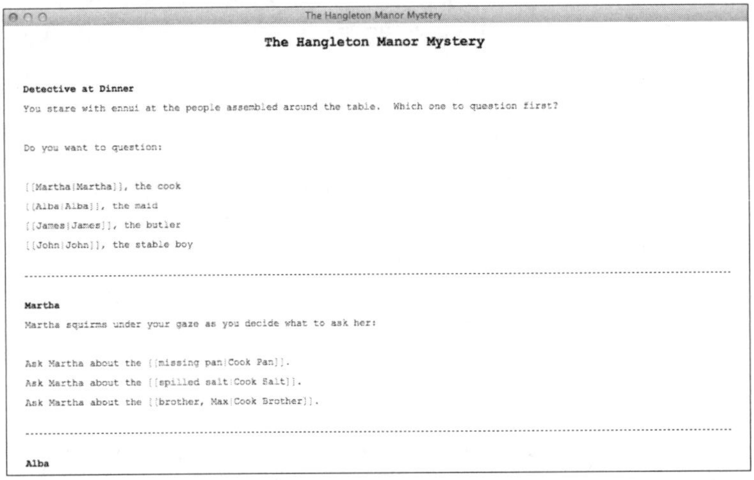

FIGURE 23.4 A plain-text copy of your story to use for proofing.

You can now copy and paste that version into a text editor, such as Notepad in Windows or TextEdit on a Mac. (Pasting it directly into a Word document removes all the formatting, so stick with using a text editor.) If it's easier for you to read and mark up your story on paper, you can print the plain-text version and write on the copy. Then transfer all your changes into the passages.

Testing Your Game

When you've taken your game as far as you can go—polishing up the text and fixing the code—it's time to line up beta testers. Beta testers will check your game on three levels: overall story, broken code, and logistics.

Who should you ask to be a beta tester? Try anyone who could be a potential player for your game, such as parents, siblings, friends, classmates, or extended family members. Aim for people who generally have a keen eye for detail and a modicum of patience. Also aim for people who are going to be supportive of your efforts and deliver criticism constructively. It's helpful to know what works and what doesn't work in a game. It's less helpful for someone to simply say, "I like it" or "It's terrible."

Questioning Beta Testers

A big mistake writers make when engaging beta testers is not giving enough guidance. Instead of giving them a general instruction such as "let me know if you find any problems," ask them to give you specific, useable feedback in three areas: overall story, broken code, and logistics.

First and foremost, have them give you feedback on the overall story. Ask them these questions so you can later turn their answers into usable information:

- Was there a moment when you felt the opening of the story ended and the conflict began?
- Was there a moment when you felt the story came to a head and the main problem in the story was resolved?
- Did you think the story moved at a good pace? Were there places in the story that were too fast or too slow?
- List all the characters in the story and write each character's personal goal next to his or her name. Did you find each character believable? Why or why not?
- Describe the setting. Were you able to hold a good mental image of the space in your mind?

You can see how these questions give the reader focus. The answers you receive from these questions tell you whether you have a story arc, good pacing, strong characters, and a vivid setting.

Next, have the beta testers give you feedback about broken code. Ask them to keep a running list of places where the code behaves strangely or where they receive an error message. Remind them before they begin that you need them to be very specific so you can find the correct passage in the future. Have them give you a snippet of text from the screen so you can use that to search the game for the correct passage.

Finally, ask the testers to give you notes about continuity and logistics. Do they enter a passage and see that the object they picked up two minutes earlier is back on the table because the description repeats? Do they keep popping in and out of a passage and see their inventory array adding dozens of copies of the same item? Do they hit dead ends, unable to solve puzzles because they're missing an important item that they can't double back and retrieve? Ask them once again to keep a list of these inconsistencies and have them give you specific snippets of text so you can enter those passages and either provide additional links or add code.

You may want to prepare a handout that you can give to beta testers along with a copy of your game. You can create a fill-in-the-blank worksheet once and reuse it with each subsequent game you make in the future.

Using Testing Notes

If you've prepared a handout or given specific instructions to your beta testers, you should now have a slew of notes giving you feedback on your game. Jump in and immediately fix any broken code or logistical errors your testers found before addressing answers to the overall story questions.

Some of the notes you receive will be a matter of opinion. One person's favorite character will be another person's grating presence in the game. But other notes, especially any points that repeat on more than one report, will give you insight into how your game will be perceived by the general public when you release it into the world.

Take these notes seriously. Address the thoughts that you think need to be addressed and leave behind the outliers. Remember that you're the author and, in the end, you get to the set the plot, the pacing, and the setting. Other people can give you advice to help you make your game stronger, but ultimately, you need to have the final opinion on what remains in the game and what goes.

Clicking Publish

Take a deep breath when you feel like your game has reached a finished state. You will always find passages to tweak and new ideas to add, but if you never declare something done, you'll never get it out into the world. So remove your hands from the keyboard and get ready for people to see your game.

Er...wait. Actually, set your hands back on the keyboard because you need to navigate back to the menu in the lower-left corner that lists the name. Click it to open the list and choose the option Publish to File, as shown in Figure 23.5, to create an individual file for your game. Save it to the Documents folder on your computer so you can find it easily in the future.

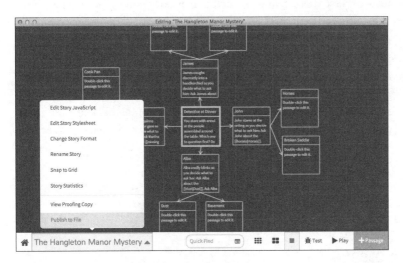

FIGURE 23.5   The Publish to File option creates an individual file of the game.

You now have an HTML file for your game, but you need a place to host it. Although Dropbox and Google Docs used to be options, changes on those platforms mean that they no longer support Twine stories. But don't worry, there are still three easy options for posting your game online.

Hosting Your Project on Philome.la

Philome.la (yes, the name of the site has a dot in the middle of the word) is a free Twine hosting site (http://www.philome.la). All you need to use it is a free Twitter account.

Log in with your Twitter account, upload the HTML file that you created when you clicked the Publish to File button, name your game, and click Publish. You can have the Philome.la Twitter account also tweet out a link to your game. You can manage or delete any games you upload to the free site.

Hosting Your Project on the Internet Fiction Database

The Internet Fiction Database (http://ifdb.tads.org), often abbreviated online as the IFDB, hosts your project for free, too. (Well, the Internet Fiction Archive actually hosts the game, but you'll access it through the IFDB site.) The IFDB is one-stop shopping for all interactive fiction games, and your game will be in good company, listed alongside the classic and new games mentioned in this book. You need to set up a free account using the Login link in the top-right corner of the screen.

The menu on the right sidebar of the site contains several subheadings, including Find, Browse, and Contribute. Navigate down to the Contribute section shown in Figure 23.6 and click Add a Game Listing.

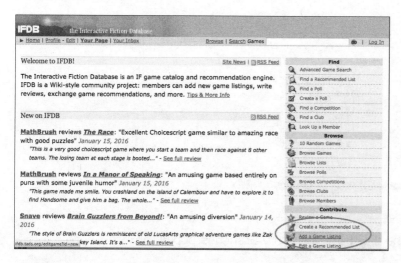

FIGURE 23.6 The front page of the Interactive Fiction Database.

This takes you to the New Game Listing page shown in Figure 23.7, which has many sections you need to fill out, including the story title and your name.

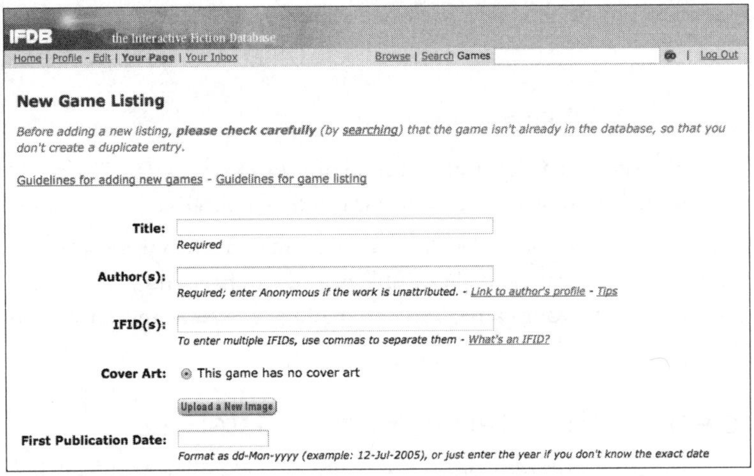

FIGURE 23.7 The New Game Listing page on the Interactive Fiction Database.

The next piece of information, the IFID, is an alphanumeric identification code that you need to get from your Twine game. Open your game and navigate to the menu in the lower-left corner of the blue grid screen that lists the name. Click it to open the list and choose the option Story Statistics. At the bottom of the pop-up box, you should see a note that begins, "The IFID for this story is..." followed by a long string of numbers and letters, seen highlighted in Figure 23.8. Copy that string of numbers and letters and paste it in the IFID box on the IFDB site.

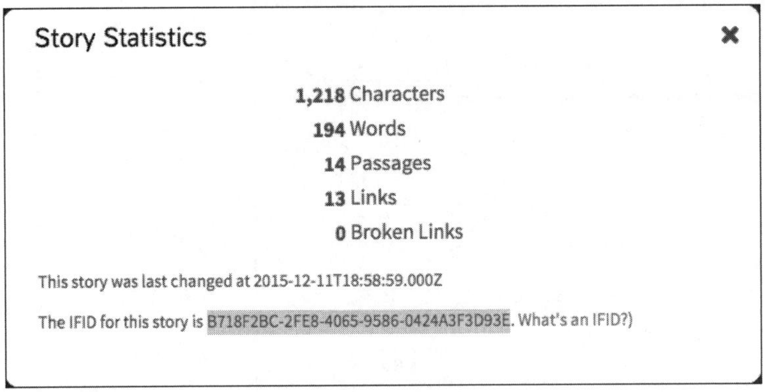

FIGURE 23.8 Get the IFID from the Story Statistics pop-up box.

Continue entering information, uploading cover art if you have any, setting the current date, and choosing a license type. The IFDB provides you with information about the various types of licenses, but most games you create will likely be Freeware. The development system, of course, is Twine, and you can find it toward the bottom of the drop-down menu list.

Write a description of your game and select a genre. Feel free to skip items such as the game's forgiveness rating or *Baf's Guide* ID. (*Baf's Guide* is now defunct.) Also skip the website and download notes and move to the Download Links option.

Under this category, you should see the option to Upload it to the IF Archive, as shown in Figure 23.9.

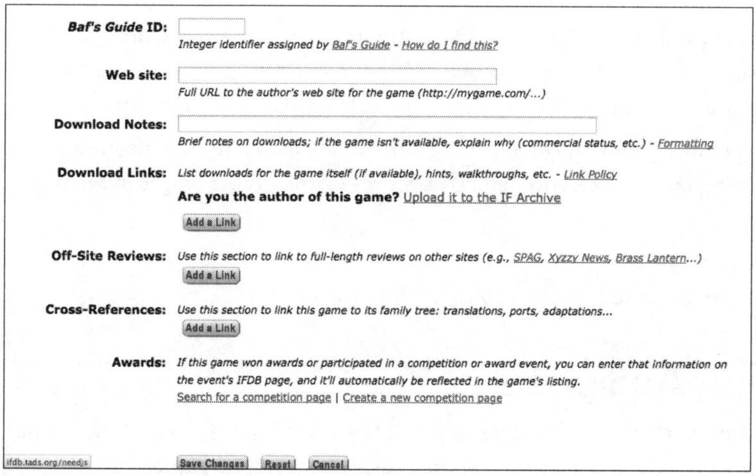

Baf's Guide ID:
Integer identifier assigned by *Baf's Guide* - *How do I find this?*

Web site:
Full URL to the author's web site for the game (http://mygame.com/...)

Download Notes:
Brief notes on downloads; if the game isn't available, explain why (commercial status, etc.) - *Formatting*

Download Links: List downloads for the game itself (if available), hints, walkthroughs, etc. - *Link Policy*
Are you the author of this game? Upload it to the IF Archive
[Add a Link]

Off-Site Reviews: Use this section to link to full-length reviews on other sites (e.g., *SPAG*, *Xyzzy News*, *Brass Lantern*...)
[Add a Link]

Cross-References: Use this section to link this game to its family tree: translations, ports, adaptations...
[Add a Link]

Awards: If this game won awards or participated in a competition or award event, you can enter that information on the event's IFDB page, and it'll automatically be reflected in the game's listing.
Search for a competition page | Create a new competition page

ifdb.tads.org/needjs   [Save Changes] [Reset] [Cancel]

FIGURE 23.9   Upload your game to the Interactive Fiction Database.

Click that option, and you are taken to a new screen that gives you the ability to upload your game. Read the page carefully so you understand what uploading your game to the site entails. Games uploaded to the IFDB should be complete and ready for the general public to play. The file will be reviewed before you receive your download link.

Hosting Your Project on Your Own Site

Of course, if you own a website, you can host your own game. You need access to the control panel (c-panel) via the hosting site (not the dashboard where you normally upload content).

Log into your hosting site and navigate to the c-panel. Click on your file management option, usually labeled something akin to File Manager. You need to upload the game into the public_html directory. Once it's uploaded, you can access the game online by typing the main URL for your site along with a slash and the game name (for example, http://melissa-fordauthor.com/Empty_Basket_Mobile.html).

Hosting the game yourself gives you ultimate control and flexibility, but it comes with a hosting charge. Still, if you own a website, it's an easy way to share your work online.

Comparing the Options

Between these three options, two of them free—Philome.la and IFDB— and one of them paid—hosting your own game—which one should you use? Philome.la is a small group, but it's easy to use, though it requires you to log in using your Twitter account. However, Philome.la does tweet your project for you, as do other Twitter accounts such as @twinethreads.

The Internet Fiction Database carries a lot of weight in the interactive fiction world, and it's the first place many people go to find games to play. Of course, posting your story there requires many more steps and a waiting period before people can access your game.

Lastly, hosting your own game gives you the ultimate control over its fate. But hosting can be costly and has a learning curve since you need to become comfortable with the hosting program.

Of course, you can try out all three options and see which one fits your needs. Which option you choose depends on exactly what you're looking for.

Reaching Your Audience

Your game is online and now it's time to find people to play it. Of course, you'll send a link to friends and family, but how do you find the general audience for your game?

Beyond connecting with people via Twitter lists or Facebook groups for interactive fiction, there are multiple sites online where interactive fiction fans gather to discuss games they're making and games they're playing.

Posting on IFDB.tads.org

Even if you don't host your game on the Interactive Fiction Database, make sure you head over to that site and fill out the Add a Game Listing information form. There is a space in that form to list where people can play your game on the Internet.

The IFDB is a meeting ground for interactive fiction enthusiasts. Not only can people find out about your game on that site, but they can review it or add it to lists, which encourages even more players to try it in the future.

Posting on Forums

There are multiple forums online where you can connect with fellow interactive fiction writers and tell them about your game as well as find others to play.

Intfiction.org (http://www.intfiction.org) is a general board for all types of interactive fiction, both parser- and choice-based. Once you make an account and are approved, you can log in and explore the bulletin boards. The Announcements and Beta Testing board is a good place to list a link to a new game.

Twine also has its own forum (http://twinery.org/forum/), as shown in Figure 23.10. It's an excellent space to ask Twine-specific questions as well as let people know about new Twine games. Because this space is specific to Twine, you'll find it a helpful space to visit to learn tricks and get feedback about your projects.

FIGURE 23.10 The Twine bulletin board at twinery.org/forum.

Joining the Gaming Community

When you've been making games for a while, you'll start connecting with other writers and hearing about game jams, competitions, and awards. Participating in game-making activities is a great way to hone your skills while meeting other people who care about interactive fiction.

Participating in Jams

Anyone can pull together a game jam, and you'll often see them listed on bulletin boards. The purpose of a game jam is to design and build a game in a short amount of time. You're usually given a topic or a set of parameters for the game, as well as a time limit. For instance, one Twine jam had a limit of 300 words, and the game had to be completed within a two-week window. What sort of game could you make if you had only 300 words to play with? How can you build complexity into a game if you can't say a lot?

Participating in game jams is a great way to challenge yourself. And don't feel shy about proposing your own game jam. What theme will you choose for the participants? How long will you give them to make their games?

Participating in Competitions

Game jams are about the fun of participation and rising to a challenge. Competitions are for measuring your game against the games of other interactive fiction writers.

The largest interactive fiction competition, IF Comp (http://www.ifcomp.org), opens every summer for entries, with voting taking place mid-fall. It's a big competition that gets coverage in the game design press, so only enter if you feel your game is complete and ready to be judged.

Smaller competitions throughout the year are listed on the boards. IntroComp, for example, is for incomplete games, while Spring Thing is a counterbalance to the excitement of IF Comp in the fall.

Earning Interactive Fiction Awards

Plenty of awards are given out for interactive fiction. Although most of the larger awards—such as *Time's* Game of the Year—look at commercial releases, the interactive fiction community has the XYZZY Awards, a long-running award ceremony for the best interactive fiction games.

Each year, the titles of new commercial or freeware games are collected, and voting commences in a number of categories, including best writing and best individual puzzle. Like most other award competitions, the XYZZY Awards (named after the magic word in the first interactive fiction game, *Adventure*) bring attention to the games involved. It's a fun way for the community to celebrate its best work.

Breaking the Rules

As this book wraps up, I'd be remiss if I didn't end this book by telling you to ignore everything you've learned up until this point.

Okay, perhaps not *everything*, but you should aim to break at least one writing rule per game. Tell instead of show, give only a vague description of the space, and make wishy-washy characters that are hard to define.

Why?

Because breaking the rules will both show you the worth of these rules and simultaneously release you from their clutches. Breaking rules will allow your creativity and imagination to guide you on your writing path.

Writing is messy, and making a game is messy. But they're good sorts of messy, offering satisfying opportunities to muck around and tear up and try to reformulate something better.

Aim to be a rule breaker in the best sense of the word: by pushing the interactive fiction medium forward, breaking new ground.

I'm always thrilled when I find an example that disproves the rule because it means that writing isn't a stagnant art, set in stone and doomed to be repeated ad infinitum. Such exceptions prove that our relationship with words is in flux. And that is a good thing because it means there are still billions of stories waiting to be written.

I promised at the beginning of this book that I would turn you into a better writer, a better reader, a more logical thinker, and a generally more inquisitive and thoughtful person. Although there is no way to measure this from afar, I'm willing to bet that writing ideas have wiggled under your skin. And once they're firmly in place, you will never walk through the world in the same way.

It's probably not the most romantic breakdown of what it means to be a writer, but at its heart, storytelling is simply about being a *noticer*, a *retainer*, and a *user*.

I bet you notice the small details of the world around you. Maybe it's a turn of phrase that someone uses that you realize defines their entire personality, or the way birds scatter when you're frantically running through a field. What other people overlook, you tend to notice.

Retain those details, either by keeping them all in your mind or by keeping a journal where you jot down all the tiny details you notice throughout the day. Those details will work their way into the stories you write, lending verisimilitude to your game. Characters feel like real people and settings feel like real places when they're based on actual details you've picked up from the people and world around you.

So what is next? Hopefully a lot more noticing, retaining, and using, which means a lot of fantastic games being released into the world for people like me to play. And I can't wait to play yours.

Index

Symbols

A

replayability
  battle scenes, 223
    continuing fights, 227-229
    starting fights, 224-227
  characters, 219-221
  creating, 214
  inventory-based, 222
  puzzles, 229-230
rescue quests, 88
researching narrative voice, 299
retrieving saved games, 321
<<return>> macro, 316
returning stasis, 99
rewarding choices, 345
rocket ship icon (Hover menu), 11
rolling dice simulation, 113-115
RPGs (role playing games), 47
rule of three, 325
rules, breaking, 394-395

S

sad endings, 281
Saint, Puck, 363
sans serif fonts, 236
Save to Disk button, 321
Saves button, 321
saving
  games, 320-321
  stories, 9
science fiction genre, 117
search quests
  conditional statements
    adding, 78-80
    hooks, 79
    multiple, 81-83
    player characters, tracking, 83-86
    structure, 78
  variable values, 71-76
  writing, 86
second-person stories, 3
seconds, counting, 350-352
selectors
  defined, 245
  setting, 245-247
  SugarCube, 364-366

sending players
  backward one passage, 315
  forward one passage, 316
  to randomly chosen passages, 310
senses, 38
sequels, creating, 282
sequencing puzzles, 59
serif fonts, 236
(set-either:) macro, 110
<<set>> macro, 268, 309-310, 328
(set:) macro, 72-75
  datamap data name values, adding, 200
  setter links, 180
(set-random:) macro, 114
setter links
  images as, 262-263
  pacing, 179-181
setting
  being the player's eyes, 36
  character traits, 206
  defined, 29
  descriptions, adding, 31-32
  descriptive words, 40-42
  drawing player attention, 40
  dynamic, 42-43
  importance, 29
  map-based games, creating, 43-45
  mazes, 46-47
  mood, 38-39
  motion, 37
  pacing, 177-181
  personal experience, 35
  player characters, 36-37
  prompts, 30
  repeating text, 32-34
  scenes. *See* exploration
  senses, 38
  static, 42-43
  variable values, 72-75
shapes (stories), 25-27
Short, Emily, 243
short stories, 171-172
showing not telling, 347-348, 354
  actions, describing, 356
  behavior, demonstrating, 358-359
  conclusions, drawing, 357

REGISTER THIS PRODUCT
SAVE 35%*
ON YOUR NEXT PURCHASE!

⌨ How to Register Your Product

- Go to quepublishing.com/register
- Sign in or create an account
- Enter ISBN: 10- or 13-digit ISBN that appears on the back cover of your product

🔓 Benefits of Registering

- Ability to download product updates
- Access to bonus chapters and workshop files
- A 35% coupon to be used on your next purchase – valid for 30 days
  To obtain your coupon, click on "Manage Codes" in the right column of your Account page
- Receive special offers on new editions and related Que products

Please note that the benefits for registering may vary by product. Benefits will be listed on your Account page under Registered Products.

We value and respect your privacy. Your email address will not be sold to any third party company.

* 35% discount code presented after product registration is valid on most print books, eBooks, and full-course videos sold on QuePublishing.com. Discount may not be combined with any other offer and is not redeemable for cash. Discount code expires after 30 days from the time of product registration. Offer subject to change.

quepublishing.com